The Humanities
through the Arts

SIXTH EDITION

The Humanities through the Arts

F. David Martin

Professor of Philosophy Emeritus
Bucknell University

Lee A. Jacobus

Professor of English
University of Connecticut

Boston   Burr Ridge, IL   Dubuque, IA   Madison, WI   New York   San Francisco   St. Louis
Bangkok   Bogotá   Caracas   Kuala Lumpur   Lisbon   London   Madrid   Mexico City
Milan   Montreal   New Delhi   Santiago   Seoul   Singapore   Sydney   Taipei   Toronto

THE HUMANITIES THROUGH THE ARTS, SIXTH EDITION
Published by McGraw-Hill, a business unit of The McGraw-Hill Companies, Inc., 1221 Avenue of the Americas, New York, NY 10020. Copyright © 2004, 1997, 1991, 1983, 1978, 1975 by The McGraw-Hill Companies, Inc. All rights reserved. No part of this publication may be reproduced or distributed in any form or by any means, or stored in a database or retrieval system, without the prior written consent of The McGraw-Hill Companies, Inc., including, but not limited to, any network or other electronic storage or transmission, or broadcast for distance learning.
Some ancillaries, including electronic and print components, may not be available to customers outside the United States.

2 3 4 5 6 7 8 9 0 VNH/VNH 0 9 8 7 6 5 4 3

Vice president and editor-in-chief: *Thalia Dorwick*
Publisher: *Christopher Freitag*
Sponsoring editors: *Allison McNamara, Joe Hanson*
Development editor: *Caroline Ryan*
Marketing manager: *Lisa Berry*
Project manager: *Holly Paulsen*
Manuscript editor: *Joan Pendleton*
Art director: *Jeanne M. Schreiber*
Design manager: *Cassandra Chu*
Cover designer: *Cassandra Chu*
Interior designer: *Claire Seng-Niemoeller*
Art manager: *Robin Mouat*
Art editor: *Robin Mouat*
Photo researcher: *Brian Pecko*
Illustrator: *Robin Mouat*
Production supervisors: *Richard DeVitto, Randy Hurst*

The text was set in 10/12 New Aster by Prographics and printed on acid-free 70# Sterling Ultra Litho Dull by Von Hoffmann Press.

Cover art: © Erich Lessing/Art Resource, New York

The credits for this book begin on page C-1, a continuation of the copyright page.

Library of Congress Cataloging-in-Publication Data

Martin, F. David.
The humanities through the arts/F. David Martin, Lee A. Jacobus. — 6th ed.
    p. cm.
 Includes bibliographical references and index.
 ISBN 0-07-240709-3
 1. Arts — Psychological aspects. 2. Art appreciation. I. Jacobus, Lee A. II. Title.

NX165.M37 2003
700′.1′04 — dc21
                                                    2003046408

www.mhhe.com

About the Authors

F. DAVID MARTIN (Ph.D., University of Chicago) taught at the University of Chicago and then at Bucknell University until his retirement in 1983. He was a Fulbright Research Scholar in both Florence and Rome from 1957 through 1959, and he has received seven other major research grants during his career as well as the Christian Lindback Award for Distinguished Teaching. Dr. Martin recently taught in the University of Pittsburgh's Semester at Sea, and is currently a consultant for Time-Warner for the development of CD-ROMs in the arts and the humanities. In addition to more than 100 articles in professional journals, Dr. Martin is the author of *Art and the Religious Experience* (Associated University Presses, 1972) and *Sculpture and the Enlivened Space* (The University Press of Kentucky, 1981). He also will be publishing shortly *Facing Death: Theme and Variations*. Although he has taught all fields of philosophy, Dr. Martin's main teaching interests have centered on the "why" questions of the arts and the humanities. Married with four children and ten grandchildren, Dr. Martin lives on the Susquehanna River in Lewisburg, Pennsylvania. His hobbies are the arts, nature, golf, and the world — especially Italy.

LEE A. JACOBUS (Ph.D., Claremont Graduate University) is Professor of English Emeritus at the University of Connecticut (Storrs). His undergraduate and master's degrees are from Brown University. He held a Danforth Teacher's Grant while earning his doctorate. Dr. Jacobus has taught at Western Connecticut State University, Columbia University, and Brown University, as well as the University of Connecticut. His specialties are Milton, Shakespeare, Joyce, and Modern Irish Literature. His publications include *Shakespeare and the Dialectic of Certainty* (St. Martin's, 1992); *Sudden Apprehension: Aspects of Knowledge in Paradise Lost* (Mouton, 1976); *John Cleveland: A Critical Study* (G.K. Hall, 1975); *Humanities: The Evolution of Values* (McGraw Hill, 1985); *Writing as Thinking* (Macmillan, 1989); *Substance, Style and Strategy* (Oxford University Press, 1999); *Literature: An Introduction to Critical Reading* (Prentice-Hall, 1996; Compact ed. 2002); and several edited volumes: *Aesthetics and the Arts* (McGraw Hill, 1968); *A World of Ideas* (Bedford/St. Martin's, 6th ed. 2002); *The Bedford Introduction to Drama* (Bedford/St. Martin's, 4th ed. 2002; Compact ed. 2002); *The Longman Anthology of American Drama* (Longman,

1982); *Teaching Literature* (Prentice-Hall, 1996). Dr. Jacobus was founder and co-editor of the scholarly journal *Lit: Literature Interpretation Theory*. He has held grants for photographic work in the northeast quadrant of Connecticut, and his photographs are in permanent collections and are published in magazines and books. In addition, he has published short fiction, poetry, numerous essays, and scholarly articles, and he had two plays showcased at the American Theatre of Actors. He currently studies piano and is working on a book of stories and a group of novels. He is married to choreographer and dancer Joanna Jacobus. They have two children and live close to New Haven.

We dedicate this study to
teachers and students of the humanities.

Brief Contents

Contents

Preface

The Humanities through the Arts offers an exploratory approach to the humanities, focusing on the special role of the arts. Examining the relation of the humanities to values, objects and events important to people, is central to this book. We also make a distinction between the role of artists and that of other humanists: Artists reveal values, while other humanists examine or reflect upon values. The goal of this book is to provide a basic program for studying values as revealed in the arts, all while keeping in mind the important question "What Is Art?" As an introduction to the humanities, this book provides the tools necessary to think critically when exploring the arts and the other humanities.

Established Features

Our examples are taken almost entirely from the Western tradition. This does not mean that other traditions are less worthy. Rather, we simply chose to concentrate on our heritage—and mainly close to our own time—because this is where we are. However, the media, elements, principles of composition, and purposes of art in the Western tradition can often be applied to other traditions. Understanding the humanities in the Western tradition is a good starting point for understanding other traditions. Our many examples are based on the standard that they best illustrate the issues discussed.

Perception Keys are included throughout the text. Concentrating on specific works of art, these boxes include questions and suggestions designed to elicit a more thoughtful analysis. The Perception Keys allow students to immediately determine the extent of their understanding and encourage a critical thinking approach to works they see on their own.

This edition continues to be closely coordinated with the Telecourse "Humanities through the Arts," based on this book. The course—produced by KOCE-TV and the Coast Community College District and distributed through Coast Telecourses—consists of thirty half-hour programs hosted by Maya Angelou. The Telecourse Student Guide to accompany *The Humanities through the Arts* (New York: The McGraw Hill Companies, 2004) was written by Richard T. Searles and revised by Joseph Rust for the Coast Community College District. This study guide continues to help students master material in the text and in the video programs by providing lesson overviews, learning objectives, assignments, additional readings, review quizzes, and suggestions for further study.

New Organization

The sixth edition has been organized into three parts.

- *Part I: Fundamentals* is the foundation for the rest of the text. In this section, we distinguish the humanities from the sciences and the arts from the other humanities. We introduce the question "What Is Art?" and discuss ways of responding to art and the vital role that criticism plays in art appreciation.
- *Part II: The Arts* includes chapters covering all of the major arts. This section has been designed for instructors to choose the order in which to cover chapters and even to skip certain chapters if necessary.
- *Part III: Interrelationships* studies the way the arts are related and, in turn, their relation to the other humanities. Chapter 13 explores how the arts relate to one another. Chapter 14 addresses what may be "artlike" and how to distinguish the arts from the artlike. Chapter 15 examines how the arts interrelate with the other humanities, particularly history, philosophy, and theology.

New Design

More color is incorporated throughout the text in an effort to be both pedagogically effective and aesthetically pleasing. In addition, many figures have been updated in order for students to experience these artworks as closely as possible without actually viewing them in person.

Additions and Updates

- In Chapter 4, "Painting," we have added a new section on media, elements, and the principles of composition. This section can also serve as a model for the other art forms. A new Chapter 14, "Is It Art or

Something Like It?," is closely tied to Chapter 2 and could be covered immediately after Part I for those that have a special interest in the philosophy of art.

- A timeline is included on the inside cover of the text to give students historical perspective. In the interests of space this timeline is not a comprehensive art history resource; it is meant to provide context for the artworks and people that are discussed in the text.

- In addition to relevant updates throughout, we have taken special care to include updated Web sites at the end of each chapter. The Internet is an incredible research tool for students and we have offered some of the best sites as recommendations for further exploration.

- Slide sets are available to all adopters of the book. Please call your local McGraw-Hill sales representative for details.

The reception of this book, since its first edition in 1975, has been enormously warming, reassuring us that the humanities thrive. We dedicate this book to the students and teachers who use it to examine their values through a lifetime of contact with the humanities.

Acknowledgments

This book is indebted to more people than we can truly credit. We are deeply grateful to the following for their help:

Bruce Bellingham, *University of Connecticut*
Michael Berberich, *Galveston College*
Barbara Brickman, *Howard Community College*
Peggy Brown, *Collin County Community College*
Lance Brunner, *University of Kentucky*
Selma Jean Cohen, editor of *Dance Perspectives*
Karen Conn, *Valencia Community College*
Harrison Davis, *Brigham Young University*
Jim Doan, *Nova University*
Roberta Ferrell, *SUNY Empire State*
Joanna Jacobus, choreographer
Marsha Keller, *Oklahoma City University*
Lee Hartman, *Howard Community College*
Deborah Jowitt, *Village Voice*
Paul Kessel, *Mohave Community College*
Edward Kies, *College of DuPage*
Marceau Myers, *North Texas State University*
Martha Myers, *Connecticut College*
William E. Parker, *University of Connecticut*
Susan Shmeling, *Vincennes University*
C. Edward Spann, *Dallas Baptist University*
Robert Streeter, *University of Chicago*
Peter Surace, *Cuyahoga Community College*
Robert Tynes, *University of North Carolina at Asheville*
Walter Wehner, *University of North Carolina at Greensboro*

We'd like to thank our editorial team at McGraw-Hill, including our former editors, Alison Meersshaert, Cheryl Mehalik, Kaye Pace, Peter Labella, Cynthia Ward, Allison McNamara, and Nancy Blaine. For this edition we would like to thank our development editors, Cynthia Ward and Caroline Ryan. We would also like to thank our production team: production editor, Holly Paulsen; manuscript editor, Joan Pendleton; design manager, Cassandra Chu; art editor, Robin Mouat; and photo researcher, Brian Pecko. Without their expertise this book could never have been put together so beautifully. We also owe special thanks to Harry Garvin and Gerald Eager, both of Bucknell University, who were steadfast critics throughout the preparation of this edition. We thank Doris Martin and Jane Baker for their scrupulous care in manuscript preparation.

Finally, we thank Associated University Presses for permission to paraphrase and quote from *Art and the Religious Experience*, 1972, and the University Press of Kentucky for permission to quote from *Sculpture and Enlivened Space*, 1981, both by F. David Martin.

PART I
Fundamentals

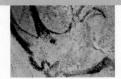

CHAPTER I

The Humanities:
An Introduction

The Humanities: A Study of Values

In the medieval period the word *humanities* distinguished that which pertained to humans from that which pertained to God. Mathematics, the sciences, the arts, and philosophy were humanities: They had to do with humans. Theology and related studies were the subjects of divinity: They had to do with God. This distinction does not have the importance it once did. Today we think of the humanities as those broad areas of human creativity and study that are distinct from mathematics and the "hard" sciences, mainly because in the humanities strictly objective or scientific standards are not usually dominant.

The separation between the humanities and the *sciences* is illustrated by the way in which values work differently in the two areas. A *value* is something we care about, something that matters. Consider, for example, the drinking of liquor: a positive value for some people, a negative value for others. The biologist describes the physiological effects. The psychologist describes the psychological effects. The sociologist takes a poll and tabulates value preferences concerning drinking. These scientists study values, but they are concerned with what "is" rather than what "ought to be." That is why they can apply strictly scientific standards to their investigations. If they make a value judgment, such as that liquor ought to be banned, they usually will be careful—as scientists—to make it clear that their pronouncements are personal value judgments rather than scientific statements. To humanists, however, the sharp separation between the "is" and the "ought," between scientific statement and value judgment, is usually not so evident, primarily because the scientific method is not so basic to their work. Most scientists and humanists will agree that we must all make value judgments and that the sciences often provide important information to help us make sound decisions. For example, if biologists discovered that liquor significantly shortens the life span, this discovery would indeed be relevant to a value judgment about banning liquor. However, such consensus seems to be lacking with respect to the relevance of the humanities to value judgments. Scientists, more than humanists, probably would be dubious about an assertion that novels such as Dostoevsky's *Brothers Karamazov* contribute important information for making sound value judgments about the banning of liquor.

The discoveries of scientists—for example, the bomb, the pill, and cloning—often have tremendous impact on the values of their society. Yet some scientists have declared that they merely make the discoveries and that others—presumably politicians—must decide how those discoveries are to be used. It is this last statement that brings us closest to the importance of the humanities. If many scientists feel they cannot judge how their discoveries are to be used, then we must try to understand why they give that responsibility to others. This is not to say that scientists uniformly turn such decisions over to others, for many of them are humanists as well as scientists. But the fact remains that governments—from that of Hitler to that of Churchill, as well as those of such nations as China, Russia, and the United States—have all made use of great scientific achievements without pausing to ask the "achievers" if they approved of the way their discoveries were being used. The questions are, Who decides how to use such discoveries? On what grounds should their judgments be based?

Studying the behavior of neutrinos or ion-exchange resins will not help us get closer to the answer. Such study is not related to the nature of humankind but to the nature of nature. What we need is a study that will get us closer to ourselves. It should be a study that explores the reaches of human feeling in relation to values—not only our own individual feelings and values but also the feelings and values of others. We need a study that will increase our sensitivity to ourselves, others, and the values in our world. To be sensitive is to perceive with insight. To be sensitive is also to feel and believe that things make a difference. Furthermore, it involves an awareness of those aspects of values that cannot be measured by objective standards. To be sensitive is to respect the humanities because, among other reasons, they help develop our sensitivity to values, to what we as individuals place importance on.

There are numerous ways to approach the humanities. The way we have chosen here is the way of the arts. One of the contentions of this book is that values are clarified in enduring ways in the arts. Human beings have had the impulse to express their values since the earliest times. Ancient tools recovered from the most recent Ice Age, for example, have features designed to express an affection for beauty as well as to provide utility.

The concept of progress in the arts is problematic. Who is to say whether the cave paintings (Figure 1-1) of 30,000 years ago in present-day France are less excellent than the work of Picasso (see Figure 1-4)? Such works surely were not made as works of art to be contemplated. To get to them in the caves is almost always difficult, and they are very difficult to see. They must have been made for some practical purpose, such as improving the prospects for the hunt. Yet these works reveal something about the power, grace, and beauty of this kind of animal. These cave paintings function now as works of art. Our species from the beginning instinctively had an interest in making revealing forms.

FIGURE 1-1
Cave painting from Chauvet
Caves, France.
(© LeSeuil/Sygma)

Among the numerous ways to approach the humanities we have chosen the way of the arts because, as we shall try to elucidate, the arts clarify or reveal values. As we deepen our understanding of the arts, we necessarily deepen our understanding of values, for that is what the arts are about. We will study our experience with works of arts as well as the values others associate with them. And in the process of doing this we will also educate ourselves about our own values.

Because a value is something that matters, engagement with art — the illuminator of values — enriches the quality of our lives significantly. Moreover, the *subject matter* of art — what it is about — is not limited to the beautiful and the pleasant, the bright sides of life. Art may also include and help us understand the dark sides — the ugly, the painful, and the tragic. And when it does and when we get it, we are better able to come to grips with those dark sides of life.

Art brings us into direct communication with others. As Carlos Fuentes said in *The Buried Mirror,* "People and their cultures perish in isolation, but they are born or reborn in contact with other men and women of another culture, another creed, another race. If we do not recognize our humanity in others, we shall not recognize it in ourselves."

Taste

Taste is an exercise in the choice of values. People who have already made up their minds about what art they like or do not like defend their choices as an expression of their taste. Some opera buffs think Italian opera is uniformly superior to opera in English, French, or German. Others claim that any opera Mozart wrote is wonderful, but all others are impossible. All of us have various kinds of limitations about the arts. Some cannot stand opera at all. Some cannot look at a painting or sculpture of a nude figure without smirking. Some think any painting is magnificent as long as it has a sunset or a dramatic sea or a battle or as long as it is abstract and goes well with the couch. Some people will read any book that deals with horse racing, has a scientific angle, or discusses their current hobby.

The taste of the mass public shifts constantly. Movies, for example, survive or fail on the basis of the number of people they appeal to. A film is good if it makes plenty of money. Consequently, film producers make every effort to cash in on current popular tastes, often by making sequels until the public's taste changes—for example, the *Batman* series (1989, 1992, 1995).

One point our study of the humanities emphasizes is that commercial success is not the most important guide to excellence in the arts. The long-term success of works of art depends on their ability to interpret human experience at a level of complexity that warrants examination and reexamination. Many commercially successful works give us what we think we want rather than what we really need with reference to insight and understanding. By satisfying us in an immediate and usually superficial way, commercial art can dull us to the possibilities of more complex and more deeply satisfying art.

Everyone has limitations as a perceiver of art. Sometimes we defend ourselves against stretching our limitations by assuming that we have developed our taste and that any effort to change it is bad form. An old saying— "Matters of taste are not disputable"—can be credited with making many of us feel very righteous about our own taste. What the saying means is that there is no accounting for what people like in the arts, for beauty is in the eye of the beholder. Thus, there is no use in trying to educate anyone about the arts. Obviously we disagree. We believe that all of us can and should be educated about the arts and should learn to respond to as wide a variety of the arts as possible: from jazz to string quartets, from Charlie Chaplin to Steven Spielberg, from Lewis Carroll to T. S. Eliot, from folk art to Picasso. Most of us defend our taste because anyone who challenges our taste challenges our deep feelings. Anyone who tries to change our responses to art is really trying to get inside our mind. If we fail to understand its purpose, this kind of persuasion naturally arouses resistance in us.

The study of the arts can involve a multitude of factual information. The dates of Beethoven's birth and death and the dates of his important compositions, as well as their key signatures and opus numbers can be verified. We can investigate the history of jazz and the claim of Jelly Roll Morton to have been its "inventor." We can decide who was or was not part of the Realistic school of painting in mid-nineteenth-century France. We can make lists of the Impressionist painters in late nineteenth-century France and those they influenced. Oceans of facts attach to every art. But our interest is not in facts alone.

For us, the study of the arts penetrates beyond facts to the values that evoke our feelings—the way a succession of Eric Clapton's guitar chords when he plays the blues can be electrifying or the way song lyrics can give us a chill. In other words, we want to go beyond the facts *about* a work of art and get to the values revealed in the work. How many times have we all found ourselves liking something that, months or years before, we could not stand? And how often do we find ourselves now disliking what we previously judged a masterpiece? Generally, we can say the work of art remains the same. It is we who change. We learn to recognize the values illuminated in such works as well as to understand the ways in which this is accomplished. Such development is the meaning of "education" in the sense in which we have been using the term.

Responses to Art

Our responses to art usually involve processes so complex that they can never be fully tracked down or analyzed. At first, they can only be hinted at when we talk about them. However, further education in the arts permits us to observe more closely and thereby respond more intensely to the content of the work. This is true, we believe, even with "easy" art, such as exceptionally beautiful works—for example, the Raphael (see Figure 14-14), Giorgione (see Figure 2-17), Cézanne (see Figure 2-4), and O'Keeffe (see Figure 4-13). Such gorgeous works generally are responded to with immediate satisfaction. What more needs to be done? If art were only of the beautiful, textbooks such as this one probably would never find many users. But we think more needs to be done, even with the beautiful. We will begin, however, with three works that obviously are not beautiful.

The Mexican painter David Alfaro Siqueiros's *Echo of a Scream* (Figure 1-2) is a highly emotional painting—in the sense that the work seems to demand a strong emotional response. What we see is the huge head of a baby crying and, then, as if issuing from its own mouth, the baby himself. What kinds of *emotions* do you find stirring in yourself as you look at this painting? What kinds of emotions do you feel are expressed in the painting? Your own emotional responses—such as shock; pity for the child; irritation at a destructive, mechanical society; or any other nameable emotion—do not sum up the painting. However, they are an important starting point, since Siqueiros paints in such a way as to evoke emotion, and our understanding of the painting increases as we examine the means by which this evocation is achieved.

PERCEPTION KEY   *Echo of a Scream*

1. Identify the mechanical objects in the painting.
2. What is the condition of these objects? What is their relationship to the baby?
3. What are those strange round forms in the upper right corner?
4. How might your response differ if the angular lines were smoothed out?
5. What is the significance of the red cloth around the baby?
6. Why are the natural shapes in the painting, such as the forehead of the baby, distorted? Is awareness of such distortions crucial to a response to the painting?

FIGURE 1-2
David Alfaro Siqueiros, *Echo of a Scream*. 1937. Enamel on wood, 48 × 36 inches (121.9 × 91.4 cm). The Museum of Modern Art, New York. Gift of Edward M. M. Warburg. (Digital image © The Museum of Modern Art, New York/Licensed by Scala/Art Resource, New York. Art © Estate of David Alfaro Siqueiros/Licensed by VAGA, New York, NY)

Study another work, very close in temperament to Siqueiros's painting: *The Eternal City* by the American painter Peter Blume (Figure 1-3). After attending carefully to the kinds of responses awakened by *The Eternal City*, take note of some background information about the painting that you may not know. The year of this painting is the same as that of *Echo of a Scream:* 1937. *The Eternal City* is a name reserved for only one city in the world—Rome. In 1937 the world was on the verge of world war: fascist Italy and Germany against the democratic nations of Europe and the Americas. In

FIGURE 1-3
Peter Blume, *The Eternal City*. 1934–1937. Dated on painting 1937. Oil on composition board, 34 × 47⅞ inches. The Museum of Modern Art, New York. Mrs. Simon Guggenheim Fund (574.1942). (Image © The Museum of Modern Art/Licensed by Scala/Art Resource, New York. Art © Estate of Peter Blume/Licensed by VAGA, New York, NY)

the center of the painting is the Roman Forum, close to where Julius Caesar, the alleged tyrant, was murdered by Brutus. But here we see fascist Blackshirts, the modern tyrants, beating people. In a niche at the left is a figure of Christ, and beneath him (hard to see) is a crippled beggar woman. Near her are ruins of Roman statuary. The enlarged and distorted head, wriggling out like a jack-in-the-box, is that of Mussolini, the man who invented fascism and the Blackshirts. Study the painting closely again. Has your response to the painting changed?

PERCEPTION KEY   Siqueiros and Blume

1. What common ingredients do you find in the Blume and Siqueiros paintings?
2. Is your reaction to the Blume similar to or quite distinct from your reaction to the Siqueiros?
3. Is the effect of the distortions similar or different?
4. How are colors used in each painting? Are the colors those of the natural world, or do they suggest an artificial environment? Are they distorted for effect?
5. With reference to the objects and events represented in each painting, do you think the paintings are comparable? If so, in what ways?
6. With the Blume, are there any natural objects in the painting that may suggest the vitality of the Eternal City? Any natural objects that may suggest the indestructibility of the Eternal City?

Before going on to the next painting, which is quite different in character, we should pause to make some observations about what we have done. With added knowledge about its cultural and political implications—what

we shall call the background of the painting—your responses to *The
Eternal City* may have changed. Ideally they should have become more focused, intense, and certain. Why? The painting is surely the same physical
object you looked at originally. Nothing has changed in that object.
Therefore, something has changed because something has been added to
you, information that the general viewer of the painting in 1937 would have
had and would have responded to more emotionally than viewers do now.
Consider how a fascist, on the one hand, or an Italian humanist and lover
of Roman culture, on the other hand, would have reacted to this painting
in 1937.

A full experience of this painting is not one thing or one system of things
but an innumerable variety of things. Moreover, "knowledge about" a work

of art can lead to "knowledge of" the work of art, which implies a richer experience. This is important as a basic principle, since it means that we can be educated about what is in a work of art, such as its shapes, objects, and *structure,* as well as what is external to a work, such as its political references. It means we can learn to respond more completely. It also means that artists such as Blume sometimes produce works that demand background information if we are to appreciate them fully. This is particularly true of art that refers to historical circumstances and personages. Sometimes we may find ourselves unable to respond successfully to a work of art because we lack the background knowledge the artist presupposes.

Picasso's *Guernica* (Figure 1-4), one of the most famous paintings of the twentieth century, is also dated 1937. Its title comes from the name of an old Spanish town that was bombed during the Spanish Civil War—the first aerial bombing of noncombatant civilians in modern warfare. Examine this painting carefully.

PERCEPTION KEY   *Guernica*

1. Distortion is powerfully evident in this painting. How does its function differ from that of the distortion in Blume's or Siqueiros's paintings?
2. Describe the objects in the painting. What is their relationship to one another?
3. Why the prominence of the lightbulb?
4. There are large vertical rectangles on the left and right sides and a very large triangle in the center. Do these shapes provide a visual order to what would otherwise be sheer chaos? If so, how? As you think about this, compare one of many studies Picasso made for *Guernica* (Figure 1-5). Does the painting possess a stronger form than the study? If so, in what ways?
5. Because of reading habits in the West, we tend initially to focus on the left side of most paintings and then move to the right, especially when the work is very large. Is this the case with your perception of *Guernica*? In the organization or form of *Guernica* is there a countermovement that, once our vision has reached the right side, pulls us back to the left? If so, what shapes in the painting cause this countermovement? How do these left–right and right–left movements affect the balance of the painting? Note that the painting is over twenty-five feet wide.
6. The bull seems to be totally indifferent to the carnage. Do you think the bull may be some kind of symbol? For example, could the bull represent the spirit of the Spanish people? Could the bull represent General Franco, the man who ordered the bombing? Or could the bull represent both? To answer these questions adequately do you need further background information, or can you defend your answers by referring to what is in the painting, or do you need to use both?
7. The bombing of Guernica occurred during the day. Why did Picasso portray it as happening at night?
8. Which are more visually dominant, human beings or animals? If you were not told, would you know that this painting was a representation of an air raid?

9. Is the subject matter—what the work is about—of this painting war? Death? Suffering? Fascism? Or some kind of combination?
10. Does *Guernica* take on more meaning for you after viewing the images of the World Trade Center, September 11, 2001? Would the bull, for example, with its implacable coldness, be associated perhaps with terrorism?
11. If Picasso were alive, do you think it likely that he would paint that horror?

The next painting (Figure 1-6) was completed in 1936 by Piet Mondrian, a very influential Dutch painter. Mondrian—with the strikingly new style of *Composition in White, Black, and Red*—became a household name. Despite the nonrepresentational character of such works, their bold colors and the apparent simplicity of design had popular appeal after a fairly short time.

PERCEPTION KEY   *Composition in White, Black, and Red*

1. If you were to comment on "distortion" in this painting, what would that imply about what the painting represents? What is represented in the painting?
2. How would your responses differ if all the black areas were repainted orange? Would the balance of the painting be distorted?
3. Suppose the horizontal black line running across the width of the painting were raised nearer to the top. Would the balance of the painting be disturbed?
4. Suppose the little black rectangle at the upper left-hand corner were enlarged. Would the balance of the painting be disturbed? How important is visual balance in this work?
5. There is no frame around this painting. Do you think there should be?
6. Do you need any historical background to appreciate this work? Is what we have said about world conditions in 1937 irrelevant to this painting? Soon after that date, Mondrian's country, Holland, partially destroyed itself by opening its dikes in an attempt to keep Hitler out. Does this fact influence the way you look at this painting?
7. Does the painting evoke strong responses in you? Do you have more difficulty articulating your responses to it than to the paintings by Siqueiros, Blume, and Picasso? If so, how is this to be explained?
8. Suppose the Mondrian were hung with its vertical lines not parallel to the lines of the wall. Would you need to straighten it? If *Echo of a Scream* were crooked on a wall, would you feel as compelled to straighten it? Explain.
9. Is it true that the painting by Mondrian is more like music than the paintings by Siqueiros, Blume, and Picasso?
10. Mondrian wanted to paint universal paintings, "pure realities" common to all people: the square; the rectangle; the vertical and the horizontal; the primary colors red, yellow, and blue; spatial relationships; features that every human being continually experiences. He wanted to make us more sensitive to these general features, independent of objects and events. Do you think Mondrian succeeded?

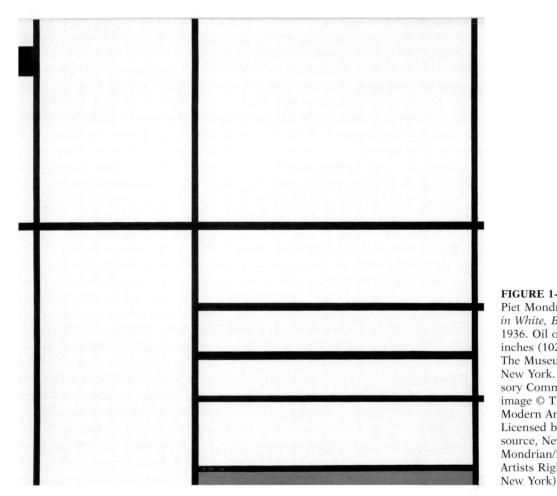

STRUCTURE AND ARTISTIC FORM

The Mondrian obviously is very different from the other paintings in subject matter. (In Chapter 4 we will analyze the subject matter of the Mondrian and abstract painting generally.) The responses you have when you look at it are probably quite different from those you had when you were viewing the other paintings, but why? You might reply that the Mondrian is pure form, an entirely *sensuous* surface. Unlike the other paintings, no objects or events are represented. And yet this painting can be very exciting. Pure form—the interrelationships of lines, colors, textures, light, and shapes—can catch and hold our attention. Most of us have the capacity to respond to pure form even in paintings in which objects and events are portrayed. Thus, responding to *The Eternal City* may involve responding not just to an interpretation of fascism taking hold in Italy but also to the sensuous surface of the painting. This is certainly true of *Echo of a Scream;* if you look again at that painting, you will see not only that its sensuous surface is interesting intrinsically but also that it deepens our response to what is represented. Painters must structure their paintings, although few painters call attention to the structure the way Mondrian does. But, because we often respond to pure form without even being conscious that it is affecting us, it is of first importance that the painter make the structure interesting.

The composition of any painting can be analyzed because any painting has to be organized: parts have to be interrelated. Moreover, it is important to think carefully about the composition of individual paintings. This is particularly true of paintings one does not respond to immediately—of "difficult" or apparently uninteresting paintings. Often the analysis of structure can help us gain access to such paintings so that they become genuinely exciting.

PERCEPTION KEY *The Eternal City*

1. Sketch the basic shapes of the painting.
2. Do these shapes relate to each other in such a way as to help reveal the obscenity of fascism? If so, how?

Artistic form is a composition or structure that makes something—a subject matter—more meaningful. The Siqueiros, Blume, and Picasso reveal something about the horrors of war and fascism. But what does the Mondrian reveal? Perhaps just the sensuous? For us, structures or forms that do not give us insight are not artistic forms. Some will argue the point. This major question will be pursued throughout the text. Hang on!

PERCEPTION

We are not likely to respond sensitively to a work of art that we do not perceive properly. What is less obvious is what we referred to previously—the fact that we can often give our attention to a work of art and still not really perceive very much. The reason for this should be clear from our previous discussion. Frequently, we need to know something about the background of a work of art that would aid our perception. Anyone who did not know who Christ was or what fascism was or what Mussolini meant to the world would have a difficult time making much sense of *The Eternal City*. But it is also true that anyone who could not perceive the composition of Blume's painting might have a completely superficial response to the painting. Such a person could indeed know all about the background and understand the symbolic statements made by the painting, but that is only part of the painting. From seeing what Mondrian can do with line, color, texture, space, and shape, and their relationships, you can understand that the formal qualities of a painting are neither accidental nor unimportant. In Blume's painting, the form acts in such a way as to focus attention and organize our perceptions by establishing the relationships between the parts.

Composition is basic to all the arts. To perceive any work of art adequately, we must perceive its structure. Examine the following poem—"l(a"—by e. e. cummings. It is unusual in its form and its effects.

l(a

le
af
fa

ll

s)
one
l

iness

This poem looks at first like a strange kind of code, like an Egyptian hieroglyph. But it is not a code — it is more like a Japanese haiku, a poem that sets a scene or paints a picture and then waits for us to get it. And to "get it" requires sensitive perception.

PERCEPTION KEY   "l(a"

1. Study the poem carefully until you begin to make out the words. What are they?
2. One part of the poem refers to an emotion; the other describes an event. What is the relationship between them?
3. Is the shape of the poem important to the meaning of the poem?
4. Why are the words of the poem difficult to perceive? Is that difficulty important to the poem?
5. Does the poem evoke an image or images?
6. With the emphasis on letters in the poem, is the use of the lowercase for the poet's name fitting?
7. Once you have perceived the words and imagery of the poem, does your response change? Compare your analysis of the poem with ours, which follows.

In this poem a word is interrupted by parentheses: "l one l iness" — "loneliness" — a feeling we have all experienced. Because of its isolating, biting power, we ordinarily do not like this feeling. Then, inside the parentheses, there is a phrase, "a leaf falls," the description of an event. In poetry such a description is usually called an image. In this poem the image illustrates the idea, or theme, of loneliness, melding the specific with the abstract. But how is this melding accomplished? First of all, notice the devices that symbolize or represent oneness, an emblem of loneliness. The poem begins with the letter "l," which in the typeface used in the original poem looks like the number "one." Even the parenthesis separating the "a" from the "l" helps accent the isolation of the "l." Then there is the "le," which is the singular article in French. The idea of one is doubled by repetition in the "ll" figure. Then cummings brazenly writes "one" and follows it by "l" and then the ultimate "iness." Furthermore, in the original edition the poem is number one of the collection. Second, notice how these representations of oneness are wedded to the image: "a leaf falls."

FIGURE 1-7
Diagram of e. e. cummings'
"l(a."

As you look at the poem, your eye follows a downward path that swirls in a pattern similar to the diagram in Figure 1-7. This is merely following the parentheses and consonants. As you follow the vowels as well, you see curves that become spirals, and the image is indeed much like that of a leaf actually falling. This accounts for the long, thin look of the poem. Now, go back to the poem and reread it. Has your response changed? If so, how?

Of course, most poems do not work in quite this way. Most poems do not rely on the way they look on the page, although this is one of the most important strategies cummings uses. But what most poets are concerned with is the way the images or verbal pictures fit into the totality of the poem, how they make us experience the whole poem more intensely. In cummings' poem the single, falling, dying leaf — one out of so many — is perfect for helping us understand loneliness from a dying person's point of view. People are like leaves in that they are countless when they are alive and together. But like leaves, they die singly. And when one person separates himself or herself from the community of friends, that person is as alone as the separate leaf.

Abstract Ideas and Concrete Images

"l(a" presents an abstract idea fused with a concrete image or word picture. It is concrete because what is described is a physical event — a falling leaf. Loneliness, on the other hand, is abstract. Take an abstract idea: love, hate, indecision, arrogance, jealousy, ambition, justice, civil rights, prejudice, revenge, revolution, coyness, insanity, or any other. Then link it with some physical object or event that you think expresses the abstract idea. "Expresses" here means simply making us see the object as portraying — and helping us understand — the abstract idea. Of course, you need not follow cummings' style of splitting words and using parentheses. You may use any way of lining up the letters and words that you think is interesting.

In *Paradise Lost* John Milton describes hell as a place with "Rocks, Caves, Lakes, Fens, Bogs, Dens, and shades of death." Now, neither you nor the poet has ever seen "shades of death," although the idea is in Psalm 23, "the valley of the shadow of death." Milton gets away with it because he has linked the abstract idea of shades of death to so many concrete images in this single line. He is giving us images that suggest the mood of hell just as much as they describe the landscape, and we realize that he gives us so many topographic details in order to get us ready for the last detail — the abstract idea of shades of death.

There is much more to be said about poetry, of course, but on a preliminary level poetry worked in much the same way in the seventeenth-century England of Milton as it does in contemporary America. The same principles are at work: Described objects or events are used as a means of bringing abstract ideas to life. The descriptions take on a wider and deeper significance — wider in the sense that the descriptions are connected with the larger scope of abstract ideas, deeper in the sense that because of these descriptions the abstract ideas become vividly focused and more meaningful. Thus cummings' poem gives us insight — a penetrating understanding — into what we all must face: the isolating loneliness of our death.

The following poem is highly complex: the memory of an older culture (simplicity, in this poem) and the consideration of a newer culture (complexity). It is an African poem by the contemporary Nigerian poet Gabriel Okara; and knowing that it is African, we can begin to appreciate the extreme complexity of Okara's feelings about the clash of the old and new cultures. He symbolizes the clash in terms of music, and he opposes two musical instruments: the drum and the piano. They stand for the African and the European cultures. But even beyond the musical images that abound in this poem, look closely at the images of nature, the pictures of the panther and leopard, and see how Okara imagines them.

PIANO AND DRUMS

When at break of day at a riverside
I hear jungle drums telegraphing
the mystic rhythm, urgent, raw
like bleeding flesh, speaking of
primal youth and the beginning,
I see the panther ready to pounce,
the leopard snarling about to leap
and the hunters crouch with spears poised;
And my blood ripples, turns torrent,
topples the years and at once I'm
in my mother's lap a suckling;
at once I'm walking simple
paths with no innovations,
rugged, fashioned with the naked
warmth of hurrying feet and groping hearts
in green leaves and wild flowers pulsing.
Then I hear a wailing piano
solo speaking of complex ways
in tear-furrowed concerto;
of far-away lands
and new horizons with
coaxing diminuendo, counterpoint,
crescendo. But lost in the labyrinth
of its complexities, it ends in the middle
of a phrase at a daggerpoint.
And I lost in the morning mist
of an age at a riverside keep
wandering in the mystic rhythm
of jungle drums and the concerto.

PERCEPTION KEY   "Piano and Drums"

1. What are the most important physical objects in the poem? What cultural significance do they have?

2. Why do you think Okara chose the drum and the piano to help reveal the clash between the two cultures? Where are his allegiances?

Such a poem speaks directly to legions of the current generation of Africans. But consider some points in light of what we have said earlier. In order to perceive the kind of emotional struggle that Okara talks about — the subject matter of the poem — we need to know something about Africa and the struggle African nations have in modernizing themselves along the lines of more technologically advanced nations. We also need to know something of the history of Africa and the fact that European nations, such as Britain in the case of Nigeria, once controlled much of Africa. Knowing these things, we know then that there is no thought of the "I" of the poem accepting the "complex ways" of the new culture without qualification. The "I" does not think of the culture of the piano as manifestly superior to the culture of the drum. That is why the labyrinth of complexities ends at a "daggerpoint." The new culture is a mixed blessing.

Ideas about Africa and slavery, for most of us, tend to be rather general. It is hard to get a fix on the horror of slavery. Now read this powerful poem by Maya Angelou.

AFRICA

Thus she had lain
sugarcane sweet
deserts her hair
golden her feet
mountains her breasts
two Niles her tears.
Thus she has lain
Black through the years.

Over the white seas
rime white and cold
brigands ungentled
icicle bold
took her young daughters
sold her strong sons
churched her with Jesus
bled her with guns.
Thus she has lain.

Now she is rising
remember her pain
remember the losses
her screams loud and vain
remember her riches
her history slain
now she is striding
although she had lain.

| PERCEPTION KEY | "Africa" |

The word *lain* is used four times and is the final word. What effect is produced by this usage? As you think about this, substitute other words. How does this change the poem?

We have argued that the perception of a work of art is aided by background information and that sensitive perception must be aware of form, at least implicitly. But we believe there is much more to sensitive perception. Somehow the form of a work of art is an artistic form that clarifies or reveals values, and our response is intensified by our awareness of those revealed values. But how does an artistic form do this? And how does this awareness come to us? In the next chapter we shall consider these questions, and in doing so we will also raise that most important question What is a work of art? Once we have examined each of the arts, it will be clear, we hope, that the principles developed in these opening chapters are equally applicable to all the arts.

Summary

Unlike scientists, humanists generally do not use strictly objective standards. The arts reveal values; other humanities study values. Artistic form refers to the structure or organization of a work of art. Values are clarified or revealed by a work of art. Judging from the most ancient of artistic efforts, we can assert that the arts represent one of the most basic of human activities. They satisfy a need to explore and express the values that link us all together. By observing our responses to a work of art and examining the means by which the artist evokes those responses, we can deepen our understanding of art. Our approach to the humanities is through the arts and our taste in art connects with our deep feelings. Yet our taste is continually improved by experience and education. Background information about a work of art and increased sensitivity to its artistic form intensify our responses.

Bibliography

Chadwick, Whitney. *Women, Art, and Society*. London: Thames and Hudson, 1990.

Dewey, John. *Art as Experience*. New York: Capricorn Books, 1934.

Jarrett, James L. *The Humanities and Humanistic Education*. Reading, Mass.: Addison-Wesley, 1973.

Kirshenblatt-Gimblett, Barbara. *Destination Culture*. Berkeley: University of California Press, 1998.

Maslow, Abraham. *New Knowledge in Human Values*. Chicago: Regnery, 1971.

Neill, Alex, and Aaron Ridley. *Arguing about Art*. New York: McGraw-Hill, 1995.

Read, Herbert. *Art and Alienation*. New York: Viking, 1969.

———. *Education through Art*, new rev. ed. New York: Pantheon, 1963.

Santayana, George. *The Sense of Beauty*, critical ed. Cambridge, Mass.: MIT Press, 1988.

Whitehead, Alfred North. *Adventures of Ideas*. New York: Free Press, 1967.

Internet Resources

ART MUSEUMS AND EXHIBITS
http://www.yahoo.com/Arts/Museums__Galleries__and_Centers

ART ON THE INTERNET
http://www.art.net/

ARTSOURCE
http://www.ilpi.com/artsource/welcome.html

BRITISH MUSEUM
http://www.British-Museum.ac.uk/

BROWSE THE ARTS
http://wwar.com/browse.html

FRENCH CAVE PAINTINGS
http://www.culture.gouv.fr/culture/arcnat/chauvet/en/index.html

METROPOLITAN MUSEUM OF ART
http://www.metmuseum.org/

MODERN MUSEUM OF ART
http://www.moma.org/

CHAPTER 2

What Is a
Work of Art?

No definition for a *work of art* seems completely adequate, and none is universally accepted. Thus we shall not propose a definition here, but rather attempt to clarify some criteria or distinctions that can help us identify works of art. Since the term "work of art" implies the concept of making in two of its words — "work" and "art" (short for "artifice") — a work of art is often said to be something made by a person. Hence sunsets, beautiful trees, "found" natural objects such as grained driftwood, "paintings" by insects or songs by birds, and a host of other natural phenomena are not considered works of art, despite their beauty. You may not wish to accept the proposal that a work of art must be of human origin, but if you do accept it, consider the construction shown in Figure 2-1, Jim Dine's *Shovel*.

Shovel is part of a valuable collection and was first shown at an art gallery in New York City. Furthermore, Dine is considered an important American artist. He did not make the shovel himself, however. Like most shovels, the one in his construction, although designed by a person, was mass-produced. Dine mounted the shovel in front of a beautifully painted panel (obviously not evident in the photograph), and presented this construction for serious consideration. The construction is described as "mixed media," meaning it consists of several materials: paint, a panel, the box beneath the shovel, wood, a cord, and the metal of the shovel. Is *Shovel* a work of art?

We can hardly discredit the construction as a work of art simply because Dine did not make the shovel; after all, we often accept objects manufactured to specification by factories as genuine works of sculpture (see the Calder construction, Figure 5-12). Collages by Picasso and Braque, which include objects such as paper and nails mounted on a panel, are generally accepted as works of art. Museums have even accepted such objects as a

FIGURE 2-1
Jim Dine, *Shovel*. 1962.
Mixed media. (Photo courtesy
Sonnabend Gallery. © 2003
Jim Dine/Artists Rights Society [ARS], New York)

signed urinal by Marcel Duchamp, one of the *Dadaist* artists of the early twentieth century, who in many ways anticipated the works of Dine, Warhol, and others in the *Pop Art* movement of the 1950s and 1960s.

Identifying Art Conceptually

Three more or less accepted criteria for determining whether something is a work of art are that (1) the object or event is made by an artist, (2) the object or event is intended to be a work of art by its maker, and (3) recognized experts agree that it is a work of art. Unfortunately, one cannot always determine these criteria by only perceiving the work. In many cases, for instance, we may confront an object such as *Shovel* and not know whether Dine constructed the shovel, thus not satisfying the first criterion that the object be made by an artist; or whether Dine intended it to be a work of art; or whether experts agree that it is a work of art. In fact, Dine did not make this particular shovel; but because this fact cannot be established by perception, one has to be told.

PERCEPTION KEY   Identifying a Work of Art

1. If Dine actually made the shovel, would *Shovel* then unquestionably be a work of art?
2. Suppose Dine made the shovel, and it was absolutely perfect in the sense that it could not be readily distinguished from a mass-produced shovel. Would that kind of perfection make the piece more a work of art or less a work of art? Suppose Dine did not make the shovel but did make the panel and the box. Then would it seem easier to identify *Shovel* as a work of art?
3. Find people who hold opposing views about whether *Shovel* is a work of art. Ask them to argue the point in detail, being particularly careful not to argue simply from personal opinion. Ask them to point out what it is about the object itself that qualifies it for or disqualifies it from being identified as a work of art.

Identifying art conceptually seems to the authors not very useful. Because someone intends to make a work of art tells us little. It is the made rather than the making that counts. To claim otherwise is called the "intentional fallacy." The third criterion—the judgment of experts—is obviously important but surely debatable.

Identifying Art Perceptually

Perception, what we can observe, and *conception,* what we know or think we know, are closely related. We often are led to see what we expect or want to see; we recognize an object because it conforms to our conception of it. For example, in architecture we recognize churches and office buildings as distinct because of our conception of what churches and office buildings are supposed to look like. The ways of identifying a work of art mentioned above depend on the conceptions of the artist and experts on art and not enough on our perceptions of the work itself. Objects and events have qualities that can be perceived without the help of artists or experts, although these specialists are often helpful. If we wish to consider the artistic qualities of objects or events, we can easily do so. Yet to do so implies an attitude or an approach.

We suggest an approach here that is simple and flexible and that depends largely on perception. The distinctions of this approach will not lead us necessarily to a definition of art, but they will offer us a way to examine objects and events with reference to whether they possess artistically perceivable qualities. And, in some cases at least, it should bring us to reasonable grounds for distinguishing certain objects or events as art. We will consider four basic terms related primarily to the perceptual nature of a work of art:

Subject matter: some value external to the work of art.

Artistic form: the organization of a medium that clarifies some subject matter.

Content: the clarified subject matter.

Participation: "thinking from" versus "thinking at."

Understanding any one of these terms requires an understanding of the others. Thus we will follow—please trust us—what may appear to be an illogical order: artistic form; participation; participation and artistic form; content; subject matter; subject matter and artistic form; and, finally, participation, artistic form, and content.

Artistic Form

All objects and events have form. They are bounded by limits of time and space, and they have parts with distinguishable relationships to one another. Form is the interrelationships of part to part and part to whole. To say that some object or event has form means it has some degree of perceptible unity. To say that something has *artistic form*, however, usually implies that there is a strong degree of perceptible unity. It is artistic form that distinguishes art from objects or events that are not works of art.

Artistic form implies that the parts we perceive — for example, line, color, texture, shape, and space in a painting — have been unified for the most profound effect possible. That effect is revelatory. Artistic form reveals, clarifies, enlightens, gives fresh meaning to something valuable in life, some subject matter. A form that lacks a significant degree of unity is unlikely to accomplish this. Our daily experiences usually are characterized more by disunity than by unity. Consider, for instance, the order of your experiences during a typical day or even a segment of that day. Compare that order with the order most novelists give to the experiences of their characters. One impulse for reading novels is to experience the tight unity that artistic form usually imposes, a unity almost none of us comes close to achieving in our daily lives. Much the same is true of music. Noises and random tones in everyday experience lack the order that most composers impose. Indeed, even nature's models of unity are usually far less strongly perceptible than the unity of most works of art.

Consider, for example, birdsongs, which are clearly precursors of music. Even the song of the meadowlark, which is longer than most birdsongs, is fragmentary and incomplete. It is like a theme that is simply a statement and repetition, lacking development or contrast. Thus the composer, finding the meadowlark's short melody monotonous when repeated again and again, enriches it by such devices as adding notes to those already sounded, varying the melody through alternation of rhythm, changing the pitch of some of the notes to higher or lower positions on the musical scale, or adding a completely different melody to set up a sense of contrast and tension with the initial melody.

Since strong, perceptible unity appears so infrequently in nature, we tend to value the perceptible unity of artistic form. Works of art differ in the power of their unity. If that power is weak, then the question arises: Is this a work of art? Consider Mondrian's painting (Figure 1-6) with reference to its artistic form. If its parts were not carefully proportioned in the overall structure of the painting, the tight balance that produces a strong unity would be lost. Mondrian was so concerned with this balance that he measured the areas of lines and rectangles to be sure they had a clear, almost mathematical, relationship to the totality. Of course, disunity or playing against expectations of unity can also be artistically useful at times. Some artists realize how strong the impulse toward unity is in those who have perceived many works of art. For some people, the contemporary attitude toward the loose organization of formal elements is something of a norm, and the highly unified work of art is thought of as old-fashioned. However, it seems that the effects achieved by a lesser degree of unity succeed only because we recognize them as departures from our well-known, highly organized forms.

Artistic form as distinct from nonartistic form, we have suggested, is likely to involve a high degree of perceptible unity. But how do we determine what is a high degree? And if we cannot be clear about this, how can this distinction be of much help in distinguishing works of art from things that are not works of art? A very strong unity does not *necessarily* identify a work of art. That formal unity must give us insight into some value. Nevertheless, a very strong unity is usually a sign that the work is likely to be art.

Consider, for example, the news photograph—taken on one of the main streets of Saigon in February 1968 by Eddie Adams, an Associated Press photographer—showing Brig. Gen. Nguyen Ngoc Loan, then South Vietnam's national police chief, killing a Vietcong captive (Figure 2-2). Adams stated that his picture was an accident, that his hand moved the camera reflexively as he saw the general raise the revolver. The lens of the camera was set in such a way that the background was thrown out of focus. The blurring of the background helped bring out the drama of the foreground scene. Does this photograph have a high degree of perceptible unity? Certainly the experience of the photographer is evident. Not many amateur photographers would have had enough skill to catch such a fleeting event with such stark clarity. If an amateur had accomplished this, we

FIGURE 2-2
Eddie Adams, *Execution in
Saigon*. 1968. Silver halide.
(© AP/Wide World Photos)

would be inclined to believe that it was more luck than skill. Adams' pride
in the photograph is even more evident. He risked his life to get it. If this
photograph had not been widely publicized and admired, we can imagine
the dismay he would have felt. But do we admire this work the way we admire Siqueiros's *Echo of a Scream*? Do we experience these two works in the
same basic way?

Compare a painting of a somewhat similar subject — Goya's *May 3, 1808*
(Figure 2-3). Goya chose the most terrible moment, that split second before
the crash of the guns. There is no doubt that the executions will go on. The
desolate mountain pushing down from the left blocks escape, while from
the right the firing squad relentlessly hunches forward. The soldiers' thick
legs — planted wide apart and parallel — support like sturdy pillars the
blind, pressing wall formed by their backs. These are men of a military machine. Their rifles, flashing in the bleak light of the ghastly lantern, thrust
out as if they belonged to their bodies. It is unimaginable that any of these
men would defy the command of their superiors. In the dead of night, the
doomed are backed up against the mountain like animals being slaughtered. One man alone flings up his arms in a gesture of utter despair — or is
it defiance? The uncertainty increases the intensity of our attention. Most
of the rest of the men bury their faces, while a few, with eyes staring out of
their sockets, glance out at what they cannot help seeing — the sprawling
dead smeared in blood.

With the photograph of the execution in Vietnam, despite its immediate
and powerful attraction, it takes only a glance or two to grasp what is presented. Undivided attention, perhaps, is necessary to become aware of

FIGURE 2-3
Francisco Goya, *May 3, 1808*.
1814–1815. Oil on canvas,
8 feet 9 inches × 13 feet
4 inches. The Prado, Madrid.
(© Scala/Art Resource, New
York)

the significance of the event, but not sustained attention. In fact, to take careful notice of all the details—such as the patterns on the prisoner's shirt—does not add to our awareness of the significance of the photograph. If anything, our awareness will be sharper and more productive if we avoid such detailed examination. Is such the case with the Goya? We believe not. Indeed, without sustained attention to the details of this work, most of what is revealed would be missed. For example, block out everything but the dark shadow at the bottom right. Note how differently that shadow appears when it is isolated. We must see the details individually and collectively, as they work together. Unless we are aware of their collaboration, we are not going to grasp fully the total form.

Close examination of the Adams photograph reveals several efforts to increase the unity and thus the power of the print. For example, the flak jacket of General Loan has been darkened so as to remove distracting details. The buildings in the background have been "dodged out" (held back in printing so that they are not fully visible). The shadows of trees on the road have been softened so as to lead the eye inexorably to the hand that holds the gun. The space around the head of the victim is also dodged out so that it appears that something like a halo surrounds the head. All this is done in the act of printing.

We are suggesting that the Goya has a much higher degree of perceptible unity than Adams' photograph, that perhaps only the Goya has artistic form. We base these conclusions on what is given for us to perceive: the fact that the part-to-part and the part-to-whole relationships are much stronger in the Goya. Now, of course, you may disagree. No judgment about such matters is indisputable. Indeed, that is part of the fun of talking about whether something is or is not a work of art — we can learn how to perceive from each other.

PERCEPTION KEY   Goya and Adams

1. Is the painting different from Adams' photograph in the way the details work together? Be specific.
2. Could any detail in the painting be changed or removed without weakening the unity of the total design? What about the photograph?
3. Does the photograph or the painting more powerfully reveal human barbarity?
4. Are there details in the photograph that distract your attention?
5. Do buildings in the background of the photograph add to or subtract from the power of what is being portrayed here? Compare the effect of the looming architecture in the painting.
6. Do the shadows on the street add anything to the significance of the photograph? Compare the shadows on the ground in the painting.
7. Does it make any significant difference that the Vietcong prisoner's shirt is checkered? Compare the white shirt on the gesturing man in the painting.
8. Is the expression on the soldier's face, along the left side of the photograph, appropriate to the situation? Compare the facial expressions in the painting.
9. Can these works be fairly compared when one is in black and white and the other is in full color?
10. What are basic differences between seeing a photograph of a real man being killed and a painting of that event?

Participation

Both the photograph and the Goya tend to grasp our attention. Initially for most of us, probably, the photograph has more pulling power than the painting, especially as the two works are illustrated here. In its setting in the Prado in Madrid, however, the size of the Goya and its powerful lighting and color draw the eye like a magnet. But the term "participate" is more accurately descriptive of what we are likely to be doing in our experience of the painting. With the painting, we must not only give but also sustain our undivided attention. If that happens, we lose our self-consciousness, our sense of being separate, of standing apart from the painting. We participate. And only by means of participation can we come close to a full awareness of what the painting is about.

Works of art are created, exhibited, and preserved for us to perceive with not only undivided but also sustained attention. Artists, critics, and philosophers of art or aestheticians generally are in agreement about this. Thus if, in order to understand and appreciate it fully, a work requires our participation, we have an indication that the work is art. Therefore — unless our analyses have been incorrect, and you should satisfy yourself about this — the Goya would seem to be a work of art. Conversely, the photograph is not as obviously a work of art as the painting, and this is the case despite the fascinating impact of the photograph. Yet these are highly tentative judgments. We are far from being clear about why the Goya requires our participation and the photograph apparently does not. Until we are clear about these "whys," the grounds for these judgments remain shaky.

Goya's painting tends to draw us on until, ideally, we become aware of all the details and their interrelationships. For example, the long dark shadow at the bottom right underlines the line of the firing squad, and the line of the firing squad helps bring out the shadow. Moreover, this shadow is the darkest and most opaque part of the painting. It has a forbidding, blind, fateful quality that, in turn, reinforces the ominous appearance of the firing squad. The dark shadow on the street just below the forearm of General Loan seems less powerful. The photograph has fewer meaningful details. Thus our attempts to keep our attention on the photograph tend to be forced—which is to say that they will fail. Sustained attention or participation cannot be achieved by acts of will. The splendid singularity of what we are attending to must fascinate and control us to the point where we no longer need to will our attention. We can make up our minds to give our undivided attention to something. But if that something lacks the pulling power that holds our attention, we cannot participate with it.

The ultimate test for recognizing a work of art, then, is how it works in us, what it does to us. *Participative experiences* of works of art are communions—experiences so full and fruitful that they enrich our lives. Such experiences are life-enhancing not just because of the great satisfaction they may give us at the moment but also because they make more or less permanent contributions to our future life. Does Mondrian's *Composition in White, Black, and Red* (Figure 1-6) heighten your perception of the relationships between sharply edged vertical and horizontal lines, the neatness and "spatial comfortableness" of these kinds of rectangles, and the rich qualities of white, black, and red? Does cummings' "l(a" heighten your perception of falling leaves and deepen your understanding of the loneliness of death? Do you see shovels differently, perhaps, after experiencing *Shovel* by Dine? If not, presumably they are not works of art. But this assumes that we have really participated with these works, that we have allowed them to work properly in our experience, so that if the meaning or content were present it had a chance to come forth into our awareness. Of the four basic distinctions—subject matter, artistic form, content, and participation—the most fundamental is participation. We must not only understand what it means to participate but also be able to participate. Otherwise, the other basic distinctions, even if they make good theoretical sense, will not be of much practical help in making art more important in our lives. The central importance of participation requires further elaboration.

Participation involves undivided and sustained attention. However, spectator attention dominates most of our experiences. Spectator attention is more commonsensical, and it works much more efficiently than participative attention in most situations. We would not get very far changing a tire if we only participated with the tire. We would not be able to use the scientific method if we failed to distinguish between ourselves and our

FIGURE 2-4
Paul Cézanne, *Mont Sainte-Victoire*. 1886–1887. Oil on canvas, 23½ × 28½ inches. The Phillips Collection, Washington, D.C.

data. Practical success on every level requires problem solving. This requires distinguishing the means from the end and then manipulating the means to achieve the end. In so doing, we are aware of ourselves as subjects distinct from the objects involved in our situation. In turn, the habit of spectator attention gets deeply ingrained in all of us because of the demands of survival. That is why, especially after we have left the innocence of childhood, participative attention is so rarely achieved. A child who has not yet had to solve problems, alternatively, is dominated by participative attention. In this sense, to learn how to experience works of art properly requires a return to the receptive attitudes of childhood, for in childhood we were likelier to think from things than at things. As children, we did not always try to dominate things but, rather, let them reveal themselves to us. Watch young children at play. Sometimes they will just push things around, but often they will let things dominate them. Then, if they are looking at flowers, for example, they will begin to follow the curves and textures with their hands, be entranced with their smell, perhaps even the taste—so absorbed that they seem to listen, as if the flowers could speak.

As participators we do not think of the work of art with reference to categories applicable to objects—such as what kind of thing it is. We grasp the work of art directly. When, for example, we participate with Cézanne's *Mont Sainte-Victoire* (Figure 2-4), we are not making geographical or geological observations. We are not thinking of the mountain as an object. For if we

FIGURE 2-5
Mont Sainte-Victoire.
(Courtesy John Rewald)

did, Mont Sainte-Victoire would pale into a mere instance of the appropriate scientific categories. We might judge that the mountain is a certain type. But in that process the vivid impact of Cézanne's mountain would dim down as the focus of our attention shifted beyond in the direction of generality. This is the natural thing to do with mountains if you are a geologist. It is also the natural thing to do with this particular colorless photograph of the mountain (Figure 2-5). The photograph lends itself to the direction of generality because its form fails to hold us to the photograph in all its specificity. But, to be only a spectator of the Cézanne would be unnatural in the sense that we would block off much of the satisfaction we might have.

When we are participators, we *"think from."* Our thoughts are dominated so much by something that we are unaware of our separation from that something. Thus the artistic form initiates and controls every thought and feeling. When we are spectators, we *"think at."*[1] Our thoughts dominate something, and we are aware of our separation from that something. We set the object into our framework. We see the Cézanne—name it, identify its maker, classify its style, recall its background information—but this approach will never get us into the Cézanne as a work of art. Of course, such knowledge can be very helpful. But that knowledge is most helpful when it

---

[1]There is evidence that the mode of "thinking from" is located mainly on the right side of the brain, whereas "thinking at" (usually described as analytic thinking) is on the left. See the fascinating study by Betty Edwards, *Drawing on the Right Side of the Brain* (New York: Putnam, 1999). Also, F. David Martin, "Spiritual Asymmetry in Portraiture," *British Journal of Aesthetics*, vol. 5, no. 1 (January 1965).

is under the control of the work of art working in our experience. This happens when the artistic form not only suggests that knowledge but also keeps it within the boundaries of the painting. Otherwise the painting will fade away. Its splendid specificity will be sacrificed for some generality. Its content or meaning will be missed.

Participators are thrust out of their ordinary, everyday, business-as-usual attitude. They are thrust out of themselves. The content of the work of art makes contact. And then the "concrete suchness" of the work of art penetrates and permeates their consciousness. Even if they forget such experiences, which is unlikely, a significant change has taken place in their perceptive organs. New sets of lenses, so to speak, have been more or less permanently built into their vision. After participating with Cézanne's *Mont Sainte-Victoire*, participators will automatically see mountains differently— something more about their colors, lines, shapes, rhythms, textures, and stability. Participative experiences transform us.

These are strong claims, and they may not be convincing. In any case, before concluding our search for what a work of art is, let us seek further clarification of our other basic distinctions—artistic form, content, and subject matter. This is worth our trouble. Even if you disagree with the conclusions, clarification helps understanding. And understanding helps appreciation.

Participation and Artistic Form

The participative experience—the undivided and sustained attention to an object or event that makes us lose our sense of separation from that object or event—is induced by strong or artistic form. Participation is not likely to develop with weak form because weak form tends to allow our attention to wander. Therefore, one indication of a strong form is the fact that participation occurs. Another indication of artistic form is the way it clearly identifies a whole or totality. In the case of the visual arts, a whole is a visual field limited by boundaries that separate that field from its surroundings. Both Adams' photograph and Goya's painting have visual fields with boundaries.

No matter what wall these two pictures are placed on, the Goya probably will stand out more distinctly and sharply from its background. Part of this is because the Goya is in vibrant color and on a large scale: eight feet nine inches by thirteen feet four inches, whereas the Adams photograph is normally exhibited as an eight- by ten-inch print. However carefully such a photograph is printed, it probably will include some random details. No detail in the Goya, though, fails to play a part in the total structure. To take one further instance, notice how the lines of the soldiers' sabers and their straps reinforce the ruthless forward push of the firing squad. The photograph, however, has a relatively weak form because a large number of details fail to cooperate with other details. For example, running down the right side of General Loan's body is a very erratic line. This line fails to tie in with anything else in the photograph. If this line were smoother, it would connect more closely with the lines formed by the Vietcong prisoner's body. The connection between killer and killed would be more vividly established. But as it is, and after several viewings, our eye tends to wander off the photograph. The unity of its form is so slack that the edges of the photograph seem to blur off into their surroundings. That is another way of saying that the form of the photograph fails to establish a clear-cut whole or identity.

Artistic form normally is a prerequisite if our attention is to be grasped and held. Artistic form makes our participation possible. Some philosophers of art, such as Clive Bell and Roger Fry, even go so far as to claim that the presence of artistic form—what they call "significant form"—is all that is necessary to identify a work of art. And by significant form, in the case of painting, they mean the interrelationships of elements: line to line, line to color, color to color, color to shape, shape to shape, shape to texture, and so on. The elements make up the artistic medium, the "stuff" the form organizes. According to Bell and Fry, any reference of these elements and their interrelationships to actual objects or events should be basically irrelevant in our awareness.

According to the proponents of significant form, if we take explicit notice of the executions as an important part of Goya's painting, then we are not perceiving properly. We are experiencing the painting not as a work of art but rather as an illustration telling a story, thus reducing a painting that is a work of art to the level of commercial communications. When the lines, colors, and the like pull together tightly, independently of any objects or events they may represent, there is a significant form. That is what we should perceive when we are perceiving a work of art, not a portrayal of some object or event. Anything that has significant form is a work of art. If you ignore the objects and events represented in the Goya, significant form is evident. All the details depend on each other and jell together, creating a strong structure. Therefore, the Goya is a work of art. If you ignore the objects and events represented in the Adams photograph, significant form is not evident. The organization of the parts is too loose, creating a weak structure. Therefore, the photograph, according to Bell and Fry, would not be a work of art. "To appreciate a work of art," according to Clive Bell, "we need bring with us nothing from life, no knowledge of its ideas and affairs, no familiarity with its emotions."

Does this theory of how to identify a work of art satisfy you? Do you find that in ignoring the representation of objects and events in the Goya much of what is important in that painting is left out? For example, does the line of the firing squad carry a forbidding quality partly because you recognize that this is a line of men in the process of killing other men? In turn, does the close relationship of that line with the line of the long shadow at the bottom right depend to some degree upon that forbidding quality? If you think so, then it follows that the artistic form of this work legitimately and relevantly refers to objects and events. Somehow artistic form, at least in some cases, has a significance that goes beyond just the design formed by elements such as lines and colors. Artistic form somehow goes beyond itself, somehow refers to objects and events from the world beyond the form. Artistic form informs us about things outside itself. These things—as revealed by the artistic form—we shall call the content of a work of art. But how does the artistic form do this?

Content

Let us begin to try to answer this question by examining more closely the meanings of the Adams photograph and the Goya painting. Both basically, although oversimply, are about the same abstract idea—barbarity. In the case of the photograph, we have an example of this barbarity. Since it is very close to any knowledgeable American's interests, this instance is likely to set off a lengthy chain of thoughts and feelings. These thoughts and feelings, furthermore, seem to lie "beyond" the photograph. Suppose a debate developed over the meaning of this photograph. The photograph itself would play an important role primarily as a starting point. From there on the photograph would probably be ignored except for dramatizing points. For example, one person might argue, "Remember that this occurred during the Tet offensive and innocent civilians were being killed by the Vietcong. Look again at the street and think of the consequences if the terrorists had not been eliminated." Another person might argue, "General Loan was one of the highest officials in South Vietnam's government, and he was taking the law into his own hands like a Nazi." What would be very strange in such a debate would be a discussion of every detail or even many of the details in the photograph.

In a debate about the meaning of the Goya, however, every detail and its interrelationships with other details become relevant. The meaning of the painting seems to lie "within" the painting. And yet, paradoxically, this meaning, as in the case of the Adams photograph, involves ideas and feelings that lie beyond the painting. How can this be? Let us first consider some background information. On May 2, 1808, guerrilla warfare had flared up all over Spain against the occupying forces of the French. By the following day, Napoleon's men were completely back in control in Madrid and the surrounding area. Many of the guerrillas were executed. And, according to tradition, Goya portrayed the execution of forty-three of these guerrillas on May 3 near the hill of Principe Pio just outside Madrid. This background information is important if we are to understand and appreciate the painting fully. Yet notice how differently this information works in our experience of the painting compared with the way background information works in our experience of the Adams photograph.

The execution in Eddie Adams' photograph was of a man who had just murdered one of General Loan's best friends and had then knifed to death his wife and six children. The general was part of the Vietnamese army fighting with the assistance of the United States, and this photograph was widely disseminated with a caption describing the victim as a suspected terrorist. What shocked Americans who saw the photograph was the summary justice that Loan meted out. It was not until much later that the details of the victim's crimes were published. A century from now, the photograph may be largely ignored except by historians of the Vietnam War. If you are dubious about this, consider how quickly most of us pass over photographs of similar scenes from World War I and even World War II. The value of the Adams photograph seems to be closely tied to its historical moment.

With the Goya, the background information, although very helpful, is not as essential. Test this for yourself. Would your interest in Adams' photograph last very long if you completely lacked background information? In the case of the Goya, the background information helps us understand the where, when, and why of the scene. But even without this information, the painting probably would still grasp and hold the attention of most of us because it would still have significant meaning. We would still have a powerful image of barbarity, and the artistic form would hold us on that image. In the Prado Museum in Madrid, Goya's painting continually draws and holds the attention of innumerable viewers, many of whom know little or nothing about the rebellion of 1808. Adams' photograph is also a powerful image, of course—and probably initially more powerful than the Goya—but the form of the photograph is not strong enough to hold most of us on that image for very long.

With the Goya, the abstract idea (barbarity) and the concrete image (the firing squad in the process of killing) are tied tightly together because the form of the painting is tight. We see the barbarity in the lines, colors, masses, shapes, groupings, and lights and shadows of the painting itself. The details of the painting keep referring to other details and to the totality. They keep holding our attention. Thus the ideas and feelings that the details and their organization awaken within us keep merging with the form. We are prevented from separating the meaning or content of the painting from its form because the form is so fascinating. The form constantly intrudes, however unobtrusively. It will not let us ignore it. We see the firing squad killing, and this evokes the idea of barbarity and the feeling of horror. But the lines, colors, mass, shapes, and shadowings of that firing squad form a pattern that keeps exciting and guiding our eyes. And then the pattern leads us to the pattern formed by the victims. Ideas of fatefulness and feelings of pathos are evoked, but they, too, are fused with the form. The form of the Goya is like a powerful magnet that allows nothing within its range to escape its pull. Artistic form fuses or embodies its meaning with itself.

In addition to participation and artistic form, then, we have come upon another basic distinction—content. Unless a work has content—meaning fused or embodied with its form—we shall say that the work is not art. Content is the meaning of artistic form. If we are correct (for our view is by no means universally accepted), artistic form always informs—has meaning or content. And that content, as we experience it when we participate, is always ingrained in the artistic form. We do not perceive an artistic form and then a content. We perceive them as inseparable. Of course, we can separate them analytically. But when we do so we are not having a participative experience. Moreover, when the form is weak—that is, less than artistic—we experience the form and its meaning separately. We see the form of the Adams photograph, and it evokes thoughts and feelings, indeed, a very powerful meaning. But the form is not strong enough to keep its meaning fused with itself. The photograph lacks content, not because it lacks meaning but because the meaning is not merged with the form. Idea and image break apart.

PERCEPTION KEY   Goya and Adams Revisited

We have argued that the painting by Goya is a work of art and the photograph by Adams is not. Even if the three basic distinctions we have made so far—artistic form, participation, and content—are useful, we may have misapplied them. Bring out every possible argument against the view that the painting is a work of art and the photograph is not a work of art.

Subject Matter

The content is the meaning of a work of art. The content is embedded in the artistic form. But what does the content interpret? We shall call it *subject matter*. Content is the interpretation—by means of an artistic form—of subject matter. Thus, subject matter is the fourth basic distinction that helps identify a work of art. Since every work of art must have a content, every work of art must have a subject matter, and this may be any aspect of experience that is of some human interest. Anything related to a human interest is a value. Some values are positive, such as pleasure and health. Other values are negative, such as pain and ill health. They are values because they are related to human interests. Negative values are the subject matter of both Adams' photograph and Goya's painting. But the photograph, unlike the painting, has no content. The less than artistic form of the photograph simply *presents* its subject matter. The form does not transform the subject matter, does not enrich its significance. In comparison, the artistic form of the painting enriches or interprets its subject matter, says something significant about it. In the photograph the subject matter is directly given. But the subject matter of the painting is not just there in the painting. It has been transformed by the form. What is directly given in the painting is the content.

The meaning or content of a work of art is what is revealed about a subject matter. But in that revelation you must imagine the subject matter. If someone had taken a news photograph of the May 3 executions, that would be a record of Goya's subject matter. The content of the Goya is its interpretation of the barbarity of those executions. Adams' photograph lacks content because it merely shows us an example of this barbarity. That is not to disparage the photograph, for its purpose was news, not art. A similar kind of photograph—that is, one lacking artistic form—of the May 3 executions would also lack content. Now, of course, you may disagree with these conclusions for very good reasons. You may find more transformation of the subject matter in Adams' photograph than in Goya's painting. For example, you may believe that transforming the visual experience in black and white distances it from reality and intensifies content. In any case, such disagreement can help the perception of both parties, provided the debate itself is focused. It is hoped that the basic distinctions we are making—subject matter, artistic form, content, and participation—will aid that focusing.

Subject Matter
and Artistic Form

Whereas a subject matter is a value that we may perceive before any artistic interpretation, the content is the significantly interpreted subject matter as revealed by the artistic form. Thus, the subject matter is never directly presented in a work of art, for the subject matter has been transformed by the form. Artistic form transforms and, in turn, informs about life. The conscious intentions of the artist may include magical, religious, political, economic, and other purposes; the conscious intentions may not include the purpose of clarifying values. Yet underlying the artist's activity—going back to cavework (Figure 1-1)—is always the creation of a form that illuminates something from life, some subject matter. Content is the subject matter detached by means of the form from its accidental or insignificant aspects. Artistic form makes the significance of a subject matter more manifest. Artistic form is the means whereby values are threshed from the husks of irrelevancies. A form that only entertains or distracts or shocks is not artistic (we will come back to this issue in detail in Chapter 14). Whereas nonartistic form merely presents a subject matter, artistic form makes that subject matter clearer and more vivid.

Artistic form draws from the chaotic state of life—which, as Van Gogh describes it, is like "a sketch that didn't come off"—a distillation. In our interpretation, Adams' photograph is like "a sketch that didn't come off," because it has numerous meaningless details. Goya's form eliminates meaningless detail. The work of art creates an illusion that illuminates reality. Thus, such paradoxical declarations as Delacroix's are explained: "Those things which are most real are the illusions I create in my paintings." Or Edward Weston's "The photographer who is an artist reveals the essence of what lies before the lens with such clear insight that the beholder may find the recreated image more real and comprehensible than the actual object." Camus asserted, "If the world were clear, art would not exist." Artistic form is an economy that produces a lucidity that enables us better to understand and, in turn, manage our lives. Hence the informing of a work of art reveals a subject matter with value dimensions that go beyond the artist's idiosyncrasies and perversities. Whether or not Goya had idiosyncrasies and perversities, he did justice to his subject matter: He revealed it. The art of a period is the revelation of the collective soul of its time.

Values in everyday situations often are confused and obscured. In art, values are clarified. Art helps us to perceive what we have missed. Anyone who has participated with cummings' "l(a" will see autumn leaves with heightened sensitivity and will understand the isolation of loneliness and death more poignantly. In clarifying values, art gives us an understanding that supplements the truths of science. Dostoevsky teaches us as much about ourselves as Freud does. All of us require something that fascinates us for a time, something out of the routine of the practical and the theoretical. Participation with works of art is especially useful in this respect, for art transforms the routine. If a work of art "works" successfully in us, it is more than a momentary delight, for it deepens our understanding

FIGURE 2-6
Kevin Carter, *Vulture and Child in Sudan*. Silver halide. (© Kevin Carter/Corbis Sygma)

of what matters. Art adds to the permanent richness of our soul's self-attainment. Art helps us arrange our environment for authentic values. Art makes civilization possible.

Participation, Artistic Form, and Content

Participation is the necessary condition that makes possible our insightful perception of artistic form and content. Unless we participate with the Goya, we will fail to see the power of its artistic form. We will fail to see how the details work together to form a totality. We also will fail to grasp the content fully, for artistic form and content are inseparable. Thus we will have failed to gain insight into the subject matter. We will have collected just one more instance of barbarity. The Goya will have basically the same effect upon us as Adams' photograph except that it will be less important to us because it happened long ago. But if, on the contrary, we have participated with the Goya, we probably will never see such things as executions in quite the same way again. The insight that we have gained will tend to refocus our vision so that we will see similar subject matters with a heightened awareness.

Look, for example, at the photograph by Kevin Carter (Figure 2-6), which was published in the *New York Times* on March 26, 1993, and which won the Pulitzer Prize for photography in 1994. The form isolates two dramatic figures. The closest is a starving Sudanese child making her way to a feeding center. The other is a plump vulture waiting for the child to die. This powerful photograph raised a hue and cry, and the *New York Times* published a commentary explaining that Carter chased away the vulture and took the child to the feeding center. Unfortunately, Carter committed suicide in July 1994.

ARTISTIC FORM: EXAMPLES

Let us examine artistic form in a series of examples taken from the work of the late Roy Lichtenstein, in which the subject matter, compared with *May 3, 1808,* is not so obviously important. With such examples, a purely formal analysis should seem less artificial. In the late 1950s and early 1960s, Lichtenstein became interested in comic strips as subject matter. The story goes that his two young boys asked him to paint a Donald Duck "straight," without the encumbrances of art. But much more was involved. Born in 1923, Lichtenstein grew up before television. By the 1930s, the comic strip had become one of the most important of the mass media. Adventure, romance, sentimentality, and terror found expression in the stories of Tarzan, Flash Gordon, Superman, Wonder Woman, Steve Roper, Winnie Winkle, Mickey Mouse, Donald Duck, Batman and Robin, and the like. Even today, despite the competition of the soap operas on television, the comic strip remains an important mass medium.

The purpose of the comic strip for its producers is strictly commercial. And because of the large market for the comic strip, a premium has always been put on making the processes of production as inexpensive as possible. And so generations of mostly unknown commercial artists, going well back into the nineteenth century, developed ways of quick, cheap color printing. They developed a technique that could turn out cartoons like the products of an assembly line. Moreover, because their market included a large number of children, they developed ways of producing images that were immediately understandable and of striking impact. As the tradition evolved, it provided a common vocabulary: Both the technique and its product became increasingly standardized. The printed images became increasingly impersonal. Wonder Woman, Bugs Bunny, Donald Duck, and Batman all seemed to come from the same hand or, rather, the same machine.

FIGURE 2-7
Pair 1a

FIGURE 2-8
Pair 1b

Lichtenstein reports that he was attracted to the comic strip by its stark simplicity—the blatant primary colors, the ungainly black lines that encircle the shapes, the balloons that isolate the spoken words or the thoughts of the characters. He was struck by the apparent inconsistency between the strong emotions of the stories and the highly impersonal, mechanical style in which they were expressed. Despite the crudity of the comic strip, Lichtenstein saw power in the strong directness of the medium. Somehow the cartoons mirrored something about our selves. Lichtenstein set out to clarify what that something was. At first people laughed, as was to be expected. He was called the "worst artist in America." Today he is considered one of our best.

The accompanying examples (Figures 2-7 through 2-16) pair the original cartoon with Lichtenstein's transformation.[2] Both the comic strips and the transformations originally were in color, and Lichtenstein's paintings are much larger than the comic strips. For the purposes of analysis, however, our reproductions are presented in black and white, and the sizes equalized. The absence of color and the reduction of size all but destroy the power of Lichtenstein's work, but these changes will help us compare the structures. They will also help us to concentrate upon what is usually the most obvious element of two-dimensional visual structure—line. The five pairs of examples have been scrambled so that either the comic strip or Lichtenstein's painting of it may be on the left or right.

---

[2]These examples were suggested to us by an article on Lichtenstein's balloons. Albert Boime, "Roy Lichtenstein and the Comic Strip," *Art Journal*, vol. 28, no. 2 (Winter 1968–69): 155–159.

Decide which are the comic strips and which are Lichtenstein's transformations. Defend your decisions with reference to the strength of organization. Presumably Lichtenstein's works will possess much stronger structures than those of the commercial artists. Be as specific and detailed as possible. For example, compare the lines and shapes as they work together—more or less—in each example. Take plenty of time, for the perception of artistic form is something that must "work" in you. Such perception never comes instantaneously. Compare your judgments with those of others.

Compare your analysis of Pair 1 with ours (Figures 2-7 and 2-8). Example *a* of Pair 1, we think, has a much stronger structure than *b*. The organization of the parts of *a* is much more tightly unified. The circles formed by the peephole and its cover in *a* have a graceful, rhythmic unity lacking in *b*. Note how in *a* the contour lines, formed by the overlapping of the cover on the right side, have a long sweeping effect. These lines look as if they had been drawn by a human hand. In *b* the analogous contours, as well as the circles to which the contours belong, look as if they had been drawn with the aid of a compass. In *a* the circular border of the cover is broken at the right edge and by the balloon above, helping to soften the hard definiteness not only of this circle but also of the contours it forms with the circle of the peephole. In *a*, also, the man's fingers and most of his face are shadowed. These contrasts help give variety and irregularity to the peephole circle, which blends in smoothly with its surroundings compared to the abrupt insularity of the peephole in *b*. Notice, too, that in *b* a white outline goes almost completely around the cover, whereas in *a* this is avoided. Moreover, the balloon in *a* overlies a significant portion of the cover. In *b* the balloon is isolated and leaves the cover almost alone.

In *a* the line outlining the balloon as it overlies the cover repeats the contours of the overlapping cover and its peephole. Rhythm depends upon repetition, and repetition unifies. But repetition that is absolutely regular is monotonous. Try tapping a pencil with a strong beat followed by a weak beat, and continue to repeat this rhythm as exactly as you can. Against your will, and unconsciously, you may desire some variations in stress. You will do this because absolute repetition becomes boring. In *a* the repetitions of the contour formed by the peephole and its cover, as well as other repetitions, have variations. The repetitions unify, whereas the variations excite interest. There are more repetitions in *b;* but, lacking variations except of the most obvious kind, these repetitions are monotonous. For example, the size of the peephole and cover appear exactly the same. In *a*, though, sometimes the peephole appears larger and sometimes the cover. This subtle variation depends on the area on which your eyes focus. And this, in turn, is controlled by the lines and shapes in dynamic interrelationship. In *b* this kind of moving control is missing.

In *a* no part remains isolated. Thus the balloon as it extends over the breadth of the painting helps bind the lower parts together. At the same

FIGURE 2-9
Pair 2a

FIGURE 2-10
Pair 2b

time, the shape and contours of the balloon help accent the shape and contours of the other details. Even the shape of the man's mouth is duplicated partially by the shape of the balloon. Conversely, the balloon in *b* is more isolated from the other details. It just hangs there. Yet notice how the tail of the balloon in *a*, just below the exclamation point, repeats the curve of the latch of the cover and also how the curve of the tail is caught up in the sweep of the curves of the peephole and cover. In *a* the latch of the cover unobtrusively helps to orbit the cover around the peephole. In *b* the latch of the cover is awkwardly large, and this helps block any sense of dynamic interrelationship between the peephole and its cover. Whereas the cover seems light and graceful in *a* and only the top of a finger is needed to turn it back, in *b* a much heavier finger is necessary. Similarly, the lines of face and hand in *a* lightly integrate, whereas in *b* they are heavy and fail to work together very well. Compare, for example, the eye in *a* with the eye in *b*. Finally, there are meaningless details in *b*—the bright knob on the cover, for instance. Such details are eliminated in *a*. Even the shape and size of the lettering in *a* belong to the whole in a way completely lacking in *b*.

Now turn to Pair 2 (Figures 2-9 and 2-10). Limit your analysis to the design functioning of the lettering in the balloons of Pair 2.

PERCEPTION KEY Comic Strip and Lichtenstein's Transformation, Pair 2

1. Does the shape of the lettering in *a* play an important part in the formal organization? Explain your reasoning.
2. Does the shape of the lettering in *b* play an important part in the formal organization? Explain your reasoning.

FIGURE 2-11
Pair 3a

FIGURE 2-12
Pair 3b

FIGURE 2-13
Pair 4a

FIGURE 2-14
Pair 4b

FIGURE 2-15
Pair 5a

FIGURE 2-16
Pair 5b

Compare your analysis of Pair 2 with ours. We think it is only in *b* that the shape of the lettering plays an important part in the formal organization. Conversely, the shape of the lettering is distracting in *a*. In *b* the bulky balloons are eliminated and only two important words are used—"torpedo" and "LOS!" The three letters of which "LOS" is composed stand out very vividly. A regular shape among so many irregular shapes, the balloon's simple shape helps the letters stand out. Also, "LOS" is larger, darker, and more centrally located than "torpedo." Notice how no word or lettering stands out very vividly in *a*. Moreover, as Albert Boime points out in his study of Lichtenstein, the shapes of the letters in "LOS" are clues to the structure of the panel:

> The "L" is mirrored in the angle formed by the captain's hand and the vertical contour of his head and in that of the periscope. The "O" is repeated in the tubing of the periscope handle and in smaller details throughout the work. The oblique "S" recurs in the highlight of the captain's hat just left of the balloon, in the contours of the hat itself, in the shadow that falls along the left side of the captain's face, in the lines around his nose and in the curvilinear tubing of the periscope. Thus the dialogue enclosed within the balloon is visually exploited in the interests of compositional structure.

Now analyze Pair 3 (Figures 2-11 and 2-12), Pair 4 (Figures 2-13 and 2-14), and Pair 5 (Figures 2-15 and 2-16).

PERCEPTION KEY Comic Strips and Lichtenstein's Transformations,
Pairs 3, 4, and 5

1. Decide once again which are the comic strips and which the transformations.
2. If you have changed any of your decisions or your reasons, how do you account for these changes?

43

Don't be surprised if you have changed some of your decisions; perhaps your reasoning has been expanded. Other people's analyses, even when you disagree with them, will usually suggest new ways of perceiving things. In the case of good criticism, this is almost always true. The correct identifications follow, and they should help you test your perceptive abilities.

Pair 1a	Lichtenstein, *I Can See the Whole Room . . . and There's Nobody in It!* 1961. Oil on canvas. © Estate of Roy Lichtenstein.
Pair 1b	Panel from William Overgard's comic strip *Steve Roper*.
Pair 2a	Anonymous comic book panel.
Pair 2b	Lichtenstein, *Torpedo . . . Los!* 1963. Magna on canvas. © Estate of Roy Lichtenstein. Courtesy of the Leo Castelli Gallery, New York.
Pair 3a	Anonymous comic book panel.
Pair 3b	Lichtenstein, *Image Duplicator*. 1963. Magna on canvas. © Estate of Roy Lichtenstein. Courtesy of the Leo Castelli Gallery, New York.
Pair 4a	Anonymous comic book panel.
Pair 4b	Lichtenstein, *Hopeless*. 1963. Magna on canvas. © Estate of Roy Lichtenstein. Courtesy of the Leo Castelli Gallery, New York.
Pair 5a	Lichtenstein, *The Engagement Ring*. 1961. © Estate of Roy Lichtenstein.
Pair 5b	Panel from Martin Branner's comic strip *Winnie Winkle*.

If you have been mistaken, do not be discouraged. Learning how to perceive sensitively takes time. Furthermore, it is not possible to decide beyond all doubt, as with the proof that $2 + 2 = 4$, whether Lichtenstein is a creator of artistic form and the comic-strip makers are not. We think it is highly probable that this is the case, but absolute certainty is not possible. And it should be noted that the comic-strip makers generally look upon Lichtenstein's work as "strongly decorative and backward looking."

PERCEPTION KEY   *I Can See the Whole Room . . . and There's Nobody In It!*
(Figure 2-7)

This painting recently sold for $1.9 million. Is this strong evidence that this painting is a work of art? Or is it quite conceivable that the art world—critics, historians, connoisseurs, and buyers—have been taken? Can you imagine any comic strip—such as Figure 2-8—bringing such a price?

The examination of these examples makes it fairly evident, we believe, that Lichtenstein was a master at composing forms. But are these paintings works of art? Do these forms inform? Do they have a content? If so, what are their subject matters? What is the subject matter of *Torpedo . . . Los!*? The aggressiveness of submarine commanders? Or, rather, the energy, passion, directness, and mechanical nature of comic strips? Or could the subject matter be made up of both these things? Perhaps there is no interpreted subject matter. Perhaps the event in the submarine is just an excuse for composing a form. Or perhaps this form is best understood and appreciated not as informing but, rather, as simply interesting and attractive. We will examine these issues in detail in Chapter 14. As you think about these questions, remember you are judging from photographs lacking color and greatly reduced in size.

SUBJECT MATTER AND CONTENT

While the male nude was a common subject in Western art well into the *Renaissance,* images of the female body have since predominated. The variety of treatment of the female nude is bewildering, ranging from the *Playboy* centerfold cliché to the radical reordering of Picasso's *Nude Under a Pine Tree.* A number of well-known female nude studies follow (Figures 2-17 through 2-24). Consider, as you look at them, how the form of the painting interprets the female body. Does it reveal it in such a way that you have an increased understanding of and sensitivity to the female body? In other words, does it have content? Also ask yourself whether the content is different in a painting by a woman than in one by a man.

Most of these paintings are very highly valued—some as masterpieces. They are highly valued because they are powerful interpretations of their subject matter, not just presentations of the human body as in *Playboy.* Think from rather than at these paintings. Then notice how different the interpretations are. Any important subject matter has many different facets. That is why shovels and soup cans have limited utility as subject matter. They have very few facets to offer for interpretation. The female nude, however, is almost limitless. The next artist interprets something about the female nude that had never been interpreted before, because the female nude seems to be inexhaustible as a subject matter.

More precisely, these paintings all have somewhat different subject matters. All are about the nude. But the painting by Giorgione is about the nude as idealized, as a goddess, as Venus. Now there is a great deal that all of us could say in trying to describe Giorgione's interpretation. We see not just a nude but an idealization that presents the nude as Venus, the goddess whom the Romans felt best expressed the ideal of woman. She represents a form of perfection which humans can only strive toward. A description of the subject matter can help us perceive the content if we have missed it. In understanding what the form worked on—that is, the subject matter—our perceptive apparatus is better prepared to perceive the *form-content,* the embodiment of the work of art's meaning and form.

The subject matter of Renoir's painting is the nude more as an earth mother. In the Modigliani, the subject matter is the sensual nude. In the Picasso, it is the nude enfleshed in her sex. In the Wesselmann, it is the nude

FIGURE 2-17
Giorgione, *Sleeping Venus*.
1508–1510. Oil on canvas,
43 × 69 inches. Gemaldega-
lerie, Dresden. (Superstock)

FIGURE 2-18
Pierre Auguste Renoir, *Bather
Arranging Her Hair*. 1893. Oil
on canvas, 36⅜ × 29⅛ inches.
National Gallery of Art,
Washington, D.C., Chester
Dale Collection.

FIGURE 2-19
Amedeo Modigliani, *Reclining Nude*. Circa 1919. Oil on canvas, 28½ × 45⅞ inches
(72.4 × 116.5 cm). The Museum of Modern Art, New York. Mrs. Simon Guggenheim
Fund. (Digital image © The Museum of Modern Art, New York/Licensed by Scala/Art
Resource, New York)

FIGURE 2-20
Pablo Picasso, *Nude under a
Pine Tree*. 1959. Oil on can-
vas, 72 × 96 inches. The Art
Institute of Chicago. Bequest
of Grant J. Pick (1965.687).
(© 2003 Estate of Pablo
Picasso/Artists Rights Society
[ARS], New York)

47

FIGURE 2-21
Tom Wesselmann, *Great American Nude*. 1977. Oil on canvas, 19½ × 54 inches. Sidney Janis Gallery, New York. (© Tom Wesselmann/ Licensed by VAGA, New York)

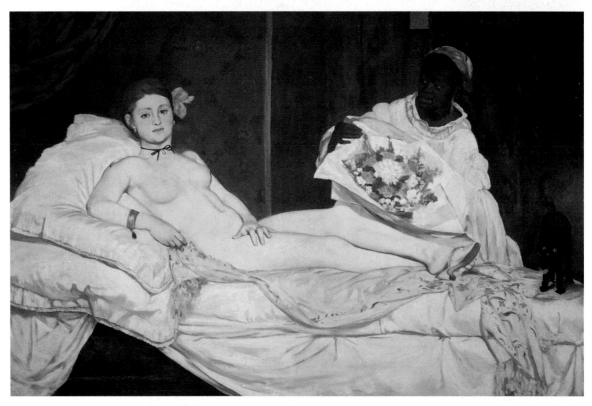

FIGURE 2-22
Edouard Manet, *Olympia*. 1863. Oil on canvas, 51¼ × 74¾ inches. Musee d'Orsay, Paris, France. (© Scala/ Art Resource, New York)

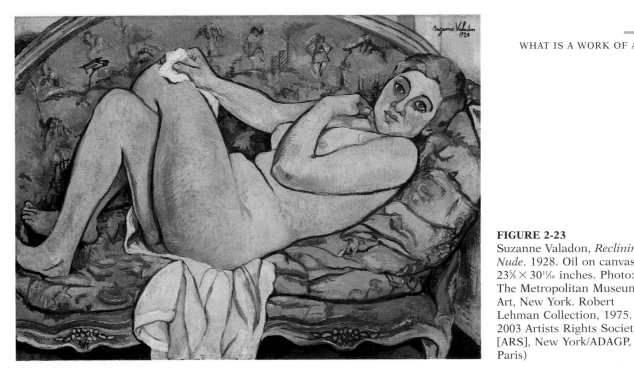

FIGURE 2-23
Suzanne Valadon, *Reclining Nude*. 1928. Oil on canvas, 23⅝ × 30¹¹⁄₁₆ inches. Photo: The Metropolitan Museum of Art, New York. Robert Lehman Collection, 1975. (© 2003 Artists Rights Society [ARS], New York/ADAGP, Paris)

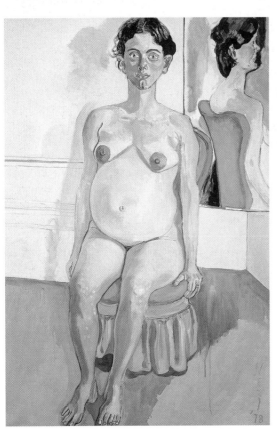

FIGURE 2-24
Alice Neel, *Margaret Evans Pregnant*. 1978. Oil on canvas, 57¾ × 38 inches. Collection, The John McEnroe Gallery. (By permission of the estate of Alice Neel, courtesy of Robert Miller Gallery, New York)

as exploited. In the Manet, it is the nude as prostitute. In all six paintings the subject matter is the female nude — but qualified: The subject matter is qualified in relation to what the artistic form focuses upon and makes lucid.

The last two paintings, by Suzanne Valadon and Alice Neel, treat the female nude differently from the others, which were painted by men. Neel's painting emphasizes an aspect of femaleness that the men usually ignore — pregnancy. Her painting does not show the alluring female but the female who is beyond allure. Valadon's nude is more traditional, but a comparison with Renoir and Giorgione should demonstrate that she is far from their ideal.

PERCEPTION KEY   The Female Nude

1. Is it clear to you that Valadon and Neel have treated the female nude very differently from the way the male painters did? What are the differences? Do these women painters treat the nude more subjectively?
2. Would you have known without being told that Valadon's and Neel's paintings were created by women? If so, how would you know this?

Summary

A work of art is a form-content. An artistic form is a form-content. An artistic form is more than just an organization of the elements of an artistic medium, such as the lines and colors of painting. The artistic form interprets or clarifies some subject matter. The subject matter, strictly speaking, is not in a work of art. When participating with a work of art, one can only imagine the subject matter, not perceive it. The subject matter is only suggested by the work of art. The interpretation of the subject matter is the content or meaning of the work of art. Content is embodied in the form. The content, unlike the subject matter, is in the work of art, fused with the form. We can separate content from form only by analysis. The ultimate justification of any analysis is whether it enriches our participation with that work, whether it helps that work "work" in us. Good analysis or criticism does just that. But, conversely, any analysis not based on participation is unlikely to be very helpful. Participation is the way — the only way — of getting into direct contact with the form-content. And so any analysis that is not based upon a participative experience inevitably misses the work of art. Participation and good analysis, although necessarily occurring at different times, always end up hand in hand.

In this chapter, we have elaborated one set of guidelines. Other sets are possible, of course. We have discussed one other set very briefly: that a work of art is significant form. If you can conceive of other sets of guidelines, make them explicit and try them out. The ultimate test is clear: Which set helps you most in appreciating works of art? We think the set we have proposed meets that test better than other proposals. But this is a large question indeed, and your decision should be delayed. In any event, we will now investigate the principles of criticism. These principles should help show us how to apply our set of guidelines to specific examples. Then we will be properly prepared to examine the extraordinary uniqueness of the various arts.

Bibliography

Aldrich, Virgil C. *The Philosophy of Art*. Englewood Cliffs, N.J.: Prentice-Hall, 1963.

Bell, Clive. *Art*. New York: Putnam, 1981.

Canaday, John. *What Is Art?* New York: Knopf, 1980.

Carroll, Noël, ed. *Theories of Art Today*. Madison: University of Wisconsin Press, 2000.

Clark, Kenneth. *The Nude*. New York: Doubleday Anchor, 1959.

Collingwood, R. G. *The Principles of Art*. Oxford, England: Clarendon Press, 1971.

Danto, Arthur C. *After the End of Art: Contemporary Art and the Pale of History*. Princeton, N.J.: Princeton University Press, 1977.

Ducasse, Curt J. *The Philosophy of Art*. New York: Dover, 1963.

Graham, Gordon. *Philosophy of the Arts: An Introduction to Aesthetics*. London: Routledge, 1997.

Kleinbauer, W. Eugene. *Modern Perspectives in Western Art History*. Toronto: University of Toronto Press, 1989.

Langer, Susanne K. *Feeling and Form*. New York: Scribner's, 1953.

Margolis, Joseph. *What, After All, Is a Work of Art?* University Park: Pennsylvania State University Press, 1999.

Maritain, Jacques. *Creative Intuition in Art and Poetry*. Princeton, N.J.: Princeton University Press, 1978.

Merleau-Ponty, Maurice. *The Primacy of Perception*. Edited by James M. Edie. Evanston, Ill.: Northwestern University Press, 1964.

Pepper, Stephen C. *The Work of Art*. Bloomington: Indiana University Press, 1955.

Perry, Gill, ed. *Gender and Art*. New Haven, Conn.: Yale University Press, 1999.

Rader, Melvin. *A Modern Book of Aesthetics*, 5th ed. New York: Holt, Rinehart and Winston, 1979.

Read, Herbert. *The Meaning of Art*. London: Faber and Faber, 1972.

Reid, Louis Arnaud. *Meaning in the Arts*. London: Allen and Unwin, 1969.

Sesonske, Alexander. *What Is Art? Aesthetic Theory from Plato to Tolstoy*. New York: Oxford University Press, 1965.

Tolstoy, Leo. *What Is Art? and Essays on Art*. Translated by Aylmer Maude. London: Bristol Classical Press, 1994.

Weiss, Paul. *Nine Basic Arts*. Carbondale: Southern Illinois University Press, 1966.

Weitz, Morris. *Philosophy of the Arts*. New York: Russell and Russell, 1964.

Internet Resources

AMERICAN SOCIETY FOR AESTHETICS
http://www.aesthetics-online.org

ARTISTS ON ART
http://www.constable.net

ARTLEX-ART DICTIONARY
http://www.artlex.com/

ART ON THE NET
http://www.art.net

YALE UNIVERSITY
http://www.library.yale.edu/Internet/arthistory.html

CHAPTER 3

Being a Critic
of the Arts

In this chapter, we are concerned with establishing the methods and means of becoming a good critic and understanding the goals of responsible *criticism*. The act of responsible criticism aims for the fullest understanding and the fullest participation possible. Being a responsible critic demands being at the height of awareness while examining a work of art in detail, establishing its context, and clarifying its achievement. It is not to be confused with popular journalism, which often sidetracks the critic into being flashy, negative, and cute.

You Are Already an Art Critic

Almost everyone operates as an art critic much of the time. Choosing a film or changing the television channel to look for something better implies a critical act. When turning a radio dial looking for good music, we become critics of music. The same is true when we stop to admire a building or a sculpture. What qualifies us to make such critical judgments? What training underlies our constant criticism of such arts as film, music, architecture, and sculpture? Experience is one factor. We have gone to movies, listened to music on the radio, and watched television since before we can remember. We can count on a lifetime of seeing architecture, of responding to the industrial design of automobiles and furniture, of seeing public sculpture. This is no inconsiderable background, and it helps us make critical judgments without hesitation.

But even though all this is true, we realize something further. Everyone has limitations as a critic. When left to our own devices we grow up with little specific critical training, even in a society rich in art, and find ourselves capable of going only so far. If we do nothing to increase our critical skills, they may not grow. By learning some principles about criticism and how to put them to work, we can develop our capacities as critics.

Participation and the Critic

One of the reasons many of us resist our roles as critics is that we value highly the participative experience we get from works of art. Criticism interferes with that participative delight. For example, most of us lose ourselves in a good film and never think about the film in an objective way. It "ruins" the experience to stop and be critical, because the act of criticism is quite different from the act of participative enjoyment. And if we were to choose which act is the most important, then, of course, we would have to stand firm behind enjoyment. Art is, above all, enjoyable. Yet the kinds of enjoyment it affords are sometimes complex and subtle. Good critics make the complexities and subtleties more understandable both to themselves and to others. In other words, by reflecting upon our participative experiences, we may help deepen our next participation. Thus the critical act is— at its very best—an act that is very much related to the act of participatory enjoyment. The reason is simple: A fine critical sense helps us develop the perceptions essential to understanding what's "going on" in a work of art.

Seeing a film twice, for instance, is often interesting. At first our personalities may melt away, and we become involved and lost in the experience. Competent and clever filmmakers can cause us to do this quickly and efficiently—the first time. But if the filmmaker is only competent and clever, as opposed to being creative, then the second time we see the film its flaws are likely to be obvious and we are likely to have a less complete participatory experience. However, when we see a really great film, then the second experience is likely to be more exciting than the first. If we have become good critics and if we have reflected wisely on our first experience, we will find that the second experience of any great work of art is likely to be more intense and our participation deeper. For one thing, our understanding of the artistic form and content is likely to be considerably more refined in our second experience and in all subsequent experiences.

It is obvious that only those works of art that are successful on most or all levels can possibly be as interesting the second time we experience them as they were the first. This presumes, however, a reliable perception of the work. For example, the first experience of most works of art will not be very satisfying—perhaps it will not produce the participative experience at all —if we fail to perceive the form-content to some significant extent. Consequently, it is possible that the first experience of a difficult poem, for instance, will be less than enjoyable. If, however, we have gained helpful information from the first experience and thus have made ourselves more sensitive to the poem, the second experience will be more satisfying.

One of the first critical questions we should ask concerns whether we actually have had a participative experience. Has the work of art taken us out of ourselves? If it is a good work of art, we should find ourselves lost in the delight of experiencing it. However, as we have been suggesting all along, if we are not so carried away by a given work, the reason may not be because it is not successful. It may be because we do not perceive all there is to perceive. We may not get it well enough for it to transport us into participation. Consequently, we have to be critical of ourselves some of the time in order to be sure we have laid the basic groundwork essential to participation. When we are sure that we have done as much as we can to prepare ourselves, then we are in a better position to decide whether the deficiency is in the work or in us. In the final analysis, we must have the participative experience if we are to fully comprehend a work of art.

Kinds of Criticism

With our basic critical purpose clearly in mind—that is, to learn, by reflecting on works of art, how to participate with them more intensely and enjoyably—let us now analyze the practice of criticism more closely. If, as we have argued in Chapter 2, a work of art is essentially a form-content, then good criticism will sharpen our perception of the form of a work of art and increase our understanding of its content.

PERCEPTION KEY   Kinds of Criticism

Seek out at least three examples of criticism from any available place, including, if you like, Chapters 1 and 2 of this book. Film or book reviews in newspapers or magazines or discussions of art in books may be used. Analyze these examples with reference to the following questions:

1. Does the criticism focus mainly on the form or the content?
2. Can you find any examples in which the criticism is entirely about the form?
3. Can you find any examples in which the criticism is entirely about the content?
4. Can you find any examples in which the focus is on neither the form nor the content but on evaluating the work as good or bad or better or worse than some other work?
5. Can you find any examples in which there is no evaluation?
6. Which kinds of criticism do you find most helpful—those bearing on form, content, or evaluation? Why?
7. Do you find any examples in which it is not clear whether the emphasis is on form, content, or evaluation?

This Perception Key points to three basic kinds of criticism: descriptive—focusing on form, interpretive—focusing on content, and evaluative—focusing on the relative merits of a work. (Historical criticism could be classified as a fourth type [see p. 99].)

DESCRIPTIVE CRITICISM

Descriptive criticism concentrates on the form of a work of art, describing, sometimes exhaustively, the important characteristics of that form in order to improve our understanding of the part-to-part and part-to-whole interrelationships. At first glance this kind of criticism may seem unnecessary.

FIGURE 3-1
Leonardo da Vinci, *Last Supper*. Circa 1495–1498. Oil and tempera on plaster, 15 feet 1⅛ inches × 28 feet 10½ inches. Refectory of Santa Maria delle Grazie, Milan. (© AKG London)

After all, the form is all there, completely given—all we have to do is observe. But most of us know all too well that we can spend time attending to a work we are very much interested in and yet not perceive all there is to perceive. We miss things, and oftentimes we miss things that are right there for us to observe. For example, were you immediately aware of the visual form of e. e. cummings' "l(a" (Figure 1-7)—the spiraling downward curve? Or in Goya's *May 3, 1808* (Figure 2-3), were you immediately aware of the way the line of the long dark shadow at the bottom right underlines the line of the firing squad?

Good descriptive critics call our attention to what we otherwise might miss in an artistic form. And even more important, they help us learn how to do their work when they are not around. We can, if we carefully attend to descriptive criticism, develop and enhance our own powers of observation. That is worth thinking about. None of us can afford to have a professional critic with us at all times in order to help us see the art around us more fully. No other learning is as likely to improve our participation with a work of art, for such criticism turns us directly to the work itself.

PERCEPTION KEY   *Last Supper*

Descriptively criticize the *Last Supper* (Figure 3-1). Point out every facet of structure that seems important. Look for shapes that relate to each other, including groupings of figures. Do any shapes stand out as unique—for example, the shapes of Christ and Judas? Describe the color relationships. Describe the symmetry, if any. Describe how the lines tend to meet in the landscape behind Christ's head. The descriptions of Goya's *May 3, 1808* (Figure 2-3) might be a helpful guide. The following distinctions should be helpful.

DETAIL, REGIONAL, AND STRUCTURAL RELATIONSHIPS

The totality of any work of art is a continuum of parts. A small part we shall call a *detail;* a large part a *region.* Significant relationships between or among details or regions we shall call *detail* or *regional relationships,* respectively. Significant relationships between or among details or regions to the totality we shall call *structural relationships.* For example, the red rectangle squeezed into the bottom of the Mondrian (Figure 1-6) relates—because of the sharp contrast in size, shape, and color—to the little black rectangle on the upper left. This is a detail relationship. The red rectangle establishes a strong base for a square (almost) with considerable area. This square with its five horizontal lines is a heavy region that contrasts with the lighter black and white square region above, both regions sharing a black horizontal. This is a regional relationship. The coordination of these two squares with the two rectangles on the left produces a strong sense of overall balance and stability. This is a structural relationship. Now the totality of the painting comes to the fore. Using these distinctions may be useful in systematizing our descriptions. Generally, they are likely to be used more implicitly than explicitly.

PERCEPTION KEY   Detail, Regional, or Structural Dominance

Whether detail, regional, or structural relationships dominate—or are equal—often varies widely from work to work. Compare Mondrian's *Composition in White, Black, and Red* (Figure 1-6), Picasso's *Guernica* (Figure 1-4), and Pollock's *Autumn Rhythm* (Figure 3-2). In which painting or paintings, if any, do detail relationships dominate? Regional relationships? Structural relationships?

Detail relationships dominate *Autumn Rhythm,* so much so that at first sight, perhaps, no structure is apparent. The loops, splashes, skeins, and blots of color were dripped or thrown on the canvas, which was laid out flat on the floor during execution. Yet there is not as much chaotic chance as one might suppose. Most of Pollock's actions were controlled accidents, the result of his awareness, developed through long trial-and-error experience, of how the motion of his hand and body along with the weight and fluidity of the paint would determine the shape and textures of the drips and splashes as he moved around the borders of the canvas. Somehow the

FIGURE 3-2
Jackson Pollack, *Autumn Rhythm*. 1950. Oil on canvas, 8 feet 9 inches × 17 feet 3 inches. Photo: The Metropolitan Museum of Art. George A. Hearn Fund, 1957 (57.92). (© 2003 The Pollack-Krasner Foundation/Artists Rights Society [ARS], New York)

endless details finally add up to a self-contained sparkling totality holding the rhythms of autumn. Yet, unlike Mondrian's painting, there are no distinct regions. Moreover, with the Mondrian the structure is so evident and so overpowering that every detail and region inevitably refers to the totality. Picasso's *Guernica*, alternatively, is more or less balanced with respect to detail, region, and structure. The detail relationships are organized into three major regions: the great triangle—with the apex at the candle and two sides sloping down to the lower corners—and the two large rectangles, vertically oriented, running down along the left and right borders. Moreover, these regions—unlike the regions of Mondrian's painting—are hierarchically ordered because the triangular region takes precedence in both size and interest, and the left rectangle, mainly because of the fascination of the impassive bull (what is he doing here?) dominates the right rectangle, even though both are about the same size. Despite the complexity of the detail relationships in *Guernica*, we gradually perceive the power of a very strong, clear structure.

INTERPRETIVE CRITICISM

Interpretive criticism explicates the content of a work of art. It helps us understand how form transforms subject matter into content: what has been revealed about some subject matter and how that has been accomplished. The content of any work of art will become clearer when the structure is perceived in relationship to the details and regions. The following examples (Figures 3-3 and 3-4) demonstrate that the same principle holds for archi-

58

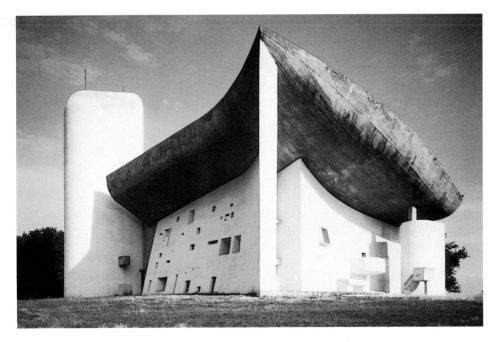

FIGURE 3-3
Le Corbusier, Notre Dame-du-Haut, Ronchamps, France, 1950–1955. (Photograph © Ezra Stoller/Esto. © 2003 Artists Rights Society [ARS], New York/ADAGP, Paris/FLC)

tecture as holds for painting. The subject matter of a building—or at least an important component of it—is usually the practical function the building serves. We have no difficulty telling which of these buildings was meant to serve as a bank and which was meant to serve as a church.

FIGURE 3-4
Louis Henry Sullivan, Guaranty (Prudential) Building, Buffalo, New York. 1894. (Buffalo and Erie County Historical Society)

PERCEPTION KEY   Sullivan and Le Corbusier

1. Which of these structures suggests solidity? Which suggests flight and motion? What have these things got to do with the function of each building?
2. Which of these buildings places more emphasis on details?
3. Which building possesses the more varied detail?
4. The entrance to the bank is off-center. Would it have been better to have it centralized? There is no centralized entrance to the church. Good or bad?
5. Explain the content of each building.

Form-Content   The interpretive critic's job is to find out as much about an artistic form as possible in order to explain its meaning. This is a particularly useful task for the critic—which is to say, for us in particular—since the forms of numerous works of art seem important but are not immediately understandable. When we look at the examples of the bank and the church, we ought to realize that the significance of these buildings is expressed by means of the *form-content*. It is true that without knowing the functions of these buildings we could appreciate them as structures without special functions, but knowing about their functions deepens our appreciation. Thus the lofty arc of Le Corbusier's roof soars heavenward more mightily when we recognize the building as a church. The form takes us up toward heaven, at least in the sense that it moves our eyes upward. For a Christian church such a reference is perfect. The bank, however, looks like a pile of square coins or banknotes. Certainly the form "amasses" something, an appropriate suggestion for a bank. We will not belabor these examples, since it should be fun for you to do this kind of critical job yourself. Observe how much more you get out of these examples of architecture when you consider each form in relation to its meaning—that is, the form as form-content. Furthermore, such analyses should convince you that interpretive criticism operates in a vacuum unless it is based on descriptive criticism. Unless we perceive the form with sensitivity—and this means that we have the basis for good descriptive criticism—we simply cannot understand the content. In turn, any interpretive criticism will be useless.

Participate with a poem by Emily Dickinson:

AFTER GREAT PAIN A FORMAL FEELING COMES

After great pain a formal feeling comes—
The nerves sit ceremonious like tombs;
The stiff Heart questions—was it He that bore?
And yesterday—or centuries before?

The feet mechanical go round
A wooden way
Of ground or air or Ought,
Regardless grown,
A quartz contentment like a stone.

This is the hour of lead
Remembered if outlived
As freezing persons recollect
The snow—
First chill, then stupor, then
The letting go.

PERCEPTION KEY   Dickinson's Poem

1. What is the subject matter?
2. Is there content, and if so what is it? What insight into the subject matter?
3. With reference to the form, what binds the following images: tombs, quartz, stone, lead? All the words are one syllable. Is this significant?
4. Who is the "He" of line 3?
5. Is the "great pain" physical or mental?

A numbed lifelessness follows the great pain—stiff heart, wooden way, quartz contentment, hour of lead, stupor, and finally a letting go, a giving up. The nerves sit "ceremoniously like tombs," like a group of mourners in a funeral setting. The tomb suggests deadness, stillness, formality, unchangeableness. The heart is so shocked that the sense of time and place is lost. Did "He" (the capital letter apparently identifies Christ) really bear the cross? And if so, when, where? The "quartz contentment" continues the suggestion of a stoniness that shuts down the nerves. Quartz is a very hard crystal. The pain is crystallized—gradually neutralized—as with someone freezing: "First chill, then stupor, then the letting go." We are given an extraordinary understanding of one way mental suffering is experienced.

You may interpret the poem differently. For example, you may not agree that the "He" refers to Christ. Perhaps the reference is to a lover who no longer loves. If so, the content or meaning of the poem is quite different. Discussion now can be especially interesting. We should compare our descriptive criticisms. If you claim that "He" was a lover, then how do you explain "He that bore? / And yesterday—or centuries before?" This kind of use of descriptive criticism is essential if varying interpretive criticisms are to be enlightening.

It is important that we grasp the relative nature of explanations about the content of artworks. Even descriptive critics, who try to tell us about what is really there, will perceive things in a way that is relative to their own perspective. In Cervantes' *Don Quixote* there is an amusing story that illustrates the point. Sancho Panza had two cousins who were expert wine tasters. However, on tasting a wine, they disagreed. One found the wine excellent except for an iron taste; the other found the wine excellent except for a leather taste. When the barrel of wine was emptied, an iron key with a leather thong was found. As N. J. Berrill points out in *Man's Emerging Mind,*

> The statement you often hear that seeing is believing is one of the most misleading ones a man has ever made, for you are more likely to see what you believe than believe what you see. To see anything as it really exists is about as hard an exercise of mind and eyes as it is possible to perform.[1]

Two descriptive critics can often "see" quite different things in an artistic form. This is not only to be expected but also desirable; it is one of the reasons great works of art keep us intrigued for centuries. But even though they may see quite different aspects when they look independently at a work of art, when they get together and talk it over, the critics will usually come to some kind of agreement about the aspects each of them sees. The work being described, after all, has verifiable, objective qualities each of us can perceive and talk about. But it has subjective qualities as well, in the sense that the qualities are observed only by "subjects."

In the case of interpretive criticism, the subjectivity and, in turn, the relativity of explanations are more obvious than in the case of descriptive criticism. The content is "there" in the form, and yet, unlike the form, it is not there in a directly perceivable way. It must be interpreted.

Interpretive critics, more than descriptive critics, must be familiar with the subject matter. Interpretive critics often make the subject matter more explicit for us at the first stage of their criticism. In doing so, they bring

---

[1]N. J. Berrill, *Man's Emerging Mind* (New York: Dodd, Mead, 1955), p. 147.

us closer to the work. Perhaps the best way initially to get at Picasso's *Guernica* (Figure 1-4) is to discover its subject matter. Is it about a fire in a building or something else? If we are not clear about this, perception of the painting is obscured. But after the subject matter has been elucidated, good interpretive critics go much further: exploring and discovering meanings about the subject matter as revealed by the form. Now they are concerned with helping us grasp the content directly, in all of its complexities and subtleties. This final stage of interpretive criticism is, undoubtedly, the most demanding of all criticism.

EVALUATIVE CRITICISM

To evaluate a work of art is to judge its merits. At first glance, this seems to suggest that *evaluative criticism* is prescriptive criticism, which prescribes what is good as if it were a medicine and tells us that this work is superior to that work.

> **PERCEPTION KEY** Evaluative Criticism I
>
> 1. Suppose you are a judge of an exhibition of painting and Figures 2-17 through 2-24 in Chapter 2 have been placed into competition. You are to award first, second, and third prizes. What would your decisions be? Why?
> 2. Suppose, further, that you are asked to judge which is the best work of art from the following selection: cummings' "l(a" (page 15), Cézanne's *Mont Sainte-Victoire* (Figure 2-5), and Le Corbusier's church (Figure 3-3). What would your decision be? Why?

It may be that this kind of evaluative criticism makes you uncomfortable. If so, we think your reaction is based on good instincts. In the first place, each work of art is such an individual thing that a relative merit ranking of several of them seems arbitrary. This is especially the case when the works are in different media and have different subject matter, as in the second question of the Perception Key. In the second place, it is not clear how such judging helps us in our basic critical purpose—to learn from our reflections about works of art how to participate with these works more intensely and enjoyably.

Nevertheless, evaluative criticism of some kind is generally necessary. We have been making such judgments continually in this book—in the selections for illustrations, for example. You make such judgments when, as you enter a museum of art, you decide to spend your time with this painting rather than that. Obviously, directors of museums must also make evaluative criticisms, because usually they cannot display every work owned by the museum. If a Van Gogh is on sale—and one of his paintings was bought recently for $82.5 million—someone has to decide its worth. Evaluative criticism, then, is always functioning, at least implicitly. Even when we are participating with a work, we are implicitly evaluating its worth. Our participation implies its worth. If it were worthless to us, we would not even attempt participation.

The problem, then, is how to use evaluative criticism as constructively as possible. How can we use such criticism to help our participation with works of art? Whether Giorgione's painting (Figure 2-17) deserves first prize over Modigliani's (Figure 2-19) seems trivial. But if almost all critics agree that Shakespeare's poetry is far superior to Edward Guest's and if we have been thinking Guest's poetry is better, we would probably be wise to do some reevaluating. Or if we hear a music critic whom we respect state that the music of the Beatles is worth listening to—and up to this time we have dismissed it—then we should indeed make an effort to listen. Perhaps the basic importance of evaluative criticism lies in its commendation of works that we might otherwise dismiss. This may lead us to delightful experiences. Such criticism may also make us more skeptical about our own judgments. If we think that the poetry of Edward Guest and the paintings of Norman Rockwell (see Figure 14-9) are among the very best, it may be helpful for us to know that other informed people think otherwise.

Evaluative criticism presupposes three fundamental standards: perfection, insight, and inexhaustibility. When the evaluation centers on the form, it usually values a form highly only if the detail and regional relationships are tightly organized. If they fail to cohere with the structure, the result is distracting and thus inhibits participation. An artistic form in which everything works together may be called perfect. A work may have perfect organization, however, and still be evaluated as poor unless it satisfies the standard of insight. If the form fails to inform us about some subject matter—if it just pleases or interests or excites us but doesn't make some significant difference in our lives—then for us that form is not artistic. Such a form may be valued below artistic form because the participation it evokes, if it evokes any at all, is not lastingly significant. Incidentally, a work lacking representation of objects and events may possess artistic form. Abstract art has a definite subject matter—the sensuous. Who is to say that the Mondrian (Figure 1-6) or the Pollack (Figure 3-2) are lesser works of art because they inform only about the sensuous? The sensuous is with us all the time, and to be sensitive to it is exceptionally life-enhancing. Finally, works of art may differ greatly in the breadth and depth of their content. The subject matter of Mondrian's *Composition in White, Black, and Red* (Figure 1-6)—the sensuous—is not as broad as the subject of Cézanne's *Mont Sainte-Victoire* (Figure 2-4). Yet it does not follow necessarily that the Cézanne is a superior work. However, the depth of penetration into the subject matter is far deeper in the Cézanne, we believe, than in the photograph of the mountain (Figure 2-5). The stronger the content—that is, the richer the insight on the subject matter—the more intense our participation, because we have more to keep us involved in the work. Such works resist monotony, no matter how often we return to them. Such works apparently are inexhaustible, and evaluative critics usually will rate only those kinds of works as masterpieces. Notice how unimportant it is how you ultimately rank these works. But notice, also, how these questions provide precise contexts for your attention.

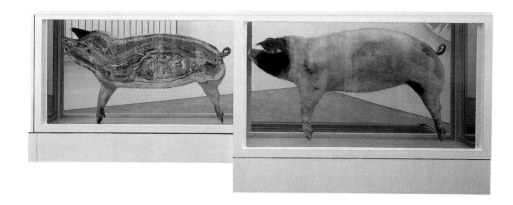

FIGURE 3-5
Damien Hirst, *This Little Piggy Went to Market, This Little Piggy Stayed Home.* 1996. Mixed media, 47¼ × 82⅝ × 23⅝ inches per tank. Courtesy Gagosian Gallery, New York. (Reproduced by permission of the artist)

> **PERCEPTION KEY**   Evaluative Criticism 2
>
> 1. Evaluate the nudes (Figures 2-17 through 2-24) with reference to the perfection of their artistic forms, the tightness of the interrelationship of details and regions to the structure.
> 2. Evaluate these works with reference to their insight. How deeply does the form inform?
> 3. Evaluate these works with reference to their inexhaustibility.

Censors of art are evaluative critics. In the autumn of 1999 the Brooklyn Museum of Art mounted a show costing $1 million called *Sensation: Young British Artists.* Works were taken from the collection of Charles Saatchi, London's most important contemporary art collector. Earlier the show had attracted record crowds in London and Berlin. The Brooklyn Museum announced that "The contents of this exhibition may cause shock, vomiting, confusion, panic, euphoria and anxiety. If you suffer from high blood pressure, a nervous disorder or palpitations, you should consult your doctor." Two examples: Damien Hirst's *This Little Piggy Went to Market, This Little Piggy Stayed at Home* (Figure 3-5) featured a pig sliced from nose to tail in formaldehyde contrasted with a whole pig also in formaldehyde. Chris Ofili produced a portrait of the Virgin Mary spotted with clumps of elephant dung (Figure 3-6). New York's mayor at the time, Rudolph Giuliani, passionately protested, "To have the government subsidize something like that is outrageous." Deputy Mayor Randy Levine announced that the city's subsidies to the museum would be suspended if the exhibit were not canceled. When huge crowds turned out and the critics pummeled Giuliani, he backed down.

> **PERCEPTION KEY**   Censorship
>
> 1. Do you agree with Giuliani's evaluative judgment? Note that Giuliani himself did not see these works.
> 2. Do you agree with Giuliani's attempt to punish the museum?

FIGURE 3-6
Chris Ofili, *Holy Virgin Mary*. 1996. Mixed media, 96 × 72 inches. Victoria-Miro Gallery, London. (© Chris Ofili, The Saatchi Gallery, London. Fotofolio. com/Artpost)

3. Do you believe that experts in the arts (including presumably museum officials) should be the ultimate evaluators of art rather than politicians who control, more or less, the finances? Discuss.

4. In 1989 the Corcoran Gallery in Washington, D.C., planned an exhibition, to be financed by the National Endowment for the Arts, featuring the homoerotic photography of Robert Mapplethorpe. Under intense pressure from certain government officials, the Gallery and the Endowment backed down. Do you think these officials were justified? Discuss.

5. Government officials of fascist and communist regimes invariably censor the arts. The movement toward government censorship seems to be increasing in this country. Good or bad? We will bring these questions to the fore again in Chapter 14.

Summary

Being a responsible critic demands being at the height of awareness while examining a work of art in detail, establishing its subject matter, and clarifying its achievement. There are three main types of criticism: descriptive, interpretive, and evaluative. Descriptive criticism focuses on form, interpretive criticism focuses on content, and evaluative criticism focuses on the relative merits of a work.

Good critics can help us understand works of art while also giving us the means or techniques that will help us become good critics ourselves. They can teach us about what kinds of questions to ask. Each of the following chapters on the individual arts is designed to do just that—to give some help about what kinds of questions a serious viewer should ask in order to come to a clearer perception and deeper understanding of any specific work. With the arts, unlike many other areas of human concern, the questions are often more important than the answers. The real lover of the arts will often be not the person with all the answers but rather the one who has the best questions. And the reason for this is not that the answers are worthless but that the questions, when properly applied, lead us to a new awareness, a more exalted consciousness of what works of art have to offer. Then when we get to the last chapter, we will be better prepared to understand something of how the arts are related to other branches of the humanities.

Bibliography

Adams, Hazard, ed. *Critical Theory since Plato*, rev. ed. Fort Worth: Harcourt Brace Jovanovich, 1992.

Aschenbrenner, Karl. *The Concepts of Criticism*. Dordrecht, The Netherlands: Reidell, 1975.

Bate, Walter Jackson, ed. *Criticism: The Major Texts*. New York: Harcourt Brace, 1952.

Beardley, Monroe. *Aesthetics: Problems in the Philosophy of Criticism*. New York: Harcourt Brace, 1961.

Boas, George. *Wingless Pegasus*. Baltimore: Johns Hopkins University Press, 1967.

Chipp, Herschel B. *Theories of Modern Art: A Source Book of Artists and Critics*. Berkeley: University of California Press, 1968.

Frye, Northrop. *Anatomy of Criticism*. Princeton, N.J.: Princeton University Press, 1990.

Greene, Theodore M. *The Arts and the Art of Criticism*. Princeton, N.J.: Princeton University Press, 1940.

Hirsch, E. D. *The Aims of Interpretation*. Chicago: University of Chicago Press, 1976.

King, Catherine, ed. *Views of Difference: Different Views of Art*. New Haven, Conn.: Yale University Press, 1999.

Krieger, Murray. *Theory of Criticism*. Baltimore: Johns Hopkins University Press, 1981.

Levich, Marvin. *Aesthetics and the Philosophy of Criticism*. New York: Random House, 1963.

Margolis, Joseph. *The Language of Art and Art Criticism: Analytic Questions in Aesthetics*. Detroit: Wayne State University Press, 1965.

Olson, Elder. *On Value Judgments in the Arts and Other Essays*. Chicago: University of Chicago Press, 1976.

Osborne, Harold. *Aesthetics and Criticism*. London: Routledge, 1955.

Richards, I. A. *Principles of Literary Criticism*. London: Kegan Paul, 1947.

Senie, Harriet, and Sally Webster. *Critical Issues in Public Art*. New York: Icon Editions, 1993.

Shrum, Wesley Monroe, Jr. *Fringe and Fortune: The Role of Critics in High and Popular Art*. Princeton, N.J.: Princeton University Press, 1966.

Sontag, Susan. *Against Interpretation and Other Essays*. New York: Farrar, Straus, and Giroux, 1964.

Wellek, René. *Concepts of Criticism*. New Haven, Conn.: Yale University Press, 1973.

AFRICAN ART

http://www.lib.virginia.edu/clemons/RMC/exhib/93.ray.aa/African.html

ART MUSEUM NETWORK

http://amn.org/

FINE ART FORUM

http://www.msstate.edu/Fineart_Online/home.html

JOURNAL OF AESTHETICS AND ART CRITICISM

http://www.aesthetics-online.org

MUSEUMS ON THE WEB

http://vlmp.museophile.com/

WEB MUSEUM

http://www.ibiblio.org/wm/

WOMEN ARTISTS

http://www.uwrf.edu/history/women/womena1.html

PART II
The Arts

CHAPTER 4

Painting

More than any other art, painting reveals the visual appearance of objects and events. The eye is the chief sense organ involved in our participation with painting and one of the chief sense organs involved in our dealings with our everyday world. But our ordinary vision of our everyday world is usually very fragmentary. We generally see scenes with their objects and events only to the degree necessary for our practical purposes. Even in such a simple act as walking on a sidewalk, we tend to ignore the colors and shapes of the environment, the possibly interesting buildings. Otherwise we would be late for our appointment or get run down by a car. We hurry on. When we are behind the wheel of a car, our lives depend on our judgment of how far away and how fast-moving that oncoming car really is. We just do not have time to enjoy its splendor of speeding color. Of course, someone else may be driving, and then the qualities of the visually perceptible may be enjoyed for their own sake. Or we may be walking leisurely in the mountains on a safe path, and then the fullness of the scene has a chance to unfold.

Our lives tend to be dominated by practical concerns to such an extent that we fail to perceive the world about us with sensitivity. Test your visual powers for yourself.

PERCEPTION KEY   Your Visual Powers

1. What are the eye colors of members of your family and your best friends?
2. Have you ever followed closely the swirl of a falling leaf?
3. Are you aware of the spatial locations of the buildings on the main street of your hometown? Are they pleasing or distressing?
4. Are you aware very often of the detailed qualities of things—such as the fluidity of water, the roughness of rocks, or the greenness of grass?

5. Take some green paint and some red paint, a brush, and paper. Or, if these are not readily available, take any materials at hand, such as marbles and chips that are green and red. Now place the green and red side by side in such a way that, as far as possible, you make the greenness of the green shine forth. Maybe this will require a different tone of green or red or a different placement. Or maybe you have to remove the red altogether and substitute another color. Notice how, as you go about this, you must really see the green. You must let the green dominate and control your seeing.

6. Are you aware very often of things as things, their "thingness"—such as the mountainness of mountains, the marbleness of marble, the glassiness of glass? Do you care about things in this sense?

7. Go into the fields and seek a rock that will enhance the appearance of an area of the yard or building or room where you live. Select both the rock and the area so that the physical qualities of the rock—its hardness, roughness or smoothness, shape, and especially its solidity—will be perceivable.

8. John Ruskin, the nineteenth-century critic, noted in his *Modern Painters* that

> there is hardly a roadside pond or pool which has not as much landscape in it as above it. It is not the brown, muddy, dull thing we suppose it to be; it has a heart like ourselves, and in the bottom of that there are the boughs of the tall trees and the blades of the shaking grass, and all manner of hues, of variable pleasant light out of the sky; nay the ugly gutter that stagnates over the drain bars in the heart of the foul city is not altogether base; down in that, if you will look deep enough, you may see the dark, serious blue of the far-off sky, and the passing of pure clouds. It is at your own will that you see in that despised stream either the refuse of the street or the image of the sky—so it is with almost all other things that we kindly despise.

Do you agree with Ruskin? If not, why not?

If you have found yourself tending to answer the questions of this Perception Key negatively or if you see the assignments about the green and the rock as being difficult and perhaps pointless, you should not be surprised or discouraged. Like the great majority of us, you probably have been educated away from sensitivity to the qualities of things and things as things. We have been taught how to manage and control things by thinking at them, as taught by the scientific method. This does not mean that such education is bad. Without this education the business of the world would come to a halt. But if not supplemented, this training may blind us like some terrible disease of the eye. For help we must go to the artists, especially the painter and the sculptor—those who are most sensitive to the visual appearances of things. With their aid, our vision can be made whole again, as when we were children. Their works accomplish this, in the first place, by making things and their qualities much clearer than they usually appear. The artist purges from our sight the films of familiarity. Second, painting, with its "all-at-onceness," more than any other art, gives us the time to allow our vision to focus and participate.

Before we analyze some of the ways painting can open our eyes and focus our vision, it will be helpful to understand something about the *media* of painting and, in turn, the visual elements of the media and the principles of their composition.

Every art has its primary media, the basic materials the artist organizes: for example, with music, sounds; with dance, bodily movement; with literature, language. Every art also has its primary *elements,* the most distinctive qualities composing the media: for example, with music, pitch and tone color; with dance, positions and shapes, emerging from movement; with literature, the sounds of words and meter. We will attempt to analyze systematically the media and the elements of painting, literature, drama, music, and film only, because with other arts that kind of analysis is too technical and specialized for our basic purpose—to deepen and widen our enjoyment of the arts. In the cases of painting, literature, and music, an examination of their media and their elements is especially instructive, for these elements lend themselves to systematic ordering. And that ordering is not so much imposed but inherent in the elements themselves. The arranging of the elements into artistic form by painters, writers, and composers is greatly aided by the powerful organizing potential of the "stuff" they work with. We, in turn, can be aided in our appreciation of these arts by understanding something about their building blocks and how they can be combined. For those interested in the media and the elements of the other arts, our very brief and oversimple presentation in this chapter might serve as a guide. However, none of the elements of the media of the other arts lend themselves to as systematic an ordering as is found in painting, literature, and music.

The most prominent media in Western painting are tempera, fresco, oil, watercolor, and acrylic. Each medium has unique qualities, potentialities, and limitations. Most media require a binder to be added to the pigment.

TEMPERA

Tempera is pigment bound by egg yolk; when applied it requires a carefully prepared surface. Thus the wood panels of Cimabue's *Madonna and Child Enthroned with Angels* (Figure 4-1) and Giotto's *Madonna Enthroned* (Figure 4-2) were first covered by linen and then dressed with several layers of gesso, an extremely fine textured, whitish mixture of very finely ground plaster and glue. The very smooth surface allows the tempera to be applied with great refinement of detail. Usually the outlines of the images to be painted are traced on the gesso by some kind of pencil-like instrument. Then the tempera—composed of approximately equal parts of pigment, yolk, and water—is applied with small, pointed brushes, the gesso tending to resist broad, sweeping brushstrokes. Tempera has a dry, flat appearance. With tempera the painter cannot reproduce the subtle qualities of light, and it is difficult to make dark colors luminous. Paint cannot be piled up for emphasis nor thinned out to throw a detail or region into the background.

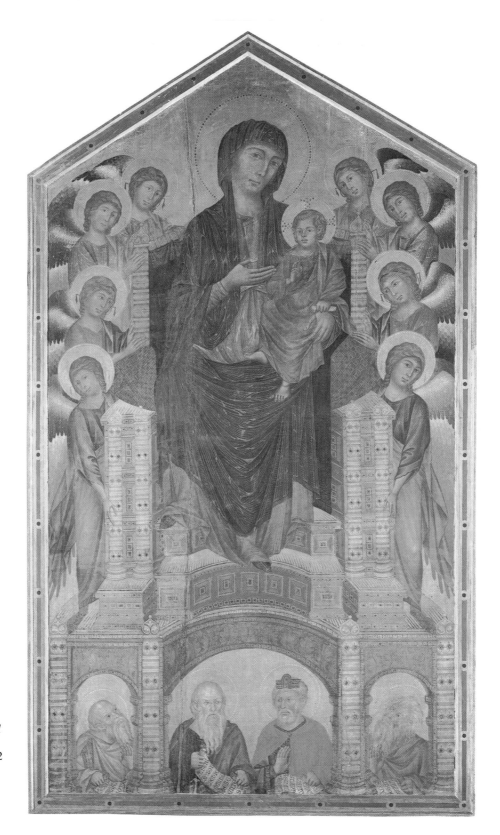

FIGURE 4-1
Cimabue, *Madonna and Child Enthroned with Angels*. Circa 1285–1290. Panel painting, 12 feet 7¾ inches × 6 feet 6⅞ inches. Uffizi, Florence. (© Scala/Art Resource, New York)

FIGURE 4-2
Giotto, *Madonna
Enthroned*. Circa 1310.
Panel painting, 10 feet
8⁷⁄₁₆ inches × 6 feet
8⅜ inches. Uffizi,
Florence. (© Alinari/
Art Resource,
New York)

Tempera does not lend itself easily to the portrayal of textures and is very difficult to correct or change because of its fast drying. Yet tempera encourages a marvelous precision of detail and subtlety of linear shaping, as in the Cimabue and the Giotto. And the purity of its colors, notably in the lighter range, can be wondrous, as with the tinted white of the inner dress of Giotto's *Madonna*. Except for *fresco*, tempera was the main medium of Western painting until the innovation of oil paint in the early fifteenth century. Tempera has been used by contemporary artists — for instance, Jacob Lawrence (Figure 4-3).

FRESCO

Wet fresco is the most enduring medium for wall painting. Painters can apply oil or other media to a wall — dry fresco — but such application is not likely to last very long, as happened unfortunately with Leonardo's *Last*

FIGURE 4-3
Jacob Lawrence, War Series
No. 3: *Another Patrol*. 1946.
Egg tempera on hardboard,
16 × 20 inches. Whitney
Museum of American Art,
New York. (© Gwendolyn
Lawrence, courtesy Jacob
and Gwendolyn Lawrence
Foundation)

Supper (Figure 3-1). Wet fresco is made by having the pigment dissolved in lime water applied to wet plaster as it is drying, the pigment penetrating usually to a depth of about one-eighth inch. Since the pigment is bound into the plaster and plaster into the wall, the pigment may last as long as the wall. The pigment usually takes on something of the luminous, crystalline whiteness of fresh plaster, as well as its grainy texture. The wall becomes both physically and psychologically an integral part of the painting. Working from a sketch or cartoon, the painter usually punches holes into the wet plaster to outline the basic shapes of the picture and then must work quickly to get the paint applied at just the right time. There is little room for error. The plaster may be too wet or too far along in drying. If a change must be made, the plaster must be knocked out and new plaster applied. Another disadvantage of wet fresco is that color changes as it dries. The painter sees the colors being applied, of course, but must imagine what they will be like when they dry. And also, unfortunately, colors may fade as they age, especially blue. Great walls and ceilings are extremely challenging, and when the painter is successful, few images are more impressive — for example, Michelangelo's Sistine Chapel.

OIL

Oil painting is a mixture of pigment, linseed oil, varnish, and turpentine, the proportions variable depending on whether thin or heavy (*impasto*) layers

FIGURE 4-4
Parmigianino, *The Madonna
with the Long Neck*. Circa
1535. Panel painting, 36⅜ ×
53¾ inches. Uffizi, Florence.
(© Erich Lessing/Art
Resource, New York)

FIGURE 4-5
Winslow Homer, *Hound and Hunter*. 1892. Oil on canvas, 28¼ × 48⅛ inches. National Gallery of Art, Washington, D.C. Gift of Stephen C. Clark. (Photograph © 2002 Board of Trustees, National Gallery of Art, Washington. Photo by Bob Grove)

FIGURE 4-6
Winslow Homer, *Sketch for "Hound and Hunter."* 1892. Watercolor, 13¹⁵⁄₁₆ × 20 inches. National Gallery of Art, Washington, D.C. Gift of Ruth K. Henschel in memory of her husband, Charles R. Henschel. (Photograph © 2002 Board of Trustees, National Gallery of Art, Washington. Photo by Dean Beasom)

are wanted. The range, richness, and subtlety of color that oil paint can produce is greater than any other medium. Since oil dries slowly, the making of a painting can proceed gradually, and changes can be made more easily than with tempera and watercolor. Oil paint can be easily diluted and applied in thin layers. And oil can be translucent, allowing a higher layer of paint to show something of a lower layer, a technique called glazing, exploited especially by the Venetians in the Renaissance (as in the Giorgione, Figure 2-17). Moreover, no medium permits a more flexible blending of colors or subtle portrayal of light and textures, as in Parmigianino's *The Madonna with the Long Neck* (Figure 4-4). The most versatile of media in the Western world, oil is the medium used most since the fifteenth century. However, the slow drying of oil paint—sometimes it can take months— can be a distinct disadvantage, and it is the messiest and smelliest of the media. Oil rarely produces the spontaneous effect of watercolor. Compare Homer's *Hound and Hunter* (Figure 4-5) in oil with the sketch in watercolor (Figure 4-6). Presumably the oil work is more finished and therefore better. But is it?

WATERCOLOR

In *watercolors*, the pigment is bound by a water-soluble adhesive, such as gum arabic, a gummy plant substance. With its flowing "watery" qualities, the medium is easily recognized. Generally watercolor is translucent so that some of the white paper can be allowed to show through. Watercolor lends itself to rapid execution in broad washes, thus appearing spontaneous and fresh, as in Homer's *Sketch*. Watercolor has a limited color range, like tempera but, unlike tempera, does not lend itself to precise detail—compare Andrew Wyeth's *Christina's World* (see Figure 14-10) with the Homer.

ACRYLIC

Many kinds of synthetic paint based on chemical compounds have been developed since the early years of the twentieth century. The most popular is *acrylic*, bound by acrylic resin, a transparent thermoplastic substance. Except for less luminosity, acrylic looks very much like oil but, unlike oil, does not darken or yellow with age. Because it dries much faster than oil, acrylic has become a favorite medium of many contemporary painters— Helen Frankenthaler, for example (Figure 4-7). However, the fast dry of acrylic makes revisions more difficult.

OTHER MEDIA

The media just described have dominated painting in the West, whereas ink has dominated painting in the East, especially in the Chinese tradition— for example in Fan K'uan's *Travelers amid Mountains and Streams* (Figure 4-8). But ink, along with many other media, is also used in the West. And in recent times various media often have been *mixed*, as in *Autumn Rhythm* (Figure 3-2). Pollock used duco and aluminum paint along with oil. Andy Warhol used acrylic and silk-screen ink in his famous *Marilyn Monroe* painting. Some of the basic kinds of *prints* (the graphic arts) are woodcut, engraving, linocut, etching, drypoint, lithography, and aquatint. Gabor Petardi in *Printmaking* describes the potentialities and limitations involved in the many kinds of printmaking. Dürer, Rembrandt, and Goya were great graphic artists, basically restricting their medium to black lines on white.

FIGURE 4-7
Helen Frankenthaler, *Flood*.
1967. Synthetic polymer on
canvas, 124 × 140 inches.
Collection of Whitney Mu-
seum of American Art. Purchase with funds from the
friends of Whitney Museum
of American Art. (Photograph
© 1997 Whitney Museum of
American Art. Art © Helen
Frankenthaler)

PIGMENT AND BINDERS

Pigment is a coloring agent. For example, when ground to powder, the stone
lapis lazuli is a dark-purplish blue. If mixed with water and applied to some
surface—such as canvas, paper, or wood—it would quickly disintegrate.
And so the mixing of some *binder*, some adhering agent, with the pigment
is necessary. The many kinds of binders include glue, egg yolk, and casein.

Elements of Painting

The elements are the basic building blocks of a medium. For painting they
are line, color, and texture.[1]

LINE

Line is a continuous marking made by a moving point on a surface. Line
outlines shapes and can contour areas within those outlines. Sometimes

---

[1]Light, shape, volume, and space often are referred to as elements, but strictly speaking they
are compounds.

FIGURE 4-8
Fan K'uan, *Travelers amid Mountains and Streams*. Eleventh century. Ink and color on silk, 81¼ × 40¾ inches. From the collection of the Chinese National Palace Museum, Taipei, Republic of China.

FIGURE 4-9
Alessandro Botticelli, *Adoration of the Magi*. Circa 1475. Tempera on panel, 43¾ × 52¼ inches. Uffizi, Florence. (© Scala/Art Resource, New York)

contour or internal lines dominate the outlines, as with the robe of Cimabue's *Madonna* (Figure 4-1). *Closed line* most characteristically is hard and sharp, as in Mondrian's *Composition in White, Black, and Red* (Figure 1-6) and Lichtenstein's *Torpedo . . . Los!* (Figure 2-10). In the Cimabue and in Botticelli's *The Adoration of the Magi* (Figure 4-9), the line is also closed but somewhat softer. *Open line* most characteristically is soft and blurry, as in Frankenthaler's *Flood* (Figure 4-7) and Renoir's *Bather Arranging Her Hair* (Figure 2-18).

Line can suggest movement. Up-and-down movement may be indicated by the vertical, as in Mondrian's *Broadway Boogie Woogie* (Figure 4-10) and tends to stress strength. Lateral movement may be indicated by the horizontal and tends to stress stability, as in the same Mondrian. Depending on the context, however, vertical and horizontal lines may appear static, as in Mondrian's *Composition in White, Black, and Red* (Figure 1-6). Generally, diagonal lines, as in Cézanne's *Mont Sainte-Victoire* (Figure 2-4), express more tension and movement than verticals and horizontals. Curving lines usually appear softer and more flowing, as in Giorgione's *Sleeping Venus* (Figure 2-17) and Modigliani's *Reclining Nude* (Figure 2-19).

An *axis line* is an imaginary line that helps determine the basic visual directions of a painting. In Goya's *May 3, 1808* (Figure 2-3), for example, two powerful axis lines move toward and intersect at the white shirt of the man

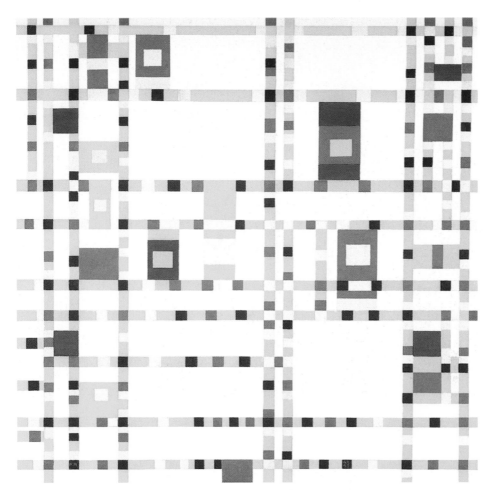

FIGURE 4-10
Piet Mondrian, *Broadway Boogie Woogie*. 1942–1943. Oil on canvas, 50×50 inches (127×127 cm). The Museum of Modern Art, New York. Given anonymously. (Digital image © The Museum of Modern Art, New York/Licensed by Scala/Art Resource, New York. Art © 2003 Mondrian/Holtzman Trust/Artists Rights Society [ARS], New York)

about to be shot: The lines of the rifles appear to converge and go on, and the line of those to be executed moving out of the ravine seems to be inexorably continuing. Axis lines are invisible vectors of visual force. Every visual field is dynamic, a field of forces directing our vision, some visible and some invisible but controlled by the visible. Only when the invisible lines are basic to the structuring of the image, as in the Goya, are they axis lines.

Since line is usually the main determinant of shapes, and shapes are usually the main determinant of detail, regional, and structural relationships, line is usually fundamental in the overall composition—Mark Rothko's *Earth Greens* (Figure 4-11) is an obvious exception. The term *linear design* is often used to describe this organizing function.

In Botticelli's *The Adoration of the Magi*, notice how finely the lines outline everything, especially the robes of the figures and the broken architecture. Every line relates to another line in precise detail, especially the contour, or internal, lines. Four basic axis lines form a large W with the Madonna and Child at its center—the focal point—and properly so since

FIGURE 4-11
Mark Rothko, *Earth Greens*.
1955. Oil on canvas, 90¼ ×
73½ inches. Museum Ludwig,
Koln. (Photograph Rhein-
isches Bildarchiv, Koln, Ger-
many. Art © 1998 Kate
Rothko Prizel & Christopher
Rothko/Artists Rights Society
[ARS], New York)

they are the most important figures. Despite the multiplicity of detail, the
axis lines tightly unify the overall structure.

In the powerful work of Jacob Lawrence, axis lines are the foundation of
most of his striking compositions. For example, in *Another Patrol* (Figure
4-3), notice how an imaginary line tracks the direction and movement
of the three sailors marching as if possessed up the gangplank of their
ship. This axis line, of course, is strengthened by the visible line that edges
the gangplank. Line is a dominant element in most African American painting of recent times, beginning with the Harlem Renaissance of the 1920s
and 30s.

PERCEPTION KEY Goya, Frankenthaler, and Cézanne

1. Goya used both closed and open line in his *May 3, 1808* (Figure 2-3). Locate these lines. Why did Goya use both kinds?
2. Frankenthaler used both closed and open lines in *Flood* (Figure 4-7). Locate these lines. Why did she use both kinds?
3. Identify outlines in Cézanne's *Mont Sainte-Victoire* (Figure 2-4). There seem to be no outlines drawn around the small bushes in the foreground. Yet we see these bushes as separate objects. How can this be? Discuss.

Cézanne's small bushes are formed by small juxtaposed greenish-blue planes that vary slightly in their tinting. These planes are hatched by brushstrokes that slightly vary the textures. And from the center of the planes to the perimeters there usually is a shading from light to dark. Thus emerges a strong sense of volume with density. We see those small bushes as somehow distinct objects, and yet we see no separating outlines. Colors and textures meet and create impressions of line. As with axis lines, the visible suggests the invisible — we project the outlines.

On occasion this kind of projection may occur when we think we see outlines of trees and other objects in the natural world. We see a tree, know it is a distinct object, and assume, of course, that it has distinct edges or outlines. But it may be that what we see are only colors, shadows, and textures. Cézanne has clarified the way we sometimes see things in the natural world. That is one of the reasons why his paintings may strike us as so fresh and true. What Cézanne has revealed is the way we sometimes see and our ignorance about how it occurs. What we are suggesting is controversial, and you may not be seeing it that way. Try to get to a museum that has a late Cézanne landscape (after 1890) and test our analysis. But above all participate. You may come out with a wonderful new lens in your eyes.

In the Asian tradition the expressive power of line is achieved generally in a very different fashion from the Western tradition. The stroke — made by flexible brushes of varying sizes and hairs — is intended to communicate the spirit and feelings of the artist, directly and spontaneously. The sensitivity of the inked brush — especially on silk — is extraordinary. The ink offers a wide range of nuances: shine, depth, pallor, thickness, and wetness. The silk has an immediate absorbent quality; the lightest touch of the brush and the slightest drop of ink registers at once, indelibly. The brush functions like a seismograph of the painter's mind.

PERCEPTION KEY Fan K'uan

Examine with a magnifying glass the brushstrokes in *Travelers amid Mountains and Streams* (Figure 4-8).

1. What different kinds of brushstrokes can you identify?
2. Why such a variety?

On the higher ranges of the mountain, broad, translucent strokes were made with wide brushes. Tiny brushes were used for dottings representing

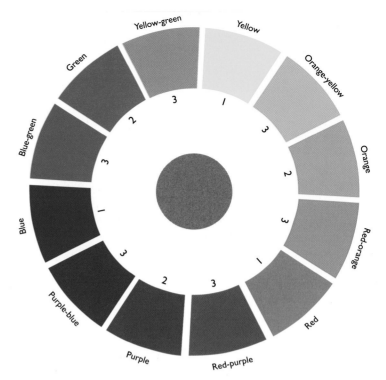

FIGURE 4-12
The color wheel.

vegetation. The sheered rocks in the lower left foreground were produced by chopping brushstrokes, the so-called ax-cut. The vegetation, especially the leaves of trees in the lower half, was produced by pointed strokes using brushes somewhat larger than those used for the dottings in the upper half. The tree trunks are smoothly brushed. The lines of the waterfall are exquisite, absolutely unchangeable. The water of the pool bounces with very light foam, line disappearing. Tiny but continuing brushstrokes barely outline the two travelers. In the Western tradition, the brushstroke usually is not as emphasized. For the most part, the brushstroke is smoothed over until the late nineteenth century. Then we have extraordinary examples of brushwork such as Van Gogh's *The Starry Night* (see Figure 13-5), which helps express frenetic disturbance.

COLOR

Color depends on light. Sunlight—*white light*—contains all the colors, the mixture preventing any color from showing. If you spin the color wheel, you get white (Figure 4-12). The component colors of white light—the spectrum—can be obtained by projecting white light through a prism. An object has a certain color because it reflects that component of white light while absorbing the others. For example, grass provides the sensation of green by reflecting that color component, absorbing all the other components.

FIGURE 4-13
Georgia O'Keeffe, *Ghost Ranch Cliffs*. 1940–1942. Oil on canvas, 16 × 36 inches. Private Collection. (© The Georgia O'Keeffe Foundation, photograph courtesy of the Gerald Peters Gallery, Santa Fe, New Mexico. © 2003 The Georgia O'Keeffe Foundation/ Artists Rights Society [ARS], New York)

Color is composed of three distinct qualities: hue, saturation, and value. *Hue* is simply the name of a color. Red, yellow, and blue are the *primary colors*. Their mixtures produce the *secondary colors:* green, orange, and purple. Further mixing produces six more, the tertiary colors. Thus the spectrum of the color wheel shows twelve hues. *Saturation* refers to the purity, vividness, or intensity of a hue. When we speak of the "redness of red," we mean its highest saturation. *Value,* or shading, refers to the lightness or darkness of a hue, the mixture in the hue of white or black. A high value of a color is obtained by mixing in white, and a low value is obtained by mixing in black. The highest value of red shows red at its lightest; the lowest value of red shows red at its darkest. *Complementary colors* are opposite each other on the color wheel—for example, red and green, orange and blue. When two complements are equally mixed, a neutral gray appears (note the gray circle within the wheel). An addition of a complement to a hue will lower its saturation. A red will look less red—will have less intensity—by even a small addition of green. And an addition of either white or black will change both the value of the hue and the saturation. *Cool colors* tend to be recessive, dominated by blue, green, and black. Blue is often associated with sky and water, as in Winslow Homer's *Sketch for "Hound and Hunter"* (Figure 4-6). Green is often associated with the earth, as in Mark Rothko's *Earth Greens* (Figure 4-11). *Warm colors* tend to be aggressive, dominated by red, yellow, and white, often associated with the sun and sunlight, as in Georgia O'Keeffe's *Ghost Ranch Cliffs* (Figure 4-13). However, given maximum saturation (intensity), a cool color can be made to come forward ahead of warm colors. For example, in Pollock's *Autumn Rhythm* (Figure 3-2), the intensity of the black helps bring it forward above the less saturated whites and tans. Warm colors can help make objects appear larger; see, for example, the breast in the Wesselmann (Figure 2-21). Cool colors can help make an object appear smaller; see for example, the pine tree in the Picasso (Figure 2-20). *Organic color* is deep, appearing to "come out" of objects, as in the Giorgione (Figure 2-17). Because of the viscosity of oil, that medium allows for the application of transparent or translucent glazes, which allow the underpainting to show; and the easy transition between lights and darks also helps make possible the depiction of depth of color. *Inorganic color* is flat, appearing to be "layered on" objects, as in the Mondrians (Figures 1-6 and 4-10). The expressive powers of colors are innumerable, and rarely can a painting be adequately described without referring to the role of color.

PERCEPTION KEY   Color and Light

1. Is the color of Rothko's *Earth Greens* (Figure 4-11) organic or inorganic? Discuss.
2. Place the eight nudes (Figures 2-17 to 2-24) in a continuum going from the one with the most organic color to the one with the least.
3. Identify any nudes in which the color dominates the lines.
4. Is the dominance of color over line, or vice versa, one clue to the meaning (content) of the Renoir nude? The Picasso nude?
5. Painters often create the impression of a light source illuminating the representation of objects and events. Select from the photographs of paintings in this book three works that most clearly illustrate the use of light as a compositional device.

TEXTURE

Texture is the surface "feel" of something. When the brushstrokes have been smoothed out, the surface is seen as smooth, as in Wesselman's *Great American Nude* (Figure 2-21) or Modigliani's *Reclining Nude* (Figure 2-19). When the brushstrokes have been left rough, the surface is seen as rough, as in Van Gogh's *The Starry Night* (see Figure 13-5) and Pollock's *Autumn Rhythm* (Figure 3-2). In these two examples, the textures are real, for if— heaven forbid!—you were to run your fingers over these paintings you would feel them as rough. Yet the surface of paintings that would be smooth to touch can render simulated textures that are rough. Thus the smooth surface of Picasso's nude portrays coarse skin.

Distinctive brushstrokes produce distinctive textures. Compare, for example, the soft hatchings of Valadon's *Reclining Nude* (Figure 2-23) with the grainy effect of most of the brushstrokes in Fan K'uan's painting (Figure 4-8). Sometimes the textural effect can be so dominant that the specific substance behind the textures is disguised, as in the background behind the head and shoulders of Renoir's *Bather* (Figure 2-18).

PERCEPTION KEY   Texture

1. Are the renditions of textures an important part in the portrayal of the eight nudes (Figures 2-17 to 2-24)? If so, in what ways?

2. Suppose the ultra-smooth surfaces of Wesselman's nude had been used by Neel. Would this have significantly changed the content of her picture? If so, explain.
3. In Pollock's *Autumn Rhythm* the impasto (the protruding paint) lays noticeably on top of a smoothly textured brownish background. Suppose there was no impasto. Would this have made a significant difference? If so, why?

Neel's nude would be greatly altered, we believe, if she had used textures such as Wesselman's. A tender, vulnerable, motherly appearance would become harsh, confident, and brazen. With the Pollock, the title brings autumn to mind; and, in turn, the laying on and drippings of heavy paint suggest vivid chaotic swirling rhythms of rain and wind-blown debris.

The medium of a painting may have much to do with textural effects. Tempera usually has a dry feel. Watercolor naturally lends itself to a fluid feel. Because they can be built up in heavy layers, oil and acrylic are useful for depicting rough textures, but of course they can be made smooth. Fresco usually has a grainy crystalline texture.

Composition

The term *composition* (in painting or any other art) refers to the ordering of relationships: among details, among regions, among details and regions, and among these and the total structure. Deliberately or more usually instinctively, artists utilize organizing principles to create forms that inform. Techniques are the ways artists go about applying the principles of composition.

PRINCIPLES

Among the basic principles of traditional painting are balance, gradation, movement and rhythm, proportion, variety, and unity. We will be discussing most of these principles in terms of the other arts as well, especially when offering descriptive criticism. The discussion that follows, however, will be restricted to painting.

- *Balance* refers to the equilibrium of opposing visual forces. Leonardo's Last Supper (Figure 3-1) is an example of symmetrical balance. Details and regions are arranged on either side of a central axis. Goya's *May 3, 1808* (Figure 2-3) is an example of asymmetrical balance, for there is no central axis.

- *Gradation* refers to a continuum of changes in the details and regions, such as the gradual variations in shape, color value, and shadowing in Siqueiros's *Echo of a Scream* (Figure 1-2).

- *Movement and rhythm* refers to the way a painting controls the movement and pace of our vision. For example, Botticelli's *Adoration of the Magi* (Figure 4-9), no matter where we start, draws our eye to the Virgin and Child and, because of the beauty of detail, does so rather slowly. The pulsing rhythm of Mondrian's *Broadway Boogie Woogie* (Figure 4-10) is much faster, for the eye is not allowed to linger, finding no detail that is particularly interesting. Note how the reds have a loud beat compared to the softer beat of the blues. Visual rhythm depends on the repetition, however varied, of details as well as regions.

- *Proportion* refers to the emphasis achieved by the scaling of sizes of shapes—for example, the way the large Madonna in the Cimabue (Figure 4-1) compares to the tiny prophets.

- *Variety* refers to the contrasts of details and regions—for example, the color and shape oppositions in the O'Keeffe (Figure 4-13).

- *Unity* refers to the togetherness, despite contrasts, of details and regions to the whole, as in Picasso's *Guernica* (Figure 1-4).

PERCEPTION KEY   Principles of Composition

After defining each principle briefly, we listed an example. Go through the color photographs of paintings in the text, and select your own example for each principle.

TECHNIQUES

Techniques are the way painters go about applying the principles of composition. Most techniques, as with principles, usually are used instinctively. It is unlikely that a painter, except perhaps a beginner, refers to a color wheel or brings to mind explicitly a principle of composition. But for us, an awareness of some of the techniques can make us more sensitive to how a painting is formed. Unless we participate with the artistic form, we miss the content. Probably the most important and interesting techniques of painting are the handling of space and shapes.

SPACE AND SHAPES

Space is difficult to explain (we will try again in the chapters on sculpture and architecture). Perhaps the best way to conceive of space is as a hollow volume available for occupation by *shapes*. Then that space can be described by referring to the distribution and relationships of those shapes in the space; for example, space can be described as crowded or open. Thus space can be conceived of not just as a hollow volume but also as the positioned interrelationships of things within that volume: We describe a space as being uncomfortable because things are in the wrong places. Or we describe another space as comfortable because things are in the right places.

Shapes in painting are areas with distinguishable boundaries, created by colors, textures, and usually—and especially—lines. A painting is a two-dimensional surface with breadth and height. But three-dimensional simulation, even in the flattest of paintings, is almost always present, even in Mondrian's *Composition in White, Black, and Red* (Figure 1-6). Colors when juxtaposed invariably move forward or backward visually. And when shapes suggest mass—three-dimensional solids—depth is inevitably seen. Furthermore, when we focus on a detail or region, there is a "punch effect"—that area is pushed back. Test the "punch" with the Mondrian.

The illusion of depth—*perspective*—can be made by various techniques, including

- Overlapping of shapes (Wesselmann, Figure 2-21)
- Making distant shapes smaller, darker, and less detailed (Siqueiros, Figure 1-2)
- Placing distant shapes higher (Goya, Figure 2-3)
- Moving from higher to lower saturation (Pollock, Figure 3-2)
- Moving from lighter to heavier textures (Cézanne, Figure 2-4)
- Shading from light to dark (Giorgione, Figure 2-17)
- Using less saturated and cooler hues in the distance (Rothko, Figure 4-11)
- Slanting lines inward—*linear perspective*—illustrated by the phenomenon of standing on railroad tracks and watching the two rails apparently meet in the distance. Sometimes the artist will make all the basic lines of a work converge toward a single *vanishing point,* a one-point perspective (as in the *Last Supper,* Figure 3-1).

PERCEPTION KEY   Composition

Choose four paintings in the text that have not been discussed so far, and try to find in them exemplifications of compositional principles and techniques.

1. Does color dominate line in any of the four?
2. Does line dominate color in any of the four?
3. Does open line dominate closed line in any of the four?
4. We have pointed out the use of axis lines in the Botticelli. Can you find any axis lines in your four choices?
5. In which of the four are textural effects most evident?
6. Which painting is most balanced?
7. Which painting is most symmetrical?
8. Which painting most shows a gradation of changes in details and regions?
9. In which painting is the sense of depth—perspective—the strongest? How is this achieved?
10. Which painting most controls the movement and rhythm of your vision along set paths?
11. Is proportion very important in any of the four?
12. Which painting possesses the most variety?
13. Which painting possesses the strongest unity?
14. Which painting seems to keep you outside the scene?
15. Which painting seems to draw you in the most?
16. Which one is the most beautiful (pleasing to your eye)?
17. If you could have one of the four on loan for your living quarters, which one would you choose? Why? Would you choose the one that is the most beautiful?
18. Which painting would likely bring the highest price? Why?

The Clarity of Painting

Examine again the photograph of Mont Sainte-Victoire (Figure 2-5). The photograph was taken many years after Cézanne was there, but, aside from a few more buildings and older trees, the scene of the photograph shows essentially what Cézanne saw. Compare the photograph of the mountain with the painting (Figure 2-4).

PERCEPTION KEY *Mont Sainte-Victoire*

1. Why did Cézanne put the two trees in the foreground at the left and right edges? Why did he have them cut off by the frame? Why did he portray the trees as if trembling?
2. In the photograph, there is an abrupt gap between the foreground and the middle distance. In the painting, this gap is filled in. Why?
3. In the painting the viaduct has been moved over to the left. Why?
4. In the painting the lines of the viaduct appear to move toward the left. Why?
5. Furthermore, the lines of the viaduct lead (with the help of an axis line) to a meeting point with the long road that runs (also with the help of an axis line) toward the left side of the mountain. The fields and buildings within that triangle all seem drawn toward that unseen apex. Why did Cézanne organize this middle ground more geometrically than the foreground or the mountain? And why is the apex of the triangle the unifying area for that region?
6. Why is the peak of the mountain in the painting given a slightly concave shape?
7. In the painting, the ridge of the mountain above the viaduct is brought into much closer proximity to the peak of the mountain. Why?
8. In the painting, the lines, ridges, and shapes of the mountain are much more tightly organized than in the photograph. How is this accomplished?

The subject matter of Cézanne's painting is surely the mountain. Suppose the title of the painting were *Trees*. This would strike us as strange because when we read the title of a representational painting we usually expect it to tell us what the painting is about—that is, its subject matter. And although the trees in Cézanne's painting are important, they obviously are not as important as the mountain. A title such as *Viaduct* would also be misleading.

The questions in the Perception Key have already hinted at some of the ways that the form reveals the essence of the mountain. But there are so many ways that a complete description is very difficult. Each aspect of the composition helps bring forth the energy of Mont Sainte-Victoire, which seems to roll down the valley and then shake the foreground trees. Everything is dominated and unified around the mountain. The rolls of its ridges are like waves of the sea, but far more durable, as we sense the impenetrable solidity of the masses underneath.

The small color shapes are something like pieces in a mosaic. These units move toward each other in receding space, and yet their intersections are rigid, as if their impact froze their movement. Almost all the colors reflect light, like the facets of a crystal, so that a solid color or one-piece effect rarely appears. And the color tones of the painting, variously modulated, are repeated endlessly. For example, the color tones of the mountain are repeated in the viaduct and the fields and buildings of the middle ground and the trees of the foreground. Cézanne's color animates everything, mainly because the color seems to be always moving out of the depth of everything rather than being laid on flat like house paint. The vibrating colors, in turn, rhythmically charge into one another and then settle down, reaching an equilibrium in which everything except the limbs of the foreground trees seems to come to rest.

Cézanne's form distorts reality in order to reveal reality. He makes Mont Sainte-Victoire far clearer in his painting than you will ever see it in nature or even in the best of photographs. Once you have participated with this and similar paintings, you will find that you may begin to see mountains like Mont Sainte-Victoire with a more sensitive and meaningful vision.

The "All-at-Onceness" of Painting

In addition to revealing the visually perceptible more clearly, paintings give us time for our vision to focus, hold, and participate. Of course, there are times when we can hold on a scene in nature. We are resting with no pressing worries and with time on our hands, and the sunset is so striking that we fix our attention on its redness. But then darkness descends and the mosquitoes begin to bite. In front of a painting, however, we find that things stand still, like the red in Mondrian's *Composition in White, Black, and Red* (Figure 1-6). Here the red is peculiarly impervious and reliable, infallibly fixed and settled in its place. It can be surveyed and brought out again and again; it can be visualized with closed eyes and checked with open eyes. There is no hurry, for all of the painting is present and, under normal conditions, it is going to stay present; it is not changing in any significant perceptual sense.

Moreover, we can hold on any detail or region or the totality as long as we like and follow any order of details or regions at our own pace. No region of a painting strictly presupposes another region temporally. The sequence is subject to no absolute constraint. Whereas there is only one route in listening to music, for example, there is a freedom of routes in seeing paintings. With *Mont Sainte-Victoire*, for example, we may focus on the foreground trees, then on the middle ground, and finally on the mountain. The next time around we may reverse the order. "Paths are made," as the painter Paul Klee observed, "for the eye of the beholder which moves along from patch to patch like an animal grazing." There is a "rapt resting" on any part, an unhurried series, one after the other, of "nows," each of which has its own temporal spread.

Paintings make it possible for us to stop in the present and enjoy at our leisure the sensations provided by the show of the visible. That is the second reason paintings can help make our vision whole. They not only clarify our world but also may free us from worrying about the future and the past, because paintings are a framed context in which everything stands still. There is the "here-now" and relatively speaking nothing but the "here-now." Our vision, for once, has time to let the qualities of things and the things themselves unfold.

Abstract Painting

Abstract, or nonrepresentational, painting may be difficult to appreciate if we are confused about its subject matter. Since no objects or events are depicted, abstract painting might seem to have no subject matter. But this is surely not the case. The subject matter is the sensuous. The sensuous is composed of visual qualities—line, color, texture, space, shape, light, shadow, volume, and mass. Any qualities that stimulate our vision are *sensa*. In representational painting, sensa are used to portray objects and events. In *abstract painting*, sensa are freed. They are depicted for their own sake. All abstract painting reveals sensa, liberating us from our habits of always identifying these qualities with specific objects and events. They make it easy for us to focus on sensa themselves even though we are not artists. Then the radiant and vivid values of the sensuous are enjoyed for their own sake, satisfying a fundamental need. Abstractions can help fulfill this need to behold and treasure the images of the sensuous. Instead of our controlling the sensa, transforming them into signs that represent objects or events, the sensa control us, transforming us into participators.

Moreover, because references to objects and events are eliminated, there is a peculiar relief from the future and the past. Abstract painting, more than any other art, gives us an intensified sense of here-now, or *presentational immediacy*. When we perceive representational paintings such as *Mont Sainte-Victoire*, we may think about our chances of getting to southern France some time in the future. Or when we perceive *May 3, 1808*, we may think about similar massacres. These suggestions bring the future and past into our participation, causing the here-now to be somewhat compromised. But with abstract painting—because there is no portrayal of objects or events that suggest the past or the future—the sense of presentational immediacy is more intense.

Although sensa appear everywhere we look, in paintings sensa shine forth. This is especially true with abstract paintings, because there is nothing to attend to but the sensa. In nature the light usually appears as external to the colors and surface of sensa. The light plays on the colors and surface. In paintings the light usually appears immanent in the colors and surface, seems to come—in part at least—through them, even in the flat polished colors of a Mondrian. When a light source is represented or suggested, as in Rembrandt's *Self Portrait* (see Figure 4-15), the light often seems to be absorbed into the colors and surfaces. There is a depth of luminosity about the sensa of paintings that rivals nature. Generally the colors of nature are more brilliant than the colors of painting; but usually in nature the sensa are either so glittering that our squints miss their inner luminosity or the sensa are so changing that we lack the time to participate and penetrate. To ignore the allure of the sensa in a painting, and, in turn, in nature, is to miss one of the chief glories life provides. It is especially the abstract painter—the shepherd of sensa—who is most likely to call us back to our senses.

Study the Mondrian (Figure 1-6) or the Rothko (Figure 4-11). Then reflect on how you experienced a series of durations—"spots of time"—that are ordered by the relationships between the regions of sensa. Compare your experience with listening to music.

PERCEPTION KEY   Rothko and Music

1 Can the varieties of pulsing color tones in the Rothko be compared with the tones of music? Do the colors suggest musical tonalities? If you have access to a musical instrument, play the tones that you find suggested by the painting.

2. If you have the opportunity of seeing any "color field" painting by Rothko, similar to *Earth Greens*, focus for a minute or so on just one color. Then focus on an adjoining color. Do you find the second color taking on a different hue? Is there a kind of visual pulsing occurring?

3. The tones of music come to us successively, and they usually interpenetrate. For example, as we hear the tone C, we also hear the preceding G, and we anticipate the coming E. Do the tones of the music interpenetrate more than the sensa of the Rothko? Do you see a succession of colors when you look at the Rothko, or do you see a color field with an "all-at-onceness"?

4. Is the process of listening to musical tones quite different from the process of seeing abstract paintings? If so, in what way?

The sensa of abstract paintings (and the same is largely true of representational paintings) are divided from one another, we think, in a different way from the more fluid progressions of music. Whereas when we listen to music the tones interpenetrate, when we see an abstract painting the sensa are more juxtaposed. Whereas the process of perceiving music is continuous, the process of perceiving abstract painting is discontinuous. Whereas music is perceived as motion, abstract painting is perceived as motionlessness. We are fascinated by the vibrant novelty and the primeval power of the red of an abstract painting for its own sake, cut off from explicit consciousness of past and future. But then, sooner or later, we notice the connection of the red to the blue, and then we are fascinated by the blue. Or then, sooner or later, we are fascinated by the interaction or contrast between the red and blue. Our eye travels over the canvas step by step, free to pause at any step as long as it desires. With music this pausing is impossible. If we hold on a tone or passage, the oncoming tones sweep by us and are lost. Music is always in part elsewhere—gone or coming—and we are swept up in the flow of process. The processes of hearing music and seeing abstract paintings are at opposite poles. Yet, as is suggested by question 2 of the Perception Key, the differences are not completely absolute.

Intensity and Restfulness

Abstract painting reveals sensa in their primitive but powerful state of innocence. In turn, this intensity of vision renews the spontaneity of our perception and enhances the tone of our physical existence. We clothe our visual sensations in positive feelings, living in these sensations instead of using them as means to ends. And such sensuous activity — sight, for once minus anxiety and eyestrain — is sheer delight. Abstract painting offers us a complete rest from practical concerns. Abstract painting is, as Matisse in 1908 was beginning to see,

> an art of balance, of purity and serenity devoid of troubling or depressing subject matter, an art which might be for every mental worker, be he businessman or writer, like an appeasing influence, like a mental soother, something like a good armchair in which to rest from physical fatigue.[2]

PERCEPTION KEY Rothko and O'Keeffe

1. Rothko's *Earth Greens* (Figure 4-11) is, we think, an exceptional example of timelessness and the sensuous. O'Keeffe's *Ghost Ranch Cliffs* (Figure 4-13) also emphasizes the sensuous, especially the rich yellows and greens. Can we compare the timelessness of these paintings? What makes one presumably more timeless?
2. Examine the sensa in the O'Keeffe. Does the fact that the painting represents real things distract you from enjoying the sensa? How crucial are the sensa to your full appreciation of the painting?
3. What difference do you perceive in Rothko's and O'Keeffe's treatment of sensa?
4. Look at the Rothko upside down. Is the form weakened or strengthened? Does it make a difference? If so, what?

The underlying blue rectangle of *Earth Greens* is cool and recessive with a pronounced vertical emphasis, accented by the way the bands of blue gradually expand upward. However, the green and rusty-red rectangles, smaller but more prominent because they stretch over most of the blue, have a horizontal "lying down" emphasis that quiets the upward thrust. The vertical and the horizontal — the simplest, most universal, and potentially the most tightly "relatable" of all axes, but in everyday experience usually cut by diagonals and oblique curves or strewn about chaotically — are brought together in perfect peace. This fulfilling harmony is enhanced by the way the lines, with one exception, of all these rectangles are soft and slightly irregular, avoiding the stiffness of straight lines that isolate. Only the outside boundary line of the blue rectangle is strictly straight, and this serves to separate the three rectangles from the outside world.

---

[2]*La grande revue,* December 25, 1908.

Within the firm frontal symmetry of the color field of this painting, the green rectangle is the most secure and weighty. It comes the closest to the stability of a square; the upper part occupies the actual center of the picture, which, along with the lower blue border, provides an anchorage; and the location of the rectangle in the lower section of the painting suggests weight because in our world heavy objects seek and possess low places. But even more important, this green, like so many earth colors, is a peculiarly quiet and immobile color. Wassily Kandinsky, one of the earliest abstract painters, finds green generally an "earthly, self-satisfied repose." It is "the most restful color in existence, moves in no direction, has no corresponding appeal, such as joy, sorrow, or passion, demands nothing." Rothko's green, furthermore, has the texture of earth, thickening its appearance. Although there are slight variations in brightness and saturation in the green, their movement is congealed in a stable pattern. The green rectangle does not look as though it wanted to move to a more suitable place.

The rusty-red rectangle, on the other hand, is much less secure and weighty. Whereas the blue rectangle recedes and the green rectangle stays put, the rusty-red rectangle moves toward us, locking the green in depth between itself and the blue. Similarly, whereas the blue is cold and the rusty-red warm, the temperature of the green mediates between them. Unlike the blue and green rectangles, the rusty-red seems light and floating, radiating vital energy. Not only is the rusty-red rectangle the smallest but also its winding, swelling shadows and the dynamism of its blurred, obliquely oriented brushstrokes produce an impression of self-contained movement that sustains this lovely shape like a cloud above the green below. This effect is enhanced by the blue, which serves as a kind of firmament for this sensuous world, for blue is the closest to darkness, and this blue, especially the middle band, seems lit up as if by starlight. Yet, despite its amorphous inner activity, the rusty-red rectangle keeps its place, also serenely harmonizing with its neighbors. Delicately, a pervasive violet tinge touches everything. And everything seems locked together forever, an image of eternity. When *Earth Greens* is turned upside down, the green rectangle weighs heavily down on the red—breaking the harmonious stability.

Representational Painting

In the participative experience with *representational paintings,* the sense of here-now, so overwhelming in the participative experience with abstractions, is somewhat weakened. Representational paintings situate the sensuous in objects and events. A representational painting, just like an abstraction, is "all there" and "holds still." But past and future are more relevant than in our experience of abstract paintings because we are seeing representations of objects and events. Inevitably we are at least vaguely aware of place and date; and, in turn, a sense of past and future is a part of that awareness. Our experience is a little more ordinary than it is when we feel the extraordinary isolation from objects and events that occurs in the perception of abstract paintings. Representational paintings always bring in some suggestion of "once upon a time." Moreover, we are kept a little closer to the experience of every day, because images that refer to objects and events usually lack something of the strangeness of the sensuous alone.

Representational painting furnishes the world of the sensuous with objects and events. The horizon is sketched out more closely and clearly, and the spaces of the sensuous are filled, more or less, with things. But even when these furnishings (subject matter) are the same, the interpretation (content) of every painting is always different. This point is clarified any time paintings of basically the same subject matter are compared, as, for example, the Madonna holding her Child, a subject matter that fascinated Florentine painters from the twelfth through the sixteenth centuries.

Comparisons of Paintings

INTERPRETATION OF THE MADONNA AND CHILD

Compare three great Florentine works that helped lead the way into the Italian Renaissance: a *Madonna and Child* (Figure 4-14) by Coppo di Marcovaldo, completed around 1275; a *Madonna and Child* (Figure 4-1) by Cimabue, completed around 1290; and a *Madonna Enthroned* (Figure 4-2) by Giotto, completed around 1310.

> **PERCEPTION KEY**   Coppo, Cimabue, and Giotto
>
> These paintings have basically the same subject matter, as their titles indicate. Yet their forms inform about their subject matter very differently. Describe the differences between the forms of these three pictures. Be as specific and detailed as possible. Then elaborate your understanding of the differences between the contents—the meanings—of these three works. Finally, compare our attempt at the same analysis. Do not, of course, take our analysis as definitive.

The figures in Cimabue's panel at first sight seem utterly lacking in human liveliness. The fine hands of the Madonna, for example, are extremely stylized. Moreover, the geometrized facial features of the Madonna, very similar to those of the angels, and the stiff, unnaturally regular features of the Child seem almost as artificial as masks. But Cimabue's *Madonna and Child* begins to grow and glow in liveliness when Cimabue's panel is juxtaposed with contemporary paintings, such as Coppo's, and only in the context of its tradition can a work of art be fully understood and in turn fully appreciated. Thus *historical criticism*—which attempts to illuminate the tradition of works of art—provides the often indispensable background information for descriptive, interpretive, and evaluative criticism. Historical criticism can be considered to be a fourth kind of criticism (see p. 55).

Coppo   Everything in this work, slightly earlier than the Cimabue and the Giotto, is subordinated to the portrayal of the theoretical, practical, and sociological expressions of the medieval Catholic conception of the sacred.

FIGURE 4-14
Coppo di Marcovaldo,
Madonna & Child. Circa
1275. Tempera, 93¾ × 53⅛
inches. Church of San
Martino ai Servi, Orvieto.
(© Scala/Art Resource,
New York)

For example, the Child is portrayed as divine, as the mediator between us and God, and as a king or prince. Conventional Christian symbols, such as halos, crowns, and the blessing gesture of the Child, dominate everything. Moreover, the sacred comes close to being represented as separate from the secular, for the Madonna and Child are flat and weightless, barely incarnated in this world. Coppo's panel is typical of the way artists of the thirteenth and the immediately preceding centuries came as close as possible to representing the sacred absolutely. The Madonna and Child, compactly and symmetrically enclosed by the angels, are interpreted more as emblems than as living embodiments of the divine. "Love not the world, neither the things that are in the world. . . . For all that is in the world . . . passeth away" (John 2:15–17). And so the human qualities of the Madonna and Child are barely recognizable. Note, for example, how the long-tailed eyes of the Madonna cannot blink and how the popping pupils stare out in a Sphinx-like glance that seems fixed forever. Her facial features are written large and seem added to rather than molded with the head. There is no hint of human affection. The spirits of this Madonna and Child belong to a supernatural world; and their bodies are hardly bodies at all but, in the words of St. Thomas Aquinas, "corporeal metaphors of spiritual things." The secular is a secondary reality. The sacred is the primary reality.

Nevertheless, the secular, even if it is more emblematic than realistic, appears very beautifully. The colors shine forth, especially the glimmering gold. We are lured by these designs beyond mere illustrations of doctrine by images. We are caught in durations of the here-now. But, unlike our experience of abstractions, these durations include, because of the conventional symbols, doctrinal interpretations of the sacred. And if we participate, we "understand"—even if we disagree—rather than having mere "knowledge of" these doctrines. The expressions of certainty, reverence, and peace in the Madonna, Child, and angels provide a context in which the intent of the Christian conventional symbols is unlikely to be mistaken by sensitive participators, even if they do not know the conventions of the symbols.

Cimabue   When we compare Cimabue's panel with Coppo's, we can readily see that something of the rigid separation between the sacred and the secular has been relaxed. Cimabue was one of the first to portray, however haltingly, the change in Florentine society toward a more secular orientation. In the twelfth and thirteenth centuries, Florence was making great strides in bending nature to human needs for the first time since the Roman Empire. A resurgence of confidence in human powers began to clash with the medieval view that people were nothing without God, that nature was valuable only as a stepping-stone to heaven, that—as St. Peter Damian in the first half of the eleventh century asserted—"the world is so filthy with vices that any holy mind is befouled by even thinking of it." The emerging view was not yet "man is the measure of all things," but the honor of being human was beginning to be taken seriously and was an idea that "was to traverse all later Italian art like the muffled, persistent sound of a subterranean river" (Malraux).

Cimabue had assimilated from a long tradition of Christian painting its conventions, technical perfection, and richness of detail. He enriched that inheritance, and in turn helped break ground for the Renaissance, by endowing the old style with more liveliness and mixing the divine into the human, as in this panel, which reveals human emotions in the Madonna. The inert passivity and the hard dogmatic grimness of the medieval style, both so evident in Coppo's work, are revitalized with a spiritual subtlety and psychic awareness, a warmth and tenderness, that make unforgettable the Madonna's benevolently inclined face, to which one returns with unwearying delight. With this face begins the scaling down of the divine into this world. The anthropocentric view — human beings at the center of things — is beginning to focus. A human face has awakened! And it leans forward to come more closely into spiritual contact with us. Its liveliness fell like a refreshing shower on a parched and long-neglected soil, and from that soil a new world began to rise.

Brown-gold tones play softly across the Madonna's features, merging them organically despite the incisive lines, setting the background for the sweeping eyebrows and large deep eye sockets that form a stage on which the pathetic eyes play their drama of tragic foreknowledge. These eyes seem to pulsate with the beat of the soul because they are more flexible than the eyes in contemporary paintings — the irises rest comfortably and dreamily within their whites; the delicately curved lids, now shortened, detach themselves gracefully to meet neatly at the inner pockets; and the doubling line of the lower lid is replaced by fragile shadows that flow into the cheeks and around the nose. Furthermore, although the Greek, or bridgeless, nose is still high and marked by a conspicuous triangle, the sensitive modeling of the nose, its dainty shape, and the tucking in of the pinched tip help blend it into the general perspective of the face. Light shadows fall under the shapely chin to the slender neck and around the cheeks to merge indistinctly with the surrounding veil, whose heavy shadows add to the contemplative atmosphere. But the full lips, depressed at the corners and tightly drawn to the left, add a contrasting touch of intensity, even grimness, to what otherwise would be pure poignancy.

The immense, exquisitely decorated throne, with the bristling and curiously vehement prophets below, enhances by its contrasting monumentality the feminine gentleness of the Madonna. Her large size relative to the angels and prophets is minimized by her robe, which, with its close-meshed lines of gold feathering over the cascading folds, is one of the loveliest in Western art. In a skillfully worked counterpoint, the angel heads and the rainbow-colored wings form an angular rhythm that tenses toward and then quietly pauses at the Madonna's head. This pause is sustained by the simple dotted edge of the centered halo and by the shape of the pedimental top of the rectangular frame. The facial features of the angels resemble the Madonna's, especially the almond-shaped eyes, separated by the stencil-like triangles, and the heavy mouths squared at the corners. Nevertheless, they lack the refined qualities and liveliness that betray so feelingly the soulful sadness of the Madonna. Now in the city of Florence

. . . Mercy has a human heart,
Pity a human face,
And Love, the human form divine,
And Peace, the human dress.

William Blake

But into this peaceful hush that spreads around her sound with anguished apprehension the tragic tones of the Pietà, like the melody of a requiem continued by our imaginations into the pregnant pause.

In Cimabue's panel, unlike Coppo's, there is no longer the sure suggestion of the sacred as almost completely separate from the secular. The sacred and the secular are only narrowly joined, but the juncture seems much more secure. The sacred is portrayed as clearly immanent in at least some things of our world—the Madonna, Child, and saints having some earthly aspects—but the emphasis, of course, is upon the transcendency of the sacred. There is not the slightest hint of the secular taking precedence over the sacred.

Giotto   According to the legend reported by Ghiberti and embellished by Vasari, Cimabue,

> going one day on some business of his own from Florence to Vespignano, found Giotto, while his sheep were browsing, portraying a sheep from nature on a flat and polished slab, with a stone slightly pointed, without having learnt any method of doing this from others, but only from nature; whence Cimabue, standing fast all in a marvel, asked him if he wished to go live with him. The child answered that, his father consenting, he would go willingly. Cimabue then asking this from Bondone, the latter lovingly granted it to him, and was content that he should take the boy with him to Florence; whither having come, in a short time, assisted by nature and taught by Cimabue, the child not only equalled the manner of his master, but became so good an imitator of nature that he banished completely that rude Greek manner and revived the modern and good art of painting, introducing the portraying well from nature of living people.[3]

The Giotto and the Cimabue, both originally placed in churches, now hang side by side in the first room of the Uffizi Gallery in Florence. The contrast between the panels is striking. Cimabue's Madonna, who seems to float into our world, is abruptly brought to earth by Giotto; or, as Ruskin puts it, now we have Mama. She sits solidly, bell-shaped, without evasion, in three-dimensional space subject to gravitational forces, her frank, focused gaze alerted to her surroundings, whereas Cimabue's Madonna is steeped in moodiness. The forms of Giotto's Madonna seem to have been drawn from nature, whereas Cimabue seems to have started from medieval forms. In subject matter Giotto seems to have begun more from "here," whereas Cimabue seems to have begun more from "hereafter."

---

[3]Giorgio Vasari, *Lives of the Most Eminent Painters,* trans. Gaston Duc Devere (London: Macmillan, 1912), vol.1, p. 72.

The eyes of Giotto's Madonna, surrounded by her high forehead and the immense cheeks, have a fascinating asymmetry that gives her face a mark of idiosyncrasy and adds to its liveliness. The fish-shaped left eye with its half-covered pupil twists to the left, so that it appears to be looking in a different direction than the more realistic right eye. The resulting tension fixes our attention and heightens our feelings of being caught in her level gaze, which gains further intensity by being the focus of the gazes of the saints and angels. Since the open space below the Madonna provides us with a figurative path of access, we are directly engaged with her in a way that Cimabue carefully avoids by, among other devices, putting the throne of his Madonna on a high-arched platform and then placing the little prophets within the arches.

The smallness of the sensual mouth of Giotto's Madonna, barely wider than the breadth of her long and snouty nose, accentuates its expressiveness. Also, for the first time, the lips of a Madonna open—however slightly, shyly revealing two teeth—as if she were about to gasp or speak. It does not matter, for the mobility of inner responsiveness is conveyed. Everything else expresses her stoicism, a rocklike kind of endurance—the untooled, centered halo, the steady gaze, the calm, impersonal expression, the cool and silvery skin color with green underpainting that suggests bone structures beneath, the heavy jaw and towerlike neck, the long unbroken verticals and broad sweeping curves of the simply colored robe and tunic, the firm hand that no longer points but holds, and above all her upright monumental massiveness, as solid as if hewn in granite. The saints and angels, compactly arranged in depth, stand on the same ground as the earthly throne. Although the saints express peace and the angels awe, they are natural beings, not imaginary supporters of a heavenly throne as in Cimabue's picture.

The Child shares with his mother the monumentality of Giotto's style—the square, forthright head, the powerful body, the physical density and solidity that make Giotto's figures so statuesque. Giotto's Child, compared with Cimabue's, seems almost coarse, especially in the shaping of the hands and feet; and the somewhat insecure placement of his body from a naturalistic standpoint is physically much more uncomfortable, primarily because such a standpoint is almost irrelevant in Cimabue's picture. The hair and ears are not so stylized as in Cimabue's Child, light and shadow sink more organically into the flesh, the eyes and nose are given the most realistic rendition since Roman times, and the expression is dynamically alert. Yet the lack of irregularity and flexibility in these less conventional features, combined with the effect of maturity in miniature, keep the Child from being a Baby. The content of Giotto's painting is clearly Christian, but not quite so obviously as in the paintings of Coppo and Cimabue. The portrayal of religious feeling is not quite so strong. For the first time in Florence there is the suggestion, however muted, of the secular challenging the sacred. If Mama gets much more earthly and independent, the sacred no longer will be so obviously in control.

Parmigianino Compare now Giotto's painting with *The Madonna with the Long Neck* (Figure 4-4), painted by Francesco Parmigianino in the waning years of the Italian Renaissance, circa 1535.

Giotto and Parmigianino

1. *The Madonna with the Long Neck* was never quite finished, and as far as we know, Parmigianino did not provide a title. Later in the sixteenth century, Giorgio Vasari, one of the first great art historians, baptized it *The Virgin and Sleeping Child*. Do you believe Parmigianino would have accepted this naming as appropriate? What about the appropriateness of its present title—*The Madonna with the Long Neck?*
2. How does the content of this picture differ from Giotto's?
3. How does Parmigianino's form accomplish a different interpretation of what apparently is the same subject matter?
4. Jacob Burckhardt, a very knowledgeable nineteenth-century critic and historian, complained of Parmigianino's "unsupportable affectation," and, somewhat more tolerantly, "the bringing of the manners of the great world divertingly into the holy scenes." Generally, until recent times, this work has been an object of derision. Why would this be so? Today the painting is generally considered to be a masterpiece. Why this radical shift in evaluative criticism?

Although natural structures in Parmigianino's painting are suggested, they are not interpreted as natural. The light is neither quite indoors nor outdoors, the perspectives are odd, gravity is defied, the bodies are artificially proportioned and drained of mass and physical power, the protagonists are psychologically detached from one another, and above all the porcelain facial features allow no hint of liveliness. The head of the Madonna is shaped like a well-wrought urn, while the ears, set out abnormally in order to emphasize their serpentine calligraphy, look like its handles. The nerveless skin is unnaturally cold and pale, glazed like ceramic, and beneath that polished surface the urn seems hollow. Hence the pure geometrical design of the fastidious lines of the eyebrows, eyes, nose, and mouth is assembled on a surface without organic foundation—no pulsating blood coursing through arteries and veins integrates these features, and no muscular structure can move them. And so the gaze down upon the Child—the most lifeless Child of the Renaissance—is too stylized and superficial to be expressive of any psychic, let alone sacramental, meaning. Like an Attic amphora, the head of the Madonna rises from its swanlike neck, while the hair decorates the lid with the preciosity of fine goldwork.

If the subject matter of *The Madonna with the Long Neck* is a sacred scene, Burckhardt's denunciation of "unsupportable affectation" would seem to be justified. If, however, the Christian symbols are no more than a support or an excuse for an interpretation of line, color, texture, shape, and light, Burckhardt's denunciation is irrelevant. To meet this painting halfway—and surely this is the responsibility of every serious perceiver—the religious symbols presumably can be dismissed, and then the subject matter can be experienced as secular. The design of this delicate work, this splendor of form shining on the proportionate parts of matter, ought to bring one to a better understanding and appreciation of the rhythmic qualities of line; the cooling, calming powers of smooth surfaces and colors; the sinuous sensuousness of spiraling shapes; and the fluidity of bulkless volumes. But this heretical design, despite its lifting flow, may not waft you to a Christian heaven on the wings of faith.

The Madonna with the Long Neck is such a magnificently secular work of art that the excommunication of the Christian symbols is rather easily accomplished, at least in our day. That is why the present title probably seems more appropriate to most of us than Vasari's title. Abstract painting has opened our eyes to the intrinsic values of the sensuous, and a strong case can be made that in a strange way *The Madonna with the Long Neck* is a kind of abstract painting. An appropriate title today might be *Sinuous Spiraling Shapes*. This is a controversial judgment. What do you think?

Determining the Subject Matter of a Painting

Study Frankenthaler's *Flood* (Figure 4-7).

PERCEPTION KEY   Frankenthaler

1. Is this painting abstract or representational? Take plenty of time before you decide, but disregard the title.
2. The title is *Flood*. Do you see a flood when you ignore the title? Do you see a flood when you take the title into consideration?
3. If you do, in fact, see a flood when taking notice of the title, does this make the painting representational?
4. If you do not see a flood, what do you see?

The third question is tricky. We suggest the following principle as a basis for answering such questions. If a work only shows (presents) but does not interpret (reveal) the objects and events that the title sometimes indicates, this is not enough to make it representational. These objects and events must be interpreted if the work is to be usefully classified as representational. Our view is that a flood in Frankenthaler's painting is interpreted, that our perception of the spreading, merging earthy stains, soft as water, intensifies our awareness of flooding, especially the rhythms of surges and backwater eddies. If this judgment is correct, the work is representational. Alternatively, your view may be that recognition of flooding in the painting only helps intensify your perception of the sensuous—the swirling rhythm of colors. If this judgment is correct, the work is abstract. As with the Parmigianino, *Flood* lies on a vague borderline between representational and abstract painting.

Sometimes, as we have seen with Frankenthaler's *Flood*, it is extremely difficult to distinguish between abstract and representational painting. Whether the recognition of objects and events in a painting intensifies perception of the sensuous may vary with the differences in temperament and background of the participators. Nevertheless, the distinction between

FIGURE 4-15
Rembrandt van Rijn, *Self Portrait*. 1659. Oil on canvas, 33¼ × 26 inches. Andrew W. Mellon Collection. National Gallery of Art, Washington, D.C.

abstract and representational painting is useful because it brings up this important fact: Whereas in abstract painting definite objects and events are not a part of the content, in representational paintings they are. Even when the distinction is difficult to make, as with *Flood*, focusing on the issue of abstraction and representation can help us clarify what is most important in any particular painting.

FIGURE 4-16
Frida Kahlo, *Self-Portrait with Thorn Necklace and Hummingbird*. 1940. Oil on masonite, 24½ × 18¾ inches. Harry Ransom Humanities Research Art Collection, The University of Texas at Austin. (© 2003 Banco de México, Diego Rivera & Frida Kahlo Museums Trust. Av. Cinco de Mayo No. 2, Centro, Del. Cuauhtémoc 06059, Mexico, D.F.)

Interpretation of the Self:
Frida Kahlo, Romaine Brooks, and Rembrandt Van Rijn

The self-portrait is a specialized genre of painting, one that often fascinates great painters. Rembrandt, for example, painted himself again and again throughout his life, leaving us a record of changing fortunes, personality, and appearances (Figure 4-15). The modern Mexican artist Frida Kahlo did much the same, giving us numerous images of herself (Figure 4-16) in often enigmatic poses and states of mind. Romaine Brooks, did relatively few self-portraits, but the one reproduced here has a strength and straightforwardness that is especially captivating (Figure 4-17).

> **PERCEPTION KEY**   Three Self-Portraits
>
> 1. Which of these paintings is more dominated by detail? How does color contribute to that domination?
> 2. If the subject matter of each painting is similar, in what lies the difference?
> 3. What is revealed by each of these paintings?
> 4. In which of these paintings does light work most mysteriously?

The appreciation of a self-portrait usually benefits from some background information. Rembrandt's self-portrait was painted when he was fifty-three. He had just ten more years to live. He made approximately a hundred self-portraits throughout his life, and this one is among the most poignant. Rembrandt had been extraordinarily successful as a painter. His impressive commissions had made him a wealthy man, but a number of years before this portrait, Rembrandt, a poor businessman, was financially ruined and had to work all the harder just to survive. The range of color in this painting is confined to earth tones, subdued, controlled, limited. His gaze is steady but not directly at the viewer — he paints himself as if he were staring into a mirror. His expression is not especially secure nor especially definite. You may decide for yourself what his expression implies, but one can see how different it is from the expressions on the faces of Kahlo and Brooks. Rembrandt is inward looking, in deep meditation. The organization of the painting differs from those of Kahlo and Brooks in that it is dark and mysterious and in some ways, perhaps, deeply religious.

Frida Kahlo was a painter and the wife of one of Mexico's most famous muralists, Diego Rivera, who was twenty years her senior. She suffered polio as a child and as a teenager was in a terrible bus and streetcar crash that left her with three fractured vertebrae, a crushed pelvis, and broken ribs. The result was a life filled with pain. She had to wear orthopedic shoes and a restraining corset that gave her almost no relief throughout her life. Moreover, her marriage to Diego Rivera involved innumerable infidelities and many stormy scenes. Yet it remained in place throughout her life. She was involved with the Communist party in Mexico in the 1940s and spent much of her time in protest against exploitation and war. Her *Self-Portrait with Thorn Necklace and Hummingbird* (Figure 4-16) connects her to the suffering of Christ, symbolized by the hummingbird. The monkey and cat were family pets and the leaves behind her are derived from Mexican folk art. Her gaze is not directly at the viewer; instead, it is distracted — possibly by psychic pain or remembrance — as if to reveal her vulnerability. The straight-on face, hair worn aloft, as she usually wore it, is unrelenting, unembarrassed, unyielding. Her eyebrows, growing together as they do, and her slight mustache were signature details in almost all her portraits — marks of psychic strength.

FIGURE 4-17
Romaine Brooks, *Self Portrait*. 1923. Oil on canvas, 46¼ × 26⅞ inches. National Museum of American Art, Smithsonian Institution, Washington, D.C. Gift of the artist. (© Smithsonian American Art Museum, Washington, D.C./Art Resource, New York)

Romaine Brooks had a difficult life as well. She had wealthy parents, but they essentially abandoned her at age six, when she was sent off to school. She was American, born in Rome, with an older, paranoid, and dangerous brother. She was taken in by her grandfather. Her mother and brother died when she was twenty-eight, leaving her independently wealthy. She married apparently for society's sake, but lived openly as a lesbian in London and Paris. She specialized in portraits, usually of friends. She seems to have willfully restricted her range of colors, which emphasize gray and black and often luminescent whites. Her self-portrait emphasizes uprightness, aloneness, and, in the essentially masculine dress, independence (Figure 4-17). The architectural details in the background imply an urban lifestyle, while the direct, unashamed look encompasses the viewer in a frank, perhaps challenging, fashion.

Some Painting Styles of the Twentieth Century

Painting, whether abstract or representational, sets forth the visually perceptible in such a way that it works in our experience with heightened intensity. Every *style* of painting finds facets of the visually perceptible that had previously been missed. For example, the painting of the past hundred years has given us, among many other styles, Impressionism, revealing the play of sunlight on color, as in the Renoir (Figure 2-18); Post-Impressionism, using the surface techniques of Impressionism but drawing out the solidity of things, as in the Cézanne (Figure 2-4); *Expressionism*, portraying strong emotion, as in the Blume (Figure 1-3); Cubism, showing the three-dimensional qualities of things as splayed out in a tightly closed two-dimensional space—without significant perspective or cast shadow—through geometrical crystallization, a technique partially exhibited in Picasso's *Guernica* (Figure 1-4); Dada, poking fun at the absurdity of everything, as in Picabia's *The Blessed Virgin* (see Figure 14-17); *Surrealism*, expressing the subconscious, as perhaps in Siqueiros (Figure 1-2); Suprematism or Constructivism, portraying sensa in movement with—as in Expressionism—the expression of powerful emotion or energy, exemplified in the Pollock (Figure 3-2); *Pop Art*, the revelation of mass-produced products, as in the Dine (Figure 2-1); and so on. And today and tomorrow, new dimensions are and will be portrayed. In Chapter 14 we will study some examples of *avant-garde* painting. Never in the history of painting has there been such rapid change and vitality. Never in history has there been so much help available for those of us who, in varying degrees, are blind to the fullness of the visually perceptible. If we take advantage of this help, the rewards are priceless.

Painting is the art that has most to do with revealing the sensuous and the visual appearance of objects and events. Painting shows the visually perceptible more clearly. Because a painting is usually presented to us as an entirety, with an all-at-onceness, it gives time for our vision to focus, hold, and participate. This makes possible a vision that is both extraordinarily intense and restful. Sensa are the qualities of objects or events that stimulate our sense organs. Sensa can be disassociated or abstracted from the objects or events in which they are usually joined. Sensa and the sensuous (the color field composed by the sensa) are the primary subject matter of abstract painting. Objects and events are the primary subject matter of representational painting.

Bibliography

Arnheim, Rudolf. *Art and Visual Perception*, new rev. ed. Berkeley: University of California Press, 1974.

Bell, Clive. *Art*. New York: Putnam, 1981.

Bryson, Norman. *Vision and Painting: The Logic of the Gaze*. New Haven, Conn.: Yale University Press, 1988.

Canaday, John. *Keys to Art*. New York: Tudor, 1964.

Clark, Kenneth. *The Nude*. New York: Doubleday Anchor, 1959.

Elsen, Albert E. *Purposes of Art*, 4th ed. New York: Holt, Rinehart and Winston, 1981.

Fine, Elsa Honig. *Women and Art*. Montclair, N.J.: Allanheld and Schram/ Prior, 1978.

Fitzhugh, Elizabeth West, ed. *Artists' Pigments: A Handbook of their History and Characteristics*. New York: Oxford University Press, 1997.

Focillon, Henri. *The Life of Forms in Art*, 2nd ed. New York: Zone Books, 1989.

Fry, Roger. *Vision and Design*. New York: New American Library, 1974.

Gombrich, E. H. *Art and Illusion*, 5th ed. London: Phaidon, 1977.

———. *The Story of Art*, 16th ed. London: Phaidon, 1995.

Gregory, R. L. *Eye and Brain*. New York: McGraw-Hill, 1966.

Hartt, Frederick. *Art: A History of Painting, Sculpture, and Architecture*, 4th ed. New York: Prentice-Hall, 1993.

Hauser, Arnold. *The Social History of Art*. 4 vols. New York: Vintage Books, 1964.

Heller, Nancy G. *Women Artists*, 3rd ed. New York: Abbeville Press, 1997.

Janson, H. W. *History of Art*, 5th ed., revised and expanded by Anthony F. Janson. London: Thames and Hudson, 1995.

McCarthy, David. *Pop Art*. New York: Cambridge University Press, 2001.

Moszuzka, Anna. *Abstract Art*. New York: Thames and Hudson, 1990.

Panofsky, Erwin. *Meaning in the Visual Arts*. Princeton, N.J.: Princeton University Press, 1995.

Patton, Sharon F. *African-American Art*. New York: Oxford University Press, 1998.

Petardi, Gabor. *Printmaking*. New York: Macmillan, 1980.

Rosenberg, Harold. *The Anxious Object*. Chicago: University of Chicago Press, 1982.

Steinberg, Leo. *Other Criteria: Confrontations with Twentieth-Century Art*. New York: Oxford University Press, 1972.

Wolfflin, Heinrich. *Principles of Art History*. Translated by W. D. Hottinger. New York: Dover, 1979.

ART SITES ON THE INTERNET

http://artsnet2.heinz.cmu.edu/artsnet/artsites

ASIAN ART GALLERY

http://www.asia-art.net

CIMABUE AND GIOTTO

http://www.dc.peachnet.edu/~shale/humanities/literature/world_literature/dante/
tour/ft_art.html
http://www.kfki.hu/~arthp/tours/giotto/index.html

INDIVIDUAL PAINTERS

http://dir.yahoo.com/Arts/Visual_Arts/Painting/Artists/Masters

FRIDA KAHLO

http://www.fbuch.com/fridaby.htm
http://members.aol.com/fridanet/kahlo.htm

THE LOUVRE

http://www.louvre.fr/louvrea.htm

REMBRANDT VAN RIJN

http://www.rembrandthuis.nl/index_en.html
http://www.ibiblio.org/wm/paint/auth/rembrandt/

MARK ROTHKO

http://www.artchive.com/artchive/R/rothko.html

SISTINE CHAPEL

http://www.christusrex.org/www1/sistine/0-Tour.html

VERMEER

http://www.ccsf.caltech.edu/~roy/vermeer/

CHAPTER 5

Sculpture

Sculpture and Touch

Sculpture, along with painting and architecture, is usually, but not very use-fully, classified as one of the visual arts. Such classification suggests that the eye is the chief sense organ involved in our participation with sculpture. Yet observe participants at an exhibition of both paintings and sculptures. Usually at least a few will touch or try to touch some of the sculptures de-spite the "Do Not Touch" signs. Some kinds of sculpture invite us to explore and caress them with our hands and even, if they are not too large or heavy, to pick them up. Constantin Brancusi noticed this and created a *Sculpture for the Blind*. Within a box with an opening at the top large enough to allow passage of the hand, he placed three-dimensional shapes of varying sizes and textures, rhythmically organized. Sculpture draws the eye to the fingers.

PERCEPTION KEY   Experiment with Touch

Using scissors cut out four approximately 6-inch cardboard squares. Shape them with curves or angles into abstract patterns (structures that do not rep-resent objects), and put one into a bag. Ask a friend to feel that sample in the bag without looking at the sample. Then ask your friend (1) to draw the pattern they felt with pencil on paper. Continue the same procedure with the other three samples. Have your friend make four samples for you, and follow the same procedures yourself. Analyze your results. How closely were the drawings imitative of the samples? What is the significance of this experiment?

Sculpture and Density

Sculpture engages our senses differently than painting. This is because sculpture occupies space as a three-dimensional *mass,* whereas painting is essentially a two-dimensional surface that can only represent ("re-present") three-dimensionality. Of course, painting can suggest density—for example, *Mont Sainte-Victoire* (Figure 2-4)—but sculpture *is* dense. Henry Moore, one of the most influential modern sculptors, states that the sculptor "gets the solid shape, as it were, inside his head—he thinks of it, whatever its size, as if he were holding it completely enclosed in the hollow of his hand." The sculptor, Moore continues, "mentally visualizes a complex form *from all round itself;* he knows while he looks at one side what the other side is like; he identifies himself with its center of gravity, its mass, its weight; he realizes its volume, as the space that the shape displaces in the air."[1] Apparently we can only fully apprehend sculpture by senses that are alive not only to visual and *tactile* (touchable) surfaces but also to the weight and volume lying behind those surfaces.

Sensory Interconnections

It is surely an oversimplification to distinguish the various arts on the basis of which sense organ is activated—for example, to claim that painting is experienced solely by sight and sculpture solely by touch. Our nervous systems are far more complicated than that. Generally no clear separation is made in experience between the faculties of sight and touch. The sensa of touch, for instance, are normally joined with other sensa—visual, aural, oral, and olfactory. Even if only one kind of sensum initiates a perception, a chain reaction triggers off other sensations, either by sensory motor connections or by memory associations. We are constantly grasping and handling things as well as seeing, hearing, tasting, and smelling them. And so when we see a thing, we have a pretty good idea of what its surface would feel like, how it would sound if struck, how it would taste, and how it would smell if we approached. And if we grasp or handle a thing in the dark, we have some idea of what its shape looks like.

As we approach a stone wall, we see various shapes. And these shapes recall certain information. We know something about how the surface of these stones would feel and that it would hurt if we walked into them. We do not know about the surface, volume, and mass of those stones by sight alone but by sight associated with manual experience. Both painting and sculpture involve sight and touch. But touch is much more involved in our participation with sculpture. If we can clarify such differences as these, our understanding of sculpture will be deeper and, in turn, our participation more rewarding.

---

[1]Henry Moore, "Notes on Sculpture," in *Sculpture and Drawings 1921–1948*, 4th rev. ed., ed. David Sylvester (New York: George Wittenborn, 1957), p. xxxiii ff.

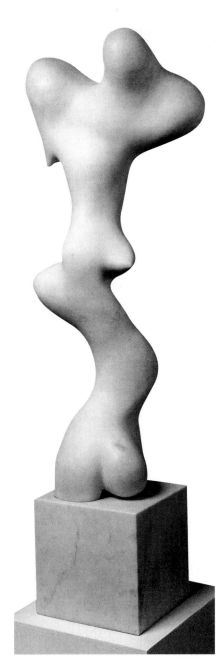

Sculpture and Painting Compared

Compare Rothko's *Earth Greens* (Figure 4-11) with Arp's *Growth* (Figure 5-1). Both works are abstract, we suggest, for neither has as its primary subject matter objects or events. Arp's sculpture has something to do with growth, of course, as confirmed by the title. But is it human, animal, or vegetable growth? Male or female? Clear-cut answers do not seem possible.

Specificity of reference, just as in the Rothko, is missing. And yet, if you agree that the subject matter of the Rothko is the sensuous, would you say the same for the Arp? To affirm this may bother you, for Arp's marble is dense material. This substantiality of the marble is very much a part of its appearance as sculpture. Conversely, *Earth Greens* as a painting — that is, as a work of art rather than as a physical canvas of such and such a weight — does not appear as a material thing. The weight of the canvas is irrelevant to our participation with *Earth Greens* as a work of art. Indeed, if that weight becomes relevant, we are no longer participating with the painting. That weight becomes relevant if we are hanging *Earth Greens* on a wall, of course, but that is a procedure antecedent to our participation with it as a painting.

Rothko has abstracted sensa, especially colors, from objects or things, whereas Arp has brought out the substantiality of a thing — the density of the marble. Earth and grass and sky are not "in" Rothko's painting. Conversely, Arp has made the marble relevant to his sculpture. This kind of difference, incidentally, is perhaps the underlying reason the term "abstract painting" is used more frequently than the term "abstract sculpture." There is an awkwardness about describing something as material as most sculpture as abstract. Picasso once remarked, "There is no abstract art. You must always start with something. There is no danger then anyway because the idea of the object will have left an indelible mark." This may be an over-statement with respect to painting, but the point rings true with sculpture. Still, the distinction between abstract and representational sculpture is worth making, just as with painting, for being clear about the subject matter of a work of art is essential to all sensitive participation. It is the key to understanding the content, for the content is the subject matter interpreted by means of the form.

PERCEPTION KEY   Rothko and Arp

1. Would you like to touch either of these works?
2. Would you expect either the Rothko or the Arp to feel hot or cold to your touch?
3. Which work seems to require the more careful placement of lighting? Why?
4. Is space perceived differently in and around these two works? If so, how?
5. Which of the two works appears to be the more unchangeable in your perception?
6. Why do the authors claim that *Earth Greens* is more abstract than *Growth*? Can you think of other reasons—for example, the shapes in the two works?

Most sculpture, whether abstract or representational, returns us to the voluminosity (bulk), density (mass), and tactile quality of things. Thus sculpture has touch or tactile appeal. Even if we do not actually handle a work of sculpture, we can imagine how it would feel with reference to its surface, volume, and weight. Sculpture brings us back into touch with

FIGURE 5-2
King Akhenaten and Queen
Nefertiti. Egyptian sunken re-
lief from El-Amarna. XVIII
dynasty. (The Metropolitan
Museum of Art)

things by allowing the thickness of things to permeate its surface. Most
sculptures make us feel them as resistant, as substantial. Hence the primary
subject matter of most abstract sculpture is the density of sensa. Sculpture
is more than skin deep. Abstract painting can only represent density,
whereas sculpture, whether abstract or representational, presents

density. Abstract painters generally emphasize the surfaces of sensa, as in *Earth Greens*. Their interest is in the vast ranges of color qualities, lines, and the play of light to bring out textural nuances. Abstract sculptors, on the other hand, generally restrict themselves to a minimal range of color, line, and textural qualities and emphasize light not only to play on these qualities but also to bring out the inherence of these qualities in things. Whereas abstract painters are shepherds of surface sensa, abstract sculptors are shepherds of depth sensa.

Sunken-Relief Sculpture

Compare Figure 5-2, a detail of an Egyptian work in limestone from about 1300 B.C., with Pollock's *Autumn Rhythm* (Figure 3-2). We usually think of sculpture, with its emphasis on density, as projecting out into space. Yet some of the lines and patches of paint in Pollock's paintings are laid on so thickly that they stand out as much as a half inch or so from the flat surface of the canvas. In the Egyptian work there is no projection whatsoever. Rather, the carving cuts grooves of various depths into the surface plane of the stone to outline each object, a technique called *sunken relief*. The firmness, clarity, and brilliance of these linear grooves in the Egyptian work are brought out by the way their sharp outside edges catch the light. Did this technique in this instance produce sculpture rather than painting? Only if it brings out in some significant sense the voluminosity or density or surface feel of its materials: Only then will the tactile as well as the visual appeal be important.

This work has significant tactile appeal, especially when you stand before it rather than seeing it in a photograph. The density of the limestone is evident. In other words, we are suggesting that this work is more than a linear drawing. Pollock's work, conversely, lacks significant tactile appeal despite the projection of its heavy, thick oils. It is conceivable that Pollock's painting could have been made in some other medium—acrylic, for example—and still be essentially the same work. It is inconceivable that the Egyptian relief could have been carved out of different material and still be essentially the same work. The surface as seen is what counts in Pollock's painting. The materials that make that surface possible are basically irrelevant in perceiving the work as painting (although for a restorer of the painting, the materials would be relevant indeed). In the Egyptian relief, the surface is perceived more tactilely than the surface of the Pollock.

Low-Relief Sculpture

Low-relief sculpture projects relatively slightly from its background plane, and so its depth dimension is very limited. Medium- and high-relief sculpture project further from their backgrounds, their depth dimensions expanded. Sculpture in the round is freed from any background plane, and so

FIGURE 5-3
Chryssa, *Times Square Sky*. 1962. Neon, aluminum, steel, 60 × 60 × 9½ inches. Collection, Walker Art Center, Minneapolis. Gift of the T. B. Walker Foundation, 1964.

its depth dimension is unrestricted. *Times Square Sky* (Figure 5-3) is, we think, most usefully classified as sculpture of the low-relief species. The materiality of the steel, the neon tubing, and especially the aluminum is brought out very powerfully by their juxtaposition. Unfortunately, this is difficult to perceive from a photograph. Because of its three-dimensionality, sculpture generally suffers even more than painting from being seen only in a photograph. Chryssa Vardea was born in Greece, and when she came to America she was fascinated by the garishness of Times Square. She worked extensively with neon lighting. In *Times Square Sky* Chryssa is especially sensitive to aluminum, the neon light helping to bring out the special sheen of that metal, which flashes forth in smooth and rough textures through subtle shadows.

Yet *Times Square Sky*, as the title suggests, is representational. The subject matter is about a quite specific place, and the content of *Times Square Sky*—by means of its form—is an interpretation of that subject matter. Times Square is walled around by manufactured products, such as aluminum and steel, animated especially at night by a chaos of flashing neon signs. Letters and words — often as free of syntax as in the sculpture — clutter that noisy space and merge with the bombarding sensa. The feel of that fascinating square is Chryssa's subject matter, just as it is in Mondrian's *Broadway Boogie Woogie* (Figure 4-10). Both works reveal something of the rhythm, bounce, color, and chaos of Times Square, but *Times Square Sky* interprets more of its physical character. Whereas Mondrian abstracts from the physicality of Broadway, Chryssa gives us a heightened sense of the way Broadway feels as our bodies are assaulted by the streets and their crowds. Those attacks — tactile, visual, aural, and olfactory — can have a metallic, mechanical, impersonal, and threatening character, and something of those menacing qualities is revealed in *Times Square Sky*. The physicality of that effect is, we suggest, what distinguishes this work as sculpture rather than painting. And yet the line here cannot be too sharply drawn. For if the neon tubing and aluminum were flattened down on the steel somewhat, or if Pollock had laid on his paints an inch or so thicker, would these works then be sculpture or painting?

Relief sculpture, except sunken relief, allows its materials to stand out from a background plane, as in *Times Square Sky*. Thus relief sculpture in at least one way reveals its materials simply by showing us — directly — their surface and something of their depth. By moving to a side of *Times Square Sky*, we can see that the steel, neon tubing, and aluminum are of such and such thickness. However, this three-dimensionality in relief sculpture, this movement out into space, is not allowed to lose its ties to its background plane. Hence relief sculpture, like painting, is usually best viewed from a basically frontal position. You cannot walk around a relief sculpture and see its back side as sculpture any more than you can walk around a painting and see its back side as painting. That is why both relief sculptures and paintings are usually best placed on walls or in niches.

High-Relief Sculpture

The Hindu deity, *Dancing Apsaras* (Figure 5-4), from a temple of the thirteenth century at Rajasthan in India, is an example of *high-relief sculpture*. Bursting with energy, the deity stands out from the wall and almost escapes from her pillar. In contrast, the small admiring handmaiden is in relatively low relief, closely integrated with the pillar. Partly because the deity is almost completely in the round, we sense her bulk and mass with exceptional force.

Sculpture in the Round

Michelangelo's *Pietà* (Figure 5-5), one of his last sculptures, circa 1550–1555, was unfinished. According to Vasari and Condivi, historians of the time, Michelangelo originally wanted to be buried at the foot of this sculpture, which was to be placed in Santa Maria Maggiore in Rome. Hence he portrayed his own features in the head of Joseph of Arimathea, the figure hovering above, and apparently was making good progress. But then a

FIGURE 5-4
Dancing Apsaras. Thirteenth century. Rajasthan, India. Relief, sandstone, 28 inches high. The Metropolitan Museum of Art, New York. Gift of Abby Aldrich Rockefeller, 1942 (42.25.18).

FIGURE 5-5
Michelangelo Buonarroti, *Pietà*. Circa 1550–1555. Marble, 7 feet 8 inches high. Opera del Duomo, Florence. (© Alinari/Art Resource, New York)

series of accidents occurred, some involuntary and some probably voluntary. In carving the left leg of Christ, a vein in the marble broke, and the leg was completely destroyed. There are also breaks above the left elbow of Christ, in his chest on the left, and on the fingers of the hand of the Virgin. The story goes that in despair Michelangelo did some of this damage himself. In any case, he gave it up as a monument for his tomb and sold it in 1561, deciding that he preferred burial in Florence.

1. Of the four figures in this statue—Joseph, Christ, the Virgin to the right, and Mary Magdalene to the left—one seems to be not only somewhat stylistically out of harmony with the other three but of lesser artistic quality. Historians and critics generally agree that this figure was not done or at least not completed by Michelangelo but rather by a second-rate sculptor, presumably Tiberio Calcagni. Which figure is this? What are your reasons for choosing it?

2. Michelangelo, perhaps more than any other sculptor, was obsessed with marble. He spent months searching the hills of Carrara near Pisa for marble blocks from which he could help sculptural shapes emerge. Something of his love for marble, perhaps, is revealed in this *Pietà*. Do you perceive this?

3. Is this sculpture in the round? The figures are freed from a base as background, and one can walk around the work. But is this *Pietà* in the round in the same way as Arp's *Growth* (Figure 5-1)?

The answer to the first question is the Magdalene. Her figure and pose, relative to the others, are artificial and stiff. Her robe—compare it with the Virgin's—fails to integrate with the body beneath. For no accountable reason she is both aloof and much smaller, and the rhythms of her figure fail to harmonize with the others. Finally, the marbleness of the marble fails to come out with the Magdalene.

In the other figures—and this is the key to the second question—Michelangelo barely allows his shapes, except for the polished surfaces of the body of Christ, to emerge from the marble block. The features of the Virgin's face, for example, are very roughly carved. It is as if she were still partially a prisoner in the stone. The Virgin is a marble Virgin; the Magdalene is a Magdalene and marble. Or, to put it another way, Michelangelo saw the Virgin in the marble and helped her image out without allowing it to betray its origin. Calcagni, or whoever did the Magdalene, saw the image of Magdalene and then fitted the marble to the image. Thus the claim that the face of the Virgin was unfinished is mistaken. It is hard to conceive, for us at least, how more chiseling or any polishing could have avoided weakening the expression of tender sorrow. The face of the Magdalene is more finished in a realistic sense, of course, but the forms of art reveal rather than reproduce reality. In the case of the body of Christ—compared with the rest of the statue except the Magdalene—the more finished chiseling and the high polish were appropriate because they helped reveal the bodily suffering.

Since there is no background plane from which the figures emerge, the *Pietà* is usually described as *sculpture in the round*. Yet when compared with Arp's *Growth* (Figure 5-1), it is obvious that the *Pietà* is not so clearly in the round. There is no "pull" around to the rough-hewn back side, except, perhaps, our need to escape from the intensity of the awesome pity. And when we do walk behind the *Pietà*, we find the back side unintegrated with the

FIGURE 5-6
Mathias Goeritz, *The Five Towers of the Satellite City*. 1957. Painted concrete pylons, 121 to 187 feet high. Near Mexico City. (Photograph from *Matrix of Man*, 1968, by Sibyl Moholy-Nagy, Praeger Publishers. Courtesy Hattula Moholy-Nagy Hug)

sides and front and of little interest. Michelangelo intended this essentially three-sided pyramid, as with practically all of his sculptures, to be placed in a niche so that it could be seen principally from the front. In this sense, the

FIGURE 5-7
Great Sphinx and Pyramid at Memphis, Egypt. IV dynasty, circa 2850 B.C. Rock-cut limestone and masonry; base of Pyramid, about 13 acres; Sphinx, 66 feet high, 172 feet long. (Egyptian State Tourist Administration)

Pietà is a transition piece between high-relief sculpture, such as the *Dancing Apsaras,* and unqualified sculpture in the round, such as *Growth.*

Sculpture and Architecture Compared

Architecture is the art of separating inner from outer space in such a way that the inner space can be used for practical purposes. There is much more to architecture than that, of course, as we shall discuss in the next chapter. But how can sculpture be distinguished from architecture? Despite the architectural monumentality of Goeritz's *The Five Towers of the Satellite City* (Figure 5-6), this is clearly sculpture because there is no inner space. But what about the Sphinx and the Pyramid at Memphis (Figure 5-7)? Like *The Five Towers of the Satellite City,* both the Sphinx and the Pyramid are among the densest and most substantial of all works. They attract us visually and tactilely. Since there is no space within the Sphinx, it is sculpture. But within the Pyramid, space was provided for the burial of the dead. There is a separation of inner from outer space for the functional use of the inner space. Yet the use of this inner space is so limited that the living often have a difficult time finding it. The inner space is functional only in a restricted sense—that is, for the dead only. Is then this Pyramid sculpture or architecture? We shall delay our answer until the next chapter. The difficulty of the question, however, points up an important factor that we should keep in mind. The distinctions between the arts that we have been and will be making are helpful in order to talk about them intelligibly, but the arts resist neat pigeonholing and any attempt at that would be futile.

Sensory Space

The space around a sculpture is sensory rather than empty. Despite its invisibility, sensory space — like the wind — is felt. Sculptures such as *Growth* (Figure 5-1) are surrounded by radiating vectors, something like the axis lines of painting. But with sculpture, our bodies as well as our eyes are directed. *Growth* is like a magnet drawing us in and around. With relief sculptures, except for very high relief such as the *Dancing Apsaras* (Figure 5-4), our bodies tend to get stabilized in one favored position. The framework of front and sides meeting at sharp angles, as in *Times Square Sky* (Figure 5-3), limits our movements to 180 degrees at most. Although we are likely to move around within this limited range for a while, our movements gradually slow down, as they do when we finally get settled in a comfortable chair. We are not Cyclops with just one eye, and so we see something of the three-dimensionality of things even when restricted to one position. But even low-relief sculpture encourages some movement of the body, because we sense that a different perspective, however slight, may bring out something we have not directly perceived, especially something more of the three-dimensionality of the materials.

When one of the authors participated with Arp's *Growth*, he had this response:

I find a warm and friendly presence. I find myself reaching toward the statue rather than keeping my distance. (If a chair were available I would not use it.) Whereas generally my perceptual relationship to a painting requires my getting to and settling in the privileged position, as when finding the best seat in the theater, my perceptual relationship to the Arp is much more mobile and flexible. The smooth rounded shapes with their swelling volumes move gently out into space, turn my body around the figure, and control the rhythm of my walking. My perception of the Arp seems to take much more time than my perception of a painting, but in fact that is not necessarily so.

The Arp seems not only three-dimensional but four-dimensional, because it brings in the element of time so discernibly — a cumulative drama. In addition to making equal demands upon my contemplation, at the same time, each aspect is also incomplete, enticing me on to the next for fulfillment. As I move, volumes and masses change, and on their surfaces points become lines, lines become curves, and curves become shapes. As each new aspect unrolls, there is a shearing of textures, especially at the lateral borders. The marble flows. The leading border uncovers a new aspect and the textures of the old aspect change. The light flames. The trailing border wipes out the old aspect. The curving surface continuously reveals the emergence of volumes and masses in front, behind, and in depth. What is hidden behind the surfaces is still perceived, for the textures indicate a mass behind them. As I move, what I have perceived and what I will perceive stand in defined positions with what I am presently perceiving. My moving body links the aspects. A continuous metamorphosis evolves, as I remember the aspects that were and anticipate the aspects to come, the leaping and plunging lights glancing off the surface helping to blend the changing volumes, shapes, and masses. The remembered and anticipatory images resonate in the present perception. My perception of the Arp is alive with motion. The sounds in the museum room are caught, more or less, in the rhythm of that motion. As I return to my starting point, I find it richer, as home seems after a journey.

FIGURE 5-8
Gaston Lachaise, *Floating Figure*. 1927. Bronze (cast in 1935), 51¾ × 96 × 22 inches (131.4 × 243.9 × 55.9 cm), weight 840 lbs (381.81 kg). The Museum of Modern Art, New York. Given anonymously in memory of the artist. (Digital image © The Museum of Modern Art, New York/Licensed by Scala/Art Resource, New York)

Sculpture and the Human Body

Sculptures generally are more or less a center—the place of most importance which organizes the places around it—of actual three-dimensional space: "more" in the case of sculpture in the round, "less" in the case of low relief. That is why sculpture in the round is more typically sculpture than the other species. Other things being equal, sculpture in the round, because of its three-dimensional centeredness, brings out the voluminosity and density of things more certainly than any other kind of sculpture. First of all, we can see and perhaps touch all sides. But, more important, our sense of density has something to do with our awareness of our bodies as three-dimensional centers thrusting out into our surrounding environment. Philosopher-critic Gaston Bachelard remarks that

> immensity is within ourselves. It is attached to a sort of expansion of being which life curbs and caution arrests, but which starts again when we are alone. As soon as we become motionless, we are elsewhere; we are dreaming in a world that is immense. Indeed, immensity is the movement of a motionless man.[2]

Lachaise's *Floating Figure* (Figure 5-8), with its ballooning buoyancy emerging with lonely but powerful internal animation from a graceful ellipse, expresses not only this feeling but also something of the instinctual longing we have to become one with the world about us. Sculpture in the round, even when it does not portray the human body, often gives us something of an objective image of our internal bodily awareness as related to its surrounding space. Furthermore, when the human body is portrayed in the round, we have the most vivid material image of our internal feelings.

---

[2]From *The Poetics of Space* by Gaston Bachelard. Translation ©1964 by the Orion Press, Inc. Reprinted by permission of Grossman Publishers.

Exercise in Drawing and Modeling

1. Take a pencil and paper. Close your eyes. Now draw the shape of a human being but leave off the arms.
2. Take some clay or putty elastic enough to mold easily. Close your eyes. Now model your material into the shape of a human being, again leaving off the arms.
3. Analyze your two efforts. Which was easier to do? Which produced the more realistic result? Was your drawing process guided by any factor other than your memory images of the human body? What about your modeling process? Did any significant factors other than your memory images come into play? Was the feel of the clay or putty important in your shaping? Did the awareness of your internal bodily sensations contribute to the shaping? Did you exaggerate any of the functional parts of the body where movement originates, such as the neck muscles, shoulder bones, knees, or ankles? Could these exaggerations, if they occurred, have been a consequence of your inner bodily sensations?

Sculpture in the Round and the Human Body

No object is more important to us than our body, and it is always with us. Yet when something is continually present to us, we find great difficulty in focusing our attention upon it. Thus we usually are only vaguely aware of air except when it is deficient in some way. Similarly, we usually are only vaguely aware of our bodies except when we feel pain or pleasure. Nevertheless, our bodies are part of our most intimate selves—we are our bodies—and, since most of us are narcissists to some degree, most of us have a deep-down driving need to find a satisfactory material counterpoint for the mental images of our bodies. If that is the case, we are lovers of sculpture in the round. All sculpture always evokes our outward sensations and sometimes our inward sensations. Sculpture in the round often evokes our inward sensations, for such sculpture often is anthropomorphic in some respect. And sculpture in the round that has as its subject matter the human body not only often evokes our inward sensations but also inter-prets them—as in the *Aphrodite* (Figure 5-9), Michelangelo's *David* (Figure 5-10), or Rodin's *Danaïde* (Figure 5-11).

Rodin, one of the greatest sculptors of the human body, wrote that

> instead of imagining the different parts of the body as surfaces more or less flat, I represented them as projections of interior volumes. I forced myself to express in each swelling of the torso or of the limbs the efflorescence of a muscle or a bone which lay beneath the skin. And so the truth of my figures, instead of being merely superficial, seems to blossom forth from within to the outside, like life itself.[3]

FIGURE 5-9
Aphrodite. First century B.C. Marble, slightly under life size. Found at Cyrene. Museo Nazionale delle Terme, Rome. (© Alinari/Art Resource, New York)

---

[3]Auguste Rodin, *Art*, trans. Romilly Fedden (Boston: Small, 1912), p. 65.

Aphrodite and Venus

The marble *Aphrodite* (Figure 5-9), slightly under life size, is a Roman copy of a Greek original of the first century B.C. It is extraordinary both for the delicacy of its carving—for most Roman copies of Greek works crudely deaden their liveliness—and the translucency of its marble, which seems to reflect light from below its surface. Compare this work with Giorgione's *Venus* (Figure 2-17).

1. In both these works, graceful lassitude and sexuality have something to do with their subject matter. Yet they are interpreted, we think, quite differently. What do you think?

2. If the head and arms of the *Venus* were obliterated, would this injure the work more than in the *Aphrodite*? If so, why? Some critics claim that the *Aphrodite* is not very seriously injured as an artistic object by the destruction of her head and arms. Yet how can this be? Suppose the *Aphrodite* were to come off her pedestal and walk. Would you not find this monstrous? Yet many people treasure her as one of the most beautiful of all female sculptures. How is this to be explained?

Aphrodite, David, and *Danaïde* present objective correlatives—images that are objective in the sense that they are "out there" and yet correlate or are similar to a subjective awareness. All three clarify internal bodily sensations as well as outward appearance. These are large claims and highly speculative. You may disagree, of course, but we hope they will stimulate your thinking.

When we participate with sculpture such as the *Aphrodite,* we find something of our bodily selves confronting us. If we demanded all of our bodily selves, we would be both disappointed and stupid. Art is always a transfor-

FIGURE 5-10
Michelangelo Buonarroti, *David*. 1501–1504. Marble, 13 feet high. Accademia, Florence. (© Alinari/Art Resource, New York)

FIGURE 5-11
Auguste Rodin, *Danaïde*. 1885. Marble, approximately 14 × 28 × 22 inches. Musée Rodin, Paris. (© Giraudon/Art Resource, New York)

mation of reality, never a duplication. Thus the absence of head and arms in the *Aphrodite* does not shock us as it would if we were confronting a real woman. Nor does their absence ruin our perception of the beauty of this statue. Even before the damage, the work was only a partial image of a female. Now the *Aphrodite* is even more partial. But, even so, she is in that partiality exceptionally substantial. The *Aphrodite* is substantial because the female shape, texture, grace, sensuality, sexuality, and beauty are interpreted by a form and thus clarified.

The human body is supremely beautiful. To begin with, there is its sensuous charm. There may be other things in the world as sensuously attractive—for example, the full glory of autumn leaves—but the human body also possesses a sexuality that greatly enhances its sensuousness. Moreover, in the human body, mind is incarnate. Feeling, thought, purposefulness—spirit—have taken shape. Thus, the absent head of the *Aphrodite* is not really so absent after all. There is a dignity of spirit that permeates her body. It is the manifestation of Aphrodite's composed spirit in the shaping of her body that, in the final analysis, explains why we are not repulsed by the absence of the head and arms.

Compare Michelangelo's *David* and *Pietà* (Figure 5-5) with the *Aphrodite*.

PERCEPTION KEY   *David, Pietà, and Aphrodite*

1. Suppose the head of the David were broken off and, like the head of *Aphrodite*, you had never seen it. Is it conceivable that a head something like that of the Christ of the *Pietà* could be satisfactorily substituted?

2. The *David*, the *Pietà*, and the *Aphrodite* are in marble, although of very different kinds. Which statue is more evocative of your outward sensations? Your inward sensations?

3. The sculptor Henry Moore claims that "sculpture is more affected by actual size considerations than painting. A painting is isolated by a frame from its surroundings (unless it serves just a decorative purpose) and so retains more easily its own imaginary scale." He makes the further claim that the actual physical size of sculpture has an emotional meaning. "We relate everything to our own size, and our emotional response to size is controlled by the fact that men on the average are between five and six feet high."[4] Does the fact that the *David* is much larger in size than the *Aphrodite* make any significant difference with respect to your tactile sensations?

Techniques of Sculpture

Sculpture in relief and in the round generally is made either by *modeling* or *carving*. Space sculpture, such as Calder's *Teodelapio* (Figure 5-12), generally is made by assembling preformed pieces of material.

---

[4]Moore, "Notes on Sculpture," p. xxxiv.

FIGURE 5-12
Alexander Calder, *Teodelapio.*
1962. Steel. Spoleto, Italy.
(Photo by Edvard Trier. Art ©
2003 Estate of Alexander
Calder/Artists Rights Society
[ARS], New York)

The modeler starts with some plastic or malleable material such as clay, wax, or plaster and creates the sculpture. If the design is complex or involves long or thin extensions, the modeler probably will have to use an internal wooden or metal support (armature) that functions something like a skeleton. Whereas *Floating Figure* (Figure 5-8) required armatures, much smaller modeled sculptures do not. In either case, the modeler builds from the inside outward to the surface finish, which then may be scratched, polished, painted, and so forth. But when nonplastic materials such as bronze are used, the technical procedures are much more complicated. Bronze cannot be built up like clay. Nor can bronze be carved like stone, although it can be lined, scratched, and so on. And so the sculptor in bronze or any material that is cast must use further processes. We present here only an oversimplified account. For those who want to pursue the techniques of sculpture further—and this can be helpful in sharpening our perceptual faculties—a large number of excellent technical handbooks are available.[5]

---

[5]For example, William Zorach, *Zorach Explains Sculpture: What It Means and How It Is Made* (New York: American Artists Group, 1947). Learning the techniques of handling various artistic media is one of the best ways of improving our perception and understanding of the arts.

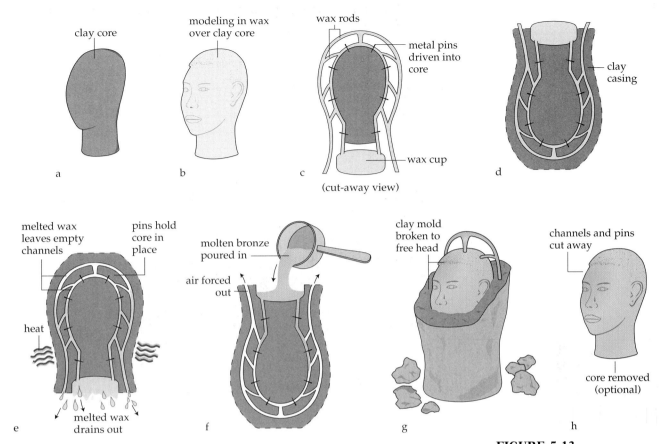

clay core

modeling in wax
over clay core

wax rods

metal pins
driven into
core

clay
casing

a   b   c   d

wax cup

(cut-away view)

melted wax
leaves empty
channels

pins hold
core in
place

molten bronze
poured in

air forced
out

clay mold
broken to
free head

channels and pins
cut away

heat

core removed
(optional)

melted wax
drains out

e   f   g   h

FIGURE 5-13
The lost-wax
casting process.

The sculptor in bronze begins with clay or some similar material and builds up a model to a more or less high degree of finish. This is a solid, or positive, shape. Then the sculptor usually makes a plaster mold—a hollow, or negative, shape—from the solid model. This negative shape is usually divisible into sections, so that the inside can easily be worked on to make changes or remove any defects that may have developed. Then, because plaster or a similar material is much better than clay for the *casting* process, the sculptor makes a positive plaster cast from his negative plaster mold and perfects its surface. This plaster cast is then given to a specialized foundry, unless the sculptor does this work for himself or herself, and a negative mold is again made of such materials as plaster, rubber, or gelatin. Inside this mold—again usually divisible into sections to allow for work in the interior—a coating of liquid wax is brushed on, normally at least one-eighth inch in thickness but varying with the size of the sculpture. After the wax dries, a mixture of materials, such as sand and plaster, is poured into the hollow space within the mold. Thus the wax is completely surrounded (Figure 5-13).

Intense heat is now applied, causing the wax to melt out through channels drilled through the outside mold, and the molds on both sides of the wax are baked hard. Then the bronze is poured into the space the wax has

131

vacated. After the bronze hardens, the surrounding molds are removed. Finally, the sculptor may file, chase, polish, or add patinas (by means of chemicals) to the surface. One of the most interesting and dramatic descriptions of casting, incidentally, can be found in the *Autobiography of Benvenuto Cellini,* the swashbuckling Renaissance sculptor whose *Perseus* was almost lost in the casting process.

The carver uses nonmalleable material, such as marble, that cannot be built up, and so the carver must start with a lump of material and work inward from the outside by removing surplus material until arriving at the surface finish. Thus for his *David* (Figure 5-10), Michelangelo was given a huge marble block that Agostino di Duccio had failed to finally shape into either a David or, more likely, a prophet for one of the buttresses of the Cathedral of Florence. Agostino's carving had reduced the original block considerably, putting severe restrictions upon what Michelangelo could do. This kind of restriction is foreign to the modeler, for there is no frame such as the limits of a marble block to prevent the expansion of the sculpture into space. And when a model is cast in materials of great tensile strength, such as bronze, this spatial freedom becomes relatively unlimited.

It should be noted that many carvers, including Michelangelo, sometimes modeled before they carved. A sketch model often can help carvers find their way around in such materials as marble. It is not easy to visualize before the fact the whereabouts of complicated shapes in large blocks of material. And once a mistake is made in nonplastic materials, it is not so easily remedied as with plastic materials. The shapes of the *David* had to be ordered from the outside inward, the smaller shapes being contained within the larger shapes. Whereas the modeler works up the most simplified and primary shapes that underlie all the secondary shapes and details, the carver roughs out the simplified and primary shapes within which all the secondary shapes and details are contained. For example, Michelangelo roughed out the head of the *David* as a solid sphere, working down in the front from the outermost planes of the forehead and nose to the outline of the eyes and then to the details of the eyes and so on. Hence the primary shape of the head, the solid sphere, is not only preserved to some extent but also points to its original containment within the largest containing shape, the block itself. Consequently, we can sense in the *David* something of the block from which Michelangelo started. This original shape is suggested by the limits of the projecting parts and the high points of the surfaces. We are aware of the thinness of the *David* as a consequence of the block Michelangelo inherited. There remains the huge imprint of that vertical block that had been sliced into. This accounts in part for the feeling we may have with some carved works of their being contained within a private space, introverted and to some extent separate. Modeled sculpture generally is more extroverted.

Alexander Calder's *Teodelapio* obviously was neither modeled nor carved. Its sheets of metal have little mass to be shaped and no interior to be structured. Although the materials of such *assemblages* exist in three-dimensional space, as does everything else in this world, they are not themselves significantly three-dimensional. Calder preformed these pieces and then assembled them, attached, furthermore, at clearly discernible joints and intersections. These pieces vividly cross and frame space, appealing more to the visual than the tactile. Calder's materials fill space only slightly, and so their tactile appeal, while still present, is considerably reduced.

Contemporary Sculpture

Developments in sculpture are emerging and changing so rapidly that no attempt can be made here even to begin to classify them adequately. But adding to the traditional species (relief sculpture and sculpture in the round), at least five new species have taken hold: space, protest against technology, accommodation with technology, machine, and earth sculpture. In most contemporary sculpture, however diverse, there is one fairly pervasive characteristic: *truth to materials,* more of a reaffirmation than an innovation.

Truth to Materials

In the flamboyant eighteenth-century *Baroque* and in some of the *Romanticism* of the later nineteenth century, respect for materials tended to be ignored. Karl Knappe referred to a "crisis" in the early twentieth century that "concerns . . . the artistic media":

> An image cannot be created without regard for the laws of nature, and each kind of material has natural laws of its own. Every block of stone, every piece of wood is subject to its own rules. Every medium has, so to speak, its own tempo; the tempo of a pencil or a piece of charcoal is quite different from the tempo of a woodcut. The habit of mind which creates, for instance, a pen drawing cannot simply be applied mechanically to the making of a woodcut; to do this would be to deny the validity of the spiritual as well as the technical tempo.[6]

PERCEPTION KEY   Truth to Materials

1. Examine the examples of twentieth-century sculpture in the text. Assuming that these examples are fairly representative, do you find a pervasive tendency to truth to materials? Do you find exceptions, and, if so, how might these be explained?
2. Henry Moore has stated that "Every material has its own individual qualities. It is only when the sculptor works direct, when there is an active relationship with his material, that the material can take its part in the shaping of an idea. Stone, for example, is hard and concentrated and should not be falsified to look like soft flesh—it should not be forced beyond its constructive build to a point of weakness. It should keep its hard tense stoniness."[7] Does *Reclining Figure* (Figure 5-14) illustrate Moore's point? If so, point out as specifically as possible how this is done.

---

[6]Karl Knappe, quoted in Kurt Herberts, *The Complete Book of Artists' Techniques* (London: Thames and Hudson, 1958), p. 16. Published in the United States by Frederick A. Praeger.
[7]Quoted by Herbert Read, *Henry Moore, Sculptor* (London: A. Zwemmer, 1934), p. 29.

FIGURE 5-14
Henry Moore, *Reclining Figure.* 1938. Green Hornton
stone, 54 inches long. (Photo
© The Tate Gallery, London/
Art Resource, New York. Reproduced by permission of
the Henry Moore Foundation)

3. Can you imagine how human figures could be made in wax, and yet truth
to wax as a material be maintained? If you think wax is a weak or even
impossible material for the sculpture of human figures, try to see a wax
work by Medardo Rosso (1858–1928). Some of his wax sculptures are in
the Hirshhorn Museum in Washington, D.C. Kiki Smith, a contemporary
sculptor, also produced a powerful group of sculptures portraying bat-
tered women, using wax as her medium.

The *Maternity Group Figure* (Figure 5-15), from Nigeria, is notable for its
respect for materials. The wood is grooved, ridged, and carved in ways that
make its woodiness all the more apparent. Societies in which technology
has not been dominant live closer to nature than we do, and so their feeling
for natural things, such as stone and wood, feathers and bone, usually is
reverent.

As *technology* has gained more and more ascendancy, reverence toward
natural things has receded. In highly industrialized societies, people tend to
revere artificial things, and the pollution of our environment is one result.
Another result is the flooding of the commercial market with imitations of
primitive sculpture, which are easily identified because of the lack of truth

to the materials (test this for yourself). Even contemporary sculptors have lost some of their innocence toward things simply because they live in a technological age. Many sculptors still possess something of the natural way of feeling things, and so they find inspiration in primitive sculpture. Despite its abstract subject matter, Barbara Hepworth's *Pelagos* (Figure 5-16) with its reverence to wood, has a close spiritual affinity to the *Maternity Group Figure*. Truth to materials sculpture is an implicit protest against technological ascendancy.

Space Sculpture

Space sculpture emphasizes spatial relationships and tends to deemphasize the density of materials. Space sculpture, however, never completely loses its ties to the materiality of its materials. Otherwise tactile qualities would be largely missing also, and then it would be doubtful if such work could usefully be classified as sculpture. The materials of *Teodelapio* (Figure 5-12), despite their thinness, appear heavy. Naum Gabo, one of the fathers of space sculpture, often uses translucent materials, as in *Spiral Theme* (Figure 5-17). Although the planes of plastic divide space with multidirectional movement, no visual barriers develop. Each plane varies in translucency as our angle of vision varies, and in seeing through each, we see them all—allowing for free-flowing transitions between the space without and the space within. In turn, the tactile attraction of the plastic, especially its smooth surface and rapid fluidity, is enhanced. As Gabo has written,

FIGURE 5-15
Maternity Group Figure. Afo peoples, Nigeria. Nineteenth century. Wood, 27¾ inches high. The Horniman Museum & Gardens, London. (31.42)

FIGURE 5-16
Barbara Hepworth, *Pelagos*. 1946. Wood with color and strings, 16 inches in diameter. (© The Tate Gallery, London/Art Resource, New York)

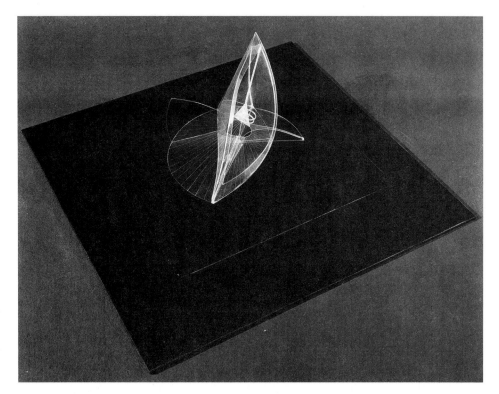

FIGURE 5-17
Naum Gabo, *Spiral Theme*. 1941. Construction in plastic, 5½ × 13¼ × 9⅜ inches (14 × 33.6 × 23.7 cm), on base 24 inches (61 cm) square. The Museum of Modern Art, New York. Advisory Committee Fund. (Digital image © The Museum of Modern Art, New York/Licensed by Scala/Art Resource, New York)

Volume still remains one of the fundamental attributes of sculpture, and we still use it in our sculptures. . . . We are not at all intending to dematerialize a sculptural work. . . . On the contrary, adding Space perception to the perception of Masses, emphasizing it and forming it, we enrich the expression of Mass, making it more essential through the contact between them whereby Mass retains its solidity and Space its extension.[8]

PERCEPTION KEY　*Reclining Figure, Pelagos,* and *Brussels Construction*

1. Compare Moore's *Reclining Figure* (Figure 5-14), Hepworth's *Pelagos* (Figure 5-16), and Rivera's *Brussels Construction* (Figure 5-18). Is there in these works, as Gabo claims for his, an equal emphasis on mass and space? If not, in which one does mass dominate space? Vice versa?

2. Moore has written that "The first hole made through a piece of stone [or most three-dimensional materials] is a revelation. The hole connects one side to the other, making it immediately more three-dimensional. A hole can itself have as much shape-meaning as a solid mass."[9] Is Moore's claim equally applicable to the Hepworth and the Rivera?

---

[8]Quoted by Herbert Read and Leslie Martin in *Gabo: Constructions, Sculpture, Drawings, Engravings* (Cambridge, Mass: Harvard University Press, 1957), p. 168.
[9]Moore, "Notes on Sculpture," p. xxxiv.

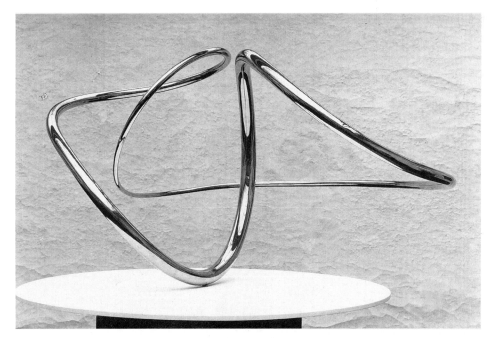

FIGURE 5-18
Jose de Rivera, *Brussels Construction*. 1958. Stainless steel. The Art Institute of Chicago. Gift of Mr. and Mrs. R. Howard Goldsmith. (© The Art Institute of Chicago)

3. How many holes are there in *Pelagos*? What is the function of the strings? Why did Hepworth color the inside white? Hepworth said, "The colour in the concavities plunged me into the depth of water, caves or shadows... the strings were the tension I felt between myself and the sea, the wind, and the hills." Are her comments helpful in responding to the work?

4. *Brussels Construction* is mounted on a flat disk turned by a low-revolution motor. Is it useful to refer to holes in this sculpture? The three-dimensional curve of *Brussels Construction* proceeds in a long, smooth, continuous flow. Does this have anything to do with the changing diameter of the chromium-plated stainless steel? Suppose the material absorbed rather than reflected light. Would this change the structure significantly? Do you think this sculpture should be displayed under diffused light or in dim illumination with one or more spotlights? Is there any reference to human life in the simplicity and elegant vitality of this work? Or is the subject matter just about stainless steel and space? Or is the subject matter about something else? Do you agree that this work is an example of space sculpture? And what about *Pelagos*? Note that there is no assemblage of pieces in the case of *Brussels Construction*, whereas, because of the addition of strings, there is some assemblage in *Pelagos*. Would you classify Figures 5-14, 5-16, 5-17, and 5-18 as space sculptures?

It seems to us that *Pelagos* and *Reclining Figure* are not space sculptures because, although they open up space within, the density of their materials dominates space. *Brussels Construction*, on the other hand, is space sculpture because the spatial relationships are at least as interesting as the stainless steel. The fact that *Pelagos* was assembled in part and *Brussels Construction* was not is not conclusive. Assemblage is the technique

FIGURE 5-19
Ernest Trova, *Study: Falling Man (Wheel Man)*. 1965. Silicon bronze, $60 \times 48 \times 20^{13}\!/_{16}$ inches. Collection, Walker Art Center, Minneapolis. Gift of the T. B. Walker Foundation, 1965.

generally used in space sculpture, but what we are perceiving and should be judging is the product, not the producing process. Of course, the producing process affects what is produced, and that is why it can be helpful to know about the producing process. That is why we went into some detail about the differences between modeling, carving, and assemblage. But the basis of a sound judgment about a work of art is that work as it is given to us in perception. Any kind of background information is relevant provided it aids that perception. But if we permit the producing process rather than the work of art itself to be the basis of our judgment, we are led away from, rather than into, the work. This destroys the usefulness of criticism.

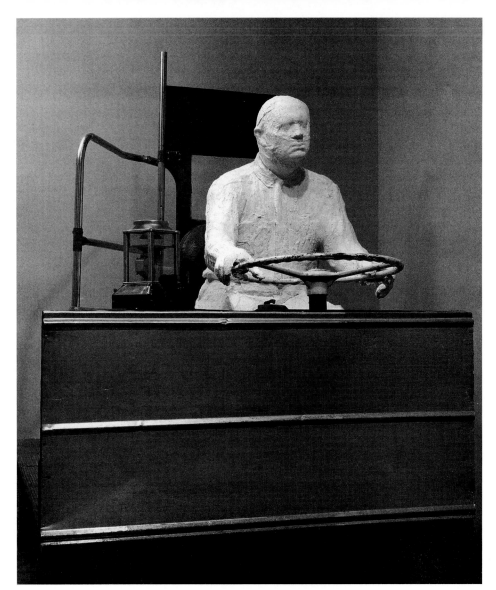

FIGURE 5-20
George Segal, *The Bus Driver.* 1962. Figure of plaster over cheesecloth with bus parts, including coin box, steering wheel, driver's seat, railing, dashboard, etc. Figure 53½ × 26⅞ × 45 inches (136 × 68.2 × 114 cm); overall 7 feet 5 inches × 4 feet 3⅜ inches × 6 feet 4¾ inches (226 × 131 × 195 cm). The Museum of Modern Art, New York. Philip Johnson Fund. (Digital image © The Museum of Modern Art, New York/Licensed by Scala/Art Resource, New York. Art © The George and Helen Segal Foundation/Licensed by VAGA, New York, NY)

Protest against Technology

Explicit social protest is part of the subject matter of the works we will discuss by Trova, Segal, and Giacometti, although perhaps only in *Wheel Man* (Figure 5-19) is that protest unequivocally directed at technology. Flaccid, faceless, and sexless, this anonymous robot has "grown" spoked wheels instead of arms. Attached below the hips these mechanisms produce a sense of eerie instability, a feeling that this antiseptically cleansed automaton with the slack, protruding abdomen may tip over from the slightest push. In this inhuman mechanical purity, no free will is left to resist. Human value, as articulated in Aldous Huxley's *Brave New World*, has been reduced to

humanpower, functions performed in the world of goods and services. Since another individual can also perform these functions, the given person has no special worth. His or her value is a unit that can easily be replaced by another.

The Bus Driver (Figure 5-20) is an example of environmental sculpture. Grimly set behind a wheel and coin box taken from an old bus, the driver is a plaster cast made in sections over a living well-greased model. Despite the "real" environment and model, the stark white figure with its rough and generalized features is both real and strangely unreal. In the air around him, we sense the hubbub of the streets, the smell of fumes, the ceaseless comings and goings of unknown customers. Yet, despite all these suggestions of a crowded, nervous atmosphere, there is a heartrending loneliness about this driver. Worn down day after day by the same grind, Segal's man, like Trova's, has been flattened into an *x* — a quantity.

In Giacometti's emaciated figures, the huge, solidly implanted feet suggest nostalgia for the earth; the soaring upward of the elongated bodies suggests aspiration for the heavens. The surrounding environment has eaten away at the flesh, leaving lumpy, irregular surfaces with dark hollows that bore into the bone. Each figure is without contact with anyone, as despairingly isolated as *The Bus Driver*. They stand in or walk through an utterly alienated space, but, unlike *Wheel Man,* they seem to know it. And whereas the habitat of *Wheel Man* is the clean, air-conditioned factory or office of *Brave New World,* Giacometti's people, even when in neat galleries, always seem to be in the grubby streets of our decaying cities. The cancer of the city has left only the armatures of bodies stained with pollution and scarred with sickness. There is no center in this city square (Figure 5-21) or any particular exit, nor can we imagine any communication among these citizens. Their very grouping in the square gives them, paradoxically, an even greater feeling of isolation. Each Giacometti figure separates a spot of space from the common place. The disease and utter distress of these vulnerable creatures demands our respectful distance, as if they were lepers to whom help must come, if at all, from some public agency. To blame technology entirely for the dehumanization of society interpreted in these sculptures is an oversimplification, of course. But this kind of work does bring out something of the horror of technology when it is misused.

FIGURE 5-22
David Smith, *Cubi X*. 1963. Stainless steel, 10 feet 1⅜ inches × 6 feet 6¾ inches × 2 feet (308.3 × 199.9 × 61 cm), including steel base 2⅞ × 25 × 33 inches (7.3 × 63.4 × 58.3 cm). The Museum of Modern Art, New York. Robert O. Lord Fund. (Digital image © The Museum of Modern Art, New York/Licensed by Scala/Art Resource, New York. Art © David Smith/Licensed by VAGA, New York, NY)

Accommodation with Technology

Many contemporary sculptors see in technology blessings for humankind. It is true that sculpture can be accomplished with the most primitive tools (that, incidentally, is one of the basic reasons sculpture in primitive cultures apparently not only precedes painting but also usually dominates both qualitatively and quantitatively). Nevertheless, sculpture in our day, far more than painting, can take advantage of some of the most sophisticated advances of technology, surpassed in this respect only by architecture.

Many sculptors today interpret the positive rather than the negative aspects of technology. This respect for technology is expressed by truth to its materials and the showing forth of its methodology.

David Smith's *Cubi X* (Figure 5-22), like Chryssa's *Times Square Sky* (Figure 5-3), illustrates truth to technological materials. But unlike Chryssa, Smith usually accomplishes this by wedding these materials to nature. The stainless steel cylinders of the *Cubi* support a juggling act of hollow rectangular and square cubes that barely touch one another as they cantilever out into space. Delicate buffing modulates the bright planes of steel, giving the illusion of several atmospheric depths and reflecting light like rippling water. Occasionally, when the light is just right, the effect is like the cascading streams of fountains, recalling the Arabic inscription on the *Fountain of the Lions* in the Alhambra, Granada: "Liquid and solid things are so closely related that none who sees them is able to distinguish which is motionless and which is flowing." Usually, however, the steel reflects with more constancy the colorings of its environment. Smith writes,

> I like outdoor sculpture and the most practical thing for outdoor sculpture is stainless steel, and I make them and I polish them in such a way that on a dull day, they take on the dull blue, or the color of the sky in late afternoon sun, the glow, golden like the rays, the colors of nature. And in a particular sense, I have used atmosphere in a reflective way on the surfaces. They are colored by the sky and the surroundings, the green or blue of water. Some are down by the water and some are by the mountains. They reflect the colors. They are designed for outdoors.[10]

But Smith's steel is not just a mirror, for in the reflections the fluid surfaces and tensile strength of the steel emerge in a structure that, as Smith puts it, "can face the sun and hold its own."

Machine Sculpture

Some avant-garde sculptors are interested in revealing the machine and its powers. For example, George Rickey's *Two Lines — Temporal I* (Figure 5-23) is kinetic, or moving, sculpture; but the motion of *machine sculpture,* unlike this work, is primarily a result of mechanical rather than natural forces. Sculptors in this tradition, going back to the ideas and work of László Moholy-Nagy after World War I, welcome the machine and its sculptural possibilities. Rivera hides his machine under *Brussels Construction* (Figure 5-18), but many machine sculptors expose their machines. They are interested not only in the power of the machine but also in the mechanisms that make that power possible. Rickey, the literary prophet of machine sculpture, writes that "A machine is not a projection of anything. The crank-shaft exists in its own right; it is the image. . . . The concreteness of machines is heartening."[11]

---

[10]David Smith in *David Smith,* ed. Cleve Gray (New York: Holt, Rinehart and Winston, 1968), p. 123.

[11]George Rickey, *Art and Artist* (Berkeley: University of California Press, 1956), p. 172.

Two Lines—Temporal I and *Homage to New York*

1. Although depending upon air currents for its motion, Rickey's *Two Lines—Temporal I* is basically a machine—two 35-foot stainless steel blades balanced on knife-edge fulcrums. Does its subject matter include more than just machinery? As you reflect about this, can you imagine perhaps more appropriate places than the Museum of Modern Art for this work?
2. Is Jean Tinguely's *Homage to New York* (Figure 5-24) an image of a machine? Or does its subject matter include more than just machinery?

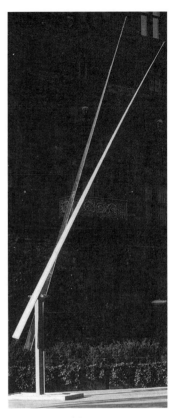

A good case can be made, we believe, for placing *Two Lines—Temporal I* in a grove of tall trees. Despite its mechanical character this work belongs in nature. Otherwise the lyrical poetry of its gentle swaying tends to be reduced to a metronome. But even in its location in New York, it is much more than just an image of machinery. *Two Lines—Temporal I* suggests something of the skeletal structure and vertical stretch of New York's buildings as well as something of the sway of the skyscrapers as we see them against the sky.

Tinguely is dedicated to humanizing the machine. His *Homage to New York* (Figure 5-24), exhibited at the Museum of Modern Art in 1960, is a better example than *Two Lines—Temporal I* of the image of the machine in its own right. The mechanical parts, collected from junk heaps and dismembered from their original machines, apparently stood out sharply, and yet they were linked together by their spatial locations, shapes, and textures, and sometimes by nervelike wires. Only the old player piano was intact. As the piano played, it was accompanied by howls and other weird sounds in irregular patterns that seemed to be issuing from the wheels, gears, and rods, as if they were painfully communicating with each other in some form of mechanical speech. Some of the machinery that runs New York City was exposed as vulnerable, pathetic, and comic, but Tinguely humanized this machinery as he exposed it. Even death was suggested, for *Homage to New York* was self-destructing: The piano was electronically wired for burning and, in turn, the whole structure collapsed.

Earth Sculpture

Another avant-garde sculpture—*earth sculpture*—even goes so far as to make the earth itself the medium, the site, and the subject matter. The proper spatial selection becomes absolutely essential, for the earth usually must be taken where it is found. Structures are traced in plains, meadows, sand, snow, and the like, in order to help make us stop and perceive and enjoy the "form site"—the earth transformed to be more meaningful. Usually nature rapidly breaks up the form and returns the site to its less ordered state. Accordingly, many earth sculptors have a special need for the photographer to preserve their art.

FIGURE 5-23
George Rickey, *Two Lines—Temporal I*. 1964. Two stainless steel mobile blades on a stainless steel base, overall height 35 feet 4⅝ inches (10.79 m); blades 31 feet ¾ inches (946.8 cm) and 31 feet 1¼ inches (948.5 cm) long; base 8 feet 11¼ inches (247 cm) high; weight 498 lbs (not including extra weights). The Museum of Modern Art, New York. Mrs. Simon Guggenheim Fund. (Digital image © The Museum of Modern Art, New York/Licensed by Scala/Art Resource, New York. Art © Estate of George Rickey/Licensed by VAGA, New York, NY)

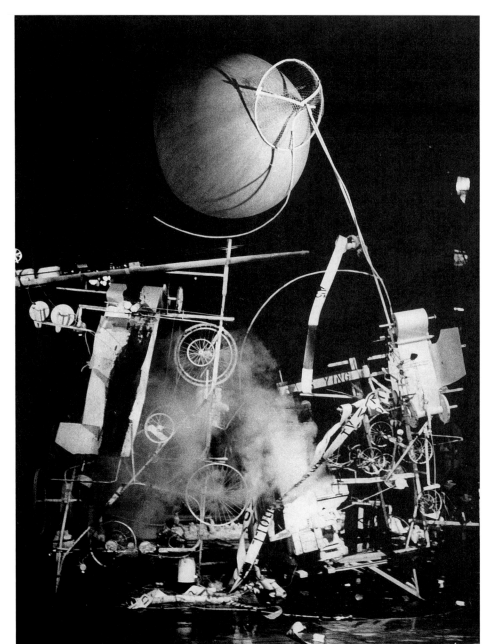

FIGURE 5-24
Jean Tinguely, *Homage to New York*. 1960. Mixed media. Exhibited at the Museum of Modern Art, New York. (Photo by David Gahr. Art © 2003 Artists Rights Society [ARS], New York/ ADAGP, Paris)

PERCEPTION KEY   Earth Sculpture

Study Michael Heizer's *Circumflex* (Figure 5-25), a 120-foot-long design "carved" out of the bed of a dry lake in Nevada.

1. Does the fact that *Circumflex* is now silted up disqualify this work as art? As you reflect about this, does the fact that the work has been elegantly photographed become relevant?

FIGURE 5-25
Michael Heizer, *Circumflex*.
1968. Massacre Creek Dry
Lake, 120 feet long.

2. Does *Circumflex* help bring out and make you notice the materiality of the earth? The line of the mountain in the far distance? The relation of the plain to the mountain?
3. Does *Circumflex* appear too large, too small, or just right in relation to the landscape?
4. Why do you think Heizer used such a long, free-flowing line juxtaposed against an almost geometrical oval?
5. Suppose works like this were found abundantly throughout the United States. Would you find this objectionable?

Sculpture in Public Places

Sculpture has traditionally shared its location with major buildings, sometimes acting as decoration on the building, as in many churches, or acting as a center point of interest, as in the original placement of Michelangelo's *David*, which was positioned carefully in front of the Palazzo Vecchio, the

FIGURE 5-26
Naum Gabo, *Rotterdam Con-struction*. 1954–1957. Steel, bronze wire, free stone sub-structure, 85 feet high. Rotterdam. (© Tom Kroeze, Rotterdam)

central building of the Florentine government. It stood as a warning not to underestimate the Florentines. Many small towns throughout the world have public sculpture that commemorates wars or other important events.

With the rise of shopping malls across the United States and much of the rest of the world, monumental sculpture has often been placed as a focal point for orienting both interior and exterior space. One interesting example is Naum Gabo's *Rotterdam Construction* (Figure 5-26) in front of De Bijenkorf, a large store in Rotterdam designed by Marcel Breuer, a monumentally successful solution to what might seem to have been an impossible commission. The open vertical construction, rooted

FIGURE 5-27
Maya Ying Lin, *Vietnam Veterans Memorial*. 1982. Black granite, V-shaped, 493 feet long, 10 feet high at center. Washington, D.C. (© David Noble/Getty Images/Taxi)

like a tree but branching out more like the cranes and bridges of Rotterdam, brings out with striking clarity the compact horizontal mass of the building. Rarely have sculpture and architecture achieved such powerful synthesis.

In contrast, one of the most popularly successful of contemporary public sculptures has been Maya Ying Lin's *Vietnam Veterans Memorial* (Figure 5-27) in Washington, D.C. Since the Vietnam War was both terribly unpopular and a major defeat, there were fears that any memorial might stir public antagonism. However, the result has been quite the opposite. The piece is a sloping black granite wall, V-shaped, which descends to ten feet below grade. On the wall are incised more than 58,000 names of dead Americans. Those who visit walk along its length, absorbing the seemingly endless list of names as they walk. The impact of the memorial grows in part because the list of names grows with each step down the slope. Visitors respond to the memorial by touching the names, sometimes taking rubbings away with them, sometimes simply weeping. Glenna Goodacre's *Vietnam Women's Memorial* (Figure 5-28) has been installed nearby. It is radically different from Lin's piece and celebrates the efforts of over 265,000 women who served in Vietnam.

FIGURE 5-28
Glenna Goodacre, *Vietnam Women's Memorial: Three Nurses and a Wounded Soldier*. 1993. Bronze. Washington, D.C. (© Bruce Burkhardt/Corbis)

PERCEPTION KEY The *Vietnam Veterans Memorial, Tilted Arc,* and the *Vietnam Women's Memorial*

1. Richard Serra's *Tilted Arc* (Figure 5-29)—a 12-foot-high, 120-foot-long wall of steel—swept across the Federal Plaza in downtown Manhattan, provoking a storm of controversy that even reached the courts. The majority of the people—apparently the great majority—who work in the buildings around the Plaza, as well as nearby dwellers, charged that the *Arc* obstructed the views; prevented comfortable access across the Plaza and to the entrance of the Jacob K. Javits Building (the main building); made large social and cultural gatherings impossible; was ugly in appearance; and attracted obnoxious graffiti. They wanted the General Services Administration, which commissioned the work, to have the sculpture removed. Serra argued that the work was site-specific—integrally related to the structures that compose the architectural environment wherein the *Arc* is placed—and that to remove it was to destroy it. A committee of distinguished critics unanimously backed Serra. Nevertheless, the General Services Administration had the sculpture removed. Do you agree with that decision? What is at stake in a confrontation of this sort? Is it appropriate for public sculpture to stir controversy?

2. What effect does public acceptance have on your attitude toward the relative success of public sculpture?

3. What shapes do the *Vietnam Veterans Memorial* and the *Arc* share? Do you think that the New York public would have been more accepting of the *Arc*

FIGURE 5-29
Richard Serra, *Tilted Arc*.
1981. Weatherproof steel, 12
feet × 120 feet × 2½ inches.
Collection: General Services
Administration, Washington,
D.C. Installed Federal Plaza,
New York City. Destroyed by
the Federal Government,
1989. (© 2003 Richard
Serra/Artists Rights Society
[ARS], New York. Photo
courtesy of Richard Serra)

had it been incised with the 58,000 names of the American dead in the Vietnam War?
4. Which of the two Vietnam works would you think is most popular with the viewing public? Which of the two would be most instantly recognizable as sculpture? Why? Is "recognizability" an important factor in evaluating sculpture?
5. Goodacre's piece has been described as "memorial statuary," similar to the angels often placed over people's graves. The realism of the sculpture has been criticized for its total lack of originality. Do you agree?

Summary

Sculpture is perceived differently from painting, engaging more acutely our sense of touch and the feeling of our body. Whereas painting is more about the visual appearance of things, sculpture is more about things as three-dimensional masses. Whereas painting only represents voluminosity and density, sculpture presents these qualities. Sculpture in the round, especially, brings out the three-dimensionality of objects. No object is more important to us than our body, and its "strange thickness" is always with us. When the human body is the subject matter, sculpture more than any other art reveals a material counterpoint for our mental images of our bodies. Traditional sculpture is made either by modeling or carving. Many contemporary sculptures, however, are made by assembling preformed pieces of material. New sculptural techniques and materials have opened up developments in avant-garde sculpture that defy classification. Nonetheless, contemporary sculptors, generally, have emphasized truth to materials, respect for the medium that is organized by their forms. Space, protest against technology, accommodation with technology, machine, and earth sculpture are five of the most important new species. Public sculpture is flourishing. We will examine a few examples of avant-garde sculpture in Chapter 14.

Bibliography

Bacholard, Gaston. *The Poetics of Space*. Translated by Maria Jolas. New York: Abrams, 1975.

Bazin, Germain. *The History of World Sculpture*. Greenwich, Conn.: New York Graphic Society, 1968.

Beardsley, John. *A Landscape for Modern Sculpture: Storm King Art Center*. New York: Abbeville Press, 1985.

Elsen, Albert E. *Origins of Modern Sculpture*. New York: Braziller, 1974.

Geist, Sidney. *Brancusi: A Study of Sculpture*. New York: Grossman, 1968.

James, Phillip, ed. *Henry Moore on Sculpture*. London: Macdonald, 1966.

Johnson, Geraldine A., ed. *Sculpture and Photography*. Cambridge: Cambridge University Press, 1998.

Kosinski, Dorothy, ed. *Sculpture in the 20th Century*. New Haven, Conn.: Yale University Press, 2001.

Krauss, Rosalind E. *Passages in Modern Sculpture*. New York: Viking, 1977.

Licht, Fred. *Sculpture: 19th and 20th Centuries*. Greenwich, Conn.: New York Graphic Society, 1967.

Martin, F. David. *Sculpture and Enlivened Space: Aesthetics and History*. Lexington, Ky.: University Press of Kentucky, 1981.

Noguchi, Isamu. *A Sculptor's World*. New York: Harper and Row, 1968.

Penny, Nicholas. *The Materials of Sculpture*. New Haven, Conn.: Yale University Press, 1966.

Read, Herbert. *The Art of Sculpture*. New York: Pantheon, 1956.

———. *Modern Sculpture*. New York: Thames and Hudson, 1985.

Read, Herbert, and Leslie Martin. *Gabo: Constructions, Sculpture, Drawings, Engravings*. Cambridge, Mass.: Harvard University Press, 1957.

Rickey, George. *Constructivism*. New York: Braziller, 1967.

Rodin, Auguste. *Art*. London: Hodder and Stoughton, 1912.

Rogers, L. R. *Relief Sculpture*. London: Oxford University Press, 1974.

Sieber, Roy, and Roslyn Adele Walker. *African Art in the Cycle of Life*. Washington, D.C.: National Museum of African Art, 1987.

Tucker, William. *Early Modern Sculpture*. New York: Oxford University Press, 1974.

Wittkower, Rudolf. *Sculpture: Processes and Principles*. New York: Harper and Row, 1977.

Zorach, William. *Zorach Explains Sculpture: What It Means and How It Is Made*. New York: American Artists Group, 1974.

Internet Resources

AFRICAN MASKS

http://community.middlebury.edu/~atherton/masking.html

AFRICAN SCULPTURE

http://www.sas.upenn.edu/African_Studies/Sculpture/menu_Sculpt.html

ALEXANDER CALDER

http://www.calder.org/

DECORDOVA MUSEUM

http://www.decordova.org/

HELLENISTIC SCULPTURE

http://www.ancientgr.com/archaeonia/arts/sculpture/hellenistic.htm

MICHELANGELO BUONARROTI

http://www.artchive.com/artchive/ftptoc/michelangelo_ext.html
http://graphics.stanford.edu/projects/mich/

HENRY MOORE

http://www.henry-moore-fdn.co.uk/hmf/

RESOURCE FOR SCULPTORS

http://www.sculptors.org

AUGUSTE RODIN

http://www.musee-rodin.fr/

CHAPTER 6

Architecture

Buildings constantly assault us. Our only temporary escape is to the increasingly less accessible wilderness. We can close the novel, shut off the music, refuse to go to a play or dance, sleep through a movie, shut our eyes to a painting or a sculpture. But we cannot escape from buildings for very long, even in the wilderness. Fortunately, however, sometimes buildings are works of art — that is, architecture. They draw us to them rather than push us away or make us ignore them. They make our living space more livable.

Centered Space

Painters do not command real three-dimensional space: They feign it. Sculptors can mold out into space, but generally they do not enfold an enclosed or inner space for our movement. The holes in the sculpture of Henry Moore (Figure 5-14), for example, are to be walked around, not into, whereas our passage through the inner spaces of architecture is one of the conditions under which its solids and voids have their effect. In a sense, architecture is a great hollowed-out sculpture that we perceive by moving about both outside and inside. Space is the material of the architect, the primeval cutter,[1] who carves apart an inner space from an outer space in such a way that both spaces become more fully perceptible and interesting.

Inner and outer space come together on the earth to form a centered and illuminated context or clearing. *Centered space* is the arrangement of things around some paramount thing — the place at which the other things seem to converge. Sometimes this center is a natural site, such as a great mountain, river, canyon, or forest. Sometimes the center is a natural site enhanced by a human-made structure. Listen to Martin Heidegger, the great German thinker, describing a bridge:

---

[1]This meaning is suggested by the Greek *architectón*.

FIGURE 6-1
Piazza before St. Peter's,
Rome. (© Anderson/Art
Resource, New York)

The bridge swings over the stream "with ease and power." It does not just connect banks that are already there. The banks emerge as banks only as the bridge
crosses the stream. The bridge designedly causes them to lie across from each
other. One side is set off against the other by the bridge. Nor do the banks stretch
along the stream as indifferent border stripes of the dry land. With the banks, the
bridge brings to the stream the one and the other expanse of the landscape lying
behind them. It brings stream and bank and land into each other's neighborhood.
The bridge gathers the earth as landscape around the stream. Thus, it guides and
attends the stream through the meadows. Resting upright in the stream's bed, the
bridge piers bear the swing of the arches that leave the stream's waters to their
own course. The waters may wander on quiet and gay, the sky's floods from storm
or thaw may shoot past the piers in torrential waves — the bridge is ready for the
sky's weather and its fickle nature. Even where the bridge covers the stream, it
holds its flow up to the sky by taking it for a moment under the vaulted gateway
and then setting it free once more.

The bridge lets the stream run its course and at the same time grants their way
to mortals so that they may come and go from shore to shore. Bridges lead in
many ways. The city bridge leads from the precincts of the castle to the cathedral
square; the river bridge near the country town brings wagons and horse teams to
the surrounding villages. The old stone bridge's humble brook crossing gives to the
harvest wagon its passage from the fields into the villages and carries the lumber
cart from the field path to the road. The highway bridge is tied into the network

of long-distance traffic, paced as calculated for maximum yield. Always and ever differently the bridge escorts the lingering and hastening ways of men to and fro, so that they may get to other banks and in the end, as mortals, to the other side.[2]

If we are near such bridges we tend to be drawn into their clearing, for centered space has an overpowering dynamism that captures both our attention and our bodies. Centered space is centripetal, insisting upon drawing us in. There is an inrush that is difficult to escape, that overwhelms and makes us acquiescent. We perceive space not as a receptacle containing things but rather as a context energized by the positioned interrelationships of things. Centered space has a pulling power that, even in our most harassed moments, we can hardly help feeling. In such places as the piazza before St. Peter's (Figure 6-1), we walk slowly and speak softly. We find ourselves in the presence of a power that is beyond our control. We feel the sublimity of space, but, at the same time, the centeredness beckons and welcomes us.

Space and Architecture

Architecture — as opposed to mere engineering — is the creative conservation of space. Architects perceive the centers of space in nature and build to preserve these centers and make them more vital. Architects are confronted by centered spaces that desire to be made, through them, into works. These spaces of nature are not offspring of architects alone but appearances that step up to them, so to speak, and demand protection. If an architect succeeds in carrying through these appeals, the power of the natural space streams forth and the work rises. Architects are the shepherds of space. In turn, the paths around their shelters lead us away from our ordinary preoccupations demanding the use of space. We come to rest. Instead of our using up space, space takes possession of us with a ten-fingered grasp. We have a place to dwell.

Chartres

On a hot summer day many years ago, following the path of Henry Adams, who wrote *Mont-Saint-Michel and Chartres,* one of the authors was attempting to drive from Mont-Saint-Michel to Chartres in time to catch the setting sun through the western rose window of Chartres Cathedral. The following is an account of this experience:

> In my rushing anxiety — I had to be in Paris the following day and I had never been to Chartres before — I became oblivious of space except as providing landmarks for my time-clocked progress. Thus I have no significant memories of the

[2]Martin Heidegger, *Poetry, Language, Thought,* Albert Hofstadter (trans.). Copyright © 1971 by Martin Heidegger. By permission of Harper & Row, Publishers, Inc., p. 152ff.

FIGURE 6-2
Chartres Cathedral. (© Lucas Abreu)

towns and countrysides I hurried through. Late that afternoon the two spires of Chartres (Figures 6-2 and 6-3), like two strangely woven strands of rope let down from the heavens, gradually came into focus. The blue dome of the sky also became visible for the first time, centering as I approached more and more firmly around the axis of those spires. "In lovely blueness blooms the steeple with metal roof" (Hölderlin). The surrounding fields and then the town, coming out now in all their specificity, grew into tighter unity with the church and sky. I recalled a passage from Aeschylus: "The pure sky desires to penetrate the earth, and the earth is filled with love so that she longs for blissful unity with the sky. The rain falling from the sky impregnates the earth, so that she gives birth to plants and grain for beasts and men." No one rushed in or out or around the church. The space around seemed alive and dense with slow currents all ultimately being pulled to and through the central portal.[3] Inside (Figure 6-4), the space, although spacious far beyond the scale of practical human needs, seemed strangely compressed, full of forces thrusting and counterthrusting in dynamic interrelations. Slowly, in the cool silence inlaid with stone, I was drawn down the long nave, fol-

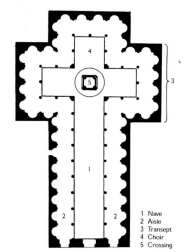

1 Nave
2 Aisle
3 Transept
4 Choir
5 Crossing

[3]Chartres, like most Gothic churches, is shaped roughly like a recumbent Latin cross:
The front (Figure 6-3)—with its large circular window shaped like a rose and the three vertical windows or lancets beneath—faces west. The apse or eastern end of the building contains the high altar. The nave is the central and largest aisle leading from the central portal to the high altar. But before the altar is reached, the transept crosses the nave. Both the northern and southern facades of the transept of Chartres contain, like the western facade, glorious rose windows. (Drawing After R. Sturgis)

FIGURE 6-3
Chartres Cathedral. The West
Front. 1194–1260. (© Scala/
Art Resource, New York)

lowing the stately rhythms of the bays and piers. But my eyes also followed the vast vertical stretches far up into the shifting shadows of the vaultings. It was as if I were being borne aloft. Yet I continued down the narrowing tunnel of the nave, but more and more slowly as the pull of the space above held back the pull of the space below. At the crossing of the transept, the flaming colors, especially the reds, of the northern and southern roses transfixed my slowing pace, and then I turned back at last to the western rose and the three lancets beneath—a delirium of color, dominantly blue, was pouring through. Earthbound on the crossing, the blaze of the Without was merging with the Within. Radiant space took complete possession of my senses. In the protective grace of this sheltering space, even the outer space which I had dismissed in the traffic of my driving seemed to converge around the center of this crossing. Instead of being alongside things—the church, the town, the fields, the sky, the sun—I was with them, at one with them. This housing of holiness made me feel at home in this strange land.

FIGURE 6-4
Chartes Cathedral. Interior.
(© A. F. Kersting)

Living Space

Living space is the feeling of the comfortable positioning of things in the environment, promoting both liberty of movement and paths as directives. Taking possession of space is our first gesture as infants, and sensitivity to the position of other things is a prerequisite of life. Space infiltrates through all our senses, and our sensations of everything influence our perception of space. A breeze broadens the spaciousness of a room that opens on a garden. A sound tells us something about the surfaces and shape of that room. A cozy temperature brings the furniture and walls into more intimate relationships. The smell of books gives that space a personality. Each of our senses helps record the positioning of things, expressed in such terms as "up-down," "left-right," and "near-far." These recordings require a reference system with a center. With abstract space, as when we estimate distances visually, the center is the zero point located between the eyes. With living space, since all the senses are involved, the whole body is a center. Furthermore, when we relate to a place of special value, such as the home, a "configurational center" is formed, a place that is a gathering point around which a field of interest is structured. If we oversimplify, we can say that for the ancient Romans, it was the city of Rome to which they most naturally belonged; Rome constituted their configurational center. For medieval people it was the church and castle, for Babbitt the office, for Sartre the café, and for de Gaulle the nation. But, for most people at almost any time, although undoubtedly more so in contemporary times, there are more than a couple of centers. Often these are more or less confused and changing. In living space, nevertheless, places, principal directions, and distances arrange themselves around configurational centers.

PERCEPTION KEY   Buildings

1. Select a house in your community that strikes you as ugly. Why do you make this judgment?
2. Do the same for an apartment house, a school building, an office building, a gas station, a supermarket, a city street, a bridge.
3. Do you have any buildings that provide a centered space? Discuss.

A building that lacks artistic qualities, even if it encloses a convenient void, encourages us to ignore it. Normally we will be blind to such a building and its space as long as it serves its practical purposes. If the roof leaks or a wall breaks down, however, then we will only see the building as a damaged instrument. A well-designed building, on the other hand, brings us into living space by centering space. Such a building clarifies earlier impressions of the scene that had been obscure and confused. The potentialities of power in the positioned interrelationships of things are captured and channeled. Our feeling for interesting, enlivened space is awakened. We become aware of the power and embrace of space. Such a building strikes a

FIGURE 6-5
The Athenian Acropolis with
the Parthenon. 447–432 B.C.
(© Dian Ellis/Photri)

bargain between what it lets us do and what it makes us do. In the piazza
before St. Peter's, we are free to wander this way or that, but always within
the draw of the powerful façade of the church and the reach of its embrac-
ing wings.

Four Necessities of Architecture

The architect's professional life is perhaps more difficult than that of any
other artist. Architecture is a peculiarly public art because buildings generally have a social function and many buildings require public funds. More
than other artists, architects must consider the public. If they do not, few
of their plans are likely to materialize. Thus architects must be psychologists, sociologists, economists, businesspeople, politicians, and courtiers.
They must also be engineers, for they must be able to design structurally
stable buildings. And then they need luck. Even as famous an architect as
Frank Lloyd Wright could not prevent the destruction, for economic reasons, of one of his masterpieces—the Imperial Hotel in Tokyo.

Architects have to take into account four basic and closely interrelated
necessities: technical requirements, function, spatial relationships, and
content. To succeed, their structures must adjust themselves to these necessities. As for what time will do to their creations, they can only hope and
prepare with foresight. Wright's hotel withstood earthquakes, but ultimately every building is peculiarly susceptible to economic demands and
the whims of future taste.

FIGURE 6-6
The Parthenon. 447–432 B.C.
(© Foto Marburg/Art
Resource, New York)

TECHNICAL REQUIREMENTS OF ARCHITECTURE

Of the four necessities, the technical requirements of a building are the most obvious. Buildings must stand and withstand. Architects must know the materials and their potentialities, how to put the materials together, and how the materials will work on a particular site. Stilt construction, for instance, will not withstand earthquakes—and so architects are engineers. But they are something more as well—artists. In solving their technical problems, they must also make their forms revelatory. Their buildings must illuminate something significant that we would otherwise fail to perceive.

Consider, for example, the relationship between the engineering requirements and artistic qualities of the Parthenon, 447–432 B.C. (Figures 6-5 and 6-6). The engineering was superb, but unfortunately the building was almost destroyed in 1687, when it was being used as an ammunition dump by the Turks and was hit by a shell from a Venetian gun. Basically the technique used was post-and-lintel (or beam) construction. Set on a base, or stylobate, columns (verticals: the posts) support the entablature (horizontals: the lintel), which, in turn, supports the *pediment* (the triangular structure) and roof (Figure 6-6).

PERCEPTION KEY   Parthenon and Chartres

Study the schematic drawing for the Doric order (Figure 6-7), the order followed in the Parthenon, and Figures 6-5 and 6-6.

1. What visual effect do the narrow vertical grooves or flutes carved into the marble columns of the Parthenon have?

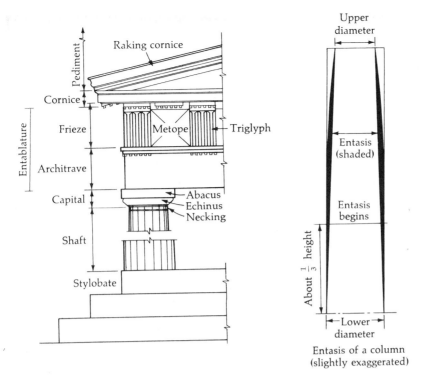

Upper diameter

Entasis (shaded)

Entasis begins

About $\frac{1}{3}$ height

Lower diameter

Entasis of a column
(slightly exaggerated)

FIGURE 6-7
Elements of the Doric order.
(Adapted from John Ives
Sewell, *A History of Western
Art*, rev. ed. New York: Holt,
Rinehart and Winston, 1961.)

2. The columns bulge or swell slightly, a characteristic called *entasis*. Can you perceive the bulge in the photographs of the Parthenon?
3. Why are the columns wider at the base than at the top?
4. Why is there a capital between the top of the shaft and the architrave (the lintels that span the voids from column to column and compose the lowest member of the entablature)?
5. The capital is made up of three parts: the circular grooves at the bottom (the necking); the bulging cushionlike molding (the echinus); and the square block (the abacus). Why the division of the capital into these three parts?
6. The columns at the corners are a couple of inches thicker than the other columns. Why?
7. The corner and adjacent columns are slightly closer together than the other columns. Is the difference perceptible in the photograph? All the columns except those in the center of each side slant slightly inward. Why?
8. Subtle refinements such as those mentioned above abound throughout the Parthenon. Few if any of them are necessary from a technical standpoint, nor were these refinements accidental. They are found repeatedly in other Greek temples of the time. Presumably, then, they are a result of a need to make the form of the temple mean something, to have it be a form-content. Presumably, as well, the Parthenon can still reveal something of the values of the ancient Greeks. What? Compare those values with the values revealed by Chartres. For example, which building seems to reveal a society that places more trust in God? And what kind of God? And in what way are the subtle refinements of the Parthenon relevant to these questions?

FIGURE 6-8
Ludwig Mies van der Rohe
and Philip Johnson, Seagram
Building, New York City.
1954–1958. (© Ezra Stoller/
Esto)

FUNCTIONAL REQUIREMENTS OF ARCHITECTURE

Architects must not only make their buildings stand but also usually stand them in such a way that they reveal their function or use. One contemporary school of architects even goes so far as to claim that form must follow function. If the form succeeds in this, that is all the form should do. In any case, a form that disguises the function of a building seems to irritate almost everyone.

If form follows function in the sense that the form stands "for" the function of its building, then conventional forms or structures are often sufficient. No one is likely to mistake Chartres Cathedral for an office building. We have seen the conventional structures of too many churches and office buildings to be mistaken about this. Nor are we likely to mistake the Seagram Building (Figure 6-8) for a church. We recognize the functions of these buildings because they are in the conventional shapes that such buildings so often possess.

> **PERCEPTION KEY**   Form, Function, Content, and Space
>
> Study Figures 6-8 and 3-3, Le Corbusier's Notre Dame-dur-Haut.
>
> 1. What is the basic function of each of these buildings?

2. How do you know what the functions are? How have the respective forms revealed the functions of their buildings? And does it seem appropriate to use the term "reveal" for Figures 6-8 and 3-3? We would argue that both works are architecture because the form of the building in Figure 3-3 is revelatory of the subject matter—of the tension, anguish, striving, and ultimate concern of religious faith, whereas in Figure 6-8 the form of the building is revelatory of the stripped-down, uniform efficiency of an American business corporation. Consider every possible relevant argument against this view.
3. If the interior of Chartres Cathedral (Figure 6-4) were remodeled into a vast dental clinic, would you feel dissatisfied with the relationship between the new interior and the old exterior? If so, why?

Study one of Frank Lloyd Wright's last and most famous works, the Solomon R. Guggenheim Museum in New York City (Figures 6-9 and 6-10), constructed in 1957–1959 but designed in 1943. Wright wrote:

Here for the first time architecture appears plastic, one floor flowing into another (more like sculpture) instead of the usual superimposition of stratified layers cutting and butting into each other by way of post-and-beam construction. The whole building, cast in concrete, is more like an egg shell—in form a great simplicity—rather than like a crisscross structure. The light concrete flesh is rendered strong enough everywhere to do its work by embedded filaments of steel either separate or in mesh. The structural calculations are thus those of can-

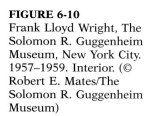

tilever and continuity rather than the post and beam. The net result of such construction is a greater repose, the atmosphere of the quiet unbroken wave: no
meeting of the eye with abrupt changes of form.[4]

The term *cantilever* refers to a structural principle in architecture in which
one end of a horizontal form is fixed—usually in a wall—while the other
end juts out over space. Steel beam construction makes such forms possible; many modern buildings, like the Guggenheim Museum, have forms
extending fluidly into space.

PERCEPTION KEY   Guggenheim Museum

1. Does the exterior of this building harmonize with the interior?
2. Does the form reveal the building as an art museum?
3. Elevators take us to the top of the building, and then we can participate with
   the exhibited works of art by walking down the spiraling ramp. This enables
   us to see each work from many perspectives. Does this seem to you to be an
   interesting, efficient, and comfortable way of exhibiting works of art?

---

[4]Reprinted from *The Solomon R. Guggenheim Museum,* copyright 1960, by permission of the
publishers, The Solomon R. Guggenheim Foundation and Horizon Press, New York, p. 16ff.

4. The front of the museum faces Fifth Avenue. The surrounding buildings are tall rectangular solids evenly lined up along the sidewalks. If possible, visit the site. Did Wright succeed in bringing his museum into a harmonious spatial relationship with these other buildings? Or was his purpose perhaps to make his museum stand out in sharp contrast, like a plant among inorganic shapes? But if so, does the museum fit successfully into the spatial context—"the power and embrace of the positioned interrelationships of things"?

5. Originally the museum was to have been situated in Central Park. Do you think a park site would have been better than its present site?

SPATIAL REQUIREMENTS OF ARCHITECTURE

Wright solved his technical problems (such as cantilevering) and his functional problems (efficient and commodious exhibition of works of art) with considerable success. Moreover, the building reveals itself as a museum. But Wright was not completely successful, it seems to us, in relating the museum to the surrounding buildings in a spatially satisfactory way. This, in turn, detracts from some of the "rightness" of the building. In any case, the technical, functional, and spatial necessities are obviously interdependent. If a building is going to be artistically meaningful—that is to say, if it is to be architecture—it must satisfy all four necessities to some extent: technical requirements, functional fitness, spatial relationships, and content. Otherwise, its form will fail to be a form-content. A building that is technically awry with poor lighting or awkward passageways or cramped rooms will distract from artistic meaning, and so usually will a form that fails to reveal the function of its building or a form that fails to fit into its spatial context. We will go about our business and ignore those kinds of structures. There is, of course, the question of the degree of success in satisfying each of the four necessities. Despite the apparent problem of its siting, Wright's museum is so successful otherwise that it would be strange indeed to describe it as just a building, something less than architecture.

REVELATORY REQUIREMENTS OF ARCHITECTURE

The function or use of a building is an essential part of the subject matter of that building, what the architect interprets or gives insight into by means of its form. The function of the Seagram Building (Figure 6-8) is to house offices. The form of that building reveals that function. But does this function exhaust the subject matter of this building? Is only function revealed? Would we, perhaps, be closer to the truth by claiming that involved with this office function are values closely associated with, but nevertheless distinguishable from, this function? That somehow other values, besides functional ones, are interpreted in architecture? That values from the architect's society somehow impose themselves, and the architect must be sensitive to them? We think that even if architects criticize or react against the values of their time, they must take account of them. Otherwise, their buildings would stand for little more than projections of their personal idiosyncrasies.

We are claiming that the essential values of contemporary society are a part of all artists' subject matter, part of what they must interpret in their work, and this—because of the public character of architecture—is especially so with architects. The way architects (and artists generally) are influenced by the values of their society has been given many explanations. According to art historian Walter Abell, the state of mind of a society influences architects directly. Historical and social circumstances generate psychosocial tensions and latent imagery in the minds of the members of a culture. Architects, among the most sensitive members of a society, release this tension by condensing this imagery in their art. The psyche of the artist, explained by Abell by means of psychoanalytic theory and social psychology, creates the basic forms of art; but this psyche is controlled by the state of mind of the artist's society, which, in turn, is controlled by the historical and social circumstances of which it is a part.

> Art is a symbolical projection of collective psychic tensions. . . . Within the organism of a culture, the artist functions as a kind of preconsciousness, providing a zone of infiltration through which the obscure stirrings of collective intuition can emerge into collective consciousness. The artist is the personal transformer within whose sensitivity a collective psychic charge, latent in society, condenses into a cultural image. He is in short the dreamer . . . of the collective dream.[5]

PERCEPTION KEY September 11, 2001

The horrifying loss of life and the destruction of the World Trade Center has caused enormous psychosocial anxiety in our society. Presumably, if Abell is correct, this social state of mind is already affecting the world of art. We will be seeing a reflection of this event in all the arts except, perhaps, in the design of skyscrapers. This is paradoxical, for among the arts it was mainly buildings that were destroyed (a few sculptures and paintings were also lost). But can an architect express terror in the design of a skyscraper and still make the building functional? Plans are now being conceived for memorials (sculpture and architecture) at the World Trade Center site. What kinds of memorials do you think would be appropriate? Discuss.

Whereas Abell stresses the unconscious tensions of the social state of mind that influence the architect's creative process, Erwin Panofsky, another art historian, stresses the artist's mental habits, conscious as well as unconscious, that act as principles to guide the architect. For example,

> We can observe [between about 1130 and 1270] . . . a connection between Gothic art and Scholasticism which is more concrete than a mere "parallelism" and yet more general than those individual (and very important) "influences" which are inevitably exerted on painters, sculptors, or architects by erudite advisors. In

---

[5]Walter Abell, *The Collective Dream in Art* (Cambridge, Mass.: Harvard University Press, 1957), p. 328.

contrast to a mere parallelism, the connection which I have in mind is a genuine cause-and-effect relation; but in contrast to an individual influence, this cause-and-effect relation comes about by diffusion rather than by direct impact. It comes about by the spreading of what may be called, for want of a better term, a mental habit—reducing this overworked cliché to its precise Scholastic sense as a "principle that regulates the act." Such mental habits are at work in all and every civilization.[6]

Whatever the explanation of the architect's relationship to society—and Abell's and Panofsky's are two of the best[7]—the forms of architecture reflect and interpret some of the fundamental values of the society of the architect. Yet, even as these forms are settling, society changes. Thus, while keeping the past immanent in the present, architecture takes on more and more the aura of the past, especially if the originating values are no longer viable or easily understandable. Anything that now exists but has a past may refer to, or function as, a sign of the past, but the forms of architecture interpret the past. Not only do the forms of architecture preserve the past more carefully than most things, for most architects build buildings to last, but these structures also enlighten that past. They inform about the values of the artists' society. Architects did the forming, of course, but from beginning to end that forming, insofar as it succeeded artistically, brought forth something of their society's values. Thus architectural forms are weighted with the past—a past, furthermore, that is more public than private. The past is preserved in the forms as part of the content of architecture.

Every stone of the Parthenon, in the way it was cut and fitted, reveals something about the values of the Age of Pericles, the fifth century B.C.— for example, the emphasis on moderation and harmony, the importance of mathematical measurement and yet its subordination to the eminence of humans and their rationality, as well as the immanence rather than the transcendence of the sacred.

Chartres Cathedral also is an exceptional example of the preservation of the past. Chartres reveals three principal value areas of that medieval region: the special importance of Mary, to whom the cathedral is dedicated; the doctrines of the cathedral school, one of the most important centers of learning in Europe in the twelfth and thirteenth centuries; and the value preferences of the main patrons—the royal family, the lesser nobility, and the local guilds. The windows of the 175 surviving panels and the sculpture, including more than 2,000 carved figures, were a bible in glass and stone for the illiterate, but they were also a visual encyclopedia for the literate. From these structures the iconographer—the decipherer of the meaning of icons or symbols—can trace almost every fundamental value of the society that created Chartres Cathedral: the conception of human history from Adam

---

[6]Erwin Panofsky, *Gothic Architecture and Scholasticism,* 2nd Wimmer Lecture, 1948. St. Vincent College. (Latrobe, Penn.: Archabbey Press, 1951, p. 20ff; New York: New American Library, 1957, p. 44).

[7]For an evaluation of these and other explanations, see F. David Martin, "The Sociological Imperative of Stylistic Development," *Bucknell Review,* vol. 11, no. 4, pp. 54–80, December 1963.

and Eve to the Last Judgment; the story of Christ from his ancestors to his Ascension; church history; ancient lore and contemporary history; the latest scientific knowledge; the curriculum of the cathedral school as divided into the trivium (grammar, logic, and rhetoric) and the quadrivium (arithmetic, geometry, astronomy, and music); the hierarchy of the nobility and the guilds; the code of chivalry and manners; and the hopes and fears of the time. Furthermore, the participator also becomes aware of a society that believed God to be transcendent but the Virgin to be both transcendent and immanent, not just a heavenly queen but also a mother. Chartres is Mary's home. For, as Henry Adams insisted, "You had better stop here, once for all, unless you are willing to feel that Chartres was made what it was, not by the artist, but by the Virgin."

Even if we disagree with Adams, we understand, at least to some extent, Mary's special position within the context of awe aroused by God as "wholly other." The architecture of Chartres does many things, but, above all, its structures preserve that awe. Something of the society of the Chartres that was comes into our present awareness with overwhelming impact. And then we can understand something about the feelings of such medieval men as Abbot Haimon of Normandy who, after visiting Chartres, wrote to his brother monks in Tutbury, England,

> Who has ever heard tell, in times past, that powerful princes of the world, that men brought up in honor and wealth, that nobles, men and women, have bent their proud and haughty necks to the harness of carts, and that, like beasts of burden, they have dragged to the abode of Christ these wagons, loaded with wines, grains, oil, stone, wood, and all that is necessary for the wants of life, or for the construction of the church . . . ? When they have reached the church, they arrange the wagons about it like a spiritual camp, and during the whole night they celebrate the watch by hymns and canticles. On each wagon they light tapers and lamps; they place there the infirm and sick, and bring them the precious relics of the saints for their relief.

PERCEPTION KEY   Values and Architecture

1. Enumerate other values in addition to the functional that may be interpreted by the form of the Seagram Building (Figure 6-8).
2. Do the same for Le Corbusier's Notre Dame-du-Haut (Figure 3-3). Is it easier to point to the values related to Le Corbusier's church? If so, how is this explained?

To participate with a work of public architecture fully, we must have as complete an understanding as possible of its subject matter—the function of the building and the relevant values of the society which subsidized the building. The more we know about the region of Chartres in medieval times, the more we will appreciate its cathedral. The more we understand our own time, the more we will appreciate the Seagram Building. Similarly, the more we understand about the engineering problems involved in a work of architecture, including especially the potentialities of its materials, the better our appreciation. And, of course, the more we know about the stylistic history of architectural details and structures and their possibilities, the deeper will be our appreciation. That tradition is a long and complex one, but you can learn its essentials in any good book on the history of architecture (see the bibliography at the end of the chapter).

Let us return again to architecture and space, for what most clearly distinguishes architecture from painting and sculpture is the way it works in space. Works of architecture separate an inside space from an outside space. They make that inside space available for human use. And in interpreting their subject matter (functions and the values of their society), architects make space "space." They bring out the power and embrace of the positioned interrelationships of things. Architecture in this respect can be divided into four main types—the earth-rooted, the sky-oriented, the earth-resting, and the earth-dominating.

Earth-Rooted Architecture

The earth is the securing agency that grounds the place of our existence, our center. In many primitive cultures it is believed that people are born from the earth. And in many languages people are the "Earth-born." In countless myths, Mother Earth is the bearer of humans from birth to death. Of all things the expansive earth, with its mineral resources and vegetative fecundity, most suggests or is symbolic of security. Moreover, since the solidity of the earth encloses its depth in darkness, the earth is also suggestive of mystery and death.

No other thing exposes its surface more pervasively and yet hides its depth dimension more completely. The earth is always closure in the midst of disclosure. If we dig below the surface, there is always a further depth in darkness that continues to escape our penetration. Thus the Earth Mother has a mysterious, nocturnal, even funerary aspect—she is also often a goddess of death. But, as the theologian Mircea Eliade points out, "even in respect of these negative aspects, one thing that must never be lost sight of, is that when the Earth becomes a goddess of Death, it is simply because she is felt to be the universal womb, the inexhaustible source of all creation."[8] Nothing in nature is more suggestive or symbolic of security and mystery than the earth. *Earth-rooted architecture* accentuates this natural symbolism more than any other art.

SITE

Architecture that is earth-rooted discloses the earth by drawing our attention to the site of the building, its submission to gravity, its raw materials, and its centrality in outer and inner space. Sites whose surrounding

---

[8]Mircea Eliade, *Myths, Dreams and Mysteries,* trans. Philip Mairet (New York: Harper, 1961), p. 188.

FIGURE 6-11
Mont-Saint-Michel. (French
Government Tourist Office)

environment can be seen from great distances are especially favorable for helping a building bring out the earth. The site of the Parthenon (Figures 6-5 and 6-6), for example, is superior in this respect to the site of Chartres (Figures 6-2 and 6-3) because the Acropolis is a natural center that dominates a widespread concave space. Thus the Parthenon is able to emphasize by continuity both the sheer heavy stoniness of the limestone cliffs of the Acropolis and the gleaming whites of Athens. In contrast, it sets off the deep blue of the Mediterranean sky and sea and the grayish greens of the encompassing mountains that open out toward the weaving blue of the sea like the bent rims of a colossal flower. All these elements of the earth would be present without the Parthenon, of course, but the Parthenon, whose columns from a distance push up like stamens of a flower, centers these elements more tightly so that their interrelationships add to the vividness of each. Together they form the ground from which the Parthenon slowly and majestically rises.

GRAVITY

The Parthenon is also exceptional in the way it manifests a gentle surrender to gravity. The horizontal rectangularity of the entablature follows evenly along the plain of the Acropolis with the steady beat of its supporting columns and quiets their upward thrust. Gravity is accepted and accentuated in this serene stability—the hold of the earth is secure.

FIGURE 6-12
Rockefeller Center, New York City. 1931–1940. (Courtesy Rockefeller Center. © Rockefeller Center Management Corporation)

The site of Mont-Saint-Michel (Figure 6-11) can also be seen from great distances, especially from the sea, and the church, straining far up from the great rock cliffs, organizes a vast scene of sand, sea, shallow hills, and sky. But the spiny, lonely verticality of the church overwhelms the pull of the earth. We are lured to the sky, to the world of light and open vastness, whereas the Parthenon draws us back into the womb of the earth. Mont-Saint-Michel discloses the earth, for both the earth and a world to be opened up require centering and thus each other, but the defiance of gravity weakens the securing sense of place. Mont-Saint-Michel rapidly moves us around its walls, when the tides permit, with a dizzying effect, whereas the Parthenon moves us around slowly and securely so that our orientation is never in doubt. The significance of the earth is felt much more deeply at the Parthenon than at Mont-Saint-Michel.

The complex of skyscrapers that composes Rockefeller Center (Figure 6-12) in New York City is an exceptional example of an architecture that allows for only a minimal submission to gravity. The surrounding buildings, unless we are high up in one nearby, block out the lower sections of the Center. If we are able to see the lower sections by getting in close, we are blocked from a clear and comprehensive view of the upper sections. The relationships between the lower and upper sections are, therefore, somewhat disconnected, and there is a sense of these tapering towers, especially the one in the center of the photograph, not only scraping but also being suspended from the sky. The Seagram Building (Figure 6-8), not far away, carries this feeling even further by the placement of the shaftlike box on stilts.

FIGURE 6-13
Frank Lloyd Wright,
Kaufman house (Falling
Water), Bear Run,
Pennsylvania. 1937–1939.
(© Scott Frances/Esto)

This apparently weightless building mitigates but does not annihilate our feeling of the earth, for despite its elegant soaring, we are aware of its base. Even at night, when the sides of this structure become dark curtains pierced by hundreds of square lights, we feel these lights, as opposed to the light of the stars, as somehow grounded. Architecture in setting up a world always sets forth the earth, and vice versa.

RAW MATERIALS

When the medium of architecture is made up totally or in large part of un-finished materials furnished by nature, especially when they are from the site, these materials tend to stand forth and help reveal the earthiness of the earth. In this respect stone, wood, and clay in a raw or relatively raw state are much more effective than steel, concrete, and glass. If the Parthenon had been made in concrete rather than in native Pentelic marble—the quarries can still be seen in the distance—the building would not grow out of the soil so organically and some of the feeling of the earth would be dissipated. Also, if the paint that originally covered much of the Parthenon had remained, the effect would be considerably less earthy than at present. Note, however, that the dominant colors were terra-cotta reds, colors of the

FIGURE 6-14
Palace of Versailles. 1661–
1687. (French Government
Tourist Office)

earth. Wright's Kaufman house (Figure 6-13) is an excellent example of the combined use of manufactured and raw materials that helps set forth the earth. The concrete and glass bring out by contrast the textures of stone and wood taken from the site, while the lacelike flow of the falling water is made even more graceful by its reflection in the smooth clear flow of concrete and glass. Like a wide-spreading plant, drawing the sunlight and rain to its good earth, this home seems to breathe within its homeland.

PERCEPTION KEY   Architecture and Materials

In his *Praise of Architecture,* the Italian architect Gio Ponti writes, "Beautiful materials do not exist. Only the right material exists. . . . Rough plaster in the right place is the beautiful material for that place. . . . To replace it with a noble material would be vulgar."

1. Do you agree with Ponti?
2. If you agree, refer to examples that corroborate Ponti's point.
3. If you disagree, refer to examples that do not corroborate. Discuss.

CENTRALITY

A building that is strongly centered, both in its outer and inner space, helps disclose the earth. Perhaps no building is more centered in its site than the Parthenon, but the weak centering of its inner space slackens somewhat the significance of the earth. Unlike Chartres, there is no strong pull into the Parthenon, and, when we get inside, the inner space, as we reconstruct it,

FIGURE 6-15
San Vitale, Ravenna, Italy.
526–547. (© Scala/Art
Resource, New York)

is divided in such a way that no certain center can be felt. There is no place to come to an unequivocal standstill as at Chartres. Even Versailles (Figure 6-14), despite its seemingly never-ending partitions of inner space, brings us eventually to somewhat of a center at the bed in Louis XIV's bedroom. Yet this centering is made possible primarily by the view from the room that focuses both the pivotal position of the room in the building and the placement of the room on a straight-line axis to Paris in the far distance. Conversely, the inner space of Chartres, most of which from the crossing can be taken in with a sweep of the eye, achieves centrality without this kind of dependence upon outside orientation. Buildings such as the Parthenon and Versailles, which divide the inner space with solid partitions, invariably are weaker in inner centrality than buildings without such divisions. The endless boxes within boxes of the Seagram Building (Figure 6-8) negate any possibility of significant inner centering, adding to the unearthiness of this cage of steel and glass.

Buildings sometimes draw us to a privileged position in their inner space, the position that gives us the best perception of that space. Then we are likely to feel the security of inner centeredness. This feeling is further enhanced when the expanses of inner space are more or less equidistant from the privileged position. *Greek-cross* buildings, in which the floor plan resembles a cross whose arms are equal in length, are likely to center us in inner space more strongly than *Latin-cross* buildings, such as Chartres (Figure 6-4). If Bramante's and Michelangelo's Greek-cross plan for St. Peter's had been carried out, the centrality of the inner space would have been greatly enhanced. It does not follow, however, that all centrally

FIGURE 6-16
San Vitale, Ravenna, Italy.
526–547. Interior. (© Scala/
Art Resource, New York)

planned buildings that open up all or almost all of the inner space will be strongly centered internally. San Vitale (Figures 6-15 and 6-16) in Ravenna, for example, is basically an octagon, but the enfolded interior spaces are not clearly outlined and differentiated. There is a floating and welling of space working out and up through the arcaded niches into the outer layers of the ambulatory and gallery that fade into semidarkness. The dazzling colors of the varied marble slabs and the mosaics lining the piers and walls add to our sense of spatial uncertainty. We can easily discover the center of San Vitale if we so desire, but there is no directed movement to it because the indeterminacy of the surrounding spaces makes the feeling of the center insecure and insignificant. The unanchored restlessness of the interior of San Vitale belies its solid weighty exterior.

Buildings in the round, other things being equal, are the most internally centered of all. In the Pantheon (Figure 6-17), almost all the inner space can be seen with a turn of the head, and the grand and clear *symmetry* of the enclosing shell draws us to the center of the circle, the privileged position, beneath the eye of the dome opening to a bit of the sky. Few buildings root us more firmly in the earth. The massive dome with its stony bluntness seems to be drawn down by the funneled and dimly spreading light falling through the eye. This is a dome of destiny pressing tightly down. We are driven earthward in this crushing ambience. Even on the outside the Pantheon seems to be forcing down (Figure 6-18). In the circular interior of Wright's Guggenheim Museum (Figure 6-10), not all of the inner space can be seen from the privileged position, but the smoothly curving ramp that comes down like a whirlpool makes us feel the earth beneath as our only support.

FIGURE 6-17
Giovanni Paolo Panini, *Interior of the Pantheon*, Rome. Circa 1734. The Pantheon itself dates from the second century after Christ. Oil on canvas, 50½ × 39 inches. National Gallery of Art, Washington, D.C. Samuel H. Kress Collection.

Whereas in buildings such as Mont-Saint-Michel and Chartres, mass seems to be overcome, the weight lightened, and the downward motion thwarted, in buildings such as the Pantheon and the Guggenheim Museum, mass comes out heavily and down.

The importance of a center, usually within a circle, as a privileged and even sacred position in relation to the earth is common among the spatial arrangements of ancient cultures—for example, Stonehenge on the Salisbury Plain of England (Figure 6-19). And the first city of Rome, according

FIGURE 6-18
The Pantheon, Rome.
117–125. Exterior. (© Canali
Photobank, Italy)

to Plutarch, was laid out by the Etruscans around a circular trench or *mundus,* over which was placed a great capstone. Around the *mundus,* the Etruscans outlined a large circle for the walls which would enclose the city. Following a carefully prescribed ritual, a deep furrow was plowed along the circle and the plow was lifted from the ground wherever a gate was to appear. This circular plan was subdivided by two main cross streets: the *cardo,* running north and south in imitation of the axis of the earth, and the *decumanus,* running east and west, dividing the city into four equal parts. These streets crossed at the site of the *mundus,* believed to be the entrance to the underworld, and the capstone was removed three times each year to allow the spirits passage between the world of the living and the world of the dead. Although such beliefs and customs have long been dead in Western civilization, we still can feel the power of the earth in circular city plans and buildings.

Sky-Oriented Architecture

Architecture that is *sky-oriented* suggests or is symbolic of a world as the generating agency that enables us to project our possibilities and realize some of them. A horizon, always a necessary part of a world, is symbolic of

FIGURE 6-19
Stonehenge, Salisbury Plain,
England. Circa 2800–1500
B.C. (Image supplied by
Aerofilms.com)

the limitations placed upon our possibilities and realizations. The light and heat of the sun are more symbolic than anything else in nature of generative power. Dante declared, "there is no visible thing in the world more worthy to serve as symbol of God than the Sun; which illuminates with visible life itself first and then all the celestial and mundane bodies." The energy of the moving sun brightens the sky that, in turn, opens up for us a spacious context or world within which we attempt to realize our possibilities. In total darkness we may be able to orient ourselves to the earth, but in order to move with direction, as do the blind, we must imagine space as open in some way, as a world enlightened with light even if our imaginations must provide that light. Total darkness, at least until we can envision a world, is terrifying. That is why, as the Preacher of Ecclesiastes proclaims, "the light is sweet, and a pleasant thing it is for the eyes to behold the sun." "The light of the living" is a common Hebrew phrase, and in Greek "to behold light" is synonymous with "to live." The light of the sky reveals space — the positioned interrelationships of things. The dome of the sky, with its limits provided by the horizon, embraces a world within which we find ourselves. But a world is above all the context for activity. A world stirs our imaginations to possibilities. A world, with its suggestion of expectation, turns our faces to the future, just as the smile of the sun lures our eyes. Architecture organizes a world, usually more tightly than nature, by centering that world

FIGURE 6-20
Antonio Gaudí, Sagrada Familia (Church of the Holy Family), Barcelona. 1883 to present. Interior. (© Vanni/ Art Resource, New York)

on the earth by means of a building. By accentuating the natural symbolism of sunlight, sky, and horizon, sky-oriented architecture opens up a world that is symbolic of our projections into the future.

Such architecture discloses a world by drawing our attention to the sky bounded by a horizon. It accomplishes this by means of making a building appear high and centered within the sky, defying gravity, and tightly integrating the light of outer with inner space. Negatively, architecture that accents a world de-emphasizes the features that accent the earth. Thus the manufactured materials, such as the steel and glass of the Seagram Building (Figure 6-8) help separate this building from the earth. Positively, architects can accent a world by turning their structures toward the sky in such a way that the horizon of the sky forms a spacious context. Architecture is an art of bounding as well as opening.

Barcelona's Antonio Gaudí created one of the most striking of modern buildings in his Sagrada Familia (Figures 6-20 to 6-22). Gaudí never lived to see the erection of the four towers that dominate the façade. The interior space is not yet covered with a roof, and this emphasizes the sky-orientation of the building. One's eye is lifted upward by about every part of the building. Under construction for over a hundred years, it may be at least

FIGURE 6-21
Antonio Gaudí, Sagrada
Familia. Interior detail.
(Lee A. Jacobus)

FIGURE 6-22
Antonio Gaudí, Sagrada
Familia. Exterior detail.
(Lee A. Jacobus)

another hundred years before the church is completed. Work proceeds slowly, guided more or less by Gaudí's general designs. Gaudí developed details and structures based on organic forms of nature through irregular sweeping lines, shapes, and volumes. Geometric designs are subordinated. Textures vary greatly, often with strong contrasts between smooth and rough; and sometimes, especially in the towers, brilliantly colored pieces of glass and ceramics are embedded, sparkling in the sunlight. The effect often is both sculptural—dense volumes activating the surrounding space—and organic, as if a forest of plants were stretching into the sky searching for sunlight. The earth, despite its necessity, is superseded. This is a building for heaven.

PERCEPTION KEY   Sagrada Familia

1. Compare Sagrada Familia with Chartres (Figures 6-2 and 6-3). How do their sky orientations differ? How are they similar? Compare the exterior facade and the four towers of Sagrada Familia to any church well known to you. What are the differences?
2. Chartres, St. Peter's (Figure 6-1), Sagrada Familia, and Notre Dame-du-Haut (Figure 3-3) are all Catholic churches. Do they each reveal different aspects of Catholicism? Discuss.

AXIS MUNDI

Early civilizations often express a need for a world by centering themselves in relation to the sky by means of an *axis mundi*. Mircea Eliade cites many instances, for example, among the nomadic Australians, whose economy is based on gathering food and hunting small game:

> According to the traditions of an Arunta tribe, the Achipla, in mythical times the divine being Numbakula cosmicized their future territory, created their Ancestor, and established their institutions. From the trunk of a gum tree Numbakula fashioned the sacred pole (*kauwa-auwa*) and, after anointing it with blood, climbed it and disappeared into the sky. This pole (the *axis mundi*) represents a cosmic axis, for it is around the sacred pole that territory becomes habitable, hence is transformed into a world. The sacred pole consequently plays an important role ritually. During their wanderings the Achipla always carry it with them and choose the direction they are to take by the direction toward which it bends. This allows them, while being continually on the move, to be always in "their world" and, at the same time, in communication with the sky into which Numbakula vanished. For the pole to be broken denotes catastrophe; it is like "the end of the world," reversion to chaos. Spencer and Gillen report that once, when the pole was broken, "the entire clan were in consternation; they wandered about aimlessly for a time, and finally lay down on the ground together and waited for death to overtake them."[9]

---

[9]Mircea Eliade, *The Sacred and the Profane*, trans. Willard R. Trask (New York: Harcourt, Brace, 1959), p. 32ff.

FIGURE 6-23
Cass Gilbert, Woolworth
Building, New York City.
1913. (Ely-Cruikshank
Company, Inc.)

When buildings accent a world, their turning to the sky usually suggests
a kind of *axis mundi*. The perpendicularity and centering of the cliffs of the
Acropolis (Figure 6-5), for example, make it a kind of natural *axis mundi*
that would open up the sky to some extent even if the Parthenon had never
been built. But the flat plains around Chartres (Figure 6-2) would rarely
turn us to the sky without the spires of the cathedral. Buildings that stretch
up far above the land and nearby structures, such as Mont-Saint-Michel
(Figure 6-11), Chartres, Rockefeller Center (Figure 6-12), and Sagrada
Familia (Figure 6-20), not only direct our eye to the sky but also act as a
center that orders the sunlight in such a way that a world with a horizon
comes into view. The sky both opens up and takes on limits. Such buildings

FIGURE 6-24
Filippo Brunelleschi, dome of the Cathedral of Florence. 1420–1436. (Italian Government Travel Office)

reach up like an *axis mundi,* and the sky reaches down to meet them in mutual embrace. And we are blessed with an orienting center, our motion being given direction and limits.

DEFIANCE OF GRAVITY

The more a building appears to defy gravity, the more it is likely to disclose the sky, for this defiance draws our eyes upward. The thrust against gravity is not simply a question of how high the building goes. Many of the skyscrapers of New York City, like the Woolworth Building (Figure 6-23), seem to stop finally not because they have reached a more or less perfect union with the sky but because the space used up had exhausted them. They hang more or less lifelessly despite their great height. They seem to have just enough strength to stand upright but no power to transcend the rudimentary laws of statics. Gravity wins out after all. The up and down frustrate each other, and their conflict dims the world that might have been.

This judgment may be unfair with reference to the Woolworth, one of the earliest of the skyscrapers and highly commended in its early days. There is undoubtedly an elegance in its "Gothic Lines." But compare the Woolworth with the Seagram Building (Figure 6-8) and Rockefeller Center (Figure 6-12). Chartres is not nearly as tall as the Woolworth Building, and yet it appears far taller. The stony logic of the press of the *flying buttresses* of Chartres and the arched roof, towers, and spires that carry on their upward thrust seem to overcome the binding of the earth, just as the stone birds on the walls seem about to break their bonds and fly out into the world. The reach up is full of vital force and finally comes to rest comfortably and securely in the bosom of the heavens. Mont-Saint-Michel is even more impressive in this respect, mainly because of the advantages of its site.

FIGURE 6-25
Michael Graves, Crown
Building, Johnstown,
Pennsylvania. 1989. (Courtesy
Crown American, Johnstown,
Pennsylvania)

Perhaps Brunelleschi's dome of the Cathedral of Florence (Figure 6-24) is the most powerful structure ever built in seeming to defy gravity and achieving height in relation to its site. The eight outside ribs spring up to the cupola with tremendous energy, in part because they repeat the spring of the mountains that encircle Florence. The dome, visible from almost everywhere in and around Florence, appears to be precisely centered in the Arno Valley, precisely as high as it should be in order to organize its sky. The world of Florence begins and ends at the still point of this dome of aspiration. In contrast, Michelangelo's dome of St. Peter's, although grander in proportions and over fifty feet higher, fails to organize the sky of Rome as firmly, mainly because the seven hills of Rome do not lend themselves to centralized organization.

PERCEPTION KEY   Architectural Centrality

1. Do you know of any building that has something of the centralizing effect of Brunelleschi's dome?
2. Why is it so much harder to achieve architectural centrality in most cities in the United States than in the old cities of Europe, such as Florence?
3. The Seagram Building (Figure 6-8), like many skyscrapers, has a flat roof. Observe the use of the flat roof in any city with a number of skyscrapers. Do you find that they dominate? Do you find pyramids or spires or domes or other kinds of structure at the top? Which do you prefer? Or do you prefer the flat top? Why?
4. Observe the pyramidal structure on top of the G.E. Building in front of the MetLife Building (see Figure 6-39). Are these structures effective in their relationship?
5. The Crown Building in Johnstown, Pennsylvania, by architect Michael Graves, has something like a Greek or Roman temple structure at the very top (Figure 6-25). It appears strangely and awkwardly placed, far above such a temple's usual location on the earth. If nothing else, the "temple," and its placement, has drawn a lot of attention. It reminds one of the Acropolis, provides a good view of the city, provides a centering axis, like the dome of

FIGURE 6-26
Hagia Sophia, Istanbul,
Turkey. 532–537; restored
558, 975. Interior. (© Hirmer
Verlag, Munich)

Florence, and can be used functionally for social purposes such as parties or a place of rest for employees. Do you think the Crown Building, with its temple, is architecturally successful? Discuss.

INTEGRATION OF LIGHT

When the light of outer space suffuses the light of inner space, especially when the light from the outside seems to dominate or draw the light from the inside, a world is accented. Inside Chartres the light through the stained glass is so majestic that we cannot fail to imagine the light outside that is generating the transfiguration inside. For a medieval man like Abbot Suger the effect was mystical, separating the earth from Heaven:

FIGURE 6-27
Ludwig Mies van der Rohe,
Farnsworth residence, Plano,
Illinois. 1950. (Jon Miller/
© Hedrich Blessing, Chicago)

When the house of God, many colored as the radiance of precious jewels, called me from the cares of the world, then holy meditation led my mind to thoughts of piety, exalting my soul from the material to the immaterial, and I seemed to find myself, as it were, in some strange part of the universe which was neither wholly of the baseness of the earth, nor wholly of the serenity of heaven, but by the grace of God I seemed lifted in a mystic manner from this lower toward the upper sphere.

For a contemporary person the stained glass is likely to be felt more as integrating rather than as separating us from a world. Hagia Sophia in Istanbul (Figure 6-26) has no stained glass, and its glass areas are completely dominated by the walls and dome. Yet the subtle placement of the relatively small windows, especially around the perimeter of the dome, seems to draw the light of the inner space up and out. Unlike the Pantheon (Figure 6-17), the great masses of Hagia Sophia seem to rise. The dome floats gently, despite its diameter of 107 feet, and the great enfolded space beneath is absorbed into the even greater open space outside. We imagine a world.

Sky-oriented architecture reveals the generative activity of a world. The energy of the sun is the ultimate source of all life. The light of the sun enables us to see the physical environment and guides our steps accordingly. "Arise, shine, for thy light is come" (Isaiah 60:1). The sky with its horizon provides a spacious context for our progress. The world of nature vaguely suggests the potentialities of the future. Architecture, however, tightly centers a world on the earth by means of its structures. This unification gives us orientation and security.

FIGURE 6-28
Philip Johnson, Wiley house,
New Canaan, Connecticut.
1953. (© Ezra Stoller/Esto)

Earth-Resting Architecture

Most architecture accents neither earth nor sky but rests on the earth, using the earth like a platform with the sky as background. *Earth-resting* buildings relate more or less harmoniously to the earth. Mies van der Rohe's residence for Edith Farnsworth (Figure 6-27) in Plano, Illinois, is an example of a very harmonious relationship. Philip Johnson's Wiley house (Figure 6-28), perhaps, is considerably less so. Generally, earth-resting buildings are not very tall, have flat roofs, and avoid strong vertical extensions such as spires and protruding chimneys. Thus—unlike sky-oriented architecture—the earth-resting type does not strongly organize the sky around itself, as with Chartres (Figure 6-2) or the Cathedral of Florence (Figure 6-24). The sky is involved with earth-resting architecture, of course, but more as backdrop.

With earth-resting architecture—unlike earth-rooted architecture—the earth does not appear as an organic part of the building, as in Wright's Kaufman house (Figure 6-13). Rather, the earth appears as a stage. Earth-resting buildings, moreover, are usually cubes that avoid cantilevering structures, as in the Kaufman house, as well as curving lines, as in the Sagrada Familia (Figure 6-20). Earth-rooted architecture seems to "hug to" the earth, as with the Pantheon (Figure 6-18), or to grow out of the earth, as with the Kaufman house. Earth-resting architecture, on the other hand, seems to "sit on" the earth. Thus, because it does not relate to its environment quite as strongly as earth-rooted and sky-oriented architecture, this kind of architecture usually tends to draw to itself more isolated attention with reference to its shape, articulation of the elements of its walls, lighting, and so on.

Earth-resting architecture is usually more appropriate than earth-rooted architecture when the site is severely bounded by other buildings. Perhaps this is a basic deficiency of Wright's Guggenheim Museum (Figure 6-9). In any case, it is obvious that if buildings were constructed close to the Kaufman house — especially earth-resting or sky-oriented types — they would destroy much of the glory of Wright's creation.

The Farnsworth residence exemplifies Mies's paradoxical doctrine that "less is more." It seems as if nothing is there that is not necessary for the technical solutions of making the building stand. Study the Wiley house (Figure 6-28) by Philip Johnson, very much in the style of Mies. The functions of this house are explicitly separated — the ground floor contains the private functions, and the open social functions are reserved for the modular glass pavilion above. Nothing seems to be there that does not work as a practical function. But is the building revelatory?

In villages, towns, and cities with climates that do not require pitched roofs, earth-resting buildings, especially among homes, are in the great majority. Usually they are the easiest and cheapest to build, and they lend themselves easily to coordination with other buildings. Check this claim with your own observations. Are we suggesting that buildings with pitched roofs are not likely to be earth-resting?

Earth-Dominating Architecture

Unlike an earth-resting building, an *earth-dominating* building does not sit on but "rules over" the earth. There is a sense of power and aggression. And unlike earth-rooted buildings, such as the Pantheon (Figure 6-18) or the Kaufman house (Figure 6-13), there is no feeling of an organic relationship between the building and the earth.

PERCEPTION KEY   Palazzo Farnese

Study the Palazzo Farnese (Figures 6-29) by Antonio da Sangallo and Michelangelo Buonarroti.

1. The façade of this building is 185 feet by 96½ feet. Is there any particular significance to the large size and proportion of these dimensions? Suppose, for example, that the construction had stopped with the second floor. Would the relationship between width and height be as right as it now appears?

2. The *cornice*—the horizontal molding projecting along the top of the building—is very large, and *quoins* (roughly cut stones) sharply accent the ends of the façade. There is a sense of heavy stability. Is this appropriate for a palace?

3. What function and what values, if any, are revealed by this building? In other words, what is the subject matter that the form informs about? And how does the form achieve its content?

4. Is the palace earth-resting or earth-dominating?

FIGURE 6-29
Antonio da Sangallo and
Michelangelo Buonarroti,
Palazzo Farnese, Rome.
1534. (© Alinari/Art
Resource, New York)

The Palazzo Farnese expresses authority. It commands the earth and every-thing around. Michelangelo's third floor, compared with Sangallo's lower floors, is even awesome, as if the power cannot be contained. Only the third floor of this mighty, sharply outlined, indestructible cube expresses movement.

Earth-dominating buildings generally are easily identified. Any work of architecture *solicits* attention. But earth-dominating buildings *demand* at-tention: Take notice! Who would fail to notice the Palazzo Farnese? Usually earth-dominating buildings are large and massive, but those features do not necessarily express earth-dominance. For example, Versailles is huge and heavy, but its vast horizontal spread has, we think, the effect of earth-resting. The earth as a platform holds its own with the palace. You can sense this much better from the ground than from the aerial photograph (Figure 6-14). Study the West Wing of the National Gallery of Art (Figure 6-30). Do you think the building is earth-resting or earth-dominating? As you think about this, compare St. Peter's (Figure 6-1). In the West, St. Peter's is probably the supreme example of earth-dominating architecture.

PERCEPTION KEY   The National Gallery and the New East Wing

In 1978 the East Wing (Figures 6-31 and 6-32)—designed by I. M. Pei and Partners—was completed, supplementing the old or West Wing of the National Gallery. Visit, if possible, both the old and new buildings and study their struc-tures carefully.

1. Does the exterior of the East Wing—a trapezoid divided into two triangular sections—reveal the function of the building as a museum? Compare with the West Wing.

FIGURE 6-30
National Gallery of Art, Washington, D.C. 1941. Mall entrance. (National Gallery of Art, Washington, D.C. Photo by Dennis Brack)

2. Both buildings utilize Tennessee pink marble from the same quarries. Does either succeed in bringing out the marbleness of this marble?
3. Is the technology that underlies the structure of the East Wing as hidden as in the West Wing?
4. Is there a draw into the entrance of the East Wing, inviting one to enter? Compare with the Mall entrance of the West Wing.
5. Do you think that architecturally the East Wing is better or worse than the West Wing? Why?

PERCEPTION KEY   Earth-Dominating Architecture

1. Try to find earth-dominating buildings in your local community. If you find them, what makes them so?
2. Can you find or can you conceive of a small building that is earth-dominating?

You may find it difficult to find earth-dominating buildings in your community. Palaces are rare, except in very wealthy communities. Few churches exert anything close to the power of St. Peter's. Indeed, for many religious traditions in the United States, such architectural display might well be considered sacrilegious. Public buildings such as courthouses tend to avoid aggressive appearance. They are expected to be traditional and democratic. And buildings of commerce—from banks to malls—are meant to invite.

FIGURE 6-31
I. M. Pei, East Wing of the
National Gallery of Art. Exterior. (© Ezra Stoller/Esto)

FIGURE 6-32
I. M. Pei, East Wing of the
National Gallery of Art. Interior. (© Ezra Stoller/Esto)

FIGURE 6-33
Richard Meier, Long Island
Federal Courthouse, Central
Islip, New York. 2000.
(© Robert Polidori)

Combinations of Types

PERCEPTION KEY   The Palazzo Farnese and the Long Island Federal Courthouse

Compare the Palazzo Farnese (Figure 6-29) with Richard Meier's Courthouse
(Figure 6-33). Both buildings are horizontally oriented cubes. Both use the
earth as a platform. Neither one uses cantilevering as with the Kaufman house
(Figure 6-13) or curving organic lines as with the Sagrada Familia (Figure
6-20). Both use the sky basically as a backdrop and thus obviously are not sky-
oriented. Would you describe the Courthouse as earth-rooted, -resting, or
-dominating? Or some kind of combination? As you think about this, note the
following features of the Courthouse as contrasted with the Palazzo Farnese:
the play of solids and voids and shadows, the deep penetration of visual space
into the interiors, the variations in the size of the rectangular divisions, the play
of details on top of the roof, the sense of structural lightness, and asymmetry.

It seems to us that the Courthouse might best be described as a combination of the earth-resting and the earth-rooted. The earth-resting features,
such as the sky as a backdrop and the platform character of the earth, are
fairly obvious. The earth-rootedness is also there, however, because of the
powerful effect of the huge rotunda that rises at the entrance like a giant
tree anchoring the building down into the earth. The Courthouse does not
just use the earth but seems to belong to it. Some critics have described the

FIGURE 6-34
Frank O. Gehry. Guggenheim
Museum Bilbao, Bilbao,
Spain. 1997. View from
across the river. (© Christian
Richters/Esto)

rotunda as a huge ugly nose that defaces a handsome face. What do you think? Meier, incidentally, is the architect of the famous Getty Museum in Los Angeles.

The problem of when to use earth-rooted, -resting, or -dominating, or sky-oriented structures or some combination is usually resolved by making the function of the building paramount. Churches and large office buildings, especially in crowded cities, lend themselves to sky-orientation. Homes in surburbia lend themselves to earth orientation, usually resting but sometimes rooted. Homes in crowded urban areas present special problems. Earth-rooted buildings, such as the Kaufman house, normally require relatively large open spaces, and to some extent the same is true of the earth-dominating. Most urban dwellings therefore are earth-resting. But as our populations have become increasingly dense, sky-oriented apartment buildings have become a common sight.

Frank Gehry's Guggenheim Museum in Bilbao, Spain, 1991–97 (Figures 6-34, 6-35, and 6-36), was the culminating architectural sensation of the twentieth century, surpassing in interest even Wright's Guggenheim of 1959. Gehry, like many contemporary architects, often uses the computer to scan models and flesh out the possibilities of his designs. The titanium-swathed structure changes drastically and yet harmoniously from every view: For example, from across the Nervion River that cuts through Bilbao the Guggenheim looks something like a whale (Figure 6-34); the locals say that from the bridge it looks like a colossal artichoke; from the south a bulging, blooming flower is suggested (Figure 6-35). The silvery skin of the

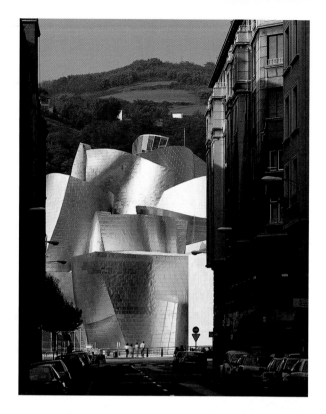

FIGURE 6-35
Frank O. Gehry. Guggenheim
Museum Bilbao, Bilbao,
Spain. 1997. View from the
south. (© Jeff Goldberg/
Esto)

FIGURE 6-36
Frank O. Gehry, Guggenheim
Museum Bilbao, Bilbao,
Spain. 1997. Interior. (©
Christian Richters/Esto)

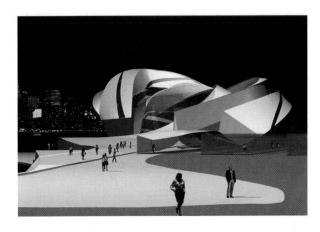

FIGURE 6-37
Peter Eisenman, Design for
the Staten Island Institute of
Arts and Sciences. 1997.
(Courtesy Eisenman
Architects)

south façade reflects colors and lights that harmonize, something like a Rothko abstraction (Figure 4-11). The billowing volumes, mainly cylindrical, spiral upward, as if blown by gently sweeping winds.

Inside (Figure 6-36), smooth curves dominate perpendiculars and right angles, propelling one leisurely from each gallery or room to another with constantly changing perspectives, orderly without conventional order.

PERCEPTION KEY   Gehry and Eisenman

1. Is the Guggenheim earth-rooted, earth-resting, earth-dominating, or sky-oriented? Could it be in some way a combination? It would be helpful if you could examine more photographs (see, for instance, *Frank O. Gehry: The Complete Works*, by Francesco Dal Co and Kurt W. Forster [New York: Monacelli Press, 1998]).
2. Avant-garde architects are producing shapes of extraordinary complexity—swoops and bends and curves—that would be impossible, perhaps, to completely conceive without the help of the computer. What do you think of Peter Eisenman's design for the Staten Island Institute of Arts and Sciences (Figure 6-37)? Do you think it likely that such structures will begin to take over from the "box" (Figures 6-8 and 6-29)? Is Eisenman's design earth-rooted, earth-resting, earth-dominating, sky-oriented, or some combination?

It seems to us that the Guggenheim Bilbao is earth-rooted from the northern perspective (Figure 6-34), the reflection in the river beautifully accenting that orientation. Yet from the southern perspective (Figure 6-35), the building is sky-oriented, its roofs appearing to stretch up the mountain like clouds tinted by the sun. Gehry has accented the natural unity of earth and sky. Eisenman's design, though, appears to be earth-resting and earth-rooted. The concrete platform distinctly separates the building from the earth. Yet the horizontally oriented roofs flare out like the leaves of great plants, tied to and dependent on the earth. It seems likely that the architecture of the twenty-first century will be moving away from the box.

More and more in recent architecture (what the academics awkwardly call "postmodern"), the four basic types of buildings are being combined in unique ways. For example, with Gehry's Guggenheim, the type shifts with one's viewing location. In contrast, with Graves' Crown Building (Figure 6-25) the combination of earth-resting and sky-orientation seems to occur no matter one's location.

Urban Planning

Nowhere has the use of space become more critical in our time than in the city. In conclusion, therefore, the issues we have been discussing about space and architecture take on special relevance with respect to city planning.

Suppose spacious parking lots were located around the fringes of the city, rapid public transportation were readily available from those lots into the city, and in the city only public and emergency transportation—most of it underground—were permitted. In place of poisonous fumes, screeching noises, and jammed streets, there could be fresh air, fountains, flowers, sculpture, music, wide-open spaces to walk and talk and enjoy, benches, and open theaters. Without the danger of being run over, all the diversified characters of a city—its theaters, opera, concert halls, museums, shops, offices, restaurants, parks, squares—could take on some spatial unity. Furthermore, we could get to those various places without nervous prostration and the risk of life and limb.

Most cities are planned either sporadically in segments or not at all. Natural features, such as rivers and hills, often distinguish living spaces from working spaces. In older cities, churches often dominate high ground. Human-made divisions, such as aqueducts, railroad tracks and trestles, bridges, and highways now largely define neighborhoods, sections, and functional spaces. The invasion of the suburban mall has threatened the old downtown business sections in most cities, and, in order to preserve those spaces from blight, imaginative schemes have been developed in some cities. San Antonio, Texas, has a waterway that slowly takes residents and visitors along a canal lined with shops and restaurants. Providence, Rhode Island, closed certain areas to automobiles and made them inviting for shoppers, especially those with strollers and children. Many cities have remodeled their inner shopping areas and made plans to keep them lively and attractive. Street music is now common in many downtown areas, such as New York, London, and Paris.

PERCEPTION KEY   City Planning

1. Do you think the city ought to be saved? Why not just spread out, without centralized functions of a city? What advantages does the city alone have? What still gives glamour to such cities as Florence, Venice, Rome, Paris, Vienna, and London?

FIGURE 6-38
St. Bartholomew's Church on Park Avenue, New York City. 1919. (Lee A. Jacobus)

2. Suppose you are a city planner for New York City, and assume that funds are available to implement your plans. What would you propose? For example, would you destroy all the old buildings? Joseph Hudnut has written, "There is in buildings that have withstood the siege of centuries a magic which is irrespective of form and technical experience . . . the wreckage of distant worlds are radioactive with a long-gathered energy."[10] Do you agree?

3. Would you allow factories within the city limits? How would you handle transportation to and within the city? For instance, would you allow expressways to slice through the city, as in Detroit and Los Angeles? If you outlawed private cars from the city, what would you do with the streets? Would you concentrate on an effective subway system? Could the streets become a unifier of the city?

The conglomerate architecture visible in Figure 6-38, surrounding a large church on Park Avenue, makes us aware that the setting of many interesting buildings so completely overwhelms them that we hardly know how to respond. An urban planner might decide to unify styles of buildings or to separate buildings so as to permit us to participate with them more individually. The scene of Figure 6-38 suggests that there has been little or no planning. Of course, some people might argue that such an accidental conglomeration is part of the charm of urban centers. One might feel, for

---

[10]Joseph Hudnut, *Architecture and the Spirit of Man* (Cambridge, Mass.: Harvard University Press, 1949), p. 15ff.

FIGURE 6-39 *(left)*
The MetLife Building, New York City. 1963. (Courtesy MetLife Media & Public Relations)

FIGURE 6-40 *(right)*
Stores and residence, Greenwich Village, New York City. (Lee A. Jacobus)

example, that part of the pleasure of looking at the church is responding to its contrast with its surroundings. For some people there is a special energy achieved in such a grouping. A consensus is unlikely. Other people are likely to find the union of old and new styles—without first arranging some kind of happy marriage—a travesty. The dome of a church capped by a sky-scraper! The church completely subdued by business! What do you think? These are the kinds of problems, along with political and social complications, that city planners must address.

Study the MetLife Building on Park Avenue (Figure 6-39). The height of certain structures can be limited so that only notable buildings are allowed to rise to great heights, as in Florence, for example. Only a few sections in New York City actually have been controlled. On Park Avenue, the buildings have height restrictions, and in some cases top stories have been removed from buildings under construction. In certain areas, the buildings on both sides of an avenue can create darkness in the middle of the day. The jam of taxis is only one symptom of the narrowness of the avenues in New York City. The architecture along this section of Park Avenue has created a space dominated by dark shadows, making the looming buildings appear threatening. Now consider the contrast in a building in the Greenwich Village section of New York City (Figure 6-40), where most of the buildings are about as tall as this one. Even though the building is by no means as sleek and mechanically elegant as the MetLife Building, it has a human scale and a humble brightness.

Three Urban Views

1. Would you prefer to live in a humble building, such as that in Figure 6-40 or in one of the buildings that create the shadows in the vicinity of the MetLife Building in Figure 6-39?
2. Do you find the placement of the building in front of the MetLife Building visually attractive? If so, why? Do you like the contrast between the pyramidal top and the flat top?
3. Suppose St. Bartholomew's Church was no longer being used for religious purposes. As a city planner, would you preserve or destroy it? Explain.

If we have been near the truth, then architects are, in a way, the shepherds of space. And to be aware of their buildings is to help, in our humble way, to preserve their work. Architects can make space a welcoming place. Such places, like a home, give us a center from which we can orient ourselves to the other places around us. And then we can feel at home anywhere.

Summary

Architecture is the creative conservation of centralized space—the power of the positioned interrelationships of things. The spatial centers of nature organize things around them, and architecture enhances these centers. Architects carve apart an inner space from an outer space in such a way that both spaces become more fully perceptible, and especially the inner space can be used for practical purposes. A work of architecture is a configurational center, a place of special value, a place to dwell. Architects must account for four basic and closely interrelated necessities: technical requirements, function, spatial relationships, and content. To succeed, their forms must adjust to these necessities. Because of the public character of architecture, moreover, the common or shared values of contemporary society usually are in a direct way a part of architects' subject matter. Architecture can be classified into four main types. Earth-rooted architecture brings out with special force the earth and its symbolisms. Such architecture appears organically related to the site, its materials, and gravity. Sky-oriented architecture brings out with special force the sky and its symbolisms. Such architecture discloses a world by drawing our attention to the sky bounded by a horizon. It accomplishes this positively by means of making a building high and centered within the sky, defying gravity, and tightly integrating the light of outer and inner space. Negatively, this kind of architecture de-emphasizes the features that accent the earth. Earth-resting architecture accents neither earth nor sky but rests on the earth, using the earth as a platform with the sky as backdrop. Earth-dominating architecture rules over the earth. There is a sense of aggression, and such buildings seem to say that humanity is the measure of all things. In recent years more and more combinations of these four types have been built.

Bibliography

Arnheim, Rudolf. *The Dynamics of Architectural Form*. Berkeley: University of California Press, 1977.

————. *The Power of the Center*. Berkeley: University of California Press, 1982.

Fletcher, Banister. *A History of Architecture on the Comparative Method*, 17th ed. New York: Scribner's, 1967.

Frampton, Kenneth. *The Poetics of Construction in Nineteenth and Twentieth Century Architecture*. Edited by John Cava. Cambridge, Mass.: MIT Press, 1996.

Giedion, Sigfried. *Space, Time and Architecture*, 5th ed. Cambridge, Mass.: Harvard University Press, 1982.

Gropius, Walter. *The New Architecture and the Bauhaus*. London: Faber and Faber, 1965.

Jordan, R. Furneaux. *A Concise History of Western Architecture*. New York: Harcourt Brace, 1978.

Heynen, Hilde. *Architecture and Modernity: A Critique*. Cambridge, Mass.: MIT Press, 1999.

Klotz, Heinrich. *The History of Postmodern Architecture*. Cambridge, Mass.: MIT Press, 1988.

Kostov, Spiro. *The City Shaped: Urban Patterns and Meanings through History*. London: Thames and Hudson, 1991.

Krell, David Farrell. *Architecture: Ecstasies of Space, Time, and the Human Body*. Albany: SUNY Press, 1997.

Le Corbusier. *Towards a New Architecture*. London: Architectural Press, 1987.

Mumford, Lewis. *The City in History*. New York: Harcourt Brace and World, 1969.

Nervi, Pier Luigi. *Aesthetics and Technology in Building*. London: Oxford University Press, 1966.

O'Gorman, James F. *ABC of Architecture*. Philadelphia: University of Pennsylvania Press, 1998.

Scully, Vincent. *Architecture: The Natural and the Man-Made*. New York: St. Martin's Press, 1991.

————. *The Earth, The Temple, and the Gods*. New Haven, Conn.: Yale University Press, 1979.

Scruton, Roger. *The Aesthetics of Architecture*. Princeton, N.J.: Princeton University Press, 1979.

Soleri, Paolo. *The City in the Image of Man*. Cambridge, Mass.: MIT Press, 1973.

Sutton, Ian. *Western Architecture: From Ancient Greece to the Present*. New York: Thames and Hudson, 1999.

Wright, Frank Lloyd. *The Living City*. New York: Horizon, 1958.

————. *Modern Architecture*. Princeton, N.J.: Princeton University Press, 1931.

AMERICAN ARCHITECTURE

http://www.bc.edu/bc_org/avp/cas/fnart/fa267/

ANCIENT GREEK ART AND ARCHITECTURE

http://harpy.uccs.edu/greek/greek.html

ARCHITECTURE SLIDE LIBRARY

http://www.mip.berkeley.edu/query_forms/browse_spiro_form.html

EUROPEAN ARCHITECTURE

http://www.bc.edu/bc_org/avp/cas/fnart/arch/

ANTONIO GAUDÍ AND ART NOUVEAU

http://www.gaudiallgaudi.com/

RENAISSANCE AND BAROQUE ARCHITECTURE

http://www.lib.virginia.edu/dic/colls/arh102/

SIR CHRISTOPHER WREN

http://www.arct.cam.ac.uk/personal-page/james/phd/wren/index.html

FRANK LLOYD WRIGHT

http://www.geocities.com/SoHo/1469/flw.html
http://www.pbs.org/flw/

CHAPTER 7

Literature

Spoken language is the basic medium of literature. As beneficiaries of the products of the printing press, invented in the fifteenth century, we rarely read aloud, and so we tend to de-emphasize the connection of literature with the sound of speech. Reading silently is faster, of course, but it may dull our ear to the sounds that "sing," the singing that helps distinguish literature from nonliterature. If you are in doubt about this, listen to a good storyteller, and observe the difference between the telling and your reading. Or get someone to read, in a foreign language you do not understand, a fine poem and a newspaper report. Or listen to a record of Dylan Thomas reciting any of his poems, especially the tones of the opening lines of "Do Not Go Gentle into That Good Night."

> Do not go gentle into that good night,
> Old age should burn and rave at close of day;
> Rage, rage against the dying of the light.

Feel your mouth, tongue, and vocal cords shaping the words, and your ear listening, as you read aloud from an old English lyric:

> The baily berith the bell away . . .

Or the first two lines of Keats' *Ode on a Grecian Urn:*

> Thou still unravish'd bride of quietness,
> Thou foster-child of silence and slow Time . . .

Or the last two lines of a poem by Emily Dickinson about a lady who bore great pain:

> And then she ceased to bear it—
> And with the Saints sat down . . .

Geoffrey Chaucer wrote down his *Canterbury Tales* for convenience, more than a century before the invention of the printing press. But he read his tales out loud to an audience of courtly listeners who were much more attuned to hearing a good story than to reading it. Today, people interested in literature are usually described as readers, which underscores the dependence we have developed on the printed word for our literary experiences. Words "sound" even when read silently, and the sound is an essential part of the sense, or meaning, of the words.

Literature, like music, dance, and film, is a serial art. In order to perceive it, we must be aware of what is happening now, remember what happened before, and anticipate what is to come. This is not so obvious with a short lyric poem or with cummings' "l(a" (page 15) because we are in the presence of something akin to a painting: It seems to be all there in front of us at once. But one word follows another; one sentence, one line, or one stanza another. There is no way to perceive the all-at-onceness of a literary work as we sometimes perceive a painting, although cummings' poem comes close.

Because of its essential sounding, literature, like painting, has a sensuous surface. And, like painting, that sensuous surface involves a subject matter. With abstract painting the subject matter is the sensuous itself— colors, lines, and the like; with representational painting, the subject matter is objects and events. Literature, like representational painting, is about objects and events, and only a smattering has as its subject matter just the sensuous sounding of the words. Words are haunted with meanings—they refer to something beyond themselves—and when words are sounded without their meanings, as when we hear a foreign language we do not understand, the soundings are usually of very little interest. The sensuousness of words, stripped of their meanings, is not nearly so rich as the sensuousness of colors or lines, stripped of their references to objects and events. Apparently no one yet has been very successful in making linguistic sensuousness by itself into works of art, although some fine poets such as Stéphane Mallarmé and Vachel Lindsay have tried. The *sine qua non* of literature is the marriage of sound and sense (reference to objects and events).

DO NOT GO GENTLE INTO THAT GOOD NIGHT

Do not go gentle into that good night,
Old age should burn and rave at close of day;
Rage, rage against the dying of the light.

Though wise men at their end know dark is right
Because their words had forked no lightning they
Do not go gentle into that good night.

Good men, the last wave by, crying how bright
Their frail deeds might have danced in a green bay,
Rage, rage against the dying of the light.

Wild men who caught and sang the sun in flight,
And learn, too late, they grieved it on its way,
Do not go gentle into that good night.

Grave men, near death, who see with blinding sight
Blind eyes could blaze like meteors and be gay,
Rage, rage against the dying of the light.

And you, my father, there on the sad height,
Curse, bless, me now with your fierce tears, I pray.
Do not go gentle into that good night.
Rage, rage against the dying of the light.

Dylan Thomas

PERCEPTION KEY   Dylan Thomas

1. What is the subject matter of Thomas's poem?
2. What is the content?
3. In the paragraph below we analyze the first stanza with reference to the merger of sound and sense. Analyze the following stanzas.

We can describe the subject matter and form, but we can only point to the content, allude to it, paraphrase it, for the content is *being said* in the poem and can only be said in the poem. There is no other way of saying it, because to change even one word changes the sound, and changing the sound changes the meaning and, in turn, the content. For example, substitute "death" for "that good night" in the first line, for that is what the phrase means literally. Notice how the rhythm of not only that line but also the two that follow is spoiled, and how the meaning of "light" in line three loses some significance because its connection with "day" (life) in the second line is loosened. Furthermore, notice how the *g* sound of "good" is tied to "gentle" in the first line, and how these soft *g* sounds help accent by contrast the hard *r* sounds of the "Rage, rage" in the third line. The sounds of these lines add weight to the words, enhance their significance, charge them with meaning. Sound and sense are trapped together in the cage of form, and they cannot be separated without loss of content. That is why literature cannot be translated without loss or change. The subject matter can be described: a boy's agony in face of his dying father's submissiveness. And much can be said about the form: the way, for instance, the sounds are organized and how they relate to the sense. But with respect to the meaning of the poem—the content—we must return to the poem and allow it to speak.

PERCEPTION KEY   "The Lotus Eaters"

The last four lines of the first section of the Choric Song of Tennyson's poem are

Here are cool mosses deep,
And thro' the moss the ivies creep,
And in the stream the long-leaved flowers weep,
And from the craggy ledge the poppy hangs in sleep.

We are given a vivid image of sleep. How is this accomplished?

The languid texture of the words, especially the soft hush of the *o*'s and *s*'s; the smoothness of the *assonance* (the sound of the vowels) and alliteration (the sound of the consonants); the slow, regular iambic rhythm (units of two syllables with the stress on the second syllable); the gradual lengthening of the lines; and the gentle tones of quietness make up the sensuous surface. The meanings of the words, as enmeshed in that sounding surface, evoke images of a calm, cool, dreamy river valley — nature "falling to sleep." We know lassitude and sleep, of course, but Tennyson presents us with an imaginary scene that shows us lassitude and sleep in such a vivid way — if we participate — that we become more sensitive to the unwinding of the tensions of life.

The "showing" in Tennyson's poem is indirect, of course, for we must imagine that river valley, and only the sounding of the language is directly perceptible. In this respect, literature always differs from representational painting, for with this kind of painting both surface and image are directly perceptible. We see Giorgione's *Sleeping Venus* (Figure 2-17); we imagine Tennyson's sleepy valley. The freedom of the literary image from the directly perceptible allows the literary imagination a much larger range than the pictorial imagination. Although literature has much less sensuous appeal than painting, the almost unlimited scope of verbal reference lays open the whole field of human experience. Listen to Marcel Proust, one of the greatest of novelists, on the scope of literature:

> [The novelist] sets free within us all the joys and sorrows in the world, a few of which, only, we should have to spend years of our actual life in getting to know, and the keenest, the most intense of which would never have been revealed to us because the slow course of their development stops our perception of them. It is the same in life; the heart changes, and that is our worst misfortune; but we learn of it only from reading or by imagination; for in reality its alteration, like that of certain natural phenomena, is so gradual that, even if we are able to distinguish, successively, each of its different states, we are still spared the actual sensation of change.[1]

More than any other art, literature, and especially the novel, reveals "all the joys and sorrows in the world." Literature — with broader scope than any other art — can bring lucidity to the vast complexities of the human spirit.

Like architecture, a work of literature is, in one sense, a construction of separable elements. The details of a scene, a character or event, or a group of symbols can be conceived of as the bricks in the wall of a literary structure. If one of these details is imperfectly perceived, our understanding of the function of that detail — and, in turn, of the total structure — will be incomplete. The *theme* (main idea) of a literary work is usually a structural decision, comparable to the architectural decision about the kind of space being enclosed. Decisions about the sound of the language, the characters, the events, the setting, are comparable to the decisions regarding the materials, size, shape, and landscape of architecture. It is helpful to think of

---

[1]*Swann's Way*, trans C. K. Scott Moncrieff (New York: Modern Library, 1928), p. 118f.

literature as works composed of elements that can be discussed individually in order to gain a more thorough perception of them. And it is equally important to realize that the discussion of these individual elements leads to a fuller understanding of the whole structure. Details are organized into parts, and these, in turn, are organized into the structure.

Our structural emphasis in the following pages will be on the narrative—both the episodic narrative, in which all or most of the parts are loosely interrelated, and the organic narrative, in which the parts are tightly interrelated. Once we have explored some of the basic structures of literature, we will examine some of the more important details. In everyday language situations, what we say is often what we mean. But in a work of literature, language is rarely that simple. Language has *denotation,* a literal level where words mean what they obviously say, and *connotation,* a subtler level where words mean more than they obviously say. When we are being denotative, we say the rose is sick and mean nothing more than that. But if we are using language connotatively, we might mean any of several things by such a statement. When the poet William Blake says the rose is sick, he is describing a symbolic rose, something very different from a literal rose (see pages 223–224). Blake may mean that the rose is morally sick, spiritually defective, and that in some ways we are the rose. The image, metaphor, symbol, and diction (word choices) are the main details of literary language that will be examined. All are found in poetry, fiction, drama, and even the essay.

Literary Structures

THE NARRATIVE AND THE NARRATOR

The *narrative* is a story told to an audience by a teller controlling the order of events and the emphasis those events receive. Most narratives concentrate upon the events. But some narratives have little action: They reveal depth of character through responses to action. Sometimes the *narrator* is a character in the fiction; sometimes the narrator pretends an awareness of an audience other than the reader. However, the author controls the narrator and through the narrator leads the reader. Participate with the following narrative poem by D. H. Lawrence:

PIANO

Softly, in the dusk, a woman is singing to me;
Taking me back down the vista of years, till I see
A child sitting under the piano, in the boom of the tingling strings
And pressing the small, poised feet of a mother who smiles as she sings.

In spite of myself, the insidious mastery of song
Betrays me back, till the heart of me weeps to belong
To the old Sunday evenings at home, with winter outside
And hymns in the cozy parlor, the tinkling piano our guide.

So now it is vain for the singer to burst into clamor
With the great black piano appassionato. The glamor
Of childish days is upon me, my manhood is cast
Down by the flood of remembrance, I weep like a child for the past.

> **PERCEPTION KEY** "Piano"
>
> 1. Which is more fully developed, events or character? Or are they roughly equally important?
> 2. What do we know about the narrator?
> 3. Is the narrator D. H. Lawrence? Does it make a significant difference to your understanding of the poem to know that answer? Why or why not?

Lawrence's poem relates events that are interesting mainly because they reveal something about the character of the narrator, especially his double focus as man and as child, with all the ambiguities that the narrator's memory evokes. If your background information includes something about the life of D. H. Lawrence, you probably will identify Lawrence as the narrator. The poem certainly has autobiographical roots: Lawrence's closeness to his mother evokes in our participation a dimension of poignancy. Yet if we did not have this information, not much would be lost. The revelation of the narrator's character is general in the sense that most of us understand and sympathize with the narrator's feelings, no matter whether the narrator is Lawrence.

The following poem is a powerful example of the way in which Sylvia Plath uses the first-person narrator while creating an "I" character who is not herself. The poem is told by someone in an iron lung:

PARALYTIC

It happens. Will it go on?—
My mind a rock,
No fingers to grip, no tongue,
My god the iron lung

That loves me, pumps
My two
Dust bags in and out,
Will not

Let me relapse
While the day outside glares by like ticker tape
The night brings violets,
Tapestries of eyes,

Lights,
The soft anonymous
Talkers: "You all right?"
The starched, inaccessible breast.

Dead egg, I lie
Whole
On a whole world I cannot touch,
At the white, tight

Drum of my sleeping couch
Photographs visit me—
My wife, dead and flat, in 1920 furs,
Mouth full of pearls,

Two girls
As flat as she, who whisper "We're your daughters."
The still waters
Wrap my lips,

Eyes, nose and ears,
A clear
Cellophane I cannot crack.
On my bare back

I smile, a buddha, all
Wants, desire
Falling from me like rings
Hugging their lights.

The claw
Of the magnolia,
Drunk on its own scents,
Asks nothing of life.

PERCEPTION KEY "Paralytic"

1. Analyze the narrative. What are the limitations of telling a story from the point of view of a person who is paralyzed?
2. What is the role of the magnolia claw—a living but not a moving instrument, (unlike people's hands)—in the poem?
3. Explore some of the implications of the fact that the narrator of the poem is an imaginary character invented by the poet. Is this information crucial to a full understanding of the poem?
4. Sylvia Plath committed suicide not long after writing this poem. Does that information add intensity to your experience of the poem?

THE EPISODIC NARRATIVE

The term *episodic* describes one of the oldest kinds of literature, embodied by *epics* such as Homer's *Odyssey*. We are aware of the overall structure of the story centering on the adventures of Odysseus, but each adventure is almost a complete entity in itself. We develop a clear sense of the character of Odysseus as we follow him in his adventures, but this does not always happen in episodic literature. The adventures sometimes are not only completely disconnected from one another, but the thread that is intended to connect everything—the personality of the *protagonist* (the main character)—also may not be strong enough to keep things together.

Sometimes the character may even seem to be a different person from one episode to the next. This is often the case in oral literature, compositions by people who told or sang traditional stories rather than by people who wrote their narratives. In oral literature, the tellers or singers may have gathered adventures from many sources and joined them in one long narrative. The likelihood of disconnectedness in such a situation is quite high. But disconnectedness is sometimes desirable. It may offer several things: compression, speed of pacing, and variety of action that sustains attention. Some of the most famous episodic narratives are novels: Cervantes' *Don Quixote,* Fielding's *Tom Jones,* Defoe's *Moll Flanders,* and Saul Bellow's *The Adventures of Augie March*.

Novels and epics are not the only literary modes to use episodic structures, nor are all episodic structures long works. One very popular episodic structure is the ballad. It usually tells a story about a hero or heroine, and it often fails to respect strict chronology or consistency of events. Since it was originally sung in the streets and byways of Europe, the ballad tends to be a casual genre. Heroes die in stanza four only to show up again hale and hearty in stanza eight. Such poems were usually the work of several wandering singers, each wishing to contribute something without undoing the work of predecessors.

THE ORGANIC NARRATIVE

The term *organic* implies close connectedness in the parts of the structure. Most novels, for example, at least until the twentieth century, move from one incident to the next chronologically, and the later incident presupposes the earlier. But even when the chronology of events is awry, the incidents may still have an organic unity because of a strong coherence of theme or character. Read aloud, for example, Langston Hughes' "Ballad of the Landlord."

BALLAD OF THE LANDLORD

Landlord, Landlord,
My roof has sprung a leak.
Don't you 'member I told you about it
Way last Week?

Landlord, Landlord.
These steps is broken down.
When you come up yourself
It's a wonder you don't fall down.

Ten bucks you say I owe you?
Ten bucks you say is due?
Well, that's Ten bucks more'n I'll pay you
Till you fix this house up new.

What? You gonna get eviction orders?
You gonna cut off my heat?
You gonna take my furniture and
Throw it on the street?

Um-huh! You talking high and mighty.
Talk on—till you get through.
You ain't gonna be able to say a word
If I land my fist on you.

Police! Police!
Come and get this man!
He's trying to ruin the government
And overturn the land!
Patrol bell!
Arrest!

Precinct Station.
Iron cell.
Headlines in press.
MAN THREATENS LANDLORD
TENANT HELD NO BAIL
JUDGE GIVES NEGRO 90 DAYS IN COUNTY JAIL.

The first five stanzas are not strictly chronological, for they might be re-arranged—especially stanzas three, four, and five—without great loss of meaning. Yet the next two stanzas and especially the last three lines clearly lay out the time frame. Moreover, each stanza is clearly allied to the others with reference to character (greedy landlord) and theme (white prejudice). The poem is basically organically structured, despite the episodic nature of the first five stanzas.

PERCEPTION KEY   "Piano" and "Paralytic"

1. Is "Piano" episodically or organically structured? What about "Paralytic"? Does the brevity of such poems negate the sense of episodes or disconnected parts?
2. Aristotle considered episodic structure to be second-rate. Why would he do so? Do you agree?

Most novels and almost all short stories are organically structured. For an example of a fine short story—Boccaccio's *The Pot of Basil*—see www. mhhe.com/humanitiesthroughthearts for the complete text and accompanying Perception Key.

THE QUEST NARRATIVE

The quest narrative is simple enough on the surface: A protagonist sets out in search of something valuable that must be found at all cost. Such, in simple terms, is the plot of almost every adventure yarn and adventure film ever written. However, where most such yarns and films content themselves with erecting impossible obstacles which the heroes overcome with courage, imagination, and skill, the quest narrative has other virtues. Herman Melville's *Moby Dick*, the story of Ahab's determination to find and kill the white whale that took his leg, is also a quest narrative. It achieves unity by focusing on the quest and its object. But at the same time it explores in great depth the psychology of all those who take part in the adventure. Ahab becomes a monomaniac, a man who obsessively concentrates on one thing. The narrator, Ishmael, is like an Old Testament prophet in that he has lived the experience, has looked into the face of evil, and has come back to tell the story to anyone who will listen, hoping to impart wisdom and sensibility to those who were not there. The novel is centered on the question of good and evil. When the novel begins, those values seem fairly clear and fairly well defined. But as the novel progresses, the question becomes murkier and murkier because the actions of the novel begin a reversal of values that is often a hallmark of the quest narrative.

Because most humans feel uncertain about their own nature—where they have come from, who they are, where they are going—it is natural that writers from all cultures should invent fictions that string adventures and character development on the thread of the quest for self-understanding. This quest attracts our imaginations and sustains our attention. Then the author can broaden and deepen the meaning of the quest until it engages our concepts of ourselves. As a result, the reader usually identifies with the protagonist.

The quest structure in Ralph Ellison's *Invisible Man* is so deeply rooted in the novel that the protagonist has no name. We know a great deal about him because he narrates the story and tells us about himself. He is black, Southern, and, as a young college student, ambitious. His earliest heroes are George Washington Carver and Booker T. Washington. He craves the dignity and the opportunity he associates with their lives. But things go wrong. He is dismissed unjustly from his college in the South and must leave home to seek his fortune. He imagines himself destined for better things and eagerly pursues his fate, finding a place to live and work up North, beginning to find his identity as a black man. He discovers the sophisticated urban society of New York City, the political subtleties of communism, the complexities of black nationalism, and the realities of his relationship to white people, to whom he is an invisible man. Yet he does not hate the whites, and in his own image of himself he remains an invisible man. The novel ends with the protagonist in an underground place he has found and which he has lighted, by tapping the lines of the electric company, with almost 200 electric lightbulbs. Despite this colossal illumination, he still cannot think of himself as visible. He ends his quest without discovering who he is beyond this fundamental fact: He is invisible. Black or white, we can identify in many ways with this quest, for Ellison is showing us that invisibility is in all of us.

| PERCEPTION KEY | The Quest Narrative |

Read a quest narrative. Some suggestions: Ralph Ellison, *Invisible Man;* Mark Twain, *The Adventures of Huckleberry Finn;* Herman Melville, *Moby Dick;* J. D. Salinger, *The Catcher in the Rye;* Graham Greene, *The Third Man;* Franz Kafka, *The Castle;* Albert Camus, *The Stranger;* and Toni Morrison, *Beloved.* How does the quest help the protagonist get to know himself or herself better? Does the quest help you understand yourself better? Is the quest novel you have read basically episodic or organic in structure?

The quest narrative is central to American culture. Mark Twain's *Huckleberry Finn* is one of the most important examples in American literature. But, whereas *Invisible Man* is an organic quest narrative, because the details of the novel are closely interwoven, *Huckleberry Finn* is an episodic quest narrative. Huck's travels along the great Mississippi River qualify as episodic in the same sense that *Don Quixote*, to which this novel is closely related, is episodic. Huck is questing for freedom for Jim, but also for freedom from his own father. Like Don Quixote, Huck comes back from his quest richer in the knowledge of who he is. One might say Don Quixote's quest is for the truth about who he is and was, since he is an old man when he begins. But Huck is an adolescent, and so his quest is for knowledge of who he is and can be.

THE LYRIC

The *lyric* structure, virtually always a poem, primarily reveals a limited but deep feeling about some thing or event. The lyric is often associated with the feelings of the poet, although we have already seen (in Plath's "Paralytic") that it is not difficult for poets to create narrators distinct from themselves and to explore hypothetical feelings.

If we participate we find ourselves caught up in the emotional situation of the lyric. It is usually revealed to us through a recounting of the circumstances the poet reflects on. T. S. Eliot speaks of an *objective correlative:* an object that correlates with the poet's feeling and helps express that feeling. Eliot has said that poets must find the image, situation, object, event, or person that "shall be the formula for that *particular* emotion" so that readers can comprehend it. This may be too narrow a view of the poet's creative process, because poets can understand and interpret emotions without necessarily undergoing them. Otherwise, it would seem that Shakespeare, for example, and even Eliot would have blown up like overcompressed boilers if they had had to experience directly all the feelings they interpreted in their poems. But, in any case, it seems clear that the lyric has feeling—emotion, passion, or mood—as basic in its subject matter.

The word "lyric" implies a personal statement by an involved writer who feels deeply. In a limited sense, lyrics are poems to be sung to music. Most lyrics before the seventeenth century were set to music—in fact, most medieval and Renaissance lyrics were written to be sung with musical accompaniment. And the writers who composed the words were usually the composers of the music—at least until the seventeenth century, when specialization began to separate those functions.

John Keats (1795–1821), an English poet of the Romantic period, died of tuberculosis. The following *sonnet*,[2] written in 1818, is grounded in his awareness of early death:

When I have fears that I may cease to be
Before my pen has glean'd my teeming brain,
Before high-piled books, in charact'ry,
Hold like rich garners the full-ripen'd grain;
When I behold, upon the night's starr'd face,
Huge cloudy symbols of a high romance,
And think that I may never live to trace
Their shadows, with the magic hand of chance;
And when I feel, fair creature of an hour!
That I shall never look upon thee more,
Never have relish in the faery power
Of unreflecting love! then on the shore
Of the wide world I stand alone, and think
Till love and fame to nothingness do sink.

PERCEPTION KEY   "When I Have Fears . . ."

1. This poem has no setting (environmental context), yet it establishes an atmosphere of uncertainty and, possibly, of terror. How does Keats create this atmosphere?
2. The poet is dying and knows he is dying—why does he then labor so over the rhyme and meter of this poem? What does the poem do for the dying narrator?

Keats interprets a terrible personal feeling. He realizes he may die before he can write his best poems. The epitaph Keats chose for his headstone just before he died is "Here lies one whose name was writ in water." He was wrong in believing that his poems would not be read by posterity. Moreover, his work is so brilliant that we cannot help wondering what else he might have done. Had Chaucer, Shakespeare, Milton, Proust, or Joyce died at twenty-six, we might not know their names, for their important work was yet to come.

It is not difficult for us to imagine how Keats must have felt. The lyric mode does not usually rely on narrative, but on our ability to respond to the circumstances described. In this poem, Keats has important resources. One is the fact that since we all will die, we can sympathize with the thought of death cutting a life's work short. The tone Keats establishes in the poem—

[2]A poem of fourteen lines typically in *iambic pentameter* with patterned rhyme, as with the Keats. An iamb is a metrical unit or foot of two syllables, the first unaccented and the second accented. Pentameter is a line of five metrical feet. Thus ˘´˘´˘´˘´˘´. *Rhyme* is the regular reoccurrence of corresponding sounds, especially at the end of lines.

one of direct speech, honestly said, not overdone or melodramatic—helps him communicate his emotions. It gives the poem an immediacy: one human being telling another something straight from the heart. Keats modulates the tone slightly, slowing things down enough at the end of the poem for us to sense and share the despairing contemplative mood "to nothingness do sink."

An entirely different mood established by quite different means characterizes the next poem. It was written in the second half of the nineteenth century by a Jesuit priest. It is very personal but also, like the psalms of the Bible, something of a prayer or hymn of praise.

PIED BEAUTY

Glory be to God for dappled things—
  For skies of couple-colour as a brinded cow;
    or rose-moles all in stipple upon trout that swim;
Fresh-firecoal chestnut-falls; finches' wings;
  Landscape plotted and pieced—fold, fallow, and plough;
    And all trades, their gear and tackle and trim.

All things counter, original, spare, strange;
  Whatever is fickle, freckled (who knows how?)
    With swift, slow; sweet, sour; adazzle, dim;

He fathers-forth whose beauty is past change:
Praise him.[3]

Gerard Manley Hopkins

PERCEPTION KEY   "Pied Beauty"

1. Hopkins reveals joy in this poem. How? Are any details inconsistent with joyousness?
2. Is the awareness of the sensory images essential in our experience of the poem?
3. Query people who have read the poem under circumstances similar to yours; then query people who come to it cold. How different is their understanding of the poem?
4. God is referred to as him rather than Him in the last line. Is this simply a printer's convention? What does it mean to call this poem a religious lyric?

The usefulness of the lyric for bringing out the significance of things as felt meditatively—Wordsworth's "emotion recollected in tranquility"—is so great that perhaps this is its most important purpose. It is a mode that in its self-awareness can explore leisurely those aspects of things that help clarify feelings. Without necessarily having a story to tell, the poet need not rush off into anything that is not central to the meditation itself. One fa-

[3]*Pied:* spotted, like "dappled" and "couple-colour." *Brinded:* spots or streaks on a buff-colored background. *Chestnut falls:* the skin of the hot chestnut, stripped off. *Plotted and pieced:* fields of different shaped rectangles. *Fold, fallow,* and *plough:* fields used for different purposes and that look different to the eye.

mous meditative poem is Walt Whitman's "A Noiseless Patient Spider," a poem that is perhaps as much a tribute to the patience of Walt Whitman as it is to the spider. Out of Whitman's contemplation of the spider comes insight into the human soul.

A NOISELESS PATIENT SPIDER

A noiseless patient spider,
I mark'd where on a little promontory it stood isolated,
Mark'd how to explore the vacant vast surrounding,
It launch'd forth filament, filament, filament, out of itself,
Ever unreeling them, ever tirelessly speeding them.

And you O my soul where you stand,
Surrounded, detached, in measureless oceans of space,
Ceaselessly musing, venturing, throwing, seeking the spheres to connect them,
Till the bridge you will need be form'd, till the ductile anchor hold,
Till the gossamer thread you fling catch somewhere, O my soul.

PERCEPTION KEY   "A Noiseless Patient Spider"

1. Whitman sees a connection between the spider and the human soul. What, exactly, is that connection? How reasonable does it seem to you? How illuminating?
2. In what sense does Witman connect people with nature in this poem? What is the meaning of such a connection?

The four lyrics that follow are notable for their rich use of *imagery* and *metaphor*. William Blake's "The Tyger" is almost surreal in its intense visual imagery, perhaps in part because Blake was by profession a visual artist and illustrated this and other poems with brilliant color and imagination. For Blake, the "tyger" represents a dark force in nature, one he attempts to understand. William Butler Yeats believed that "The Lake Isle of Innisfree" was the first poem in which he achieved genuine poetic music. Interestingly, the poem has been set to music by several composers. Its imagery, derived from its rural location in the west of Ireland, is contrasted with imagery of the urban London environment ("pavements gray") where the poem was written. Siegfried Sassoon's "Attack" is in stark contrast with these lyrics, focusing as it does on the machinery of war. Sassoon survived the war, but his work is forever connected with it. Louise Glück's "Vespers" is one of her several meditative religious poems. This one seems to be addressed specifically to God and relies on the richness of agricultural imagery for its effect. Implied in the poem's imagery is a serious question that Glück poses but does not resolve.

THE TYGER

Tyger! Tyger! burning bright
In the forests of the night,
What immortal hand or eye
Could frame thy fearful symmetry?

In what distant deeps or skies
Burnt the fire of thine eyes?
On what wings dare he aspire?
What the hand dare seize the fire?

And what shoulder, and what art,
Could twist the sinews of thy heart?
And when thy heart began to beat,
What dread hand? and what dread feet?

What the hammer? what the chain?
In what furnace was thy brain?
What the anvil? what dread grasp
Dare its deadly terrors clasp?

When the stars threw down their spears,
And water'd heaven with their tears,
Did he smile his work to see?
Did he who made the Lamb make thee?

Tyger! Tyger! burning bright
In the forests of the night,
What immortal hand or eye
Dare frame thy fearful symmetry?

William Blake

THE LAKE ISLE OF INNISFREE

I will arise and go now, and go to Innisfree,
And a small cabin build there, of clay and wattles made:
Nine bean-rows will I have there, a hive for the honeybee,
And live alone in the bee-loud glade.

And I shall have some peace there, for peace comes dropping slow,
Dropping from the veils of the morning to where the cricket sings;
There midnight's all a glimmer, and noon a purple glow,
And evening full of the linnet's wings.

I will arise and go now, for always night and day
I hear lake water lapping with low sounds by the shore;
While I stand on the roadway, or on the pavements gray,
I hear it in the deep heart's core.

William Butler Yeats

ATTACK

At dawn the ridge emerges massed and dun
In the wild purple of the glow'ring sun,
Smoldering through spouts of drifting smoke that shroud
The menacing scarred slope; and, one by one,
Tanks creep and topple forward to the wire.
The barrage roars and lifts. Then, clumsily bowed
With bombs and guns and shovels and battle-gear,
Men jostle and climb to meet the bristling fire.
Lines of gray, muttering faces, masked with fear,

They leave their trenches, going over the top,
While time ticks blank and busy on their wrists,
And hope, with furtive eyes and grappling fists,
Flounders in mud. O Jesus, make it stop!

Siegfried Sassoon

VESPERS

More than you love me, very possibly
you love the beasts of the field, even,
possibly, the field itself, in August dotted
with wild chicory and aster:
I know. I have compared myself
to those flowers, their range of feeling
so much smaller and without issue; also to white sheep,
actually gray: I am uniquely
suited to praise you. Then why
torment me? I study the hawkweed,
the buttercup protected from the grazing herd
by being poisonous: is pain
your gift to make me
conscious in my need of you, as though
I must need you to worship you,
or have you abandoned me
in favor of the field, the stoic lambs turning
silver in twilight; waves of wild aster and chicory shining
pale blue and deep blue, since you already know
how like your raiment it is.

Louise Glück

PERCEPTION KEY   Varieties of Lyric

1. What feelings (emotions, passions, or moods) does each poem evoke?
2. Which two lyrics seem most different to you? What constitutes their differences? Comment on use of language, rhythm, imagery.
3. Of these four lyrics, which would you most want to set to music? If possible, either sing that lyric yourself (make up your own tune or rely on a tune you know) or listen to someone sing the lyric. What difference in emotional response do you detect in listening to the lyric as it is sung? Comment on the relationship of the music to the words of the lyric.
4. Lyrics are often noted for their appeal to our emotions. Which of these poems appeals to you most powerfully? Compare your choice with the choices of others. What factors seem to affect the differences in yours and your peers' choices?
5. Comment on the poems whose imagery seems to you to be most powerful. What senses do these images appeal to? How does the imagery help convey the significance of the poem?

Literary Details

So far we have been analyzing literature with reference to structure, the overall order. But within every structure are details that need close examination in order to properly perceive the structure.

Language is used in literature in ways that differ from everyday uses. This is not to say that literature is artificial and unrelated to the language we speak but, rather, that we sometimes do not see the fullest implications of our speech and rarely take full advantage of the opportunities language affords us. Literature uses language to reveal meanings that are usually absent from daily speech.

Our examination of detail will be restricted to image, metaphor, symbol, and diction. They are central to literature of all *genres*.

IMAGE

An image in language asks us to imagine or "picture" what is referred to or being described. An image appeals essentially to our sense of sight, but sound, taste, odor, and touch are sometimes involved. One of the most striking resources of language is its capacity to help us reconstruct in our imagination the "reality" of perceptions. This resource sometimes is as important in prose as in poetry. Consider, for example, the following passage from Joseph Conrad's *Youth*:

> The boats, fast astern, lay in a deep shadow, and all around I could see the circle of the sea lighted by the fire. A gigantic flame arose forward straight and clear. It flares fierce, with noises like the whirr of wings, with rumbles as of thunder. There were cracks, detonations, and from the cone of flame the sparks flew upwards, as man is born to trouble, to leaky ships, and to ships that burn.

PERCEPTION KEY   Conrad's *Youth*

1. Which of our senses is most powerfully appealed to in this passage?
2. How does this passage differ from the average, nonliterary description of a burning boat? If possible read a newspaper description of a burning boat (or perhaps one written by you or one of your friends) that does not try to involve the reader in the occurrence itself. What are the differences between it and Conrad's passage? Compare especially the use of images.

In *Youth* this scene is fleeting, only an instant in the total structure of the book. But the entire book is composed of such details, helping to engage the reader's participation.

Virginia Woolf, in the following passage from her novel *To the Lighthouse*, has Lily thinking about Mrs. Ramsay's thoughts on her philosopher-husband's mind. In the process, she constructs images that reflect the activity of the bees in her garden as well as the activity of Mr. Ramsay's thoughts.

Nothing happened. Nothing! Nothing! as she leant her head against Mrs. Ramsay's knee. And yet, she knew knowledge and wisdom were stored up in Mrs. Ramsay's heart. How then, she had asked herself, did one know one thing or another thing about people, sealed as they were? Only like a bee, drawn by some sweetness or sharpness in the air intangible to touch or taste, one haunted the dome-shaped hive, ranged the wastes of the air over the countries of the world alone, and then haunted the hives with their murmurs and their stirrings; the hives, which were people. Mrs. Ramsay rose. Lily rose. Mrs. Ramsay went. For days there hung about her, as after a dream some subtle change is felt in the person one has dreamt of, more vividly than anything she said, the sound of murmuring and, as she sat in the wicker arm-chair in the drawing-room window she wore, to Lily's eyes, an august shape; the shape of a dome.

In this passage, the dome-shaped hive is metaphorically related to the dome-shaped head of Mr. Ramsay, whose thoughts, like bees, "range the wastes of the air over the countries of the world alone." The murmurings and stirrings of the bees that sound in her garden are appropriate to the murmurings and stirrings of the thoughts of the philosopher. The use of the verb "rose" in "Mrs. Ramsay rose. Lily rose." also implies a garden image, just as does the name Lily, Mrs. Ramsay's friend. Lily is a painter; and when she reflects on this moment, she imagines Mrs. Ramsay as "an august shape; the shape of a dome," which for the reader of the novel underscores Mrs. Ramsay's own intelligence, which Mr. Ramsay usually downplays. These images are subtle, like most of Woolf's imagery, and they intensify the significance of the story, which helps us understand the values of the socially devalued world of Mrs. Ramsay.

IN A STATION OF THE METRO

The apparition of these faces in the crowd.
Petals on a wet, black bough.

The Metro is the Paris subway. The poem makes no comment about the character of these faces. The poem simply asks us to "image" the scene; we must reconstruct it in our imagination. And in doing so we visualize with clarity one aspect of the appearance of these faces: They are like petals on a wet, black bough. Such comparisons are metaphoric.

Archibald MacLeish, poet and critic, points out in *Poetry and Experience* that not all images in poetry work metaphorically — that is, as a comparison of two things. This may be the case even when the images are placed side by side. Thus in a grave in John Donne's "The Relic" "a loving couple lies," and there is this marvelous line: "A bracelet of bright hair about the bone. . . ." The image of a bracelet of bright hair is coupled with an image of a bone. The images lie side by side, tied by the *b* sounds. Their coupling is startling because of the immediacy of their contrasting associations: vital life and inevitable death. There is no metaphor here (something like something else in some significant way). There is simply one image juxtaposed beside another. We hear or read through the sounds — but never leave them — into their references, through the references to the images they create, through the images to their relationship, and finally to the poignant meaning: Even young girls with golden hair die. We all know that, of course, but now we face it, and feel it, because of the meaning generated by those images lying side by side: life, death, beauty, and sorrow bound together in that unforgettable grave.

John Donne

1. Suppose the word "blonde" were substituted for "bright." Would the meaning of the line be enhanced or diminished? Why?
2. Suppose the word "white" were placed in front of "bone." Would the meaning of the line be enhanced or diminished? Why?

In his use of imagery, Pound was influenced by Chinese and Japanese poets. The following poem is by the Chinese poet Tu Mu (803–852):

THE RETIRED OFFICIAL YÜAN'S HIGH PAVILION

The West River's watershed sounds beyond the sky.
Shadows of pines in front of the studio sweep the clouds flat.
Who shall coax me to blow the long flute
Leaning together on the spring wind with the moonbeams for our toys?

"The Retired Official Yüan's High Pavilion"

1. Obviously images are basic to this poem. How do they work in your imagination?
2. Do the images of Tu Mu's poem work more like the images of Donne's poem or those of Pound's? Explain.

METAPHOR

Metaphor helps writers intensify language. Metaphor is a comparison designed to heighten our perception of the things compared. Poets or writers will usually let us know which of the things compared is the main object of their attention. For example, in the following poem Shakespeare compares his age to the autumn of the year and himself to a glowing fire that consumes its vitality. The structure of this sonnet is marked by developing one metaphor in each of three quatrains (a group of four rhyming lines) and a couplet that offers a kind of summation of the entire poem.

SONNET 73

That time of year thou mayst in me behold
When yellow leaves, or none, or few, do hang
Upon those boughs which shake against the cold,
Bare ruined choirs, where late the sweet birds sang.
In me thou see'st the twilight of such day
As after sunset fadeth in the west,
Which by and by black night doth take away,
Death's second self, that seals up all in rest.
In me thou see'st the glowing of such fire

That on the ashes of his youth doth lie,
As the death-bed whereon it must expire,
Consumed with that which it was nourished by.
    This thou perceiv'st, which makes thy love more strong,
    To love that well which thou must leave ere long.

            William Shakespeare

PERCEPTION KEY   Shakespeare's 73rd Sonnet

1. The first metaphor compares the narrator's age with autumn. How are "yellow leaves, or none" appropriate for comparison with a man's age? What is implied by the comparison? The "bare ruined choirs" are the high place in the church—what place, physically, would they compare with in a man's body?
2. The second metaphor is the "sunset" fading "in the west." What is this compared with in a man's life? Why is the imagery of the second quatrain so effective?
3. The third metaphor is the "glowing" fire. What is the point of this metaphor? What is meant by the fire's consuming "that which it was nourished by"? What is being consumed here?
4. Why does the conclusion of the poem follow logically from the metaphors developed in the first three quatrains?

The standard definition of the metaphor is that it is a comparison made without any explicit words to tell us a comparison is being made. The *simile* is the kind of comparison that has explicit words: "like," "as," "than," "as if," and a few others. We have no trouble recognizing the simile, and we may get so used to reading similes in literature that we recognize them without any special degree of awareness.

Although there is some difference between a metaphor and a simile, basically both are forms of comparison for effect. Our discussion, then, will use the general term "metaphor" and use the more specific term "simile" only when necessary. However, symbols, which are also metaphoric, will be treated separately, since their effect is usually much more specialized than that of the nonsymbolic metaphor.

The use of metaphor pervades all cultures. Daily conversation—none too literary—nevertheless is full of metaphoric language used to emphasize our points and give color and feeling to our speech (check this for yourself). The Chinese poet Li Ho (791–817) shows us the power of the metaphor in a poetic tradition very different from that of the West.

THE GRAVE OF LITTLE SU

I ride a coach with lacquered sides,
My love rides a dark piebald horse.
Where shall we bind our hearts as one?
On West Mound, beneath the pines and cypresses.
    (Ballad ascribed to the singing girl Little Su, circa 500 A.D.).

Dew on the secret orchid
No thing to bind the heart to.
Misted flowers I cannot bear to cut.
Grass like a cushion,
The pine like a parasol:
The wind is a skirt,
The waters are tinkling pendants.
A coach with lacquered sides
Waits for someone in the evening.
Cold blue candle-flames
Strain to shine bright.
Beneath West Mound
The wind puffs the rain.

Little Su was important to the narrator, but the portrayal of his feeling for her is oblique—which is, perhaps, why so many metaphors appear in such a short poem. Instead of striking bluntly and immediately, the metaphoric language resounds with nuances, so that we are aware of its cumulative impact only after reading and rereading.

Metaphor pervades poetry, but we do not always realize how extensive the device is in other kinds of literature. Prose fiction, drama, essays, and almost every other form of writing use metaphors. Poetry in general, however, tends to have a higher metaphoric density than other forms of writing, partly because poetry is somewhat distilled and condensed to begin with. Rarely, however, is the density of metaphor quite as thick as in "The Grave of Little Su."

Since literature depends so heavily on metaphor, it is essential that we reflect on its use. One kind of metaphor tends to evoke an image and involves us mainly on a perceptual level—because we perceive in our imagination something of what we would perceive were we there. This kind we shall call a *perceptual metaphor*. Another kind of metaphor tends to evoke ideas, gives us information that is mainly conceptual. This kind of metaphor we shall call a *conceptual metaphor*. To tell us the pine is like a parasol is basically perceptual: Were we there, we would see that the cone shape of the pine resembles that of a parasol. But to tell us the wind is a skirt is to go far beyond perception and simple likeness. The metaphor lures us to reflect upon the suggestion that the wind resembles a skirt, and we begin to think about the ways in which this might be true. Then we are lured further—this is an enticing metaphor—to explore the implications of this truth. If the wind is like a skirt, what then is its significance in the poem? In what ways does this conceptual metaphor help us to understand the poet's insights at the grave of Little Su? In what ways does the perceptual metaphor of the pine and parasol help us?

The answer to how the wind is a skirt is by no means simple. Its complexity is one of the precious qualities of this poem. It is also one of the most precious possibilities of strong conceptual metaphors generally, for then one goes beyond the relatively simple perceptual comparison into the more suggestive and significant acts of understanding. We suggest, for instance, that if the wind is like a skirt, it clothes a girl: Little Su. But Little

Su is dead, so perhaps it clothes her spirit. The comparison then is between the wind and the spirit. Both are impossible to see, but the relationships between their meanings can be understood and felt.

The same kind of complexity is present in Tu Mu's poem, "The Retired Official Yüan's High Pavilion." The last line suggests that the moonbeams are toys. The metaphor is quiet, restrained, but as direct as the wind–skirt metaphor. Moreover, the last line suggests that the wind is something that can be leaned against. Turn back to that poem to see just how these metaphors expand the mysterious quality of the poem.

SYMBOL

The *symbol* is a further use of metaphor. Being a metaphor, it is a comparison between two things; but unlike most perceptual and conceptual metaphors, only one of the things compared is clearly stated. The symbol is clearly stated, but what it is compared with (sometimes a very broad range of meanings) is only hinted at. For instance, the white whale in Herman Melville's novel *Moby Dick* is a symbol both in the novel and in the mind of Captain Ahab, who sees the whale as a symbol of all the malevolence and evil in a world committed to evil. But we may not necessarily share Ahab's views. We may believe that the whale is simply a beast and not a symbol at all. Or, we may believe that the whale is a symbol for nature, which is constantly being threatened by human misunderstanding. Such a symbol can mean more than one thing. It is the peculiar quality of most symbols that they do not sit still; even their basic meanings keep changing. Symbols often are vague and ambiguous. The context in which they appear usually helps guide us to their meaning. It is said that many symbols are a product of the subconscious, which is always treating things symbolically and always searching for implicit meanings. If this is so, it helps account for the persistence of symbols in even the oldest literature.

Perhaps the most important thing to remember about the symbol is that it implies rather than explicitly states meaning. We sense that we are dealing with a symbol in those linguistic situations in which we believe there is more being said than meets the eye. Most writers are quite open about their symbols, as William Blake was in his poetry. He saw God's handiwork everywhere, but he also saw forces of destruction everywhere. Thus his poetry discovers symbols in almost every situation and thing, not just in those situations and things that are usually accepted as meaningful. The following poem is an example of his technique. At first the poem may seem needlessly confusing, because we do not know how to interpret the symbols. But a second reading begins to clarify their meaning.

THE SICK ROSE

O rose, thou art sick!
  The invisible worm,
That flies in the night,
  In the howling storm,

Has found out thy bed
Of crimson joy;
And his dark secret love
Does thy life destroy.

William Blake

PERCEPTION KEY "The Sick Rose"

1. The rose and the worm stand as opposites in this poem, symbolically antagonistic. In discussion with other readers, explore possible meanings for the rose and the worm.
2. The bed of crimson joy and the dark secret love are also symbols. What are their meanings? Consider them closely in relation to the rose and the worm.
3. What is not a symbol in this poem?

Blake used such symbols because he saw a richness of implication in them that linked him to God. He thus shared in a minor way the creative act with God and helped others understand the world in terms of symbolic meaningfulness. For most other writers, the symbol is used more modestly to expand meaning, encompassing deep ranges of suggestion. The symbol has been compared with a stone dropped into the still waters of a lake: The stone itself is very small, but the effects radiate from its center to the edges of the lake. The symbol is dropped into our imagination, and it, too, radiates with meaning. But the marvelous thing about the symbol is that it tends to be permanently expansive: Who knows where the meaningfulness of Blake's rose ends?

Prose fiction has made extensive use of the symbol. In Melville's *Moby Dick,* the white whale is a symbol, but so, too, are Ahab and the entire journey they undertake. The quest for Moby Dick is itself a symbolic quest. The albatross in Samuel Coleridge's "The Ancient Mariner" is a symbol, and so is the Ancient Mariner's stopping one of the wedding guests to make him hear the entire narrative. In these cases the symbols operate both structurally, in the entire narrative, and in the details.

In Dostoevsky's *Crime and Punishment,* the murderer-to-be, Raskolnikov, has a symbolic dream shortly before he kills the old woman, Alena. In the dream Raskolnikov is a child again, walking through city streets with his father:

Suddenly there was a great explosion of laughter that drowned everything else: the old mare had rebelled against the hail of blows and was lashing out feebly with her hoofs. Even the old man could not help laughing. Indeed, it was ludicrous that such a decrepit old mare could still have a kick left in her.

Two men in the crowd got whips, ran to the horse, one on each side, and began to lash at her ribs.

"Hit her on the nose and across the eyes, beat her across the eyes!" yelled Mikolka.

"Let's have a song, lads!" someone called from the wagon, and the others joined in. Somebody struck up a coarse song, a tambourine rattled, somebody else whistled the chorus. The fat young woman went on cracking nuts and giggling.

. . . The boy ran towards the horse, then round in front, and saw them lashing her across the eyes, and actually striking her very eyeballs. He was weeping. His heart seemed to rise into his throat, and tears rained from his eyes. One of the whips stung his face, but he did not feel it; he was wringing his hands and crying aloud. He ran to a grey-haired, grey-bearded old man, who was shaking his head in reproof. A peasant-woman took him by the hand and tried to lead him away, but he tore himself loose and ran back to the mare. She was almost at her last gasp, but she began kicking again.

"The devil fly away with you!" shrieked Mikolka in a fury.

He flung away his whip, stooped down and dragged up from the floor of the cart a long thick wooden shaft, grasped one end with both hands, and swung it with an effort over the wretched animal.

Cries rose: "He'll crush her!" "He'll kill her!"

"She's my property," yelled Mikolka, and with a mighty swing let the shaft fall. There was a heavy thud.[4]

The symbolism of this passage becomes clearer in the context of the entire novel. Raskolnikov is planning a brutal murder of an aged shopkeeper. Only a couple of pages later, Raskolnikov reflects on his dream:

"God!" he exclaimed, "is it possible, is it possible, that I really shall take an axe and strike her on the head, smash open her skull . . . that my feet will slip in warm, sticky blood, and that I shall break the lock, and steal, and tremble, and hide, all covered in blood . . . with the axe . . . ? God, is it possible?"[5]

PERCEPTION KEY   *Crime and Punishment*

1. What does the old mare symbolize in Raskolnikov's dream? What does the entire situation symbolize?
2. Sample opinion from others and explore the effectiveness of having the beating of the horse revealed in a dream. Is this weaker or stronger in symbolic value than if the scene had actually taken place on the streets in front of Raskolnikov? Why?
3. How much does this symbolic action reveal about Raskolnikov? Does he seem—considering what he is actually about to do—different as a boy than as an adult? How would you characterize his sensitiveness and his compassion?
4. Dostoevsky uses the dream as a symbol. Are any of your dreams symbolic?

The problem most readers have with symbols centers on either the question of recognition—is this a symbol?—or the question of what the symbol stands for. Usually an author will use something symbolically in situations that are pretty clearly identified. Blake does not tell us that his rose and worm are symbolic, but we readily realize that the poem says very little worth listening to if we do not begin to go beyond its literal meaning.

_____

[4]From Dostoevsky's *Crime and Punishment*, translated by J. L. Coulson, published by Oxford University Press, 1953. Reprinted by permission of the publisher.
[5]Ibid.

The fact that worms kill roses is more important to gardeners than it is to readers of poetry. But that there is a secret evil that travels mysteriously to kill beautiful things is not as important to gardeners as to readers of poetry.

Some less experienced readers tend to see everything as symbolic. This is as serious a problem as being unable to identify a symbol at all. The best rule of thumb is based on experience. Symbols are very much alike from one kind of literature to another. Once you begin to recognize symbols — the several presented here are various enough to offer a good beginning — other symbols and symbolic situations will be clearer and more unmistakable. But the symbol should be compelling. The situation should be clearly symbolic before we dig in to explore what the symbols mean. Not all black objects are symbolic of death; not all predators are symbolic of evil. Moreover, all symbols should be understood in the context in which they appear. Their context in the literature is what usually reveals their meaning, as we can see from the dream of Raskolnikov.

In those instances in which there is no evident context to guide us, we should interpret symbols with extreme care and tentativeness. Symbolic objects usually have a fairly well understood range of meaning that authors such as Blake depend on. For instance, the rose is often thought of in connection with beauty, romance, love. The worm is often thought of in connection with death, the grave, and — if we include the serpent in the Garden of Eden (Blake, of course, had read Milton's *Paradise Lost*) — the worm also suggests evil, sin, and perversion. Most of us know these things. Thus the act of interpreting the symbol is usually an act of bringing this knowledge to the forefront of our minds so we can use it in our interpretations.

DICTION

Diction refers to the choice of words. But because the entire act of writing involves the choice of words, the term "diction" is usually reserved for literary acts (speech as well as the written word) that use words chosen especially carefully for their impact. The diction of a work of literature will sometimes make that work seem inevitable, as if there were no other way of saying the same thing, as in Hamlet's: "To be or not to be." Try saying that in other words.

Sometimes artificially formal diction is best, as it often is in the novels of Henry James; other times conversational diction works best, as in the novels of Ernest Hemingway. Usually, as Joseph Conrad asserts in one of his famous Prefaces, there is "the appeal through the senses." Diction, he says,

> must strenuously aspire to the plasticity of sculpture, to the colour of painting, and to the magic suggestiveness of music—which is the art of arts. And it is only through complete, unanswering devotion to the perfect blending of form and substance; it is only through an unremitting never-discouraged care for the shape and ring of sentences that an approach can be made to plasticity, to colour, that the light of magic suggestiveness may be brought to play for an evanescent instant over the commonplace surface of words . . . of the old, old words, worn thin, defaced by ages of careless usage.

In Robert Herrick's poem, we see an interesting example of the poet calculating the effect of specific words in their context. Most of the words in "Upon Julia's Clothes" are single-syllable words, such as "then." But the few polysyllables — "vibration" with three syllables and the most unusual four-syllable word, "liquefaction" — lend an air of intensity and special meaning to themselves by means of their syllabic contrast. There may also be an unusual sense in which those words act out or imitate what they describe.

UPON JULIA'S CLOTHES

Whenas in silks my Julia goes,
Then, then, methinks, how sweetly flows
That liquefaction of her clothes.

Next, when I cast mine eyes, and see
That brave vibration, each way free,
O, how that glittering taketh me!

                    Robert Herrick

PERCEPTION KEY   "Upon Julia's Clothes"

1. The implications of the polysyllabic words in this poem may be quite different for different people. Read the poem aloud with a few people. Ask for suggestions about what the polysyllables do for the reader. Does their complexity enhance what is said about Julia? Their sounds? Their rhythms?
2. Read the poem to some listeners who are not likely to know it beforehand. Do they notice such words as "liquefaction" and "vibration"? When they talk about the poem, do they observe the use of these words? Compare their observations with those of students who read the poem in this book.

We have been giving examples of detailed diction. Structural diction produces a sense of linguistic inevitability throughout the work. The careful use of structural diction can sometimes conceal a writer's immediate intention, making it important for us to be explicitly aware of the diction until it has made its point. Jonathan Swift's essay, *A Modest Proposal*, is a classic example. Swift most decorously suggests that the solution to the poverty-stricken Irish farmer's desperation is the sale of his infant children — for the purpose of serving them up as plump, tender roasts for Christmas dinners in England. The diction is so subtly ironic that it is with some difficulty that many readers finally realize Swift is writing *satire*. By the time one reaches the following passage, one should surely understand the *irony*:

I have been assured by a very knowing American of my acquaintance in London, that a young healthy child well nursed is at a year old a most delicious, nourishing, and wholesome food, whether stewed, roasted, baked, or boiled; and I make no doubt that it will equally serve in a fricasee or a ragout.

There are many kinds of diction available to the writer, from the casual and conversational to the archaic and the formal. Every literary writer is sensitive, consciously or unconsciously, to the issues of diction, and every piece of writing solves the problem in its own way. When the choice of words seems so exact and right that the slightest tampering diminishes the value of the work, then we have literature of high rank. Then, to paraphrase Robert Frost, "Like a piece of ice on a hot stove the poem rides on its own melting." No writer can tell you exactly how he or she achieves "inevitability," but much of it depends upon sound and rhythm as it relates to sense.

Lincoln's Gettysburg Address, November 1863, was given four months after the most dramatic battle of the Civil War, which killed or wounded close to 50,000 men. Work on the cemetery was still not complete. There were 15,000 spectators. Lincoln read 272 words in two minutes.

> Four score and seven years ago our fathers brought forth on this continent a new nation, conceived in Liberty, and dedicated to the proposition that all men are created equal.
>
> Now we are engaged in a great civil war, testing whether that nation, or any nation so conceived and so dedicated, can long endure. We are met on a great battle-field of that war. We have come to dedicate a portion of that field, as a final resting place for those who here gave their lives that that nation might live. It is altogether fitting and proper that we should do this.
>
> But, in a larger sense, we can not dedicate—we can not consecrate—we can not hallow—this ground. The brave men, living and dead, who struggled here, have consecrated it, far above our poor power to add or detract. The world will little note, nor long remember what we say here, but it can never forget what they did here. It is for us the living, rather, to be dedicated here to the unfinished work which they who fought here have thus far so nobly advanced. It is rather for us to be here dedicated to the great task remaining before us—that from these honored dead we take increased devotion to that cause for which they gave the last full measure of devotion—that we here highly resolve that these dead shall not have died in vain—that this nation, under God, shall have a new birth of freedom—and that government of the people, by the people, for the people, shall not perish from the earth.

Study the address with great care, especially with reference to structural diction, before proceeding to the Perception Key. Notice how there is a division into three parts (paragraphs), in which the first refers to the past, the second to the present, the third to the future. The first refers to birth, the second to death, the third to rebirth.

PERCEPTION KEY   The Gettysburg Address and Diction

1. Are there examples in the address of poor diction? Of excellent diction? Be specific. Try to substitute other words that would be better. For example, what about "Eighty-seven years ago"? Or "that government of the citizens . . . shall not perish from the earth"?

2. You may have been taught that it is clumsy to repeat a word more than once or twice in a paragraph. Lincoln uses "here" eight times and a form of "dedicate" six times. Are these repetitions clumsy? Do they have something to do with structural diction? Is structural diction vital to the address? If so, how?

3. Can you discover something like a musical beat? In reading the Address out loud is there a pronounced rhythm that helps tie the words together? If so, does this rhythm resonate at all with the rhythms of some of the Psalms of the Bible?

4. Are there any images, metaphors, or symbols?

5. In his first inaugural address, Lincoln used the word "union" twenty times and never the word "nation." In the Gettysburg Address he used "nation" five times and "union" not once. Why?

6. The last sentence is described by some critics as one of the most wondrous in all literature. Do you agree? If so, why?

7. Many critics describe the address as superb political rhetoric (persuasion) but not literature. If you disagree, what is the subject matter? What is the content?

We shall close this chapter with three translations of Psalm 23, a work that in its original Hebrew is almost universally referred to as a work of art.

My shepherd is the living Lord; nothing, therefore, I need.
In pastures fair, with waters calm, he set me for to feed.
He did convert and glad my soul, and brought my mind in frame
To walk in paths of righteousness for his most holy name.
Yea, though I walk in the vale of death, yet will I fear none ill;
Thy rod, thy staff doth comfort me, and thou art with me still.
And in the presence of my foes, my table thou has spread;
Thou shalt, O Lord, fill full my cup and eke anoint my head.
Through all my life thy favor is so frankly showed to me
That in thy house forevermore my dwelling place shall be.

Sternhold and Hopkins, 1567

The Lord is my shepherd, I shall not want.
He maketh me to lie down in green pastures: he leadeth me beside
the still waters.
He restoreth my soul: he leadeth me in the paths of righteousness
for his name's sake.
Yea, though I walk through the valley of the shadow of death,
I will fear no evil: for thou art with me; thy rod and thy staff they
comfort me.
Thou preparest a table before me in the presence of mine enemies:
thou anointest my head with oil; my cup runneth over.
Surely goodness and mercy shall follow me all the days of my life:
and I will dwell in the house of the Lord forever.

King James Version, 1611

Because the Lord acts as my shepherd, I don't need anything.
He lets me lie down in green pastureland and walk near quiet rivers.
He restores my soul and leads me on the right path in his name.
Yes, even though I walk through some tough neighborhoods,
I'm not afraid of anyone because God is with me.
He makes a table ready for me in front of those who despise me.
God anoints me with oil and gives me more than enough of everything.
I expect God will look after me through all the days of my life
And when I die, I will live with God forever.

Andre James, 1995

PERCEPTION KEY   Psalm 23

1. Compare the Sternhold–Hopkins version with the King James version. What word choices are particularly strong or weak in either version? Does the lack of rhyme in the King James version weaken or strengthen the meaning? Explain.
2. Compare the rhythms of the three versions. Which is more effective? Why? Which is most poetic in feel? Which most prosaic?
3. As an experiment, read the Sternhold–Hopkins version to friends and ask them what the name of the piece is. Does it come as a surprise when they realize which psalm it is?
4. Try your hand at revising the Sternhold–Hopkins version. "Translate" it into contemporary English. Ask others to do the same. Compare the best translation with the King James version.
5. What is it about the diction of the King James version that apparently makes it so effective? Be specific.

Summary

Our emphasis throughout this chapter has been on literature as the wedding of sound and sense. Literature is not passive; it does not sit on the page. It is engaged actively in the lives of those who give it a chance. A reading aloud of some of the literary samples in this chapter — especially the lyric — clarifies this point.

We have been especially interested in two aspects of literature: its structure and its details. Any artifact is composed of an overall organization that gathers details into some kind of unity. It is the same in literature, and before we can understand how writers reveal the visions they have of their subject matter we need to be aware of how details are combined into structures. The use of image, metaphor, symbol, and diction, as well as other details, determines in an essential sense the content of a work of literature.

Structural strategies, such as the choice between a narrative or a lyric, will determine to a large extent how details are used. There are many kinds of structures besides the narrative and the lyric, although these two offer convenient polarities that help indicate the nature of literary structure. It would be useful for any student of literature to discover how many kinds of narrative structures — in addition to the already discussed episodic, organic, and quest structures—can be used. And it also would be useful to determine how the different structural strategies tend toward the selection of different subject matters. We have made some suggestions as starters: pointing out the capacity of the narrative for reaching into a vast range of experience, especially for revealing its psychological truths, and the capacity of the lyric for revealing feeling.

Bibliography

Auerbach, Erich. *Mimesis*. Princeton, N.J.: Princeton University Press, 1973.

Bodkin, Maud. *Archetypal Patterns in Poetry*. New York: AMS Press, 1978.

Booth, Wayne. *The Rhetoric of Fiction*, 2d ed. Harmondsworth, England: Penguin, 1987.

Brooks, Cleanth. *The Well-Wrought Urn*. London: Reynal and Hitchcock, 1947.

Burke, Kenneth. *The Philosophy of Literary Form*. Baton Rouge: Louisiana State University Press, 1941.

Eagleton, Terry. *Literary Theory: An Introduction*. Oxford, England: Oxford University Press, 1983.

Eco, Umberto. *Interpretation and Overinterpretation*. Cambridge, England: Cambridge University Press, 1992.

Eliot, T. S. *Selected Essays: New Edition*. New York: Harcourt Brace and World, 1978.

Fish, Stanley. *Is There a Text in This Class?* Cambridge, Mass.: Harvard University Press, 1980.

Forster, E. M. *Aspects of the Novel*. New York: Harcourt Brace and World, 1973.

Frye, Northrop. *Anatomy of Criticism*. Princeton, N.J.: Princeton University Press, 1990.

Groden, Michael, and Martin Kreisworth. *The Johns Hopkins Guide to Literary Theory and Criticism*. Baltimore, Md.: Johns Hopkins University Press, 1994.

Hirsch, E. D. *The Aims of Interpretation*. Chicago: University of Chicago Press, 1978.

James, Henry. *The Art of the Novel*. New York: Scribner's, 1978.

Leavis, F. R. *The Great Tradition*. New York: New York University Press, 1973.

Lentricchia, Frank. *After the New Criticism*. Chicago: University of Chicago Press, 1980.

———. *Criticism and Social Change*. Chicago: University of Chicago Press, 1983.

Moller, Lis. *The Freudian Reading*. Philadelphia: University of Pennsylvania Press, 1991.

Newton, K. M. *Twentieth-Century Literary Theory*. London: Macmillan, 1988.

Quashie, Kevin Everod, Joyce Lausch, and Keith D. Miller. *New Bones: Contemporary Black Writers in America*. Upper Saddle River, N.J.: Prentice-Hall, 2001.

Qusby, Ian. *The Cambridge Guide to Literature in English*, 2d ed. New York: Cambridge University Press, 1994.

Robinson, Jontyle Theresa. *Bearing Witness: Contemporary Works by African American Women Artists*. New York: Rizzoli, 1996.

Rose, Jacqueline. *The Haunting of Sylvia Plath*. Cambridge, Mass.: Harvard University Press, 1991.

Scholes, Robert. *Textual Power*. New Haven, Conn.: Yale University Press, 1985.

Stoll, E. E. *From Shakespeare to Joyce*. New York: Doubleday, 1944.

Wellek, René, and Austin Warren. *Theory of Literature*, 3rd ed. New York: Harcourt Brace Jovanovich, 1984.

Wimsatt, William K., and Cleanth Brooks. *Literary Criticism: A Short History*. Chicago: University of Chicago Press, 1983.

Internet Resources

THE ACADEMY OF AMERICAN POETS
http://www.poets.org

BARTLEBY.COM: GREAT BOOKS ONLINE
http://www.bartleby.com

LINKS TO CLASSIC LITERATURE
http://dir.yahoo.com/Arts/Humanities/Classics/

ESSAYS ABOUT CONTEMPORARY SPANISH AMERICAN WOMEN WRITERS
http://www.monmouth.edu/~pgacarti/

LINKS TO LITERARY SITES
http://www.concordance.com

ONLINE LITERATURE LIBRARY
http://www.literature.org/index.html

THE POETRY AND LITERATURE CENTER OF THE LIBRARY OF CONGRESS
http://www.loc.gov/poetry/

POETRY ARCHIVES (THE ESERVER POETRY COLLECTION)
http://eserver.org/poetry/

POETRY NEWSLETTER (NEW POEMS BY YOUNG POETS)
E-mail poetrylist@aol.com to subscribe

POETRY ONLINE: THE INTERNATIONAL LIBRARY OF POETRY
http://www.poetry.com

PROJECT GUTENBERG (SOURCE FOR CLASSIC LITERATURE ONLINE)
http://www.gutenberg.org/

WOMEN IN LITERATURE
http://digital.library.upenn.edu/women/

CHAPTER 8

Drama

Drama is a species of literature whose basic medium is spoken language acted. Drama can be read, somewhat like a poem or a novel. But the word "drama" comes from a Greek word meaning "act." Drama is spoken language, produced for public exhibition, usually upon a stage. The script of a play, like a score of music, is designed for performance. From that script a director must develop a synthesis of related resources—acting, scenery, lighting, perhaps music, dance, and even film. Drama as a complete work of art exists in the presentation. Its success depends on interpreters, such as directors, designers, and actors, who intervene between the dramatist and the audience. Unfortunately, for most of us the stage, unlike books or records or film, is not easily available. Rarely can we choose to see a play, as one may choose a poem, to suit our immediate preference. We have to take what is offered. Thus, much of the time we have to read the drama and re-create in our imaginations something of what the play on the stage would be like. This requires considerable initiation. We learn both from our theater experiences and, we hope, from a text such as this. Drama uses the resources of the theater to portray human action in such a way that we gain deeper understanding of human experience.

Imitation and Realism

Generally, drama is a form of narrative, but its mode of expression is a showing as well as a telling. Drama exhibits events at the moment of their occurring, vividly, with immediate impact. No other art comes closer to life; hence, drama, more than any other art, led Aristotle in the fourth century B.C. to his theory of drama as the imitation of nature—nature being life in general, not just the outdoors. In his *Poetics*, Aristotle claimed that *tragedy* is the imitation (mimesis) of human action. From other comments, we can

FIGURE 8-1
Anna Deavere Smith. (Courtesy Berkeley Repertory Theatre. Photo by Ken Friedman, 1996)

assume he meant to include comedy and other forms of drama. Just what Aristotle meant by imitation is open to different interpretations. For instance, certain kinds of drama imitate an action by allusion. The musical dramas *Godspell, Jesus Christ Superstar,* and *Your Arms Too Short to Box with God* all allude to the story of Christ. They do not, however, aim at representing the gospels with accuracy. Because they imitate an action by allusion, they can omit much and admit purposeful distortion. Another way of imitating an action is by reenacting, which requires more accuracy. Historical plays, such as Shakespeare's *Henry V,* strive for enough accuracy to resemble reasonably what had happened. Plays on the assassinations of Lincoln, John F. Kennedy, and Malcolm X all depend on historical accuracy to some extent. Numerous one-person dramas such as Hal Holbrook's imitation of Mark Twain, Julie Harris's imitation of Emily Dickinson, and James Whitmore's imitations of Will Rogers and Harry Truman are particularly popular on television.

Anna Deavere Smith (Figure 8-1), in two extraordinary one-woman performances—*Fires in the Mirror: Crown Heights, Brooklyn, and Other Identities* and *Twilight: Los Angeles, 1992*—takes the roles of dozens of ordinary people, male and female, of various ages and races, and convinces her audiences that she speaks with their voices. Her focus is on racial and religious violence in Brooklyn—the death of a black youth and the killing of a Jewish rabbinical student in the ensuing riots. The Los Angeles riots of 1992 were sparked by the failure to convict the policemen who beat Rodney King and then were further inflamed by the sight on television of Reginald

Denney being hauled by rioters from his truck and beaten. These events generated intense emotional reponses from the entire nation. Smith interprets those events from a variety of realistic points of view.

However, no matter how realistically events are portrayed on stage, they cannot duplicate the actions we experience in our ordinary lives outside the theater. Audiences are necessarily called upon to exercise what Coleridge called the "willing suspension of disbelief"; that is, we must agree to imagine that the events on stage are actually occurring in ancient Greece, or Denmark, even though we are simultaneously aware that we are seated in a theater in our own hometown in the twenty-first century.

Realism is not a very useful standard for evaluating drama. In real life we do not observe the lives of others by looking through an imaginary "fourth wall," nor is our conversation consistently relevant to a central theme. If absolute realism were achieved in drama, we would abominate it. If characters really went to sleep onstage or really got drunk and forced us to wait for them to sober up, we would have much more realism, but the drama would be much less interesting. Drama—or any other art, for that matter—should be only realistic enough to allow a meaningful revelation of the subject matter.

The history of drama is filled with amusing anecdotes about the extent to which a drama has been realistic enough to cause an audience to mistake drama for real life. For instance, when Arthur Miller's *Death of a Salesman* (1949) played to early audiences that included salesmen at a New York convention, stories circulated that several salesmen in the audience leaped up in anguish to help the hero, Willy Loman, by offering good business advice to help him from losing his territory. These are breakdowns of a distance that we ought to maintain with all art, and they help explain why realism has limits. Our awareness of the difference between life and art is sometimes described as "aesthetic distance." Maintaining that distance implies, paradoxically, the possibility of truly participating with the drama, since it implies the loss of the self-conscious self that participation demands. When spectators leap onstage to right the wrongs of drama, they show that there has been no loss of self. Indeed, because they see themselves as capable of changing the action, they are projecting their own ego into—rather than participating with—the actors in the dramatic action unfolding before them.

There is one realistic restraint that allows for little compromise—the capacity of an average audience for sustained concentration. Most plays run for approximately two hours, with intermissions as concessions to the need for mental and physical relaxation. Thus a drama must unfold rapidly and be interesting at all times. Perhaps a novel may occasionally make us nod. We can take a break. But if a drama nods, we leave. Furthermore, the drama must be comprehensible, independent of extended explanations, and this independence must be accomplished mainly through the conduct and speech of the actors. Dramatists must leave the significance of what is happening largely to inference, whereas novelists, for example, have many leisurely ways of reflecting about the significance of the action. Nevertheless, there are conventions, such as the *soliloquy*—an extended speech by a character alone with the audience—which allow for reflection and explanation within the drama.

Aristotle and the Elements of Drama

The basic *elements of drama* (following the analyses of Aristotle) are, in descending order of importance, plot, character, thought, dialogue, spectacle, and music. *Plot* refers to the action, the activities of the characters. *Character* refers to the personality and morality of the personae of the play. They make the plot go. The most important characters are called the protagonists. *Thought* refers to the thinking that explains the motivations and the actions of the characters. Dialogue refers to the spoken words, the diction. *Spectacle* refers to the places of the action, the *setting*. Music refers to the singing and dancing of the chorus, an element that largely disappears after the classical Greek period (sixth to fourth centuries B.C.). Aristotle's analysis centered on tragedy. The subject matter of tragedy is the tragic — intense sorrow and suffering.

Plot is a series of events: incident, rising action, climax, falling action, *denouement*. For Aristotle the tragic hero is in search of truth. The moment of truth — the climax — is called *recognition*. When the protagonist's fortunes turn from good to bad — the *reversal* — doom follows. The strongest effect of tragedy occurs when the recognition and the reversal occur at the same time, as in Sophocles' *Oedipus Rex*.

The protagonist in the most powerful tragedy fails not only because of fate but also because of a fatal *flaw in character (hamartia)*, a disregard of human limitations: The protagonist brings his misfortune upon himself. In *Oedipus Rex*, for example, the courageous impetuosity of Oedipus, which served him well in most circumstances, leads to disaster in a different kind of circumstance. Sophocles shows us that such horror can befall anyone. We pity Oedipus, and we fear for him. While arousing pity and fear, the play also helps us understand the causes of those feelings. Thus the pity and fear are purged (*catharsis*). The drama helps us understand the complexities of human nature and the power of our inescapable destinies.

PERCEPTION KEY   Shakespeare and Arthur Miller

Read or, if possible, see Shakespeare's *Hamlet, Macbeth, Othello,* or *King Lear*. Compare one of these tragedies with Arthur Miller's *Death of a Salesman*. Does Aristotle's analysis of the downfall of the protagonist ring true for both Shakespeare and Miller?

If the protagonist was not heroic, well above the common man or woman, Aristotle thought that our pity and fear would be weaker and thus the tragedy less powerful. Aristotle's theories have been modified in many ways since his time. In the eighteenth century, for example, some of his observations were hardened into rules of "unities." Thus there should be only one plot, and action should take place in one locale and be completed in one day. In our time, these unities are rarely observed. Moreover, the tragic protagonist is often just an ordinary person, such as Willy Loman in *Death of a Salesman*. But Aristotle's theory of tragedy still remains the foundation for understanding drama, including comedy. (If you are especially interested in drama, you should study Aristotle's *Poetics* very carefully.)

SOLILOQUY AND MONOLOGUE

Many dramatic techniques have been changed or developed since Aristotle's time. For example, in early Greek plays such as those of Aeschylus, Sophocles, and Euripides, a chorus, usually accompanied by music and dancing, sometimes was used to comment on the action and sometimes became an acting force. In Shakespeare's time, the soliloquy occasionally took over the function of the chorus.

Soliloquies are asides, a form of dialogue in which a character delivers a speech to the audience, or into space, as a mode of reflective discourse. The soliloquy has special force because it may be assumed in most instances that since no other characters are nearby, the character delivering the soliloquy can be trusted to tell the truth. *Hamlet* is especially noted for its soliloquies. His most famous speech is a soliloquy beginning

To be, or not to be, that is the question:
Whether 'tis nobler in the mind to suffer
The slings and arrows of outrageous fortune,
Or to take arms against a sea of troubles,
And by opposing end them. [3.1.57–61]

Monologues differ from soliloquies in that in a monologue one character speaks at great length, perhaps taking up an entire act or even an entire play. Brian Friel's *The Faith Healer* is exceptional for its three long monologues by three characters, none of whom appears on stage with anyone else. A soliloquy, which is also delivered by one character, is usually an interruption of an action that consists of dialogue among the characters. Dialogue can be brisk and snappy, with short speeches delivered in rapid fire, or it can be marked by expansive passages that give the character an opportunity to speak extensively and then listen to an extensive response.

PERCEPTION KEY   The Soliloquy

A soliloquy occurs when a character in a drama reveals his or her thoughts to the audience but not to the other characters. Study the use of the soliloquy in a couple of plays—for example, Shakespeare's *Hamlet* (3.3.73–96, 4.4.32–66) and Tennessee Williams' *The Glass Menagerie* (Tom's opening speech; Tom's long speech in scene 5; and his opening speech in scene 6). What does the soliloquy accomplish? Suppose their use was greatly expanded; would it enliven the drama? Do you find its use awkward?

An Alternative Theory

We lack space to study the many alternative theories that attempt to explain tragedy. But—even as oversimplified—the theory of G. W. F. Hegel, the nineteenth-century German philosopher, requires attention, for his explanation of tragedy is exceptionally interesting and quite different from Aristotle's. Hegel argues that it is not the *tragic flaw* of a protagonist that leads to the tragic. Rather, all of us inhabit a world where one's good intentions inevitably collide with the good intentions of someone else. Being finite, we cannot avoid these collisions. Thus the tragic is our fate. Even if Oedipus possessed no tragic flaw, his "good" inevitably would have collided with the "good" of his parents and others. Tragedy, according to Hegel, reveals our sorrows and the sufferings as inevitable.

PERCEPTION KEY   Hegel

1. Hegel, if our interpretation is accurate, apparently presumes that all human beings have good intentions. But what about Iago in *Hamlet*? Or Hitler or Stalin?
2. Examine Miller's *Death of a Salesman*. Is Hegel's explanation of that tragedy more illuminating than Aristotle's?
3. Hegel presumably would have argued that the tragic end of Romeo and Juliet is due not to tragic flaws, but rather to the collision of good intentions. Romeo and Juliet had no tragic flaws—they were simply caught in a web of fate from which there was no escape. Which explanation is more illuminating—the Aristotelian or the Hegelian? What about a combination of the two? Discuss.

Archetypal Patterns

Certain structural principles tend to govern the shape of dramatic narrative, just as they do the narrative of fiction. The discussion of episodic and organic structures in the previous chapter has relevance for drama as well. However, drama originated from ancient rituals and sometimes seems to maintain a reference to those rites. For example, the ritual of sacrifice—which implies that the individual must be sacrificed for the commonweal of society—seems to find its way into a great many dramas, both old and new. Such a pattern is archetypal—a basic psychological pattern that people apparently react to on a more or less subconscious level. These patterns are deep in the *myths* that have permeated history. We feel their importance even if we do not recognize them consciously.

Archetypal drama aims at symbolic or mythic interpretations of experience. For instance, one's search for personal identity, for self-evaluation, since it seems to be a pattern repeated in all ages, can serve as a primary archetypal structure for drama. This particular *archetype* is the driving force in Sophocles' *Oedipus Rex*, Shakespeare's *Hamlet*, August Wilson's *The Piano Lesson*, Arthur Miller's *Death of a Salesman*, and many more plays—notably, but by no means exclusively, in tragedies. (As we shall see, *comedy* also often uses this archetype.) One reason this archetype is so powerful is that it involves large risks. Most of us are content to watch other people discover their own identities, since there is an implied terror in finding that we may not be the delightful, humane, and wonderful person we want others to think we are.

The power of the archetype derives, in part, from our recognition of a pattern that has been repeated by the human race throughout history. The psychologist Carl Jung, whose work spurred critical awareness of archetypal patterns in all the arts, believed that the greatest power of the archetype lies in its capacity to reveal through art the "imprinting" of human experience. Maud Bodkin, a critic who developed Jung's views, explains the archetype this way:

> The special emotional significance going beyond any definite meaning conveyed [Jung] attributes to the stirring in the reader's mind, within or beneath his conscious response, of unconscious forces which he terms "primordial images" or archetypes. These archetypes he describes as "psychic residua of numberless experiences of the same type," experiences which have happened not to the individual but to his ancestors, and of which the results are inherited in the structure of the brain.[1]

The quest narrative (Chapter 7) is an example of an archetypal structure, one that recurs in drama frequently. For instance, Hamlet is seeking the truth about his father's death (Aristotle's recognition), but in doing so he is also trying to discover his own identity as it relates to his mother. Sophocles' *Oedipus* is the story of a man who kills his father, marries his mother, and suffers a plague on his lands. He discovers the truth (recognition again), and doom follows (Aristotle's reversal). He blinds himself and is ostracized. Freud thought the play so archetypal that he saw in it a profound human psychological pattern, which he called the Oedipus complex: the desire of a child to get rid of the same-sex parent and to have a sexual union with the parent of the opposite sex. Not all archetypal patterns are so shocking, but most reveal an aspect of basic human desires. Drama—because of its immediacy and compression of presentation—is, perhaps, the most powerful means of expression for such archetypes.

Some of the more important archetypes include those of an older man, usually a king in ancient times, who is betrayed by a younger man, his trusted lieutenant, with regard to a woman. This is the theme of Lady Gregory's *Diarmuid and Grania*. The loss of innocence, a variation on the Garden of Eden theme, is another favorite, as in Strindberg's *Miss Julie* and Ibsen's *Ghosts* and *The Wild Duck*. Tom Stoppard's *Arcadia* combines two archetypes: loss of innocence and the quest for knowledge. However, no archetype seems to rival the quest for self-identity with reference to prevalence. That quest is so common that it is even parodied, as in Oscar Wilde's *The Importance of Being Earnest*.

The four seasons set temporal dimensions for the development of archetypes because the seasons are intertwined with patterns of growth and

---

[1]Maud Bodkin, *Archetypal Patterns in Poetry* (New York: Oxford University Press, 1934), p. 1.

decay. The origins of drama, which are obscure beyond recall, may have been linked with rituals associated with the planting of seed, the reaping of crops, and the entire complex issue of fertility and death. In *Anatomy of Criticism*, Northrop Frye associates comedy with spring, romance with summer, tragedy with autumn, irony and satire with winter. His associations suggest that some archetypal drama may be rooted in connections between human destiny and the rhythms of nature. Such origins may account for part of the power that archetypal drama has on our imaginations, for the influences that derive from such origins presumably are deeply pervasive in all of us. These influences may also help explain why tragedy usually involves the death of a hero—although, sometimes, as in the case of Oedipus, death is withheld—and why comedy frequently ends with one or more marriages, as in Shakespeare's *As You Like It, Much Ado about Nothing*, and *A Midsummer Night's Dream*, with their suggestions of fertility. Such drama seems to thrive on seasonal patterns and on the capacity to excite in us a recognition of events that on the surface may not seem important but that underneath have profound meaning.

PERCEPTION KEY   Archetypes

1. You may wish to supplement the comments above by reading the third chapter of Northrop Frye's *Anatomy of Criticism* or the *Hamlet* chapter in Francis Fergusson's *The Idea of a Theater*. Discuss archetypes with friends interested in the concept.

2. Whether or not you do additional reading, consider the recurrent patterns you have observed in dramas—include television dramas or television adaptations of drama. Can you find any of the patterns we have described? Do you see other patterns showing up? Do the patterns you have observed seem basic to human experience? For example, do you associate gaiety with spring, love with summer, death with fall, and bitterness with winter? If so, what are the origins of these associations for you? Do you believe these origins are shared by most people?

Genres of Drama: Tragedy

Carefully structured plots are basic for Aristotle, especially for tragedies. The action must be probable or plausible, but not necessarily historically accurate. Although noble protagonists are essential for great tragedies, Aristotle allows for tragedies with ordinary protagonists. In these the plot is much more the center of interest than character. Then we have what may be called action dramas, never, according to Aristotle, as powerful as character dramas, other things being equal. Action dramas prevail on the popular stage and television. But when we turn to the great tragedies that most define the genre, we think immediately of great characters: Oedipus, Agamemnon, Prometheus, Hamlet, Macbeth, King Lear.

Modern drama tends to avoid traditional tragic structures because modern concepts of morality, sin, guilt, fate, and death have been greatly altered. Modern psychology explains character in ways the ancients either would not have understood or would have disputed. It has been said that

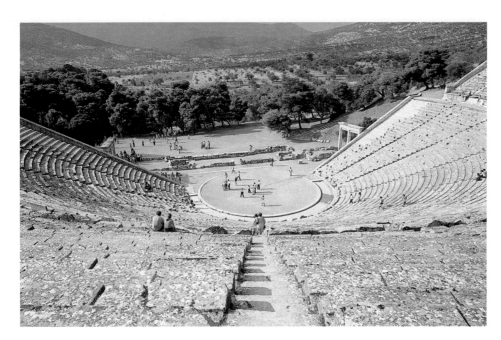

FIGURE 8-2
Theater at Epidaurus, Greece.
Circa 350 B.C. (J. Allan Cash
Ltd., London)

there is no modern tragedy because there can be no character noble enough to engage our heartfelt sympathy. Moreover, the acceptance of chance as a force equal to fate in our lives has also reduced the power of tragedy in modern times. Even myth—which some modern playwrights like O'Neill still use—has a diminished vitality in modern tragedy. It may be that the return of a strong integrating myth—a world vision that sees the actions of humanity as tied into a large scheme of cosmic or sacred events—is a prerequisite for producing a drama that we can recognize as truly tragic, at least in the traditional sense. This may be an overstatement. What do you think?

THE TRAGIC STAGE

Our vision of tragedy comes from its two great ages—in ancient Greece and Renaissance England. These two historical periods shared certain basic ideas: for instance, that there is a "divine providence that shapes our ends," as Hamlet says, and that fate is immutable, as the Greek tragedies tell us. Both periods were marked by considerable prosperity and public power, and both ages were deeply aware that sudden reversals in prosperity could change everything. In addition both ages had somewhat similar ideas about the way a stage should be constructed. The relatively temperate climate of Greece permitted an open amphitheater, with seating on three sides of the stage. The Greek architects often had the seats carved out of hillside rock, and their attention to acoustics was so remarkable that even today in some of the surviving Greek theaters, as at Epidaurus (Figure 8-2), a whisper on the stage can be heard in the farthest rows. The Elizabethan stages were roofed wooden structures jutting into open space enclosed by stalls in which the well-to-do sat (the not-so-well-to-do stood around the stage), providing for sight lines from three sides. Each kind of theater was similar to a modified theater-in-the-round, such as is used occasionally today. A glance at Figures 8-2, 8-3, and 8-4 shows that the Greek and Elizabethan theaters were very different from the standard theater of our time—the *proscenium* theater.

The proscenium acts as a transparent "frame" separating the action taking place on the stage from the audience. The Greek and Elizabethan stages are not so explicitly framed, thus involving the audience more directly spatially and, in turn, perhaps, emotionally. With the Greek theater, the area on which the action took place was a circle, called the orchestra. The absence of a separate stage put the actors on the same level as those seated at the lowest level of the audience.

FIGURE 8-3
Modern rendering of DeWitt's 1596 drawing of the interior of an Elizabethan theater. (Courtesy University of Utrecht)

PERCEPTION KEY   The Proscenium Stage

Test the preceding observations by examining your own experience in the theater. What is the effect of setting apart the dramatic action of a play by framing it with a proscenium? Do you know of any plays that are weakened because of the proscenium frame? Explain.

SHAKESPEARE'S *ROMEO AND JULIET*

For a contemporary audience, *Romeo and Juliet* is probably easier to participate with than most Greek tragedies because, among other reasons, its tragic hero and heroine, although aristocratic, are not a king and queen. Their youth and innocence add to their remarkable appeal. The play presents the archetypal story of lovers whose fate—mainly because of the hatred their families bear one another—is sealed from the first. The archetype of lovers who are not permitted to love enacts a basic struggle among forces that lie so deep in our psyche that we need a drama such as this to help reveal them. It is the struggle between light and dark, between the world in which we live on the surface of the earth with its light and openness, and the world of darkness, the underworld of the Greeks and the Romans, and the hell of the Christians. Young lovers represent life, the promise of fertility, and the continuity of the human race. Most of us who are no longer in the bloom of youth were once such people, and we can both sympathize with and understand their situation. Few subject matters could be more potentially tragic than that of young lovers whose promise is plucked by death.

The play begins with some ominous observations by Montague, Romeo's father. He points out that when Romeo, through love of a girl named Rosaline (who does not appear in the play), comes home just before dawn, he locks "fair daylight out," making for himself an "artificial night." In other words, Montague tells us that Romeo stays up all night, comes home, pulls down the shades, and converts day into night. These observations seem innocent enough unless one is already familiar with the plot; then it seems a clear and tragic irony: that Romeo, by making his day a night, is already foreshadowing his fate. After Juliet has been introduced, her nurse wafts her offstage with an odd bit of advice aimed at persuading her of the wis-

FIGURE 8-4
Auditorium and proscenium, Royal Opera House, Covent Garden, London. (Woodmansterne Publications, England)

dom of marrying Count Paris, the man her mother has chosen. "Go, girl, seek happy nights to happy days." At first glance, the advice seems innocent. But with knowledge of the entire play, it is prophetic, for it echoes the day/night imagery Montague has applied to Romeo. Shakespeare's details invariably tie in closely with the structure. Everything becomes relevant.

Much of the play takes place at night, and the film version by Franco Zeffirelli was particularly impressive for exploiting the spectacle, one of Aristotle's basic elements of tragedy. Spectacle includes all the visual and sounding features of a production, which, in their richness or starkness, can intensify the drama. Zeffirelli skillfully exploited the dramatic use of lighting, costuming, and music.

PERCEPTION KEY   Drama and Music

1. Is music in a film production likely to be a more important element than in a stage production? Why or why not?
2. If you are able to see Zeffirelli's film of *Romeo and Juliet,* judge the effectiveness of the music.

When Romeo first speaks with Juliet, not only is it night but they are in Capulet's orchard: symbolically a place of fruitfulness and fulfillment. Romeo sees her and imagines her, not as chaste Diana of the moon, but as his own luminary sun: "But soft! What light through yonder window breaks? / It is the East, and Juliet is the sun!" He sees her as his "bright angel." When she, unaware he is listening below, asks, "O Romeo, Romeo!

FIGURE 8-5
Romeo and Juliet. E. H. Sothern and Julia Marlow. (Theatre Collection, The New York Public Library for the Performing Arts, Lincoln Center)

Wherefore art thou Romeo? / Deny thy father and refuse thy name," she is touching on profound concerns. She is, without fully realizing it, asking the impossible: that he not be himself. The denial of identity often brings great pain, as witness Oedipus, who at first refused to believe he was his father's child. When Juliet asks innocently, "What's in a name? That which we call a rose / By any other name would smell as sweet," she is asking that he ignore his heritage. The mythic implications of this are serious and, in this play, fatal. Denying one's identity is rather like Romeo's later attempt to deny day its sovereignty.

When they finally speak, Juliet explains ironically that she has "night's cloak to hide me" and that the "mask of night is upon my face." We know, as she speaks, that eternal night will be on that face, and all too soon. Their marriage, which occurs offstage as Act Two ends, is also performed at night in Friar Lawrence's cell, with his hoping that the heavens will smile upon "this holy act." But he is none too sure. And before Act Three is well under way the reversals begin. Mercutio, Romeo's friend, is slain because of Romeo's intervention. Then Romeo slays Tybalt, Juliet's cousin, and finds himself doomed to exile from both Verona and Juliet. Grieving for the dead Tybalt and the banished Romeo, Juliet misleads her father into thinking the only cure for her condition is a quick marriage to Paris, and Romeo comes to spend their one night of love together before he leaves Verona. Naturally they want the night to last and last — again an irony we are prepared for — and when daylight springs, Romeo and Juliet have a playful argument over whether it is the nightingale or the lark that sings. Juliet wants him to stay, so she defends the nightingale; he knows he must go, so he points to the lark and the coming light. Then both, finally, admit the truth. His line is "More light and light—more dark and dark our woes."

Another strange archetypal pattern, part of the complexity of the subject matter, has begun here: the union of sex and death as if they were aspects of the same thing. In Shakespeare's time death was a metaphor for making love, and often when a singer of a love song protested that he was dying, he expected everyone to understand that he was talking about the sexual act. In *Romeo and Juliet* sex and death go together, both literally and symbolically. The first most profound sense of this appears in Juliet's pretending death in order to avoid marrying Paris. She takes a potion from Friar Lawrence—who is himself afraid of a second marriage because of possible bigamy charges—and appears, despite all efforts of investigation, quite dead (Figure 8-5).

When Romeo hears that she has been placed in the Capulet tomb, he determines to join her in death as he was only briefly able to do in life. The message Friar Lawrence had sent by way of another friar explaining the counterfeit death did not get through to Romeo. And it did not get through because genuine death, in the form of plague, had closed the roads to Friar John. When Romeo descends underground into the tomb he must ultimately fight Paris, although he does not wish to. After killing Paris, Romeo sees the immobile Juliet. He fills his cup (a female symbol) with poison and drinks. When Juliet awakes from her potion and sees both Paris and Romeo dead, she can get no satisfactory answer for these happenings from Friar Lawrence. His fear is so great that he runs off as the authorities bear down on the tomb. This leaves Juliet to give Romeo one last kiss on his still warm lips, then plunge his dagger (a male symbol) into her heart and die.

Earlier, when Capulet thought his daughter was dead, he exclaimed to Paris, "O son, the night before thy wedding day / Hath Death lain with thy wife. There she lies, / Flower as she was, deflowered by him. / Death is my son-in-law, Death is my heir." At the end of the play, both Juliet and his real son-in-law, Romeo, are indeed married in death. The linkage of death and sex is ironically enacted in their final moments, which include the awful misunderstandings that the audience beholds in sorrow, that make Romeo and Juliet take their own lives for love of one another. And among the last lines is one that helps clarify one of the main themes: "A glooming peace this morning with it brings. / The sun for sorrow will not show his head." Theatergoers have mourned these deaths for generations, and the promise that these two families will now finally try to get along together in a peaceful manner does not seem strong enough to brighten the ending of the play.

PERCEPTION KEY   Tragedy

1. While participating with *Romeo and Juliet,* did you experience pity and fear for the protagonists? Catharsis (the purging of those emotions)?
2. Our discussion of the play did not treat the question of the tragic flaw (hamartia): the weakness of character that brings disaster to the main characters. One of Romeo's flaws may be rashness—the rashness that led him to

kill Tybalt and thus be banished. But he may have other flaws as well. What might they be? What are Juliet's tragic flaws, if any?

3. In scenes such as that where Romeo views the apparently dead Juliet (see Figure 8-5), the film version focuses narrowly on the two and brings us close in. On the stage, the surrounding space cannot be completely abolished (even with highly concentrated lighting), and we cannot be brought as close in. In this respect, does this flexibility give film a distinct advantage over the stage play? Discuss.

4. You may not have been able to see *Romeo and Juliet*, but perhaps other tragedies are available. Try to see any of the tragedies by Aeschylus, Sophocles, or Shakespeare; Ibsen's *Ghosts;* John Millington Synge's *Riders to the Sea;* Eugene O'Neill's *Long Day's Journey into Night;* Tennessee Williams' *The Glass Menagerie;* or Miller's *Death of a Salesman.* Analyze the issues of tragedy we have raised. For example, decide whether the play is archetypal. Are there tragic flaws? Are there reversals and recognitions of the sort Aristotle analyzed? Did the recognition and reversal occur simultaneously? Are the characters important enough—if not noble enough—to excite your compassion for their sorrow and suffering?

5. If you were to write a tragedy, what kind of tragic protagonist would you choose? What kind of plot? Imagine a drama based on the love of an Israeli girl and a Palestinian boy? Would something like the plot of *Romeo and Juliet* be helpful in writing the play? Would Aristotle favor this? Why or why not?

Comedy: Old and New

Ancient Western comedies were performed at a time associated with wine making, thus linking the genre with the wine god Bacchus and his relative Comus—from whom the word "comedy" comes. Comedy, like tragedy, achieved institutional status in ancient Greece. Some of the earliest comedies, along with satyr plays, were frankly phallic in nature, and many of the plays of Aristophanes, the master of *Old Comedy,* were raucous and coarse. Plutarch was offended by plays like *The Clouds, The Frogs, The Wasps,* and especially *Lysistrata,* the world's best-known phallic play, concerning a situation in which the women of a community withhold sex until the men agree not to wage any more war. At one point in the play, the humor centers on the men walking around with enormous erections under their togas. Obviously Old Comedy is old in name only, since it is still present in the routines of nightclub comedians and the bawdy entertainment halls of the world.

In contrast, the *New Comedy* of Menander, with titles such as *The Flatterer, The Lady from Andros, The Suspicious Man,* and *The Grouch,* his only surviving complete play, concentrated on the more common situations in the everyday life of the Athenian. It also avoided the brutal attacks on individuals, such as Socrates, which characterize much Old Comedy. Historians credit Menander with developing the comedy of manners, the kind of drama that satirizes the manners of a society as the basic part of its subject matter.

Old Comedy is associated with our modern farce, burlesque, and the broad humor and make-believe violence of slapstick. New Comedy tends to be suave and subtle. Concentrating on manners, New Comedy developed *type characters*, for they helped focus upon the foibles of social behavior. Type characters, such as the gruff and difficult man who turns out to have a heart of gold, the good cop, the bad cop, the ingenue, the finicky person, or the sloppy person—all these work well in comedies. Such characters can become *stereotypes*—with almost totally predictable behavior patterns— although the best dramatists usually make them complex enough so that they are not completely predictable.

Comedy makes us laugh. If a man slips on a banana peel and very awkwardly regains his balance, we laugh. But if he breaks his leg, we do not laugh. The humorous has something to do with gracelessness, behavior that is not under our control but that does not have tragic consequences. When we behave in an antisocial way—for example, with sloppy table manners— we are liable to be laughed at. We do not enjoy that, so we may mend our ways. Comedy satirizes and criticizes antisocial behavior, as Henri Bergson brilliantly analyzed in *Laughter*. Whereas Old Comedy often indulges in wild exaggeration, New Comedy is usually subtler. Comedy, more than any other art, is the arena of oddball activity.

There is, however, another important dimension to comedy. The comic vision celebrates life and fecundity. Typically in comedy all ends well; conflicts are resolved; and, as often in Shakespeare's comedies, the play concludes with feasting, revelry, and a satisfying distribution of brides to the appropriate suitors. We are encouraged to imagine that they will live happily ever after.

PERCEPTION KEY   Type Characters

1. Television comedies thrive on types and stereotypes. If you have seen some of the characters from the following series you may be able to describe their type: George or Kramer in *Seinfeld* (Figure 8-6); Chandler, Joey, Monica, Rachel, Ross, and Phoebe in *Friends;* Daphne, Frasier, Martin, Niles, and Roz in *Frasier*. What makes them interesting? Are any of these characters completely predictable in their behavior; that is, are they stereotypes?

2. New Comedy usually uses types and stereotypes to make socially interesting points. Do series such as *Seinfeld, Friends*, and *Frasier* do this?

3. Are type and stereotype characters graceless in some way? Is being almost or totally predictable in behavior often funny? If so, why? Is awkward behavior often funny? If so, why?

4. A British channel paid a high price for the rights to broadcast *Seinfeld*. The show was a total failure. Do you think there is such a thing as a national sense of humor?

Both Old and New Comedy, despite, or perhaps because of, the humor, can have serious meaning. Comedy is a powerful reformer of society, which is one of the reasons dictators are so quick to censor the comic dramatist. We love to be laughed with but hate to be laughed at. No normal person likes to be seen as ridiculous. When comedy reveals aspects of ourselves that are laughable, we try to change. Think about how the comedians lampooned Vice President Al Gore and George W. Bush during the 2000 presidential campaign, leading to changes in their behavior.

FIGURE 8-6
A still from *Seinfeld*. (Courtesy Castle Rock Entertainment, Beverly Hills, California, photograph by Byron Cohen)

Comedy, like tragedy, may use archetypal patterns. For example, there is the pattern pointing toward marriage and the new life made possible by the hoped-for fruitfulness of such a union. The forces of society, personified often by a parent or controlling older person, are usually pitted against the younger characters who wish to be married. Thus one of the most powerful archetypal patterns of comedy is a variant of the generation gap. The "parent" can be any older person who blocks the younger people, usually by virtue of controlling their inheritance or their wealth. When the older person wishes to stop a marriage, he or she becomes the blocking character. This character, for reasons that are usually social or simply mercenary, does everything possible to stop the young people from getting together.

Naturally, the blocking character fails. But the younger characters do not merely win their own struggle. They usually go on to demonstrate the superiority of their views over those of the blocking character. For example, they may demonstrate that true love is a better reason for marrying than merging two neighboring estates. One common pattern is for two lovers to decide to marry regardless of their social classes. The male, for instance, may be a soldier or a student but not belong to the upper class to which the female belongs. But usually at the last minute through the means of a birthmark (as in *The Marriage of Figaro;* see Chapter 13) or the admission of another character who knew all along, the lower-class character will be shown to be a member of the upper class in disguise. Often the character himself will not know the truth until the last minute in the drama. This is a variant of Aristotle's recognition, although it does not have unhappy consequences.

In all of this, New Comedy is usually in tacit agreement with the ostensible standards of the society it entertains. It only stretches the social standards and is thus evolutionary rather than revolutionary.

Blocking characters are often eccentrics, like Archie Bunker, whose behavior is marked by an extreme commitment to a limited perspective. They may be misers, for example, whose entire lives are devoted to mercenary goals, although they may not be able to enjoy the money they heap up; or malcontents, forever looking on the dark side of humanity; or hypochondriacs, whose every move is dictated by their imaginary illnesses. Such characters are so rigid that their behavior is a form of vice. The effort of the younger characters is often to reform the older characters, educating them away from their entrenched and narrow values toward accepting the idealism and hopefulness of the young people who, after all, are in line to inherit the world that the older people are reluctant to turn over. Few generations give way without a struggle, and this archetypal struggle on the comic stage may serve to give hope to the young when they most need it, as well as possibly help to educate the old so as to make the real struggle less terrible.

PERCEPTION KEY   Old and New Comedy

Studying comedy in the abstract is difficult. It is best for you to test what has been discussed above by comparing our descriptions and interpretations with your own observations. If you have a chance to see some live comedy on stage, use that experience, but if that is impossible, watch some television comedy.

1. Is there criticism of society? If so, is it savage or gentle?
2. Are there blocking characters? Do they function somewhat in the ways described above? Are there any new twists?
3. Do you find examples of the generation gap? Are they similar to the archetypal pattern of the blocking character opposing the marriage of younger people? Do you observe any modern variations of this archetype?
4. See or read at least two comedies. How many type or stereotype characters can you identify? Is there an example of the dumb blonde? The braggart tough guy? The big lover? The poor but honest fellow? The dumb cop? The absent-minded professor? Do types or stereotypes dominate? Which do you find more humorous? Why?

Tragicomedy: The Mixed Genre

On the walls beside many stages, especially the ancient, we find two masks: the tragic mask with a downturned mouth and the comic mask with an upturned mouth. If there were a third mask, it would probably have an expression of bewilderment, as if someone had just asked a totally unanswerable question. Mixing the genres of tragedy and comedy in a drama may give such a feeling. Modern audiences are often left with many unanswered questions when they leave the theater. They are not always given resolutions that wrap things up neatly. Instead, *tragicomedy* tends, more than either tragedy or comedy, to reveal the *ambiguities* of the world. It does not usually end with the finality of death or the promise of a new beginning. It usually ends somewhere in between.

The reason tragicomedy has taken some time to become established as a genre may have had something to do with the fact that Aristotle did not provide an analysis, an extraordinary example of a philosopher having great influence on the arts. Thus for a long time tragicomedy was thought of as a mixing of two pure genres and consequently inferior in kind. The mixing of tragedy and comedy is surely justified, if for no other reason than the mixture works so well, as proved by most of the marvelous plays of Chekhov. This mixed genre is a way of making drama truer to life. As playwright Sean O'Casey commented to a college student, "As for the blending 'Comedy with Tragedy,' it's no new practice—hundreds have done it, including Shakespeare. . . . And, indeed, Life is always doing it, doing it, doing it. Even when one lies dead, laughter is often heard in the next room. There's no tragedy that isn't tinged with humour, no comedy that hasn't its share of tragedy—if one has eyes to see, ears to hear." Much of our best modern drama is mixed in genre so that, as O'Casey points out, it is rare to find a comedy that has no sadness to it, or a tragedy that is unrelieved by laughter.

A Play for Study: *The Rising of the Moon*

Isabella Augusta Gregory, known as Lady Gregory, was a founder of the celebrated Abbey Theatre in Dublin in the 1890s. Her comedies were essential to the success of what has come to be known as the Irish Dramatic Renaissance. *The Rising of the Moon* is one of her most popular short plays and illustrates many of the principles discussed in these pages. It is a play about two characters on opposite sides of a political upheaval. One, the policeman, must maintain the social order under which the English rule Ireland. The other, "a Ragged Man," is determined to change the social order to permit the Irish to rule Ireland. Out of this opposition of forces a remarkable outcome changes the balance of power and points to the future.

Lady Gregory (1852–1932)
THE RISING OF THE MOON   (1907)

Persons

SERGEANT POLICEMAN B
POLICEMAN X A RAGGED MAN

Scene: *Side of a quay in a seaport town. Some posts and chains. A large barrel. Enter three policemen. Moonlight.*

(Sergeant, who is older than the others, crosses the stage to right and looks down steps. The others put down a pastepot and unroll a bundle of placards.)

POLICEMAN B: I think this would be a good place to put up a notice. *(He points to barrel.)*

POLICEMAN X: Better ask him. *(Calls to Sergeant.)* Will this be a good place for a placard?

(No answer.)

POLICEMAN B: Will we put up a notice here on the barrel?

(No answer.)

SERGEANT: There's a flight of steps here that leads to the water. This is a place that should be minded well. If he got down here, his friends might have a boat to meet him; they might send it in here from outside.

POLICEMAN B: Would the barrel be a good place to put a notice up?

SERGEANT: It might; you can put it there.

(They paste the notice up.)

SERGEANT *(reading it):* Dark hair—dark eyes, smooth face, height five feet five—there's not much to take hold of in that—It's a pity I had no chance to seeing him before he broke out of jail. They say he's a wonder, that it's he makes all the plans for the whole organization. There isn't another man in Ireland would have broken jail the way he did. He must have some friends among the jailers.

POLICEMAN B: A hundred pounds is little enough for the Government to offer for him. You may be sure any man in the force that takes him will get promotion.

SERGEANT: I'll mind this place myself. I wouldn't wonder at all if he came this way. He might come slipping along there *(points to side of quay)*, and his friends might be waiting for him there *(points down steps)*, and once he got away it's little chance we'd have of finding him; it's maybe under a load of kelp he'd be in a fishing boat, and not one to help a married man that wants it to the reward.

POLICEMAN X: And if we get him itself, nothing but abuse on our heads for it from the people, and maybe from our own relations.

SERGEANT: Well, we have to do our duty in the force. Haven't we the whole country depending on us to keep law and order? It's those that are down would be up and those that are up would be down, if it wasn't for us. Well, hurry on, you have plenty of other places to placard yet, and come back here then to me. You can take the lantern. Don't be too long now. It's very lonesome here with nothing but the moon.

POLICEMAN B: It's a pity we can't stop with you. The Government should have brought more police into the town, with *him* in jail, and at assize° time too. Well, good luck to your watch.

(They go out.)

SERGEANT *(walks up and down once or twice and looks at placard):* A hundred pounds and promotion sure. There must be a great deal of spending in a hundred pounds. It's a pity some honest man not to be better of that.

(A Ragged Man appears at left and tries to slip past. Sergeant suddenly turns.)

SERGEANT: Where are you going?

MAN: I'm a poor ballad-singer, your honor. I thought to sell some of these *(holds out bundle of ballads)* to the sailors.

(He goes on.)

SERGEANT: Stop! Didn't I tell you to stop? You can't go on there.

MAN: Oh, very well. It's a hard thing to be poor. All the world's against the poor!

SERGEANT: Who are you?

MAN: You'd be as wise as myself if I told you, but I don't mind. I'm one Jimmy Walsh, a ballad-singer.

SERGEANT: Jimmy Walsh? I don't know that name.

MAN: Ah, sure, they know it well enough in Ennis. Were you ever in Ennis, sergeant?

SERGEANT: What brought you here?

MAN: Sure, it's to the assizes I came, thinking I might make a few shillings here or there. It's in the one train with the judges I came.

SERGEANT: Well, if you came so far, you may as well go farther, for you'll walk out of this.

MAN: I will, I will; I'll just go on where I was going.

(Goes toward steps.)

SERGEANT: Come back from those steps; no one has leave to pass down them tonight.

MAN: I'll just sit on the top of the steps till I see will some sailor buy a ballad off me that would give me my supper. They do be late going back to the ship. It's often I saw them in Cork carried down the quay in a handcart.

SERGEANT: Move on, I tell you. I won't have anyone lingering about the quay tonight.

MAN: Well, I'll go. It's the poor have the hard life! Maybe yourself might like one, sergeant. Here's a good sheet now. *(Turns one over.)* "Content and a pipe"—that's not much. "The Peeler° and the goat"—you wouldn't like that. "Johnny Hart"—that's a lovely song.

SERGEANT: Move on.

MAN: Ah, wait till you hear it. *(Sings.)*
There was a rich farmer's daughter lived near the town of Ross;

---

assize: Judicial inquest.

Peeler: Policeman

> She courted a Highland soldier, his name was
> Johnny Hart;
> Says the mother to her daughter, "I'll go distracted
> mad
> If you marry that Highland soldier dressed up in
> Highland plaid."

SERGEANT: Stop that noise.

(Man wraps up his ballads and shuffles toward the steps.)

SERGEANT: Where are you going?

MAN: Sure you told me to be going, and I am going.

SERGEANT: Don't be a fool. I didn't tell you to go that way; I told you to go back to the town.

MAN: Back to the town, is it?

SERGEANT *(taking him by the shoulder and shoving him before him):* Here, I'll show you the way. Be off with you. What are you stopping for?

MAN *(who has been keeping his eye on the notice, points to it):* I think I know what you're waiting for, sergeant.

SERGEANT: What's that to you?

MAN: And I know well the man you're waiting for—I know him well—I'll be going.

(He shuffles on.)

SERGEANT: You know him? Come back here. What sort is he?

MAN: Come back is it, sergeant? Do you want to have me killed?

SERGEANT: Why do you say that?

MAN: Never mind. I'm going. I wouldn't be in your shoes if the reward was ten times as much. *(Goes on off stage to left.)* Not if it was ten times as much.

SERGEANT *(rushing after him):* Come back here, come back. *(Drags him back.)* What sort is he? Where did you see him?

MAN: I saw him in my own place, in the County Clare. I tell you you wouldn't like to be looking at him. You'd be afraid to be in the one place with him. There isn't a weapon he doesn't know the use of, and as to strength, his muscles are as hard as that board *(slaps barrel).*

SERGEANT: Is he as bad as that?

MAN: He is then.

SERGEANT: Do you tell me so?

MAN: There was a poor man in our place, a sergeant from Ballyvaughan.—It was with a lump of stone he did it.

SERGEANT: I never heard of that.

MAN: And you wouldn't, sergeant. It's not everything that happens gets into the papers. And there was a

policeman in plain clothes, too. . . . It is in Limerick he was. . . . It was after the time of the attack on the police barrack at Kilmallock. . . . Moonlight . . . just like this . . . waterside. . . . Nothing was known for certain.

SERGEANT: Do you say so? It's a terrible county to belong to.

MAN: That's so, indeed! You might be standing there, looking out that way, thinking you saw him coming up his side of the quay *(points)*, and he might be coming up this other side *(points)*, and he'd be on you before you knew where you were.

SERGEANT: It's a whole troop of police they ought to put here to stop a man like that.

MAN: But if you'd like me to stop with you, I could be looking down this side. I could be sitting up here on this barrel.

SERGEANT: And you know him well, too?

MAN: I'd know him a mile off, sergeant.

SERGEANT: But you wouldn't want to share the reward?

MAN: Is it a poor man like me, that has to be going the roads and singing in fairs, to have the name on him that he took a reward? But you don't want me. It'll be safer in the town.

SERGEANT: Well, you can stop.

MAN *(getting up on barrel):* All right, sergeant. I wonder, now, you're not tired out, sergeant, walking up and down the way you are.

SERGEANT: If I'm tired I'm used to it.

MAN: You might have hard work before you tonight yet. Take it easy while you can. There's plenty of room up here on the barrel, and you see farther when you're higher up.

SERGEANT: Maybe so. *(Gets up beside him on barrel, facing right. They sit back to back, looking different ways.)* You made me feel a bit queer with the way you talked.

MAN: Give me a match, sergeant *(he gives it and man lights pipe)*; take a draw yourself? It'll quiet you. Wait now till I give you a light, but you needn't turn round. Don't take your eye off the quay for the life of you.

SERGEANT: Never fear, I won't. *(Lights pipe. They both smoke.)* Indeed it's a hard thing to be in the force, out at night and no thanks for it, for all the danger we're in. And it's little we get but abuse from the people, and no choice but to obey our orders, and never asked when a man is sent into danger, if you are a married man with a family.

MAN *(sings):* As through the hills I walked to view the hills and shamrock plain,

I stood awhile where nature smiles to view the rocks
  and streams,
On a matron fair I fixed my eyes beneath a fertile
  vale,
And she sang her song it was on the wrong of poor
  old Granuaile.

SERGEANT: Stop that; that's no song to be singing in
  these times.

MAN: Ah, sergeant, I was only singing to keep my heart
  up. It sinks when I think of him. To think of us two
  sitting here, and he creeping up the quay, maybe, to
  get to us.

SERGEANT: Are you keeping a good lookout?

MAN: I am; and for no reward too. Amn't I the foolish
  man? But when I saw a man in trouble, I never
  could help trying to get him out of it. What's that?
  Did something hit me?

(Rubs his heart.)

SERGEANT *(patting him on the shoulder):* You will get
  your reward in heaven.

MAN: I know that, I know that, sergeant, but life is
  precious.

SERGEANT: Well, you can sing if it gives you more
  courage.

MAN *(sings):* Her head was bare, her hands and feet
  with iron bands were bound,
Her pensive strain and plaintive wail mingles with
  the evening gale,
And the song she sang with mournful air, I am old
  Granuaile.
Her lips so sweet that monarchs kissed . . .

SERGEANT: That's not it. . . . "Her gown she wore was
  stained with gore." . . . That's it—you missed that.

MAN: You're right, sergeant, so it is; I missed it.
  (Repeats line.) But to think of a man like you knowing a song like that.

SERGEANT: There's many a thing a man might know
  and might not have any wish for.

MAN: Now, I daresay, sergeant, in your youth, you used
  to be sitting up on a wall, the way you are sitting up
  on this barrel now, and the other lads beside you,
  and you singing "Granuaile"? . . .

SERGEANT: I did then.

MAN: And the "Shan Van Vocht"? . . .

SERGEANT: I did then.

MAN: And the "Green on the Cape"?

SERGEANT: That was one of them.

MAN: And maybe the man you are watching for tonight
  used to be sitting on the wall, when he was young,
  and singing those same songs. . . . It's a queer

world. . . .

SERGEANT: Whisht! . . . I think I see something coming. . . . It's only a dog.

MAN: And isn't it a queer world? . . . Maybe it's one of
  the boys you used to be singing with that time you
  will be arresting today or tomorrow, and sending
  into the dock. . . .

SERGEANT: That's true indeed.

MAN: And maybe one night, after you had been singing,
  if the other boys had told you some plan they had,
  some plan to free the country, you might have joined
  with them . . . and maybe it is you might be in trouble now.

SERGEANT: Well, who knows but I might? I had a great
  spirit in those days.

MAN: It's a queer world, sergeant, and it's little any
  mother knows when she sees her child creeping on
  the floor what might happen to it before it has gone
  though its life, or who will be who in the end.

SERGEANT: That's a queer thought now, and a true
  thought. Wait now till I think it out. . . . If it wasn't
  for the sense I have, and for my wife and family, and
  for me joining the force the time I did, it might be
  myself now would be after breaking jail and hiding
  in the dark, and it might be him that's hiding in the
  dark and that got out of jail would be sitting up here
  where I am on this barrel. . . . And it might be myself would be creeping up trying to make my escape
  from himself, and it might be himself would be keeping the law, and myself would be breaking it, and
  myself would be trying to put a bullet in his head, or
  to take up a lump of stone the way you said he
  did . . . no, that myself did. . . . Oh! *(Gasps. After a
  pause.)* What's that? *(Grasps man's arm.)*

MAN *(jumps off barrel and listens, looking out over
  water):* It's nothing, sergeant.

SERGEANT: I thought it might be a boat. I had a notion
  there might be friends of his coming about the quays
  with a boat.

MAN: Sergeant, I am thinking it was with the people
  you were, and not with the law you were, when you
  were a young man.

SERGEANT: Well, if I was foolish then, that time's gone.

MAN: Maybe, sergeant, it comes into your head sometimes, in spite of your belt and your tunic, that it
  might have been as well for you to have followed
  Granuaile.

SERGEANT: It's no business of yours what I think.

MAN: Maybe, sergeant, you'll be on the side of the country yet.

SERGEANT *(gets off barrel)*: Don't talk to me like that. I have my duties and I know them. *(Looks round.)* That was a boat; I hear the oars.

(Goes to the steps and looks down.)

MAN *(sings)*: O, then, tell me, Shawn O'Farrell,
  Where the gathering is to be.
In the old spot by the river
  Right well known to you and me!
SERGEANT: Stop that! Stop that, I tell you!
MAN *(sings louder)*: One word more, for signal token,
  Whistle up the marching tune,
With your pike upon your shoulder,
  At the Rising of the Moon.
SERGEANT: If you don't stop that, I'll arrest you.

(A whistle from below answers, repeating the air.)

SERGEANT: That's a signal. *(Stands between him and steps.)* You must not pass this way. . . . Step farther back. . . . Who are you? You are no ballad-singer.
MAN: You needn't ask who I am; that placard will tell you. *(Points to placard.)*
SERGEANT: You are the man I am looking for.
MAN *(takes off hat and wig. Sergeant seizes them)*: I am. There's a hundred pounds on my head. There is a friend of mine below in a boat. He knows a safe place to bring me to.
SERGEANT *(looking still at hat and wig)*: It's a pity! It's a pity. You deceived me. You deceived me well.
MAN: I am a friend of Granuaile. There is a hundred pounds on my head.
SERGEANT: It's a pity, it's a pity!
MAN: Will you let me pass, or must I make you let me?
SERGEANT: I am in the force. I will not let you pass.
MAN: I thought to do it with my tongue. *(Puts hand in breast.)* What is that?
VOICE OF POLICEMAN X *(outside)*: Here, this is where we left him.
SERGEANT: It's my comrades coming.
MAN: You won't betray me . . . the friend of Granuaile. *(Slips behind barrel.)*
VOICE OF POLICEMAN B: That was the last of the placards.
POLICEMAN X *(as they come in)*: If he makes his escape it won't be unknown he'll make it.

(Sergeant puts hat and wig behind his back.)

POLICEMAN B: Did anyone come this way?
SERGEANT *(after a pause)*: No one.

POLICEMAN B: No one at all?
SERGEANT: No one at all.
POLICEMAN B: We had no orders to go back to the station; we can stop along with you.
SERGEANT: I don't want you. There is nothing for you to do here.
POLICEMAN B: You bade us to come back here and keep watch with you.
SERGEANT: I'd sooner be alone. Would any man come this way and you making all that talk? It is better the place to be quiet.
POLICEMAN B: Well, we'll leave you the lantern anyhow.

(Hands it to him.)

SERGEANT: I don't want it. Bring it with you.
POLICEMAN B: You might want it. There are clouds coming up and you have the darkness of the night before you yet. I'll leave it over here on the barrel. *(Goes to barrel.)*
SERGEANT: Bring it with you, I tell you. No more talk.
POLICEMAN B: Well, I thought it might be a comfort to you. I often think when I have it in my hand and can be flashing it about into every dark corner *(doing so)* that it's the same as being beside the fire at home, and the bits of bogwood blazing up now and again.

(Flashes it about, now on the barrel, now on Sergeant.)

SERGEANT *(furious)*: Be off the two of you, yourselves and your lantern!

(They go out. Man comes from behind barrel. He and Sergeant stand looking at one another.)

SERGEANT: What are you waiting for?
MAN: For my hat, of course, and my wig. You wouldn't wish me to get my death of cold?

(Sergeant gives them.)

MAN *(going toward steps)*: Well, good night, comrade, and thank you. You did me a good turn tonight, and I'm obliged to you. Maybe I'll be able to do as much for you when the small rise up and the big fall down . . . when we all change places at the Rising *(waves his hand and disappears)* of the Moon.
SERGEANT *(turning his back to audience and reading placard)*: A hundred pounds reward! A hundred pounds! *(Turns toward audience.)* I wonder, now, am I as great a fool as I think I am?

1. *Plot:* What is the primary action of the drama? What happens to whom?
2. *Character:* To what extent do these characters seem archetypal? In what ways do they surprise us? Do they surprise themselves?
3. *Ideas:* What are the most important ideas presented to the audience in this drama? In what ways can you see conflicts implicit in these ideas? What resolutions of these conflicts seem possible?
4. *Setting:* The action takes place at night during the "rising of the moon." Why is darkness important to the drama, and how is the rising of the moon a metaphor for action?
5. *Genre:* Is this play a tragedy, comedy, or tragicomedy?

Experimental Drama

The twentieth century saw exceptional experimentation in drama in the Western world. Samuel Beckett wrote plays with no words at all, as in *Acts without Words*. One of his plays, *Not I,* has an oversized mouth talking with a darkened, hooded figure, thus reducing character to a minimum. In *Waiting for Godot,* plot was greatly reduced in importance. In *Endgame* two of the characters are immobilized in garbage cans. Beckett's experiments have demonstrated that even when the traditional elements of drama are de-emphasized or removed, it is still possible for drama to evoke intense participative experiences. Beckett has been the master of refining away. He subscribes to the catch phrase "less is more" of Mies van der Rohe.

Another important thrust of experimental drama has been to assault the audience. Antonin Artaud's "Theater of Cruelty" has regarded audiences as comfortable, pampered groups of privileged people. Peter Weiss's play — *The Persecution and Assassination of Marat as Performed by the Inmates of the Asylum at Charenton under the Direction of the Marquis de Sade* (or *Marat/Sade*) — obviously was influenced by Artaud's anti-establishment thinking. Through a depiction of insane inmates contemplating the audience at a very close range (Figure 8-7), it sought to break down the traditional security associated with the proscenium theater. *Marat/Sade* ideally was performed in a theater-in-the-round with the audience sitting on all sides of the actors and without the traditional fanfare of lights dimming for the beginning and lighting up for the ending. The audience is deliberately made to feel uneasy throughout the play. The depiction of intense cruelty within the drama is there because, according to Weiss, cruelty underlies all human events, and the play attempts a revelation of that all-pervasive cruelty. The audience's own discomfort is a natural function of this revelation.

Marat/Sade has usually been performed without a proscenium frame, but, nonetheless, on a stage, a space set apart from those watching. In the "Theater of the Absurd," sometimes, the separation between actors and audience is completely abolished, as in Jack Gelber's *The Connection* (1960s). The play was about a group of addicts waiting for their dealer to show up,

FIGURE 8-7
Marat/Sade. The Academy
Theatre production, Atlanta,
Georgia. (Courtesy Atlanta
History Center)

and it was specifically designed to seem like a non-play. Gelber was in the
audience—clearly identified as the author—complaining about the way
the production was distorting his play.

Richard Schechner's *Dionysus in '69* also did away with spatial separation. The space of the theater was the stage space, with a design by Jerry
Rojo that made players and audience indistinguishable. The play demanded
that everyone become part of the action; in some performances—and in
the filmed performance—most of the players and audience ended the

FIGURE 8-8
Robert Wilson in *Hamlet: A Monologue* at Alice Tully Hall. (© Sara Krulwich/The New York Times)

drama with a modern-day orgiastic rite. Such experimentation, indeed, seems extreme. But it is analogous to other dramatic events in other cultures, such as formal religious and celebratory rites.

Another significant aspect of the contemporary experimental drama is the tendency to interpret freely the written text. The director tends to become more identified with the play than the author. Andrei Serban, the director of such productions in the 1980s as *Agamemnon* and *The Cherry Orchard*, reinterprets these plays so freely that the authors, Aeschylus and Chekhov, hardly get a notice. When Brecht's *Three-Penny Opera* was performed, Richard Foreman, director of the highly experimental Hysteric-Ontological Theater in New York, dominated the play so much that the original text was almost ignored.

Robert Wilson, known for his daylong dramas and extraordinary staging of modern operas, performed *Hamlet* as a monologue in 1995 (Figure 8-8). Dressed in black, alone on stage, he played Hamlet as a man who reviewed his life moment by moment, reenacting the scenes of the play and telling the entire story from his point of view. Wilson depended on intense music and sounds, such as explosions and clanging, as well as on unusual lighting effects. *Hamlet* invites experimentation. Tom Stoppard interpreted the action from the point of view of Rosencrantz and Guildenstern in *Rosencrantz and Guildenstern Are Dead* (1966); Heiner Müller produced a wildly Expressionist version called *Hamletmachine* (1977); and Lee Blessing produced a fascinating version called *Fortinbras* (1991), which tells the story of the play from the point of view of Horatio, the only major character left at the end of the play.

PERCEPTION KEY   Experimental Drama

Should you have the chance to experience a drama produced by any of the directors or groups mentioned above, try to distinguish its features from those of the more traditional forms of drama. What observations can you add to those made above? Consider the kinds of satisfaction you can get as a participant. Is experimental drama as satisfying as traditional drama? What are the differences? To what extent are the differences to be found in the details? The structure? Are experimental dramas likely to be episodic or organic? Why?

Summary

The subject matter of drama is the human condition as represented by action. By emphasizing plot and character as the most important elements of drama, Aristotle helps us understand the priorities of all drama, especially with reference to its formal elements and their structuring. Aristotle's theory of tragedy focuses on the fatal flaw of the protagonist. Hegel's theory of tragedy focuses on the collision of good intentions. Tragedy and comedy both have archetypal patterns that help define them as genres. Some of the archetypes are related to the natural rhythms of the seasons and focus, in the case of tragedy, on the endings of things, such as death, and, in the case of comedy, on the beginnings of things, such as marriage. The subject matter of tragedy is the tragic—sorrow and suffering. The subject matter of comedy is the comic—oddball behavior and joy.

Comedy has several distinct genres. Old Comedy revels in broad humor. New Comedy satirizes the manners of a society; its commentary often depends on type and stereotype characters. Tragicomedy combines both genres to create a third genre. The ambiguity implied by tragedy joined with comedy makes this a particularly flexible genre, suited to a modern world that lives in intense uncertainty. The experiments in modern drama have broken away from traditional drama, creating fascinating insights into our time. The human condition shifts from period to period in the history of drama, but somehow the constancy of human concerns makes all great dramatists our contemporaries.

Bibliography

Aristotle. *Aristotle's Theory of Poetry*. Translated by S. H. Butcher. New York: Dover, 1951.

Bentley, Eric. *The Playwright as Thinker*. New York: Harcourt Brace and World, 1967.

Bergson, Henri. *Laughter*. New York: Arden Library, 1983.

Brockett, Oscar. *History of the Theatre*, 7th ed. Boston: Allyn and Bacon, 1995.

Burkman, Katherine. *The Arrival of Godot*. Rutherford, N.J.: Fairleigh Dickinson University Press, 1986.

Cameron, Kenneth M., and Theodore Hoffman. *A Guide to Theater Study*, 2d ed. New York: Macmillan, 1974.

Dihle, Albrecht. *A History of Greek Literature*. New York: Routledge, 1994.

Esslin, Martin. *The Theatre of the Absurd*, 3rd ed. New York: Penguin, 1991.

Fergusson, Francis. *The Idea of a Theater*. Princeton, N.J.: Princeton University Press, 1972.

Gassner, John. *Masters of the Drama*, 3rd ed. New York: Dover, 1954.

Gassner, John, and Ralph Allen. *Theatre and Drama in the Making*. 2 vols. Boston: Houghton Mifflin, 1964.

Jacobus, Lee. *The Bedford Introduction to Drama*, 4th ed. New York: St. Martin's Press, 2001.

———. *Shakespeare and the Dialectic of Certainty*. New York: St. Martin's Press, 1992.

Kernodle, George. *Invitation to the Theatre*. San Diego, Calif.: Harcourt Brace Jovanovich, 1985.

Mason, Jeffrey D. *Melodrama and the Myth of America*. Bloomington: Indiana University Press, 1993.

Nicoll, Allardyce. *The Theory of the Drama*. New York: Crowell, 1931.

Orr, John. *Tragicomedy and Contemporary Culture: Play and Performance from Beckett to Shepard*. Ann Arbor: University of Michigan Press, 1990.

Potts, L. J. *Comedy*. London: Hutchinson, 1966.

Roose-Evans, James. *Experimental Theatre: From Stanislavsky to Today*, rev. ed. London: Studio Vista, 1973.

Steiner, George. *The Death of Tragedy*. New York: Knopf, 1961.

Wilson, Edwin. *The Theatre Experience*. New York: McGraw-Hill, 1976.

Internet Resources

AMERICAN ASSOCIATION FOR COMMUNITY THEATRE

http://www.aact.org/

CLASSICAL GREEK AND ROMAN THEATRE

http://www.didaskalia.net/
http://www.classics.ox.ac.uk/apgrd/index.html

JAPANESE THEATRE

http://www.theatrehistory.com/asian/japanese.html

SCOTT'S THEATRE LINK

http://www.theatre-link.com/

MR. WILLIAM SHAKESPEARE AND THE INTERNET

http://shakespeare.palomar.edu

THEATRE HISTORY

http://www.theatrehistory.com/index.html

WOMEN OF COLOR, WOMEN OF WORDS—AFRICAN AMERICAN FEMALE PLAYWRIGHTS

http://www.scils.rutgers.edu/~cybers/home.html

CHAPTER 9

Music

Music is one of the most powerful of the arts partly because sounds — more than any other sensory stimulus — create in us involuntary reactions, pleasant or unpleasant. Live concerts, whether of the Boston Symphony, Wynton Marsalis at Lincoln Center, or Bruce Springsteen and the E Street Band on tour, usually excite delight in their audiences. Yet, in all cases the audiences rarely analyze the music. It may seem difficult to connect analysis with the experience of listening to music, but everyone's listening, including the performer's, benefits from a thorough understanding of some of the fundamentals of music.

Hearing and Listening

Music can be experienced in two basic ways: "hearing" or "listening." *Hearers* do not attempt to perceive accurately either the structure or the details of the form. They hear a familiar *melody* such as the Beatles' "Strawberry Fields," which may trigger associations with John Lennon, early rock and roll, and perhaps even the garden in Central Park dedicated to his memory. But aside from the melody, little else — such as the details of chord progression, movement toward or away from tonic and dominant — is heard. The case is much the same with classical music. Most hearers prefer richly melodic music, such as Tchaikovsky's Fifth Symphony, whose second movement especially contains lush melodies that can trigger romantic associations. But when one asks hearers if the melody was repeated exactly or varied, or whether the melody was moved from one instrument family to another, they cannot say. They are concentrating on the associations evoked by the music rather than on the structure of the music. A hearer of hard rock is likely to attend as much to the performer as to the sonic effects. Powerful repetitive rhythms and blasting sounds trigger visceral responses so strong that dancing or motion — often wild — becomes imperative. Another kind of hearer is "suffused" or "permeated" by music, bathing in sensuous sounds, as many people will do with their earphones tuned to soft rock, new age, or easy-listening sounds. In this nonanalytic but attractive state of mind the music spreads through the body rhythmically, soothingly. It feels great, and that is enough.

The *listeners,* conversely, concentrate their attention upon the form, details as well as structure. They could answer questions about the structure of Tchaikovsky's Fifth Symphony. And a listener, unlike a hearer, would be aware of the details and structure of works such as the Rolling Stones' "Sympathy for the Devil." Listeners focus upon the form that informs, that creates content. Listeners do not just listen: They listen for something—the content.

PERCEPTION KEY   Hearing and Listening

1. Play one of your favorite pieces of music. Describe its overall organization or structure. Is there a clear melody? Is there more than one melody? If so, are they similar to one another or do they contrast with each other? Is the melody repeated? Is it varied or the same? Do different instruments play it? If there are lyrics, are they repeated?

2. Describe details such as what kind of rhythm is used. Is it varied? How? Is there harmony? What kind of instruments are played? How do these details fit into the structure?

3. Play the first movement of Beethoven's Third Symphony (the *Eroica*). Answer the same questions for this piece as were asked in questions 1 and 2. Later, we will analyze this symphony. You may wish to compare your responses now with those you have after you have studied the work.

4. Do such questions annoy you? Would you rather just experience the music as physically stimulating? Or as a means to daydreaming? Or as sensuously suffusing?

5. Are you basically a hearer or a listener? Are you sometimes one and then the other? Which would you rather be most of the time? And at what times? Why?

If you find that you cannot answer the first three questions or find them annoying, then indeed you are a hearer. Even the most avid listeners will be hearers under certain circumstances. No one is always up for concentrated attention. And although one can *hear* the Mozart in the background of a loud cocktail party, no one can *listen*. If you are usually a hearer even when the circumstances allow for listening, it is our hope that we can help you toward being a listener. And if you are a listener, we hope to make you and ourselves better ones. The content of music gives generous gifts, provided we are prepared to receive them.

The Elements of Music

Before we go further, we will introduce some of the important terms and concepts essential to a clear discussion of music. We begin with some definitions and then analyze the basic musical elements of tone, consonance,

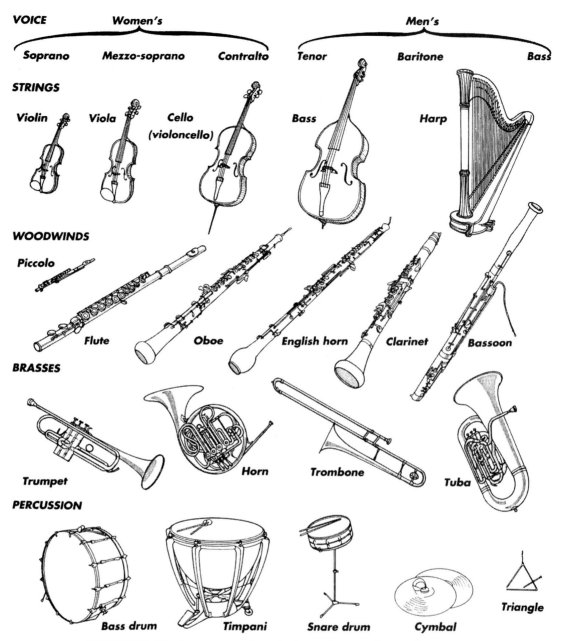

FIGURE 9-1. The key sources of musical tone in an orchestra (instruments not to scale). Calmann & King, Ltd.

dissonance, rhythm, tempo, melody, counterpoint, harmony, dynamics, and contrast. A common language about music is prerequisite to any intelligible analysis.

A sound that has one definite frequency or that is dominated by one definite frequency is a *tone*. Most music is composed of a succession of tones. Musical patterns are heard because of our ability to hear tones and remember them as they are played in succession. Tones on a musical instrument—except for pure tones—will have subordinate, related tones, or partials, sounding simultaneously, although not as loudly as the primary tone. Our ear is used to hearing a primary tone with fainter partials; therefore, when electronic instruments produce a pure tone—that is, with no partials—it may sound very odd to us. All instruments differ in the intensity or loudness of each of the partials. Consequently, a trumpet or a piano playing C will each have its distinctive timbre, or tone color, because of the variation in intensity of the simultaneously sounding partials that accompany the primary tone. (Figure 9-1 shows many of the various instruments that contribute to an orchestra.)

CONSONANCE

When two or more tones are sounded simultaneously and the result is pleasing to the ear, the resultant sound is said to be consonant. The phenomenon of *consonance* may be qualified by several things. For example, what sounds dissonant or unpleasant often becomes more consonant after repeated hearings. Thus, the sounds of the music of a different culture may seem dissonant at first but consonant after some familiarity develops. Also, there is the influence of context: A combination of notes or chords may seem dissonant in isolation or within one set of surrounding notes and consonant within another set. In the C major scale, the strongest consonances will be the eighth (C + C′) and the fifth (C + G), with the third (C + E), the fourth (C + F), and the sixth (C + A) being only slightly less consonant. Use Figure 9-2 if helpful, and sound the chords above on a piano.

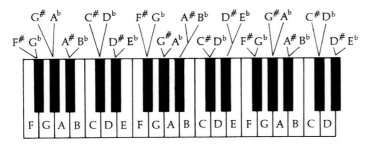

FIGURE 9-2
Notes of the piano keyboard.

DISSONANCE

Just as some tones sounding together tend to be soothing and pleasant, other tones sounding together tend to be rough and unpleasant. This unpleasantness is a result of wave interference and a phenomenon called "beating" which accounts for the roughness we perceive in *dissonance*. The most powerful dissonance is achieved when notes close to one another in pitch are sounded simultaneously. The second (C + D) and the seventh (B + C) are both strongly dissonant. Dissonance is important in building musical tension, since the desire to resolve dissonance with consonance is strong in most listeners. There is a story that Mozart's wife would retaliate against her husband after some quarrel by striking a dissonant chord on the piano. Wolfgang would be forced to come from wherever he was to play a resounding consonant chord to relieve the unbearable tension.

RHYTHM

Rhythm refers to the temporal relationships of sounds. Our perception of rhythm is controlled by the accent or stress on given notes and their duration. In the waltz, the accent is heavy on the first note (of three) in each musical measure. In most jazz music, the stress falls on the second and fourth notes (of four) in each measure. Marching music, which usually has six notes in each measure, emphasizes the first and fourth notes.

TEMPO

Tempo is the speed at which a composition is played. We perceive tempo in terms of beats, just as we perceive the tempo of our heartbeat as seventy-two pulses per minute, approximately. Many tempos have descriptive names indicating the general time value. *Presto* means "very fast"; *allegro* means "fast"; *andante* means "at a walking pace"; *moderato* means at a "moderate pace"; *lento* and *largo* mean "slow." Sometimes metronome markings are given in a score, but musicians rarely agree on any exact time figure. Tension, anticipation, and one's sense of musical security are strongly affected by tempo.

MELODIC MATERIAL: MELODY, THEME, AND MOTIVE

Melody is usually defined as a group of notes played one after another, having a perceivable shape or having a perceivable beginning, middle, and end. Usually a melody is easily recognizable when replayed. Vague as this definition is, we rarely find ourselves in doubt about what is or is not a melody. We not only recognize melodies easily but also can say a great deal about them. Some melodies are brief, others extensive; some slow, others fast; some bouncy, others somber. A melodic line is a vague melody, without a quite clear beginning, middle, and end. A *theme* is a melody that undergoes significant modifications in later passages. Thus, in the first movement of the *Eroica*, the melodic material is more accurately described as themes than melodies. On the other hand, the melodic material of "Swing Low, Sweet Chariot" (see Figure 9-5) is clear and singable. A *motive* is the briefest intelligible and self-contained fragment or unit of a theme — for example, the famous first four notes of Beethoven's Symphony no. 5.

In the Middle Ages the monks composing and performing church music began to realize that powerful musical effects could be obtained by staggering the melodic lines. This is called *counterpoint*—a playing of one or more motives, themes, or melodies against each other, as in folk songs such as "Row, Row, Row Your Boat." It implies an independence of simultaneous melodic lines, each of which can, at times, be most clearly audible. The opposition of melodic lines creates tension by virtue of their competition for our attention.

HARMONY

Harmony is the sounding of tones simultaneously. It is the vertical dimension, as with a chord (Figure 9-3), as opposed to the horizontal dimension, as with a melody. The harmony that most of us hear is basically chordal. A *chord* is a group of notes sounded together that has a specific relationship to a given key: The chord C-E-G, for example, is a major triad in the *key* of C major. At the end of a composition in the key of C, the major triad will emphasize the sense of finality—more than any other technique we know.

G or treble clef

F or bass clef

FIGURE 9-3
Harmony—the vertical element.

Chords are particularly useful for establishing *cadences:* progressions to resting points that release tensions. Cadences move from relatively unstable chords to stable ones. You can test this on a piano by first playing the notes C-F-A together, then playing C-E-G (consult Figure 9-2 for the position of these notes on the keyboard). The result will be obvious. The first chord establishes tension and uncertainty, making the chord unstable, while the second chord resolves the tension and uncertainty, bringing the sequence to a satisfying conclusion. You probably will recognize this progression as one you have heard in many compositions—for example, the "Amen" that closes most hymns. The progression exists in every key with the same sense of moving to stability.

In Figure 9-4 chords open the chorus of the "Battle Hymn of the Republic." Notice in the first chord the octave C interval in the bass clef and the third plus the fifth interval (E and G) in the treble clef, a very stable interval. Thus at the outset of the piece a strong equilibrium is established by the harmony. Whatever may happen in the middle of the composition, we will expect the end to be just as stable. A glance at the last measure shows this to be the case. Whereas the opening included two Cs, an E, and a G, the final harmony dispenses with the G and substitutes another C, adding even more stability to the ending.

Battle Hymn of the Republic

Attributed to William Steffe (Words by Julia Ward Howe)

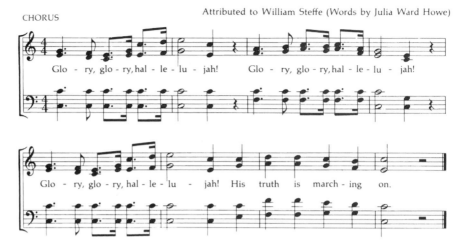

FIGURE 9-4
"Battle Hymn of the Republic." (Attributed to William Steffe. Words by Julia Ward Howe).

Harmony is based on apparently universal psychological responses. The smoothness of consonance and the roughness of dissonance seem to be just as perceptible to the non-Western as to the Western ear. The effects may be different due to cultural conditioning, but they are predictable within a limited range. One anthropologist, when told about a Samoan ritual in which he was assured he could hear original Samoan music—as it had existed from early times—hauled his tape recorder to the site of the ceremonies, waited until dawn, and when he heard the first stirrings turned on his machine and captured the entire group of Samoans singing "You are my sunshine, my only sunshine." The anthropologist was disappointed, but his experience underscores the universality of music.

DYNAMICS

One of the most easily perceived elements of music is dynamics: loudness and softness. Composers explore *dynamics*—as they explore keys, tone colors, melodies, rhythms, and harmonies—to achieve variety, to establish a pattern against which they can play, to build tension and release it, and to provide the surprise which can delight an audience. Two terms, *piano* ("soft") and *forte* ("loud"), with variations such as *pianissimo* ("very soft") and *fortissimo* ("very loud"), are used by composers to identify the desired dynamics at a given moment in the composition. A gradual building up of loudness is called a *crescendo*, whereas a gradual building down is called a decrescendo. Most compositions will have some of each, as well as passages that sustain a dynamic level.

CONTRAST

One thing that helps us value dynamics in a given composition is the composer's use of contrast. But contrast is of value in other ways. When more than one instrument is involved, the composer can contrast timbres. The brasses, for example, may be used to offer tonal contrast to a passage that may have been played by the strings. The percussion section, in turn, can contrast with both those sections, with high-pitched bells and low-pitched kettledrums covering a wide range of pitch and timbre. The woodwinds create very distinctive tone colors, and the composer writing for a large orchestra can use all of the families of instruments in ways designed to exploit the differences in the sounds of these instruments even when playing the same notes.

Composers may approach rhythm and tempo with the same attention to contrast. Most symphonies begin with a fast movement (usually labeled *allegro*) in the major key, followed by a slow movement (usually labeled *andante*) in a related or contrasting key, then a third movement with bright speed (often labeled *presto*), and a final movement that resolves to some extent all that has gone before—again at a fast tempo *(molto allegro)*, although sometimes with some contrasting slow sections within it, as in Beethoven's *Eroica*.

The Subject Matter of Music

If music is like the other arts, it has a content that is achieved by the form's transformation of some subject matter. However, some critics have denied that music has a subject matter, while others have suggested so many different possibilities as to create utter confusion. Our theory identifies two basic kinds of subject matter: feeling (emotions, passions, and moods) and sound. The issues are extremely complex and there is little consensus, but we hope our approach at least will be suggestive.

It is difficult for music to refer to objects and events outside itself. Therefore it is difficult to think of music as having the same kind of subject matter as a representational painting, a figurative sculpture, or a realistic novel. Nonetheless, composers have tried to circumvent this limitation by a number of means. One is to use sounds that imitate the sounds we experience outside music: bird songs and clocks in Haydn's symphonies, a thunderstorm in Beethoven's Symphony no. 6, sirens in Charles Ives's works. Limited as such imitation may be, it represents an effort to overcome the abstract nature of music and to give it a recognizable subject matter.

Another means is a program—usually in the form of a descriptive title, a separate written description, or an accompanying narrative, as in songs or opera. *La Mer,* by Claude Debussy, has a program clearly indicated by its title, *The Sea,* and its subtitles: "From Dawn to Noon at Sea," "Gambols of the Waves," and "Dialogue between the Wind and the Sea." Debussy tried to make *La Mer* refer to events that happen outside music. His success depends on our knowing the program and its relationship to the music. But even if we make the connections, there is a problem involved with stating flatly that the sea is the subject matter of *La Mer*. The sea cannot be perceived in listening to *La Mer* in anything like the way it can be perceived imaginatively from a literary description or the way it can be perceived more directly in a painting. If *La Mer* were a work that used the actual sounds of the sea (as with a tape recording) or closely imitated them—the crashing of waves, the roaring of winds, and similar sounds—the problem would be simplified. But the same kind of musical sounds found in *La Mer* is also found in other compositions by Debussy that have nothing to do with the sea.

It seems, therefore, that *La Mer* is an interpretation not of the sea but, rather, of our impressions of the sea, and the fact that Debussy is often referred to as an Impressionist is supporting evidence. Thus the subject matter of *La Mer* can be said to be the feelings evoked in him by the sea. The content of the music is the interpretation of those feelings. Given close attention to the program, this suggestion seems to pose few difficulties. But much music has no program, and *La Mer* can be enjoyed by those unaware of its program. Consequently, there may be some general feelingful character to the music that can be appreciated apart from any recognition that the swelling of a theme implies the swelling of a sea wind, that the crash of the orchestra suggests the crash of a wave, or that long, quiet passages suggest calm stretches of the sea. Apparently those who do not know the program may still recognize general feeling qualities in these same passages despite the fact that they do not relate these qualities to their feelings about the sea. There seems to be a general relationship, but not necessarily a strict relationship, between the structures of our feelings and the structures of music.

Feelings

Feelings are composed basically of sensations, emotions, passions, and moods. Any awareness of our sense organs, whether internal or external, being stimulated is a sensation. *Emotions* are strong sensations felt as related to a specific and apparent stimulus. *Passions* are emotions elevated to great intensity. *Moods,* in contrast, are sensations that arise from no specific or apparent stimulus, as when one awakens with a feeling of lassitude or gloom. Generally moods, although often long-lasting, are not felt as strongly as emotions and passions. Sometimes moods are evoked by emotions and passions and mix in with them so thoroughly that we are unaware of their origin. This often seems to happen when we listen to music. For example, a number of vibrant chordal progressions may evoke joyful emotions that—taken in their entirety—evoke a mood of well-being.

Music seems to be able to interpret and thus clarify our feelings primarily because in some important ways the structures of music parallel or are congruent with the structures of feelings. A rushing, busy passage can suggest unease or nervousness so powerfully that we sense unease to be a quality of the music itself, as well as feeling unease within ourselves. A slow passage in a minor key, such as a funeral march, can suggest gloom; a sprightly passage in a major key, such as a dance, can suggest joy. These extremes, and others like them, are obvious and easy for most listeners to comprehend. But there are innumerable subtleties and variations of feelings between these extremes, none of which can be named or discussed as easily as those mentioned. How can music interpret such feelings?

First of all, the exceptional power of sound to evoke feeling has been recognized by innumerable philosophers of art. John Dewey observes:

> Sounds come from outside the body, but sound itself is near, intimate; it is an excitation of the organism; we feel the clash of vibrations throughout the whole body. . . . A foot-fall, the breaking of a twig, the rustling of underbrush may signify attack or even death from hostile animal or man. . . . Vision arouses emotion in the form of interest—curiosity solicits further examination . . . or it institutes a balance between withdrawal and forward exploring action. It is sound that makes us jump.[1]

Second, feeling is heightened when a tendency to respond is in some way arrested or inhibited. Suspense is often fundamental to a feelingful response. Musical stimuli activate tendencies that are frustrated by means of deviations from the expected, and then these partially blocked tendencies are usually followed by meaningful resolutions. We hear a tone or tonal pattern and find it lacking in the sense that it demands other tones, for it seems to need or anticipate further tones that will presumably resolve its "need-fulness."

Third, it may be that musical structures possess, at least at times, more than just a general resemblance to the structures of feelings. Susanne Langer maintains that

> the tonal structures we call "music" bear a close logical similarity to the forms of human feelings—forms of growth and attenuation, flowing and stowing, conflict and resolution, speed, arrest, terrific excitement, calm, or subtle activation and dreamy lapses—not joy and sorrow perhaps, but the poignancy of either and both—the greatness and brevity and eternal passing of everything vitally felt. Such is the pattern, or logical form, of sentience, and the pattern of music is that same form worked out in pure, measured sound and silence. Music is a tonal analogue of emotive life.[2]

These examples of the close similarity between the structures of music and feelings are fairly convincing because they are extreme. Most listeners agree that some music has become associated with gloomy moods, while other music has become associated with exhilaration. Much of this process of association undoubtedly is the result of cultural conventions that we unconsciously accept. But presumably there is something in the music that is the basis for these associations, and Langer has made a convincing case that the basis is in the similarity of structures. It is unlikely, indeed, that a bouncy, dynamic trumpet passage would ever be associated with peaceful feelings. Such a passage is more likely to be associated with warlike alarms and uncertainties. Soft vibrating string passages, on the other hand, are more likely to be associated with less warlike anxieties. The associations of feelings with music, in other words, do not seem to be entirely conventional or arbitrary. The associations are made because music sounds the way feel-

---

[1] John Dewey, *Art as Experience* (New York: Milton Balch, 1934), p. 237.
[2] Susanne Langer, *Feeling and Form* (New York: Scribner's, 1953), p. 27.

ings feel. Music is "shaped" like the "shapes" of our feelings. Or, more precisely, the tonal structures of music and the inner or subjective structures of feelings can be significantly similar.

Music creates structures that are something like what we feel during nonmusical experiences. We perceive outside something of what we usually perceive inside. When we listen to the anguish of the funeral march in the second movement of Beethoven's *Eroica,* we perceive the structures of anguish but not what evoked the anguish. Beethoven interprets and, in turn, clarifies those structures, gives us insight into them. Anguish is a very unpleasant feeling, but when we listen to Beethoven's funeral march we normally feel pleasant emotions. For now we are not asked to be anguished, but to observe and interpret anguish musically. That insight dissipates—to a large extent, although probably never wholly—the pain. Understanding tragic music brings satisfaction, analogous to the satisfaction that comes from understanding tragic drama. But there is a fundamental difference: Tragic drama is about what causes painful feelings; tragic music is about the structure of painful feelings. The subject matter of tragic drama is the outside world; the subject matter of tragic music is the inside world.

Music has the capacity to clarify the nuances of feeling. When we speak in terms of nuances or when we suggest that music can clarify subtle feelings, we are no longer referring to nameable feelings such as joy, sadness, uncertainty, anxiety, and security. Music is, perhaps, richest in its ability to clarify feelings for which we have no names at all. One reason we return to a favorite piece of music again and again may be that it, and it alone in many cases, can interpret for us feelings that we could not otherwise identify. One of the results of participating with such music is the revelation of the unnameable feelings that refine and enlarge our life of feeling.

Music sometimes makes us recognize feelings we do not know we had. We feel a sorrow we have no name for, but we can say that it feels like the funeral march of the *Eroica.* Or, we feel a joy we have no name for, but we can say that it feels like the exuberant last movement of Mozart's *Jupiter* Symphony. And those who have participated with the *Eroica* and the *Jupiter* will understand more definitively what is meant than if we simply say "We are sad," or "We are joyful." No art reaches into our life of feeling more deeply than music.

Two Theories: Formalism and Expressionism

Music apparently not only evokes feeling in the listener but also reveals the structures of those feelings. Presumably, then, the form of *La Mer* not only evokes feelings analogous to the feelings the sea arouses in us but also interprets those feelings and gives us insight into them. The Formalists of music, such as Eduard Hanslick and Edmund Gurney,[3] deny this connection of music with nonmusical situations. For them, the apprehension of

---

[3]Eduard Hanslick, *The Beautiful in Music,* trans. Gustav Cohen (London: Novello, 1891), and Edmund Gurney, *The Power of Sound* (London: Smith, Elder, 1880).

the tonal structures of music is made possible by a unique musical faculty that produces a unique and wondrous effect, and they refuse to call that effect feeling since this suggests alliance with everyday feelings. They consider the grasp of the form of music so intrinsically valuable that any attempt to relate music to anything else is spurious.

As Igor Stravinsky, one of the greatest composers of the twentieth century, insisted, "Music is by its very nature essentially powerless to express anything at all."[4] In other words, the Formalists deny that music has a subject matter and, in turn, this means that music has no content, that the form of music has no revelatory meaning. We think that the theory of the Formalists is plainly inadequate, but it is an important warning against thinking of music as a springboard for hearing, for nonmusical associations and sentimentalism. Moreover, much work remains — building on the work of philosophers of art such as Dewey and Langer — to make clearer the mechanism of how the form of music evokes feeling and yet at the same time interprets or gives us insight into those feelings.

Much simpler — and more generally accepted than either the Formalist theory of Hanslick and Gurney or our own theory — is the Expressionist theory: Music evokes feelings. Composers express or communicate their feelings through their music to their audience. We should experience, more or less, the same feelings as the composer. But Mozart was distraught both psychologically and physically when he composed the *Jupiter* Symphony, one of his last and greatest works, and melancholy was the pervading feeling of his life shortly before his untimely death. Yet where is the melancholy in that symphony? Certainly there is melancholy in his *Requiem,* also one of his last works. But do we simply undergo melancholy in listening to the *Requiem?* Is it only evoked in us and nothing more? Is there not a transformation of melancholy? Does not the structure of the music — "out there" — allow us to perceive the structure of melancholy and thus understand it better? If so, then the undoubted fact that the *Requiem* gives extraordinary satisfaction to most listeners is given at least partial explication by our theory that music reveals as well as evokes emotion.

Sound

Apart from feelings, sound might also be thought of as one of the subject matters of music, because in some music it may be that the form gives us insight into sounds. This is somewhat similar to the claim that colors may be the subject matter of some abstract painting (see pages 94–95). The tone C in a musical composition, for example, has its analogue in natural sounds, as in a bird song, somewhat the way the red in an abstract painting has its analogue in natural colors. However, the similarity of a tone in music to a tone in the nonmusical world is rarely perceived in music that emphasizes tonal relationships. In such music, the individual tone usually is so caught up in its relationships with other tones that any connection with

---

[4]Igor Stravinsky, *An Autobiography* (New York: Simon and Schuster, 1936), p. 83.

sounds outside the music seems irrelevant. It would be rare, indeed, for someone to hear the tone C in a Mozart sonata and associate it with the tone C of some bird song.

Tonal relationships in most music are very different in their context from the tones of the nonmusical world. Conversely, music that does not emphasize tonal relationships—such as many of the works of John Cage—can perhaps give us insight into sounds that are noises rather than tones. Since we are surrounded by noises of all kinds—humming machines, people talking, and banging garbage cans, to name a few—we usually turn them off in our conscious mind so as not to be distracted from more important matters. This is such an effective turnoff that we are surprised and sometimes delighted when a composer introduces such noises into a musical composition. Then, for once, we listen to rather than away from them, and then we may discover these noises to be intrinsically interesting.

PERCEPTION KEY   The Subject Matter of Music

1. Select two brief musical compositions you like and participate with them. Then analyze each one with the following questions in mind. Do these pieces evoke feelings? Are there passages that evoke emotions? passions? moods? Do the structures of these pieces appear similar to the structures of emotions, passions, or moods? Be as specific as possible. Do you "live through" the feelings the music evokes? In other words, are they essentially the same feelings you experience in everyday situations? Or do they differ because their structures are perceptible in the music?

2. In a small group, present a very brief piece of popular music that you think has feeling as part of its subject matter. What degree of agreement do you find concerning what that feeling is? Is there general agreement relative to whether the feeling is emotion, passion, or mood? Listen to Tchaikovsky's *1812 Overture*, the "Tuba Mirum" from Berlioz's *Requiem*, Beethoven's *Grosse Fuge* (Great Fugue) Op. 133, or "Der Erlkönig" (The Erlking), a song by Franz Schubert. Ask the same questions as in question 1. Are the answers more complex? If so, why?

3. Analyze the Beatles' "Strawberry Fields" and/or the Rolling Stones' "Sympathy for the Devil." Ask the same questions as in question 1.

4. Listen to a John Cage or a Spike Jones recording that uses everyday sounds, such as barking dogs or car horns. With a group, discuss the value of such music for making one more aware of the characteristics and qualities of sounds we usually take for granted.

Tonal Center

A composition written mainly in one scale is said to be in the key that bears the name of the tonic or tonal center of that scale. A piece in the key of F major uses the scale of F major, although in longer, more complex works, such as symphonies, the piece may use other related keys in order to achieve variety. The tonal center of a composition in the key of F major is the tone F. We can usually expect such a composition to begin on F, to end on it, and to return to it frequently to establish stability. Each return to F builds a sense of security in the listener, while each movement away usually builds a sense of insecurity or tension. The listener perceives the tonic as the basic tone because it establishes itself as the anchor, the point of reference for all the other tones.

After beginning with A in the familiar melody of "Swing Low, Sweet Chariot" (Figure 9-5), the melody immediately moves to F as a weighty rest point. The melody rises no higher than D and falls no lower than C. (For convenience, the notes are labeled above the notation in the figure.) Most listeners will sense a feeling of completeness in this brief composition as it comes to its end. But the movement in the first four bars, from A downward

Swing Low, Sweet Chariot

FIGURE 9-5
"Swing Low, Sweet Chariot," African American spiritual.

to C, then upward to C, passing through the tonal center F, does not suggest such completeness; rather, it prepares us to expect something more. If you sing or whistle the tune, you will see that the long tone, C, in bar 4 sets up an anticipation that the next four bars attempt to satisfy. In bars 5 through 8 the movement downward from D to C, then upward to A, and finally to the rest point at F suggests a temporary resting point. When the A sounds in bar 8, however, we are ready to move on again with a pattern that is similar to the opening passage: a movement from A to C and then downward through the tonal center, as in the opening four bars. Bar 13 is structurally repetitious of bar 5, moving from D downward, establishing firmly the tonal center F in the last note of bar 13 and the first four tones of bar 14. Again, the melody continues downward to C, but when it returns in measures 15 and 16 to the tonal center F, we have a sense of almost total stability. It is as if the melody has taken us on a metaphoric journey: showing us at the beginning where "home" is; the limits of our movement away from home; and then the pleasure and security of returning to home.

The tonal center F is home, and when the lyrics actually join the word *home* in bar 4 with the tone C, we are a bit unsettled. This is a moment of instability. We do not become settled until bar 8, and then again in bar 16, where the word *home* falls on the tonal center F, which we have already understood — simply by listening — as the real home of the composition. This composition is very simple, but also subtle, using the resources of tonality to excite our anticipations for instability and stability.

PERCEPTION KEY   "Swing Low, Sweet Chariot"

1. What is the proportion of tonic notes (F) to the rest of the notes in the composition? Can you make any judgments about the capacity of the piece to produce and release tension in the listener on the basis of the recurrence of F?
2. Are there any places in the composition where you expect F to be the next note but it is not? If F is always supplied when it is expected, what does that signify for the level of tension the piece creates?
3. On the one hand, the ending of this piece produces a strong degree of finality. On the other hand, in the middle section the sense of finality is much less complete. Is this difference between the middle section and the ending effective? Explain.
4. Does this music evoke feeling in you? If so, what kind of feeling? Does the music interpret this feeling, help you understand it? If so, how does the music do this?
5. Would a piece that always produces what is expected be interesting? Or would it be a musical cliché? What is a musical cliché?

Musical Structures

The most familiar musical structures are based on repetition — especially repetition of melody, harmony, rhythm, and dynamics. Even the refusal to repeat any of these may be effective mainly because repetition is usually anticipated by the listener. Repetition in music is of particular importance because of the serial nature of the medium — linear, with one musical moment following another. The ear cannot retain sound patterns for very long, and thus it needs repetition to help hear the musical relationships.

THEME AND VARIATIONS

A theme and variations on that theme constitute a favorite structure for composers, especially since the seventeenth century. We are usually presented with a clear statement of the theme that is to be varied. The theme is sometimes repeated so that we have a full understanding, and then modifications of the theme follow. "A" being the original theme, the structure unfolds as A^1-A^2-A^3-A^4-A^5 . . . and so on to the end of the variations. Some marvelous examples of structures built on this principle are Bach's *Art of Fugue*, Beethoven's *Diabelli Variations*, Brahms' *Variations on a Theme by Joseph Haydn*, and Elgar's *Enigma Variations*.

If the theme is not carefully perceived when it is originally stated, the listener will have little chance of hearing how the variations relate to the theme. Furthermore, unless one knows the structure is theme and variations, much of the delight of the variations will be lost. Theme and variations is a structure that many arts can employ, especially the dance.

RONDO

The first section or refrain of a *rondo* will include a melody and perhaps a development of that melody. Then, after a contrasting section or episode with a different melody, the refrain is repeated. Occasionally, early episodes are also repeated, but usually not so often as the refrain. The structure of the rondo is sometimes in the pattern A-B-A-C-A—either B or D—and so on, ending with the refrain A. Some rondos will end on an episode instead of a refrain, although this is unusual. The rondo may be slow, as in Mozart's *Hafner Serenade,* or it may be played with blazing speed, as in Weber's *Rondo Brilliante*. The rondo may suggest a question–answer pattern, as in the children's song "Where Is Thumbkin?" Sometimes the A-B organization is reversed, so that the refrain comes second each time. The first and third movements of Vivaldi's *Four Seasons,* Haydn's *Gypsy Rondo,* Pachelbel's *Dance Rondo,* and the second movement of Beethoven's Symphony no. 4 are all fine examples of the rondo.

FUGUE

The *fugue,* a specialized structure of counterpoint, was developed in the seventeenth and eighteenth centuries and is closely connected with Bach and his *Art of Fugue*. Most fugues feature a melody—called the "statement"—which is set forth clearly at the beginning of the composition, usually with the first note the tonic of its key. Thus, if the fugue is in C major, the first note of the statement is likely to be C. Then that same melody more or less—called the "answer"—appears again, usually beginning with the dominant note (the fifth note) of that same key. The melodic lines of the statements and answers rise to command our attention and then submerge into the background as episodes of somewhat contrasting material intervene. Study the diagram in Figure 9-6 as a suggestion of how the statement, answer, and episode at the beginning of a fugue might interact. As the diagram indicates, the melodic lines often overlap, as in the popular song "Row, Row, Row Your Boat."

The fugue, like theme and variations, is a repetitive structure, for the statements, answers, and episodes generally are very similar to each other.

Sometimes they share the same pattern of ascending or descending tones. Often they have similar rhythms. In some cases the answer appears like a mirror image of the statement, or sometimes the answer may be an upside-down image of the statement. Sometimes the statements and answers are jammed together, in a device called the stretto (narrow passage), usually used near the conclusion of the fugue. Sometimes fugues exist not as independent compositions, but as part of a larger composition. Many symphonies, for example, have fugal passages as a means of development. Sometimes those fugal passages become the basis for independent fugues. Thus Beethoven's *Grosse Fuge* in B♭ was originally composed as a section within a string quartet.

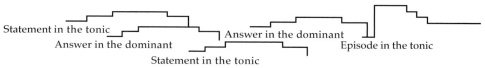

Statement in the tonic
Answer in the dominant
Answer in the dominant
Statement in the tonic
Episode in the tonic

FIGURE 9-6
The fugue.

SONATA FORM

The eighteenth century brought the *sonata form* to full development, and many contemporary composers still find it very useful. Its overall structure basically is *A-B-A*, with these letters representing the main parts of the composition and not just melodies, as for the rondo. The first A is the exposition, with a statement of the main theme in the tonic key of the composition and usually a secondary theme or themes in the dominant key (the key of G, for example, if the tonic key is C). A theme is a melody that is not merely repeated, as it usually is in the rondo, but is instead developed in an important way. In the A section, the themes are usually restated but not developed very far. This full development of the themes occurs in the B, or development, section, with the themes normally played in closely related keys. The development section explores contrasting dynamics, timbres, tempos, rhythms, and harmonic possibilities inherent in the material of the exposition. In the third section, or recapitulation, the basic material of the first section or exposition is more or less repeated, usually in the tonic key. After the contrasts of the development section, this repetition in the home key has the quality of return and closure.

The sonata form is ideal for revealing the resources of melodic material. For instance, when contrasted with a very different second theme, the principal theme of the exposition may take on a surprisingly new quality, as in the opening movement of Beethoven's *Eroica*. We sense that we did not fully grasp the principal theme the first time. This is one of the major sources of satisfaction for the careful listener. Statement, contrasting development, and restatement is a useful pattern for exploring the resources of almost any basic musical material, especially the melodic.

The symphony is usually a four-movement structure often employing the sonata form for its opening and closing movements. The middle movement or movements normally are contrasted with the first and last movements in dynamics, tempos, timbres, harmonies, and melodies. The listener's ability to perceive how the sonata form functions within most symphonies is essential if the total structure of the symphony is to be comprehended.

Sonata Form

1. Listen to and then examine closely the first movement of a symphony by Haydn or Mozart. That movement with few exceptions will be a sonata form. If a score is available it can be helpful. (You do not have to be a musician to read a score.) Identify the exposition section—which will come first—and the beginning of the development section. Then identify the end of the development and the beginning of the recapitulation section. At these points you should perceive some change in dynamics, tempo, and movements from home key or tonic to contrasting keys and back to the tonic. You need not know the names of those keys in order to be aware of the changes. They are usually easily perceptible.

2. Once you have developed the capacity to identify these sections, describe the characteristics that make each of them different. Note the different characteristics of melody, harmony, timbre, dynamics, rhythm, tempo, and contrapuntal usages.

3. When you have confidence in your ability to perceive the sonata form, do some comparative studies. Take the first movement of a Haydn symphony—Symphony no. 104 in D major, the *London,* for example—and compare its first movement with any of the first movements of Brahms' four symphonies. All these movements are sonata forms, but notice how differently they are structured and how much more difficult it is to know where you are with the Brahms. The sonata form allows for great variability. For example, most of Haydn's early symphonies, up to around Symphony no. 70, are monothematic; that is, only one theme appears in the exposition. Mozart's, Beethoven's, and Brahms' sonata forms, on the other hand, are very rarely monothematic.

FANTASIA

Romantic composers, especially in the period from 1830 to 1900, began working with structures much looser than in earlier periods. We find compositions with terms such as rhapsodies, nocturnes, aubades, and fantasias. The names are impressionistic and vague, suggesting perhaps that their subject matter may be moods. The *fantasia* may be the most helpful of these to examine, since it is to the sonata form what free verse is to the sonnet. The word *fantasia* implies fancy or imagination, which suggests, in turn, the fanciful and the unexpected. It is not a stable structure, and its sections cannot be described in such conventional terms as A-B-A. The fantasia usually offers some stability by means of a recognizable melody of a singable quality, but then it often shifts to material that is less identifiable, tonally certain, and harmonically secure. The succession of motives (brief musical units) is presented without regard for predetermined order. However, there are controls in terms of pacing, the relationship of motives, the harmonic coloring, dynamics, and rhythms. Sometimes the fantasia will explore a wide range of feelings by contrasting fast and slow, loud and soft, rich and spare harmonies, and singable melodies with those less singable.

Many of Robert Schumann's best works are piano pieces he called fantasias. Mozart's Fantasia in C minor is an excellent example of the mode, but probably most of us are more familiar with Moussorgsky's fantasia: *A Night on Bald Mountain*, which was used in Walt Disney's *Fantasia*, a 1940 film.

THE SYMPHONY

The symphony marks one of the highest developments in the history of Western instrumental music. The symphony has proved to be so flexible a structure that it has flourished in every musical era since the *Baroque* period in the early eighteenth century, especially with the works of Handel and C. P. E. Bach. The word *symphony* implies a "sounding together." From its beginnings, through its full and marvelous development in the works of Haydn, Mozart, Beethoven, and Brahms, the symphony was particularly noted for its development of harmonic structures. Harmony is the sounding together of tones that have an established relationship to one another. Because of its complexity, harmony is a subject most composers must study in great depth during their apprentice years.

The symphony as it existed in the Baroque period of the late seventeenth and early eighteenth centuries, the Classical period of the late eighteenth and early nineteenth centuries, and the Romantic period of the nineteenth and early twentieth centuries, has undergone great changes. Many of these can be traced to developing concepts of harmony, most of which are extremely complex and not fully intelligible without considerable analysis. Triadic harmony (which means the sounding of three tones of a specific chord, such as the basic chord of the key C major, C-E-F, or the basic chord of the key F major, F-A-C) is common to most symphonies, especially before the twentieth century. Even in classical symphonies, however, such as Mozart's, the satisfaction that the listener has in triadic harmony is often withheld by the composer in order to develop musical ideas that will resolve their tensions only in a full, resounding chordal sequence of triads.

The symphony usually depends on thematic development. All the structures that we have discussed—theme and variations, rondo, fugue, and sonata form—develop melodic material, and some or all of them are often included in the symphony. Because it is a much larger structure with usually three or four movements, the symphony lends itself to expansive developments of musical material. In general, as the symphony evolved into its conventional structure in the time of Haydn and Mozart, the four movements were ordered as follows: first movement, sonata form; second movement, A-B-A or rondo; third movement, minuet; fourth movement, sonata form or rondo. There were exceptions to this order even in Haydn's and Mozart's symphonies, and in the Romantic and following periods the exceptions increased as the concern for conventions decreased.

The relationships between the movements of a symphony are flexible. The same melodic or key or harmonic or rhythmic approach may not prevail in all the movements. The sequence of movements may then seem arbitrary. On the other hand, there are some symphonies that develop similar material through all movements, and then the sequence may seem less, if at all, arbitrary. This commonality of material is relatively unusual because three or four movements can rapidly exhaust all but the most sustaining and profound material. One's ear can get tired of listening to the same material for an extended time. The preferred method, until the twentieth century, was to follow the conventional patterns of tempo throughout, using appropriate melodies and harmonies in each movement, which is to say material best suited for fast or slow tempos.

A comparison of the tempo markings of several symphonies by important composers usually shows several similarities: fast opening and closing movements with at least one slower middle movement. One of the most important connecting devices holding the movements of a symphony together is the convention of altering the tempo in patterns similar to those listed below. An alteration of tempo can express a profound change in the feeling of a movement. The predictable alteration of tempo is one of the things our ear depends upon for finding our way through the whole symphony. In such large structures, we need all the signposts we can get, since it is easy to lose one's way through a piece that may last almost an hour. The following tempo markings are translated loosely:

Haydn, Symphony in G major, no. 94, the *Surprise*
1. *Adagio, vivace* (slowly, lively)
2. *Andante* (moderately slow)
3. *Allegretto* (dancelike)
4. *Allegro molto* (very fast)

Mozart, Symphony in C major, no. 41, the *Jupiter*
1. *Allegro vivace* (fast and lively)
2. *Andante cantabile* (slow and songlike)
3. *Allegretto* (dancelike)
4. *Allegro molto* (very fast)

Beethoven, Symphony in C minor, no. 5
1. *Allegro con brio* (fast, breezy)
2. *Andante con moto* (slowly with motion)
3. *Allegro, scherzo* (fast, with dance rhythm)
4. *Allegro, presto* (fast, very quick)

Brahms, Symphony in E minor, no. 4
1. *Allegro non assai* (fast, but not very)
2. *Andante moderato* (moderately slow)
3. *Presto giocoso* (fast and jolly)
4. *Allegro energetico e patetico* (fast, with energy and feeling)

The tempo markings in these and other symphonies, including those of modern composers, like Ives and Stravinsky, suggest that each movement is designed with other movements in mind. That is, each movement offers a contrast to those that come before or after it. Composers of symphonies have many means at their disposal besides tempo to achieve contrast, especially rhythm. The first movement is often written in 4/4 time, which means that there are four quarter notes in each measure, with the first especially and the third usually getting accents. The rhythms of the second movement are so varied that no general pattern is discernible. The third movement, especially in the early period of the symphony (Haydn and Mozart) is a dancelike minuet — 3/4 time, three quarter notes to a measure, with the first note receiving the accent. Occasionally in the second and third movements, march time is used, either 6/8 time or 2/4 time. In 6/8 time there are six eighth notes to a measure, with the first and fourth receiving the accent. In 2/4 time the first of the two quarter notes receives the accent. Sometimes this produces the "oom-pah" sound we associate with marching bands. The fourth movement, usually a sonata form or a rondo, normally returns to 4/4 time.

Contrast is also achieved by varying the dynamics, with opposing loud and soft passages likely to be found in any movement. We might expect the middle movements, which are normally shorter than the first and last, to use less dynamic shifting. We usually expect the last movement to build to a climax that is smashing and loud. Variations in the length of movements add to contrast. And since the symphony is usually played by a large orchestra, the composer has a variety of instrumental families to depend on for adding contrast of tone colors. A theme, for instance, can be introduced by the violins, passed on to the woodwinds, then passed on to the horns, only to return to the violins. Secondary themes can be introduced by flutes or piccolos so as to contrast with the primary themes developed by other families of instruments. A secondary theme is often very different in length, pitch, and rhythmic character from a primary theme, thus achieving further contrast. Sometimes a theme or a developmental passage is played by a single instrument in a solo passage and then with all the instruments in that family playing together. Once the theme has been introduced by a single instrument or a small group, it may be played by the entire orchestra. These contrasts should hold our attention — for otherwise we miss much of what is going on — helping us grasp the melodic material by showing us how it sounds in different timbres and ranges of pitch (higher in the flutes, lower in the cellos). The exceptional possibilities for achieving contrast in the symphony account, in part, for its sustaining success over the centuries.

We readily perceive contrasts in tempo, time signature, dynamics, and instrumentation, even if we are not trained and do not have access to the score of the composition. But there are subtler means of achieving contrast. For one thing, even within a specific movement, a composer will probably use a number of different keys. Usually they are closely related keys, such as C major followed by G major, or F major followed by C major. The dominant tone is the fifth tone, and one of the most convenient ways of moving from key to key is to follow the cycle of fifths, confident that each new key will clearly relate to the key that precedes it. Distant keys, A major to, say, D minor, can produce a sense of incoherence or uncertainty. Such motions between keys often are used to achieve this effect.

The average listener cannot always tell just by listening that a passage is in a new key, although practiced musicians can tell immediately. The exploration of keys and their relationship is one of the more interesting aspects of the development portions of most symphonies. The very concept of development, which means the exploration of a given material, is sometimes best realized by playing the same or similar material in different keys, finding new relationships among them. Our awareness of an especially moving passage is often due to the subtle manipulation of keys that analysis with a score might help us better understand. For the moment, however, let us concentrate on what the average listener can detect in the symphony.

The Symphony

Listen to a symphony by Haydn or Mozart (they established the form for us). Then analyze as you listen intermittently, jotting down notes on each movement with the following questions in mind:

1. Is the tempo fast, medium, or slow? Is it the same throughout? How much contrast is there in tempo within the movement? Between movements?
2. Can you hear differences in time signature—such as the difference between waltz time and marching time?
3. How much difference in dynamics is there in a given movement? From one movement to the next? Are some movements more uniform in loudness than others?
4. What variations do you perceive in instrumentation? If you have a difficult time distinguishing among instruments, use the families of instruments sketch (Figure 9-1).
5. Identify melodic material as treated by single instruments, groups of instruments, or the entire orchestra.
6. Are you aware of the melodic material establishing a tonal center, moving away from it, then returning? (Perhaps only practiced listeners will be able to answer this in the affirmative.)
7. Are you surprised by any passage within a movement? Why?
8. As a movement is coming to an end, is your expectation of the finale carefully prepared for by the composer? Is your expectation frustrated in any fashion? Is this effective or not? Explain.
9. Can you identify or describe the subject matter of each movement? Of the whole symphony?
10. Can you describe the content of each movement? Of the whole symphony?

Beethoven's Symphony in E♭ Major, No. 3, *Eroica*

Beethoven's "heroic" symphony is universally acclaimed by musicians and critics as a symphonic masterpiece. It has some of the most daring innovations for its time, and it succeeds in powerfully unifying its movements by developing similar material throughout, especially melodic and rhythmic. The symphony was finished in 1804 and was intended to celebrate the greatness of Napoleon, whom Beethoven regarded as a champion of democracy and the common man. But when Napoleon declared himself emperor in May 1804, Beethoven, his faith in Napoleon betrayed, was close to destroying the manuscript. However, the surviving manuscript indicates that he simply tore off the dedication page and substituted the general title *Eroica*.

The four movements of the symphony follow the tempo markings we would expect of a classical symphony, but there are a number of important ways in which the *Eroica* is unique in the history of musical structures. The first movement, marked *allegro con brio* (fast, breezy), is a sonata form with the main theme of the exposition based on a triadic chord in the key of E♭ major that resoundingly opens the movement. The development section introduces a number of related keys, and the recapitulation ultimately returns to the home key of E♭ major. There is a *coda* (a section added to the end of the recapitulation) so extended that it is something of a second development section as well as a conclusion. After avoidance of the home key in the development, the E♭ major finally dominates in the recapitulation and the coda. The movement is at least twice as long as the usual first movements of earlier symphonies, and no composer before had used the coda in such a developmental way. Previously the coda was quite short and repetitive. The size of the movement, along with the tight fusion of themes and their harmonic development into such a large structure, were very influential on later composers. The feelings that are evoked and revealed are profound and enigmatic.

The slow second movement is dominated by a funeral march in 2/4 time, with a very plaintive melody and a painfully slow tempo (in some performances), and an extremely tragic mood prevails. In contrast with the dramatic and vivid first movement, the second movement is sobering, diminishing the reaches of power explored in such depth in the first movement. The second movement uses a fugue in one of its later sections, even though the tempo of the passage is so slow as to seem to "stretch time." Despite its exceptional slowness, the fugue, with its competing voices and constant, roiling motion, seems appropriate for suggesting heroic, warlike feelings. The structure is a rondo: A-B-A'-C-A''-B'-D-A-''', A being the theme of the funeral march, and following A's being variations. The other material, including the fugue in C, offers some contrast, but because of its close similarity to the march theme, it offers no resolution.

The relief comes in the third movement, marked *scherzo,* which is both lively (*scherzo* means a joke) and dancelike. The movement is derivative from the first movement, closely linking the two in an unprecedented way. The time signature is the same as a minuet, 3/4, and the melodic material is built on the same triadic chord as in the first movement. And there is the same rapid distribution from one group of instruments to another. However, the third movement is much briefer than the first, while only a little briefer than the last.

The finale is marked *allegro molto* (very fast). A theme and variation movement, it is a catchall. It includes two short fugues, a dance using a melody similar to the main theme of the first movement, which is not introduced until after a rather decorative opening, and a brief march. Fast and slow passages are contrasted in such a fashion as to give us a sense of a recapitulation of the entire symphony. The movement brings us triumphantly to a conclusion that is profoundly stable. At this point, we can most fully appreciate the powerful potentialities of the apparently simple chord-based theme of the first movement. Every tonal pattern that follows is ultimately derivative, whether by approximation or by contrast, and at the end of the symphony the last triumphal chords are characterized by total inevitability and closure. The feelings evoked and revealed defy description, although there surely is a progression from yearning to sorrow to joy to triumph.

The following analysis will be of limited value without your listening carefully to the symphony more than once. If possible use a score, even if you have no musical training. Ear and eye can coordinate with practice.

LISTENING KEY: THE SYMPHONY

BEETHOVEN, SYMPHONY NO. 3, OPUS 55, *EROICA*

Performed by George Szell and the Cleveland Orchestra. CBS Compact Disc MYK 3722. (This disc is available for use with this book.)

Listen to the symphony using the timings of the compact disc. Before reading the following discussion, listen to the symphony. Then after studying the analysis, the "thinking at," listen again, this time participatively. Your enjoyment will likely be much greater.

Movement I: *Allegro Con Brio*. Fast, Breezy.

Sonata form, 3/4 time, E♭ major. Timing: 14:46, Track 1.

FIGURE 9-7
Opening chord in E♭ major (0:01).

The first two chords are powerful, staccato, isolated, and compressed (Figure 9-7). They are one of the basic chords of the home key of E♭ major: G-E♭-B♭-G. Then at the third measure (Figure 9-8) the main theme, generated from the opening chord of the symphony, is introduced. Because it is stated in the cellos, it is low in pitch and somewhat portentous, although not threatening. Its statement is not quite complete, for it unexpectedly ends on a C♯ (♯ is the sign for sharp). The horns and clarinets take the theme at bar 15 (0:19), only to surrender it at bar 20 (0:23) to a group of ascending tones closely related to the main theme.

FIGURE 9-8
Main theme, cellos (0:04).

The second theme is in profound contrast to the first. It is a very brief and incomplete pattern (and thus could also be described as a motive) of three descending tones moved from one instrument to another in the woodwinds, beginning with the oboes at bar 45 (Figure 9-9). This theme is

FIGURE 9-9
Second theme, oboes at bar 45 (0:54).

unstable, like a gesture that needs something to complete its meaning. And the following motive of dotted eighth notes at bars 60 through 64 played by flutes and bassoons (Figure 9-10) is also unstable.

FIGURE 9-10
Flutes and bassoons at bars 60 through 64 (1:14).

This is followed by a rugged rhythmic passage, primarily audible in the violins, preparing us for a further incomplete thematic statement at bar 83, a very tentative, delicate interlude. The violin passage that preceded it

FIGURE 9-11
Violin passage preceding bar 83 (1:19).

(Figure 9-11) functions here and elsewhere as a link in the movement between differing material. Getting this passage firmly in your memory will help you follow the score, for it returns dependably.

Many passages have unsettling fragments, such as the dark, brooding quality of the cello and contrabass motive shown in Figure 9-12, which sounds as a kind of warning, as if it were preparing us for something like the funeral march of the second movement. It repeats much later in variation at bar 498, acting again as an unsettling passage. Many other passages also appear to be developing into a finished statement, only to trail off. Some commentators have described these passages as digressions, but this is misleading, because they direct us to what is coming.

FIGURE 9-12
Cello and bass motive (1:57).

The exposition starts to end at bar 148 (3:03), with a long passage in B♭, the measures from 148 to 152 hinting at the opening theme, but they actually prepare us for a dying-down action that joins with the development. In George Szell's rendition, as in most recordings, the repeat sign at 156 is ignored. Instead, the second ending (bars 152 to 159) is played, and this passage tends to stretch and slow down, only to pick up when the second theme is played again in descending patterns from the flutes through all the woodwinds (3:16).

The development section is colossal, from bars 156 to 394, beginning at 3:18. The main theme reoccurs first at 178 (3:48) in shifting keys in the cellos, then is played again in B♭ from 186 to 194 (3:55), very slow and drawn out. Contrasting passages mix in so strongly that we must be especially alert or we will fail to hear the main theme. The momentum speeds up around bar 200 (4:16), where the main theme is again played in an extended form in the cellos and the contrabasses. The fragmented motives contribute to a sense of incompleteness, and we do not have the fullness of the main theme to hold on to. The fragmentary character of the second theme is also emphasized, especially between bars 220 and 230 (4:39). When we reach the crashing discords at bar 275 (5:44), the following quieting down is a welcome relief. The subsequent passage is very peaceful and almost without direction until we hear again the main theme in B♭ at bar 300 (6:21), then again at 312 (6:37) in the cellos and contrabasses. The music builds in loudness, quiets down, and then the main theme is stated clearly in the bassoons, preparing for an extended passage that includes the main theme in the woodwinds building to a mild climax in the strings at bar 369 (Figure 9-13).

FIGURE 9-13
Strings at bar 369 (7:53).

The remainder of this passage is marvelously mysterious, with the strings maintaining a steady tremolo and the dynamics brought down almost to a whisper. The horn enters in bar 394 (8:24), playing the main theme in virtually a solo passage. Bars 394 and 395 are two of the most significant measures of the movement because of the way in which they boldly announce the beginning of the recapitulation. The horns pick up the main theme again at bar 408 (8:32), loud and clear, and begin the restatement of the exposition section. The recapitulation begins at bar 394 (8:24) and extends to bar 575 (12:05). It includes a brief development passage, treating the main theme in several unusual ways, such as the tremolo statement in the violins at bars 559 to 565 (Figure 9-14).

FIGURE 9-14
Violins at bars 559 through 564 (11:50).

The long, slow, quiet passages after bar 575 (12:05) prepare us for the incredible rush of power that is the coda—the "tail" or final section of the movement. The triumphal quality of the coda—which includes extended development, especially of the main theme—is most perceptible, perhaps, in the juxtaposition of a delightful, running violin passage from bar 631 to bar 639 (13:31), with the main theme and a minimal variation played in the horns. It is as if Beethoven is telling us that he has perceived the musical problems that existed with his material, mastered them, and now is celebrating with a bit of simple, passionate, and joyous music.

PERCEPTION KEY   Movement I

1. Describe the main theme and the second theme. What are their principal qualities of length, "tunefulness," range of pitch, rhythm, and completeness? Could either be accurately described as a melody? Which is easier to whistle or hum? Why could the second theme be plausibly described as a motive? Do the two themes contrast with each other in such a way that the musical quality of each is enhanced? If so, how?

2. What are the effects of hearing the main theme played in different keys, as in bars 3 to 7 (0:04), bars 184 to 194 (3:55), and bars 198 to 206 (4:16)? All these passages present the theme in the cellos and contrabasses. What are the effects of the appearance of the theme in other instrumental families, such as the bassoons at bar 338 (7:12) in the development section and the

horns at bar 408 (8:32) in the recapitulation section? Does the second theme appear in a new family of instruments in the development section?

3. How clearly perceptible do you find the exposition, development, recapitulation, and coda sections? Can you describe, at least roughly, the feeling qualities of each of these sections?

4. Many symphonies lack a coda. Do you think Beethoven was right in adding a coda, especially such a long and involved one? If so, what does it add?

5. If possible, record the movement on a tape recorder, but begin with the development section, then follow with the recapitulation, exposition, and coda sections. Does listening to this "reorganization" help clarify the function of each section? Does it offer a better understanding of the movement as it was originally structured? Does this "reorganization" produce significantly different feeling qualities in each section?

Movement II: *Marcia Funebra. Adagio Assai.* Funeral March, Very Slow.
Rondo, 2/4 time. Timing: 15:34; Track 2.

A funeral march in 2/4 time, the movement begins with its first theme in the opening bars shown in Figure 9-15, extremely slow, quiet, and brooding. The rhythm limps. The second theme, a plaintive descending passage in the violins beginning at bar 17 (Figure 9-16), is no less unrelieved in its sadness. Its very limited range, from B♭ to E♭, then back down to B♭, adds a closed-in quality. At bar 69 (4:19), the second, or B, section begins, ending at bar 105 (6:28). Then the funeral theme is restated very quietly in the violins. This is the A′ section of the rondo, ending at bar 113. A brief fugue appears at bar 114 (7:09), beginning the C section with material from the second theme inverted in the second violins (Figure 9-17).

FIGURE 9-15
Second movement opening bars (0:02).

FIGURE 9-16
Violins at bar 17 (1:02).

FIGURE 9-17
Beginning of a brief fugue at bar 114 (7:09).

The tempo picks up considerably at this point, with some passages echoing the full orchestral timbres of the first movement. The flutes contribute an interesting contrast in sixteenth notes in a descending pattern beginning with bar 168 (10:11), continuing through the beginning of the A″ section, which is announced by a restatement of the funeral theme at bar 172 (10:25), but this time in the bassoons, horns, cellos, and contrabasses. The second theme is restated totally in the B′ section, beginning at bar 182. The next section, D, begins at bar 211 with a surprise, a new melody in the violins (Figure 9-18).

FIGURE 9-18
New melody. Violins at bars 211 through 217 (13:37).

This melody is not developed and thus is not a theme. The melody is relatively bright, emphasizing by contrast the plaintiveness of the themes. To emphasize this contrast, Beethoven brings back the funeral theme for the last time, A‴, at bar 238 (14:43), but in fragmented form. Now it has lost some of its power. The movement ends with no dramatic finale, but rather a simple pair of rising passages at bars 246 and 247. There remains a sense of unfulfillment. We anticipate the opening passage of the next movement.

PERCEPTION KEY   Movement II

1. Are the dynamics of the second movement very different from the dynamics of the first movement? If so, in what ways?
2. The use of contrast in the second movement is much more restricted than in the first movement. What is the effect of this difference?
3. Are the sections of the rondo A-B-A′-C-A″-B′-D-A‴ as clearly defined as the exposition, development, recapitulation, and coda sections of the first movement? What effect does Beethoven achieve by bringing the funeral theme back again and again? Do you begin to anticipate its return?

Movement III: *Scherzo. Allegro Vivace.* Fast and Lively.

Scherzo, 3/4 time. Timing: 5:32; Track 3.

The sections of the third movement are relatively easy to hear: A-B (trio)-A′-coda. The theme of the A sections begins immediately in the first six bars with soft, rapidly paced notes, followed in bars 7 to 10 with a sharp, punctuating motive (Figure 9-19) in the oboes, succeeded by a delightful descending passage that concludes the theme in bar 14. Everything that

FIGURE 9-19
Beginning of third movement. Oboes at bar 7 (0:07).

comes after in the A section is derivative from the three parts of this theme. Notice especially the repetition of the motive in bars 85 to 88 (0:41), 265 to 268 (4:01), and 299 to 302 (4:18). The trio (named for the tradition of having three voices play in harmony) begins with its theme announced by the horns (Figure 9-20). Although the rhythmic pattern of this theme is not

FIGURE 9-20
Horn passage stating the principal theme of the trio (2:31).

287

reminiscent of the main theme of the first movement, the notes G-C-E-G are very reminiscent. Also, the sonorities recall the first movement, especially the horns playing alone. After a contrasting woodwind interlude from bars 205 to 216 (3:03), the horns come back with a strong fanfarelike passage leading to the conclusion of the trio. The A′ section beginning in bar 255 (3:56) is essentially a repeat of the A section except that it contains more allusions to the full orchestral passages of the first movement. Because of the familiarity of this section, we feel at ease, comfortable, in recognizable territory. These allusions of A′ are more solid harmonically than in A, relying much more on the main key, E♭. The very brief finale, or coda, bars 423 to 442 (5:21), is steady in its rhythm, building to a powerful closure.

PERCEPTION KEY   Movement III

1. Examine the two principal themes in this movement. Do they contrast with each other as much as the themes of the first two movements?
2. The movement is marked scherzo, a dancelike rhythm. Do you sense dance-like passages here? Does the movement suggest a dance to you?
3. What are the feelings characteristics of this movement? Compare with the first two movements.

Movement IV: *Finale. Allegro Molto*. Very Fast.
Theme and variations, 2/4 time. Timing: 11:28; Track 4.

This theme and variation movement opens with the strings in a loud, rushing passage of eleven bars. Then the strings play a theme quite different from anything we have yet heard. This theme is both mysterious and suggestive of things to come, particularly as it diminishes to almost silence—followed by the plucking of single notes. The pattern of these notes (Figure 9-21) looks and sounds like a cross between the first theme of the first movement and the first theme of the third movement.

FIGURE 9-21
Fourth movement. Opening passage for violins (0:13).

This passage sounds playful, as if it were designed to represent the tread of toy soldiers. But this theme, called the bass theme, is countered by another, more important, theme, the melody theme, which begins at bar 76 (1:57), stated in the woodwinds (Figure 9-22). The violins restate this melody theme at bar 103 (2:20). We call one theme the melody theme and the other the bass theme because Beethoven used an extraordinary bit of ingenuity here. He took these themes, which were closely combined in one of his earlier contradances (Figure 9-23), varied them slightly, and separated them for use as the two distinctive themes of the movement.

FIGURE 9-22
Melody theme at bar 76 (1:57).

FIGURE 9-23
Melody and bass themes of the contradance.

Beethoven develops a fugue on the bass theme shortly thereafter, beginning at bar 117 (2:41) with the cellos (Figure 9-24) and then moving to the clarinets and bassoons. At bar 175 (3:30) the melody theme again comes

FIGURE 9-24
Cellos at bar 117 (2:41).

into dominance. At bar 211 (3:46) the bass theme takes over in a marchlike passage, building up energy and anticipation, with rhythms that are reminiscent of the ending of the first movement. The melody theme dominates again at bar 257 (4:44), in the violins and the flutes. Another fugal passage begins at bar 278 (5:09), using both themes, either entirely or in part, moving from one family of instruments to another. The effect of this passage, even though the themes are in the home key, is again to excite anticipation.

At bar 348 (6:15) an andante, or slow, passage begins, marked *con expressione* (with expression), meaning that the music based on the melody theme should be played lyrically, which is not quite what we might anticipate by the preceding fugue. The slow, songlike quality of this passage is something of a surprise, a distinct contrast to the marches and fugues that usually belong to a symphony celebrating the heroic. Marches, driving orchestral passages, warlike fugues, and intense rhythms seem more appropriate to a symphony inspired by Napoleon. But, quite possibly, this last songlike passage hints at a romantic quality the hero should also have. Even Napoleon had his Josephine.

But this romanticism diminishes rapidly with the descending violin passage at bar 380 (8:04). The melody theme is heard in the horns in a very stately fashion, and although the pace does not pick up quickly, the dynamics build steadily, suggesting an official ceremony. A number of brief interludes develop earlier thematic material. Despite the fragmentary quality of these interludes, the steady building of dynamic intensity and pitch by the entire orchestra suggests that we are coming to a powerful conclusion. Yet we hardly know when to expect it. But when we hear the opening passages of the movement repeated at bar 431 (10:41), with an increase of the tempo to *presto* (extremely fast), we sense that we are coming to the end of the entire symphony. Even when the very last *presto* passages are played considerably slower than marked, the straightforwardness of the finale is inevitably complete.

PERCEPTION KEY　Movement IV

1. Many of the contrasts in this movement are achieved by using different structures — such as the fugue, march, and dance — to rework the two basic themes. Are these contrasts clearly audible to you? If not, keep listening.
2. Compare the bass and melody themes for their relative qualities of length, "tunefulness," range of pitch, rhythm, and completeness. What do you discover? If you did question 1 of the Perception Key for the first movement, you will have a basis of comparison already in your mind. What are the differences between the themes of this fourth movement and the themes of the first movement?
3. Compare your sense of closure and finality at the end of the first and fourth movements. Is there a profound difference?

Before going on to the next Perception Key, give your ear a rest for a brief time. Then, come back to the symphony and listen to it all the way through. Sit back and enjoy it. Then consider the following questions.

PERCEPTION KEY　The *Eroica*

1. In what ways are the four movements tied together? Does a sense of relatedness develop for you?
2. Is the symphony properly named? What qualities do you perceive in it that seem "heroic"?
3. Comment on the use of dynamics throughout the whole work. Comment on variations in rhythms.
4. Is there a consistency in the thematic material used throughout the symphony? Are there any inconsistencies?
5. Do you find that fatigue affects your responses to the second movement or any other portion of the symphony? The act of creative listening can be very tiring. Could Beethoven have taken that into consideration?
6. Are you aware of a variety of feeling qualities in the music? Does there seem to be an overall plan to the changes in these qualities as the symphony unfolds?
7. What kind of feelings (emotion, passion, or mood) did the *Eroica* arouse in you? Did you make discoveries of your inner life of feeling because of your responses to the *Eroica*?

Summary

We began this chapter by suggesting that feelings and sounds are the primary subject matters of music. This implies that the content of music is a revelation of feelings and sounds—that music gives us a more sensitive understanding of them. However, as we indicated in our opening statements, there is considerable disagreement about the subject matter of music, and, therefore, there is disagreement about the content of music. If music does reveal feelings and sounds, the way it does so is still one of the most baffling problems in the philosophy of art.

Even a brief survey of the theories about the content of music is beyond our scope here, but given the basic theory of art as revelation, as we have been presupposing in this book, a couple of examples of how that theory might be applied to music are relevant. In the first place, some music apparently clarifies sounds as noises. For example, John Cage, at times, uses devices such as a brick crashing through a glass. By putting such noises into a composition, Cage brackets out the everyday situation and helps us listen "to" rather than listen "through" such noises. In this way he clarifies those noises. His musical form organizes sounds and sometimes silences before and after the noise of the breaking glass in such a way that our perception of the noise of breaking glass is made more sensitive. Similar analyses can be made of the sounds of musical instruments and their interrelationships in the structures in which they are placed.

Second, there seems to be some evidence that music gives us insight into our feelings. It is not ridiculous to claim, for example, that one is feeling joy like that of the last movement of Mozart's *Jupiter* symphony, or sadness like the second movement—the funeral march—of Beethoven's *Eroica* symphony. In fact, joy and sadness are general terms that only very crudely describe our feelings. We experience all kinds of different joys and different sadnesses, and the names language gives to these are imprecise. Music, with its capacity to evoke feelings, and with a complexity of detail and structure that in many ways is greater than that of language, may be able to reveal or interpret feeling with much more precision than language. Perhaps the form of the last movement of the *Jupiter* symphony—with its clear-cut rising melodies, bright harmonies and timbres, brisk strings, and rapid rhythms—is somehow analogous to the form of a certain kind of joy. Perhaps the last movement of the *Eroica* is somehow analogous to a different kind of joy. And if so, then perhaps we find revealed in those musical forms clarifications or insights about joy. Such explanations are highly speculative. However, they not only are theoretically interesting but also may intensify one's interest in music. There is mystery about music, unique among the arts; that is part of its fascination.

Bibliography

Abraham, Gerald. *The Concise Oxford History of Music*. New York: Oxford University Press, 1979.

Apel, Willi. *New Harvard Dictionary of Music*. Cambridge, Mass.: Harvard University Press, 1996.

Bovers, Jane, and Judith Tick. *Women Making Music 1150–1950*. Urbana: University of Illinois Press, 1985.

Bowman, Wayne D. *Philosophic Perspectives on Music*. New York: Oxford University Press, 1998.

Copland, Aaron. *What to Listen For in Music*. New York: McGraw-Hill, 1989.

Dalhaus, Carl. *Esthetics of Music*. Translated by William Austin. Cambridge, England: Cambridge University Press, 1982.

Hindemith, Paul. *Composer's World*. Cambridge, Mass.: Harvard University Press, 1952.

Kostelanetz, Richard, ed. *Writing about John Cage*. Ann Arbor: University of Michigan Press, 1993.

Levinson, Jerold. *Music in the Moment*. Ithaca, N.Y.: Cornell University Press, 1998.

May, Elizabeth, ed. *Music of Many Cultures*. Berkeley: University of California Press, 1980.

Meyer, Leonard B. *Emotion and Meaning in Music*. Chicago: University of Chicago Press, 1956.

———. *Explaining Music*. Berkeley: University of California Press, 1973.

The New Grove Dictionary of Opera. London: Macmillan, 1993.

Nicholls, David, ed. *The Cambridge History of American Music*. Cambridge, England: Cambridge University Press, 1998.

Pendle, Karen. *Women and Music*. Bloomington: Indiana University Press, 1991.

Presley, Horton. *Principles of Music and Visual Arts*. Lanham, Md.: University Press of America, 1986.

Radocy, Rudolph, and J. David Boyle. *Psychological Foundations of Musical Behavior*. Springfield, Ill.: Charles C. Thomas, 1979.

Rosen, Charles. *The Classic Style*. New York: Viking, 1971.

Sadie, Stanley, ed. *The New Grove Dictionary of Music and Musicians*. London: Macmillan, 1980.

Scruton, Roger. *The Aesthetics of Music*. New York: Oxford University Press, 1997.

Stravinsky, Igor, and Robert Craft. *Expositions and Developments*. Garden City, N.Y.: Doubleday, 1962.

Tovey, Donald F. *Beethoven*. New York: Oxford University Press, 1965.

———. *Essays in Musical Analysis*. New York: Oxford University Press, 1981.

AFRICAN MUSIC ARCHIVE

http://ntama.uni-mainz.de/~ama/

AMERICAN MUSIC CENTER

http://www.amc.net/

LUDWIG VAN BEETHOVEN

http://www.kingsbarn.freeservice.co.uk/
http://web02.hnh.com/composer/btm.asp?fullname=Beethoven,%20Ludwig%20van
http://www.madaboutbeethoven.com/

THE UNHEARD BEETHOVEN

http://www.unheardbeethoven.org

THE BLUES

http://bluesnet.hub.org/

CLASSICAL MUSIC (GENERAL SOURCE FOR CLASSICAL MUSIC)

http://dir.yahoo.com/Entertainment/Music/Genres/Classical/Organizations/

INDIANA UNIVERSITY MUSIC LIBRARY

http://www.music.indiana.edu/muslib.html

JAZZ LINKS (LATIN JAZZ, SWING, MODERN, ETC.)

http://dir.yahoo.com/Entertainment/Music/Genres/Jazz/

LINKS TO POPULAR MUSIC AND OTHER GENRES

http://music.lycos.com/

CHAPTER 10

Dance

Dance—moving bodies shaping space—shares common ground with kinetic sculpture. In abstract dance the center of interest is upon visual patterns, and thus there is common ground with abstract painting. Dance, however, usually includes a narrative, performed on a stage with scenic effects, and thus has common ground with drama. Dance is rhythmic, unfolding in time, and thus has common ground with music. Most dance is accompanied by music, and dance is often incorporated in opera.

Subject Matter of Dance

At its most basic level, the subject matter of dance is abstract motion, as in much of the work of the Pilobolus Dance Company. Pilobolus specializes in finding interrelationships of bodies in motion, often producing remarkable abstract shapes and patterns. The medium of the dance is the human body, whose movements on stage often produce sympathetic "movements" in the audience. Our feelings show vividly in our movements and gestures. Thus, a much more pervasive subject matter of the dance is feeling. This is what, generally speaking, dance is basically about. The body exhibits feelings less abstractedly than in music, for now they are "embodied." Our instinctive ability to identify with other human bodies is so strong that the perception of feelings exhibited by the dancer often evokes something of those feelings in ourselves. The choreographer, creator of the dance, interprets those feelings. And if we participate, we may understand those feelings and ourselves with greater insight. In Paul Sanasardo's *Pain,* for example, the portrayal of this feeling is so powerful that few in any audience can avoid some sense of pain. Yet, the interpretation of pain by means of the dancing bodies gives us an objective correlative, a shaping "out there" that makes it possible for us to understand something about pain rather than simply undergoing it. Figure 10-1 shows Sanasardo's depiction of pain, but only with the moving dance can its interpretation occur.

FIGURE 10-1
Judith Blackstone and Paul
Sanasardo in *Pain*. (Paul
Sanasardo Dance Company,
photograph by Fred Fehl)

PERCEPTION KEY   Feeling and Dance

The claim that dance can interpret the inner life of feeling with exceptional power implies, perhaps, that no other art excels dance in this respect. Can you think of any examples—restricting your analysis to the feeling of pain—that would disprove this claim? What about feelings other than pain? Compare dance and music in terms of their power to reveal the inner life of feeling.

States of mind are a further dimension that may be the subject matter of dance. Feelings, such as pleasure and pain, are relatively transient, but states of mind involve attitudes, tendencies that engender certain feelings on the appropriate occasions. A state of mind is a disposition or habit that is not easily superseded. For example, jealousy usually involves a feeling so strong that it is best described as a passion. Yet, jealousy is more than just a passion, for it is an orientation of mind that is relatively enduring. Thus, José Limón's *The Moor's Pavane* explores the jealousy of Shakespeare's *Othello*. In Limón's version, Iago and Othello dance around Desdemona and seem to be directly vying for her affections. *The Moor's Pavane* represents an interpretation of the states of mind Shakespeare dramatized, although it can stand independently of the play and make its own contribution to our understanding of jealousy.

Since states of mind are felt as enduring, the serial structure of the dance is an appropriate vehicle for interpreting that endurance. The same can be said of music, of course, and its serial structure, along with its rhythmic nature, is the fundamental reason for the wedding of music with dance. Even silence in some dances seems to suggest music, since the dancer exhibits visual rhythm, the rising and falling of stress that we hear in music. But the showing of states of mind is achieved only partly through the elements dance shares with music. More basic is the body language of the dancing bodies. Perhaps nothing—not even spoken language—exhibits states of mind more clearly or strongly.

PERCEPTION KEY Body Language and States of Mind

1. Represent one of the following states of mind by bodily motion: love, jealousy, self-confidence, pride. Have others do the same. Do you find such representations difficult to perceive when others do them?
2. Try to move in such a way as to represent no state of mind at all. Is it possible? Discuss this with your group.
3. Representing or portraying a state of mind allows one to recognize that state. Interpreting a state of mind gives one insight into that state. In any of the experiments above, did you find any examples that went beyond representation and involved revelation? If so, what made this possible? What does artistic form have to do with this?
4. Is it possible for you to recognize a state of mind such as jealousy being represented without having that state of mind being evoked in you? Is it possible for you not only to recognize but also to gain insight about a state of mind without that state of mind being evoked in you?

Narrative provides one obvious subject matter for many dances. Thus Robert Helpmann's ballet *Hamlet* uses Shakespeare's play as its subject matter. Viewers of the dance who know the play will see an interpretation of a drama, while others will see the interpretation of a tragic situation. In either case, feelings and states of mind relevant to the narrative are given vivid embodiment in the dancers' movements and gestures. Helpmann's *Hamlet* interprets the inner life of a tragic drama. Shakespeare's *Hamlet* provides the events that cause those reactions. In the dance, what is revealed is not so much why something happened, but rather the inner-life reactions to the happening.

Form

The subject matter of dance can be moving visual patterns, feelings, states of mind, narrative, or various combinations of these. The form of the dance—its details and structure—gives us insight into the subject matter. But the form of dance is not as clearly perceptible as it usually is in painting, sculpture, and architecture. The visual arts normally "sit still" long enough for us to reexamine everything. But dance moves on relentlessly, like literature in recitation, drama, and music, preventing us from reexamining its details and organization. We can only hope to hold in memory a detail for comparison with an ensuing detail, and those details as they help create the structure.

Therefore, one prerequisite for a thorough enjoyment of the dance is the development of a memory for the dance movements. The dance will usually help us in this task by the use of repetitive movements and variations on them. It can do for us what we cannot do for ourselves: present once again details for our renewed consideration. Often the dance builds tension by withholding movements we want to have repeated; sometimes it creates unusual tension by refusing to repeat any movement at all. Repetition or the lack of it—as in music or any serial art—becomes one of the most important structural features of the dance.

Most of the dance performed on television or produced on stage will make use of a number of basic compositional principles. Careful repetition of movements is often patterned on the repetition in the music to which the dancers perform. The musical structure of A-B-A is common to the dance: A melody is played (A), followed by a period of development (B), finally ending with a recapitulation of the melody (A). Movements performed at the beginning of a dance, the A section, are often developed, enlarged, and modified in the B section, and are repeated at the end of the dance during the second A section.

Further, dance achieves a number of kinds of balance. In terms of the entire stage, usually a company of dancers balance themselves across the space allotted to them, moving forward, backward, left, and right as well as in a circle. Centrality of focus is important in most dances and helps us unify the shapes of the overall dance. The most important dancers are usually at the center of the stage, holding our attention while subordinate groups of dancers balance them on the sides of the stage. Balance is also a structural consideration for both individual dancers (see Figure 10-6) and groups (see Figure 10-3).

The positions of the ballet dancer illustrated in Figure 10-5 also imply basic movements for the dancer, movements that can be maneuvered, interwoven, set in counterpoint, and modified as the dance progresses. As we experience the dance, we develop an eye for the ways in which these movements combine to create the dance. Modern dance develops a different vocabulary of dance, as one can see from the illustrations in Figures 10-1 and 10-7 through 10-12.

Dance and Ritual

Since the only requirement for dance is a body in motion and since all cultures have this basic requirement, dance probably precedes all other arts. In this sense dance comes first. And when it comes first, it is usually connected to a ritual that demands careful execution of movements in precise ways to achieve a precise goal. The dances of most cultures were originally connected with either religious or practical acts, both often involving magic. Early dance often religiously celebrates some tribal achievement. At other times the dance is expected to have a specific practical effect. In this kind of dance—the Zuni rain dance, for instance—the movement is ritually ordered and expected to be practically effective as long as the dance is performed properly.

Some dance has sexual origins and often is a ritual of courtship. Since this phenomenon has a correlative in nature—the courtship dances of birds and some other animals—many cultures occasionally imitated animal dances. Certain movements in Mandan Indian dances, for instance, can be traced to the leaps and falls of western jays and mockingbirds who, in finding a place to rest, will stop, leap into the air while spreading their wings for balance, then fall suddenly, only to rise into the air again. Some modern dancers send their students to the zoo to observe birds, leopards, and other animals so that they can represent them onstage.

Today at Native American powwows, fancy dance competitions are frequently held, giving dancers an opportunity to use complex costuming and dance steps. These dances are not ordinarily expected to produce ritual results, but they derive from such dances and echo their movements.

Dance of all kinds draws much of its inspiration from the movements and shapes of nature: the motion of a stalk of wheat in a gentle breeze, the scurrying of a rabbit, the curling of a contented cat, the soaring of a bird, the falling of a leaf. These kinds of events have supplied dancers with ideas and examples for their own movement. A favorite shape for the dance is that of the spiral nautilus, so often seen in shells, plants, and insects:

This shape is apparent in individual movement (see Figures 10-1 and 10-5) just as it is in the movement of groups of dancers whose floor pattern may follow the spiral pattern (see Figure 10-3). The circle is another of the most pervasive shapes of nature. The movements of planets and stars suggest circular motion, and, more mundanely, so do the rings working out from a stone dropped in water. In a magical-religious way, circular dances sometimes have been thought to bring the dancers—and therefore humans in general—into a significant harmony with the divine forces in the universe. The planets and stars are heavenly objects in circular motion, so it was reasonable for early dancers to feel that they could align themselves with these divine forces by means of dance.

INDIAN DANCE

Some of the most complex and exquisite dances performed in the world today originated in India, which continues to preserve its traditional music and dance. The dancers in Figure 10-2 are performing part of a lengthy dance that retells the story of the *Mahabharata*, one of India's greatest epics, dealing with Lord Krishna and the primary forces of nature. Like ballet

FIGURE 10-2
Indian Dance: A Kathakali
performance from the
Mahabharata. (© Jack
Vartoogian/FrontRow
Photos)

dancers, the Kathakali dancers follow set movements, with the addition of complex finger and hand movements, all of which have significance. The hand gestures are called mudras. There are twenty-eight of them, and they can be combined to produce at least eight hundred distinctive meanings. Dancers begin working with the mudras early as children and practice endlessly in an effort to master the mudras with perfection. The control the dancers must have over their bodies to perform the complex dances matches the message of the *Mahabharata:* that the individual must practice self-control in order to be truly free. The dance and the drama are truly intertwined in the Kathakali renditions of the epic.

THE ZUNI RAIN DANCE

Tourists can see rain dances in the American Southwest even today. The floor pattern of the dance is not circular but a modified spiral, as can be seen in Figure 10-3. The dancers, properly costumed, form a line and are led by a priest, who at specific moments spreads cornmeal on the ground, symbolizing his wish for the fertility of the ground. The ritual character of the dance is clearly observable in the pattern of motion, with dancers beginning by moving toward the north, then turning west, south, east, north, west, south, and ending toward the east. The gestures of the dancers, like the gestures in most rituals, have definite meanings and functions. For

FIGURE 10-3
Arapahoe and Shoshone dancers at the Windriver Reservation. (© John Running)

example, the dancers' loud screams are designed to awaken the gods and arrest their attention, the drumbeat suggests thunder, and the dancers' rattles suggest the sound of rain.

PERCEPTION KEY   Dance and Contemporary Rituals

1. Contemporary rituals such as some weddings and funerals involve motion that can be thought of as dance motion. Can you think of other contemporary rituals that involve dance motion? Do we need to know the meanings of the ritual gestures in order to appreciate the motion of the ritual?
2. How much common ground do we share with early dancers in trying to give meaning to our gestures, either in a generally accepted dance situation or out of it?
3. Do we have dances that can be considered as serving functions similar to those of the dances we have described? Consider, for instance, the dancing that accompanied the tearing down of the Berlin Wall or the dancing that sometimes spontaneously breaks out at rock concerts. Are there other instances?

Social Dance

Social dance is not specifically theatrical or artistic, as are ballet and modern dance. Folk and court dances are often done simply for the pleasure of the dancers. Because we are more or less familiar with square dances, round dances, waltzes, and a large variety of contemporary dances done at parties, we have some useful points of reference for the social dance in general.

FIGURE 10-4
Pieter Breughel the Elder,
The Wedding Dance. Circa
1566. Oil on panel, 47 × 62
inches. (Photograph © 2003
The Detroit Institute of the
Arts, city of Detroit purchase)

COUNTRY AND FOLK DANCE

Social dance is not dominated by religious or practical purposes, although
it may have secondary purposes such as meeting people or working off ex-
cess energy. More importantly, it is a form of recreation and social enjoyment. Country dance—for example, the English Playford dances—is a
species of folk dance that has traces of ancient origins, because country
people tended to perform dances in specific relationship to special periods
in the agricultural year, such as planting and harvesting.

Folk dances are the dances of the people—whether ethnic or regional in
origin—and they are often very carefully preserved, sometimes with con-
tests designed to keep the dances alive. When they perform, the dancers
often wear the peasant costumes of the region they represent. Virtually
every nation has its folk dance tradition (see Figure 10-4.)

THE COURT DANCE

The court dances of the Middle Ages and Renaissance developed into more
stylized and less openly energetic modes than the folk dance, for the court
dance was performed by a different sort of person and served a different
purpose. Participating in court dances signified high social status. Some of
the favorite older dances were the volta, a favorite at Queen Elizabeth's
court in the sixteenth century, with the male dancer hoisting the female
dancer in the air from time to time; the pavane, a stately dance popular in

the seventeenth century; the minuet, popular in the eighteenth century, performed by groups of four dancers at a time; and the eighteenth-century German allemande—a dance performed by couples who held both hands, turning about one another without letting go. These dances and many others were favorites at courts primarily because they were enjoyable—not because they performed a religious or practical function. Because the dances were also pleasurable to look at, it very quickly became a commonplace at court to have a group of onlookers as large as or larger than the group of dancers. Soon professional dancers appeared at more significant court functions, such as the Elizabethan and Jacobean masques, which were mixed-media entertainments in which the audience usually took some part—particularly in the dance sequences.

PERCEPTION KEY Social Dance

1. How would you evaluate rock dancing? Why does rock dancing demand loud music? Does the performing and watching of spontaneous and powerful muscular motions account for some of the popularity of rock dancing? If so, why? Why do you think the older generations generally dislike, if not hate, both rock music and rock dancing? Is rock dancing primarily a mode to be watched or danced? Or is it both? Explain what the viewer and the dancer, respectively, might derive from the experience of rock dancing. Substitute rap for rock and answer the same questions.

2. Try to see an authentic folk dance. Describe the basic differences between folk dance and rock dance. Is the basic subject matter of the folk dance visual patterns, or feelings, or states of mind, or narrative? Or some combination of these? If so, what is the mix? Answer the same questions for rock dances and rap.

3. Do you believe that rock and rap dances are basically entertainment, lacking artistic form and content?

4. Break and swing dancing for the young; square and ballroom dancing for the old. Why the divided generational appeal? Country dance seems to appeal to both young and old. Why?

Ballet

The origins of ballet usually are traced to the early seventeenth century, when dancers performed interludes between scenes of an opera. Eventually the interludes grew more important, until finally ballets were performed independently. In the eighteenth century, the *en pointe* (or *on point*) technique was developed, with female dancers elevated on their toes to emphasize airy, floating movements. This has remained the technique to this day and is one of the important distinctions between ballet and modern dance, which avoids *en pointe* almost entirely.

Today there is a vocabulary of movements that all ballet dancers must learn, since these movements constitute the fundamental elements of every ballet. They are as important as the keys and scales in music, the

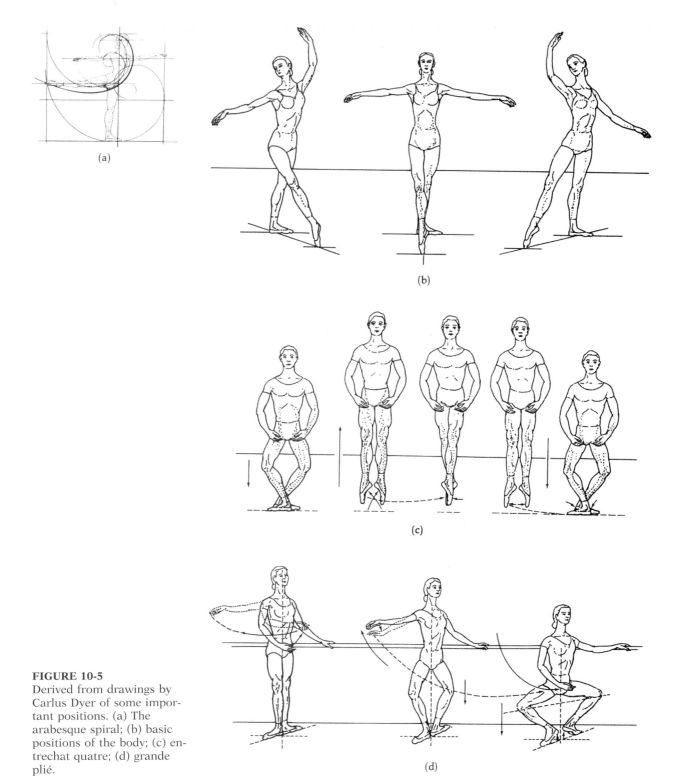

(a)

(b)

(c)

FIGURE 10-5
Derived from drawings by Carlus Dyer of some important positions. (a) The arabesque spiral; (b) basic positions of the body; (c) entrechat quatre; (d) grande plié.

(d)

303

vocabulary of tones constantly employed in most musical composition. Figure 10-5 shows a number of the more important ballet positions. There are, of course, many more.

A considerable repertory of ballets has been built up in the last three centuries, but many ballets have been lost to us through the lack of a system of notation with which to record them. Today most dance is recorded on videotape and film, although there is a system — *Labanotation* — that can be used effectively by experts for recording a dance. Some of the ballets many of us are likely to see are Lully's *Giselle; Les Sylphides,* with music by Chopin; Tchaikovsky's *Nutcracker, Swan Lake,* and *Sleeping Beauty; Coppelia,* with music by Delibes; and *The Rite of Spring,* with music by Stravinsky. All these ballets — like most ballets — have a *pretext,* a narrative line or story around which the ballet is built. In this sense, the ballet has as its subject matter a story that is interpreted by means of stylized movements such as the *arabesque,* the bourrée, and the relévé to name a few. Our understanding of the story is basically conditioned by our perception of the movements that present the story to us. It is astounding how, without having to be obvious and without having to resort very often to everyday gestures, ballet dancers can present a story to us in an intelligible fashion. Yet, it is not the story or the movement that constitutes the ballet: It is the meld of story and movement.

PERCEPTION KEY   Narrative and Bodily Movement

1. Without training we cannot perform ballet movements, but all of us can perform some dance movements. By way of experiment and simply to increase understanding of the meld of narrative and movement, try representing a narrative by bodily motion to a group of onlookers. Choose a narrative poem from our chapter on literature, or choose a scene from a play that may be familiar to you and your audience. Let your audience know the pretext you are using, since this is the normal method of most ballets. Avoid movements that rely exclusively on facial expressions or simple mime to communicate story elements. After your presentation, discuss with your audience their views about your success or failure in presenting the narrative. Discuss, too, your problems as a dancer, what you felt you wanted your movement to reveal about the narrative. Have others perform the experiment, and discuss the same points.

2. Even the most rudimentary movement attempting to reveal a narrative will bring in interpretations that go beyond the narrative alone. As a viewer, discuss what you believe the other dancers added to the narrative.

SWAN LAKE

One of the most popular ballets of all time is Tchaikovsky's *Swan Lake (Le Lac des Cygnes),* composed from 1871 to 1877 and first performed in 1894 (Act 2) and 1895 (complete). The choreographers were Leon Ivanov and Marius Petipa. Tchaikovsky originally composed the music for a ballet to be performed for children, but its fascination has not been restricted to young audiences. With Margot Fonteyn and Rudolf Nureyev, the reigning dancers

FIGURE 10-6
Margot Fonteyn and Rudolf
Nureyev in *Swan Lake*.
(Dance Collection, The New
York Public Library for the
Performing Arts, Lincoln
Center)

in this ballet in modern times, *Swan Lake* has been a resounding favorite on television and film, not to mention repeated sellout performances in dance theaters the world over (Figure 10-6).

Act 1 opens with the principal male dancer, the young Prince Siegfried, attending a village celebration. His mother, the Queen, finding Siegfried sporting with the peasants, decides that it is time for him to marry some- one of his own station and settle into the nobility. After she leaves, a *pas de trois*—a dance with three dancers, in this instance Siegfried and two maids—is interrupted by the Prince's slightly drunk tutor, who tries to take part in some of the dancing but is not quite able. When a flight of swans is seen overhead, the prince resolves to go hunting.

The opening scene of Act 2 is on a moonlit lake, with the arch magician, Rothbart, tending his swans. The swans, led by Odette, are maidens he has enchanted. They can return to human form only at night. Odette's move- ments are imitated by the entire group of swans, movements that are clearly influenced by the motions of the swan's long neck and by the movements we associate with birds—for example, an undulating motion executed by the dancers' arms and a fluttering executed by the legs. Siegfried comes upon the swans and restrains his hunters from shooting at them. He falls in love with Odette, now in her human form, all of whose motions are char- acterized by the softness and grace of a swan. Siegfried learns that Odette is enchanted and that she cannot come to the ball at which the Queen has planned to arrange his marriage. Siegfried also learns that if he vows his love to her and keeps his vow, he can free her from the enchantment. She warns him that Rothbart will do everything to trick him into breaking the vow, but Siegfried is determined to be steadfast. As dawn arrives, the lovers part and Rothbart retrieves his swans.

Act 3 commences with the ball the Queen has arranged for presenting to Siegfried a group of princesses from whom he may choose. Each princess, introduced in lavish native costume with a retinue of dancers and retainers, dances the folk dance of her country, such as the allemande, the czardas, the tarantella. But suddenly Rothbart enters in disguise with his own daughter, Odile, who looks exactly like Odette. Today, most performances require that Odette and Odile be the same dancer, although the parts were originally written for two dancers. Siegfried and Odile dance the famous Black Swan *pas de deux,* a dance notable for its virtuosity. It features almost superhuman leaps on the part of Siegfried, and it also involves thirty-two rapidly executed whipping turns (fouettés) on the part of Odile. Her movement is considerably different in character from that of Odette. Odile is more angular, less delicate, and in her black costume seems much less the picture of innocence Odette had seemed in her soft white costume. Siegfried's movements suggest great joy at having Odette, for he does not realize that this is really Odile, the magician's daughter.

When the time comes for Siegfried to choose among the princesses for his wife, he rejects them all and presents Odile to the Queen as his choice. Once Siegfried has committed himself to her, Rothbart exults and takes Odile from him and makes her vanish. Siegfried, who has broken his vow to Odette, realizes he has been duped and ends the act by rushing out to find the real Odette.

Like a number of other sections of the ballet, Act 4 has a variety of versions that interpret what is essentially similar action. Siegfried, in finding Odette by the lake at night, sacrifices himself for her and breaks the spell. They are joined in death and are beyond the power of the magician. Some versions of the ballet aim for a happy ending and suggest that though Siegfried sacrifices himself for Odette, he does not die. In this happy-ending version, Odette, upon realizing that Siegfried had been tricked, forgives him. Rothbart raises a terrible storm in order to drown all the swans, but Siegfried carries Odette to a hilltop, where he is willing to die with her if necessary. This act of love and sacrifice breaks the spell and the two of them are together as dawn breaks.

Another version concentrates on spiritual victory and reward after death in a better life than that which was left behind. Odette and the swans dance slowly and sorrowfully together, with Odette rising in a stately fashion in their midst. When Siegfried comes, he begs her to forgive him, but nothing can break the magician's spell. Odette and he dance, they embrace, she bids him farewell and casts herself mournfully into the lake, where she perishes. Siegfried, unable to live without her, follows her into the lake. Then, once the lake vanishes, Odette and Siegfried are revealed in the distance, moving away together as evidence that the spell was broken in death.

The late John Cranko produced a more tragic version with the Stuttgart Ballet in the 1970s. Siegfried is drowned in the rising of the lake—presented most dramatically with long bolts of fabric undulating across the stage. Odette is whisked away by Rothbart and condemned to keep waiting for the hero who can be faithful to his vow. This version is particularly gloomy, since it reduces the heroic stature of Siegfried and renders his sacrifice useless. The hero who can rescue Odette must be virtually superhuman.

The story of *Swan Lake* has archetypal overtones much in keeping with the Romantic age in which it was conceived. John Keats, who wrote fifty years before this ballet was created, was fascinated by the ancient stories of men who fell in love with supernatural spirits, which is what the swan-Odette is, once she has been transformed by magic. Likewise, the later Romantics were fascinated by the possibilities of magic and its implications for dealing with the forces of good and evil. In his *Blithedale Romance,* Nathaniel Hawthorne wrote about a hypnotist who wove a weird spell over a woman. The story of Svengali and his ward Trilby was popular everywhere, seemingly attesting to the fact that strange spells could be maintained over innocent people. This interest in magic and the supernatural is coupled with the Wagnerian interest in heroism and the implications of the sacrifice of the hero for the thing he loves. Much of the power of the idea of sacrifice derives from the sacrifice of Christ on the cross. But Tchaikovsky—like Wagner, whose hero in the *Ring of the Niebelungs* is also a Siegfried, whose end with Brünnhilde is similar to the ending in *Swan Lake*—concentrates on the human valor of the prince and its implication for transforming evil into good.

PERCEPTION KEY *Swan Lake*

1. If you can see a production or video of *Swan Lake,* focus on a specific act and comment in a discussion with others on the suitability of the bodily movements for the narrative subject matter of that act. Are feelings or states of mind interpreted as well as the narrative? If so, when and how?
2. If someone who has had training in ballet is available, you might try to get him or her to present a small portion of the ballet for your observation and discussion. What would be the most important kinds of questions to ask such a person?

Modern Dance

The origins of *modern dance* are usually traced to the American dancers Isadora Duncan and Ruth St. Denis. They rebelled against the stylization of ballet, with ballerinas dancing on their toes and executing the same basic movements in every performance. Duncan insisted on natural movement, often dancing in bare feet with gossamer drapery that showed her body and legs in motion (Figure 10-7). She felt that the emphasis ballet places on the movement of the arms and legs was wrong. Her insistence on placing the center of motion just below the breastbone was based on her feeling that

FIGURE 10-7
Isadora Duncan in *La Marseillaise*. (Dance Collection, The New York Public Library for the Performing Arts, Lincoln Center)

the torso had been neglected in the development of ballet. She believed, too, that the early Greek dancers, whom she wished to emulate, had placed their center of energy at the solar plexus. Her intention was to return to natural movement in dance, and this was one effective method of doing so.

The developers of modern dance who followed Duncan (she died in 1927) built on her legacy. In her insistence on freedom with respect to clothes and conventions, she infused energy into the dance that no one had ever seen before. Although she was a native Californian, her successes and triumphs were primarily in foreign lands, particularly in France and Russia. Her performances differed greatly from the ballet. Instead of developing a dance built on a pretext of the sort that underlies *Swan Lake,* Duncan took more abstract subject matters—especially moods and states of mind—and expressed her understanding of them in dance.

Duncan's dances were lyrical, personal, and occasionally extemporaneous. Since she insisted that there were no angular shapes in nature, she would permit herself to use none. Her movements tended to be ongoing and rarely came to a complete rest. An interesting example of her dance, one in which she does come to a full rest, is recounted by a friend. It was performed in a salon for close friends, and its subject matter seems to be human emergence on the planet:

> Isadora was completely covered by a long loose robe with high draped neck and long loose sleeves in a deep muted red. She crouched on the floor with her face resting on the carpet. In slow motion with ineffable effort she managed to get up on her knees. Gradually with titanic struggles she rose to her feet. She raised her arms toward heaven in a gesture of praise and exultation. The mortal had emerged from primeval ooze to achieve Man, upright, liberated, and triumphant.[1]

Martha Graham, Erick Hawkins, José Limón, Doris Humphrey, and other innovators who followed Isadora developed modern dance in a variety of directions. Graham, who was also interested in Greek origins, created some dances on themes of Greek tragedies, such as her *Medea*. In addition to his *Moor's Pavane*, Limón is well known for his interpretation of Eugene O'Neill's play *The Emperor Jones*, in which a black slave escapes to an island only to become a despised and hunted tyrant. These approaches are somewhat of a departure from Duncan, as they tend to introduce the balletic pretext into modern dance. Humphrey, who was a little older than Graham and Limón, was closer to the original Duncan tradition in such dances as *Water Study, Life of the Bee*, and *New Dance*, a 1930s piece that was successfully revived in 1972.

PERCEPTION KEY   Pretext and Movement

1. Devise a series of movements that will take about one minute to complete and that you are fairly sure do not tell a story. Then perform these movements for a group and question them on the apparent pretext of your movement. Do not tell them in advance that your dance has no story. As a result of this experiment, ask yourself and the group whether it is possible to create a sequence of movements that will not suggest a story line to some viewers. What would this mean for dances that try to avoid pretexts? Can there really be abstract dance?
2. Without explaining that you are not dancing, represent a familiar human situation to a group by using movements that you believe are not dance movements. Is the group able to understand what you represented? Do they think you were using dance movements? Do you believe it possible to have movements that cannot be included in a dance? Are there, in other words, non-dance movements?

---

[1]From Kathleen Cannell, "Isadorable Duncan," *Christian Science Monitor*, December 4, 1970. Reprinted by permission from The Christian Science Monitor. © 1970 The Christian Science Publishing Society. All rights reserved.

FIGURE 10-8
The Alvin Ailey City Center Dance Theater, New York. *Revelations*, "Wading in the Water." (© Jack Vartoogian/ FrontRow Photos)

ALVIN AILEY'S *REVELATIONS*

One of the classics of modern dance is Alvin Ailey's *Revelations* (Figure 10-8), based largely on African American spirituals and experience. It was first performed in January 1960, and hardly a year has gone by since without its having been performed to highly enthusiastic crowds. Ailey refined *Revelations* somewhat over the years, but its impact has brought audiences to their feet for standing ovations at almost every performance. Since Ailey's early death, the company has been directed by Judith Jamison, one of the great dancers in Ailey's company.

Some of the success of *Revelations* stems from Ailey's choice of the deeply felt music of the spirituals to which the dancers' movements are closely attuned. But, then, this is also one of the most noted qualities of a ballet like *Swan Lake*, which has one of the richest orchestral scores of any ballet. Music, unless it is program music, is not, strictly speaking, a pretext for a dance, but there is a perceptible connection between, say, the rhythmic characteristics of a given music and a dance composed in such a way as to take advantage of those characteristics. Thus, in *Revelations* the energetic movements of the dancers often appear as visual, bodily transformations of the rhythmically charged music.

Try to see *Revelations*. We will point out details and structures of which an awareness may prove helpful for refining your experience not only of this dance but of modern dance in general. Beyond the general pretext of *Revelations* — that of African American experience as related by spirituals—each of its separate sections has its own pretext. But none of them is as tightly or specifically narrative as is usually the case in ballet. In *Revelations* only generalized situations act as pretexts.

The first section of the dance is called "Pilgrim of Sorrow," with three parts: "I Been Buked," danced by the entire company (about twenty dancers, male and female); "Didn't My Lord Deliver Daniel," danced by only a few dancers; and "Fix Me Jesus," danced by one couple. The general pretext is the suffering of African Americans, who are, like the Israelites of the Old Testament, taking refuge in their faith in the Lord. The most dramatic moments in this section are in "Didn't My Lord Deliver Daniel," a statement of overwhelming faith characterized by close ensemble work. The in-line dancers parallel the rhythms of the last word of the hymn: "Dan´-i-el´," accenting the first and last syllables with powerful rhythmic movements.

The second section, titled "Take Me to the Water," is divided into "Processional," danced by eight dancers; "Wading in the Water," danced by six dancers; and "I Want to Be Ready," danced by a single male dancer. The whole idea of "Take Me to the Water" suggests baptism, a ritual that affirms faith in God—the source of energy of the spirituals. "Wading in the Water" is particularly exciting, with dancers holding a stage-long bolt of light-colored fabric to represent the water. The dancers shimmer the fabric to the rhythm of the music and one dancer after another crosses over the fabric, which symbolizes at least two things: the waters of baptism and the Mosaic waters of freedom. It is this episode that originally featured the charismatic Judith Jamison in a long white gown holding a huge parasol as she danced. Donna Wood performs the role in the illustration (Figure 10-8).

The third section is called "Move, Members, Move," with the subsections titled "Sinner Man," "The Day Is Past and Gone," "You May Run Home," and the finale "Rocka My Soul in the Bosom of Abraham." In this last episode a sense of triumph over suffering is projected, suggesting the redemption of a people by using the same kind of Old Testament imagery and musical material that opened the dance. The entire section takes as its theme the life of people after they have been received into the faith, with the possibilities of straying into sin. It ends with a powerful rocking spiritual that emphasizes forgiveness and the reception of the people (the "members") into the bosom of Abraham, according to the prediction of the Bible. This ending features a large amount of ensemble work and is danced by the entire company, with rows of male dancers sliding forward on their outspread knees and then rising all in one sliding gesture, raising their hands high. "Rocka My Soul in the Bosom of Abraham" is powerfully sung again and again until the effect is almost hypnotic.

The subject matter of *Revelations* is in part that of feelings and states of mind. But it is also more obviously that of the struggle of a people as told—on one level—by their music. The dance has the advantage of a powerfully engaging subject matter even before we witness the interpretation of that subject matter. And the way in which the movements of the dance are closely attuned to the rhythm of the music tends to give most viewers a very intense participation, since the visual qualities of the dance are so powerfully reinforced by the aural qualities of the music. Not all modern dance is characterized by this reinforcement, but most show dance and most dance in filmed musicals encourage a similar closeness of movement and music.

MARTHA GRAHAM

Quite different from the Ailey approach is the "Graham technique," taught in Graham's own school in New York as well as in colleges and universities across the country. Like Ailey, Graham was a *virtuoso* dancer and organized her own company. After Isadora Duncan, no one has been more influential in modern dance. Graham's technique is reminiscent of ballet in its rigor and discipline. Dancers learn specific kinds of movements and exercises designed to be used both as preparation for and part of the dance. Graham's contraction, for example, is one of the most common movements one is likely to see. It is the sudden pulling in of the diaphragm with the resultant relaxation of the rest of the body. This builds on Duncan's emphasis on the solar plexus, but adds to that emphasis the systolic and diastolic rhythms of heartbeat and pulse. The movement is very effective visually as well as being particularly flexible in depicting feelings and states of mind. It is a movement unknown in ballet, from which Graham always wished to remain distinct.

At times Graham's dances have been very literal, with narrative pretexts quite similar to those found in ballet. *Night Journey,* for instance, is an interpretation of *Oedipus Rex* by Sophocles. The lines of emotional force linking Jocasta and her son-husband Oedipus are strongly accentuated by the movements of the dance as well as by certain props on stage, such as ribbons that link the two together at times. In Graham's interpretation, Jocasta becomes much more important than she is in the original drama. This is partly because Graham saw the female figures in Greek drama—such as *Phaedra* (Figure 10-9)—as much more fully dimensional than we have normally understood them. By means of dancing their roles, she was able to develop the complexities of their character. In dances such as her *El Penitente,* Graham experimented with states of mind as the subject matter. Thus the featured male dancer in loose white trousers and tunic, moving in slow circles about the stage with a large wooden cross, is a powerful interpretation of penitence.

FIGURE 10-9
Martha Graham in *Phaedra*.
(© Martha Swope)

PILOBOLUS DANCE COMPANY

The more innovative dance companies, such as Pilobolus and the Mark Morris Company, often surprise audiences with abstract dances: moving bodies creating visual patterns as the primary subject matter. The dances of these companies usually have no pretexts—or at least none that could be interpreted in the narrative fashion of *Swan Lake*. The Pilobolus Company began in 1970 at Dartmouth, with four gymnastic male dancers. The choreographer Alison Chase directed the company in a series of dances that depended on the balance and leverage principles of gymnastics, producing shapes and movement that startled the dance world. The principle of balance and leverage is illustrated in Figure 10-10, a moment from *Monkshood's Farewell* (1974), one of their first efforts at producing a dance that had an extended development suggesting a narrative.

MARK MORRIS DANCE GROUP

The Mark Morris Dance Group was created—"reluctantly," he has said—in 1980 because he found he could not do the dances he wanted with other existing companies. Morris and his company were a sensation from the first, performing to rave reviews in New York from 1981 to 1988. In 1988 the company shocked the dance world by accepting an invitation from Brussels to take up residence at Théâtre Royal de la Monnaie, where the famed and well-loved ballet company of Maurice Béjart had thrilled a very demanding audience.

FIGURE 10-10
Monkshood's Farewell.
Pilobolus Dance Company.
(© Tim Matson)

Morris's first dance in Brussels was a theatrical piece with an intricate interpretation of Handel's music to John Milton's lyric poems: *L'Allegro, il Penseroso, ed il Moderato*. The title refers to three moods: happiness, melancholy, and restfulness. The interpretation of the state of mind associated with happiness is clearly evident in the movement patterns in Figure 10-11. The dance was produced again in Edinburgh in 1994 and at Lincoln Center in 1995. David Dougill commented on the "absolute rightness to moods and themes" with Milton's poems and Handel's music. Morris left Brussels in 1991 and again centers his work in New York.

TWYLA THARP

Tharp has developed a style pleasing to both serious critics and dance amateurs. A thoughtful student of the philosophy of dance, she includes a playful spontaneity that seems appropriately modern. She also has taken advantage of the new opportunities for dance on television, particularly the Public Broadcasting Corporation's *Dance in America* series, which has been very popular and critically successful. For television productions, she often uses cuts from newsreel films along with her dancers' interpretations of 1930s dances. She has been particularly successful in adapting jazz of the 1920s and 1930s to dance; for example, *Sue's Leg* features the music of "Fats" Waller (Figure 10-12). *Bix Pieces* was inspired by the cornetist Bix

FIGURE 10-11
L'Allegro, il Penseroso, ed il Moderato. Mark Morris Dance Group. (Klaus Lefebvre)

FIGURE 10-12
Sue's Leg. Choreography,
Twyla Tharp; costumes,
Santo Loquasto; lighting,
Jennifer Tipton; dancers
(l. to r.) Kenneth Rinker,
Rose Marie Wright, Twyla
Tharp, Tom Rawe. (Courtesy
Twyla Tharp Dance Founda-
tion, photograph by Tom
Berthiaume)

Beiderbecke, one of the first romantic, self-destructive young musicians of the twentieth century. *Eight Jelly Rolls,* premiered in 1971, and also televised, is a brilliant series of interpretations of eight songs written by the legendary Jelly Roll Morton, who claimed to have invented jazz. Tharp's interest in sequential dances — *Ocean's Motion,* a suite of dances to the music of Chuck Berry; *Raggedy Dances,* to ragtime tunes; and *Assorted Quarters,* to classical music — shows a virtuoso ability to explore feelings and states of mind as related to music.

Television has had a significant impact on dance performances since the early 1970s, making them much more available to the public. Tharp has been foremost among those experimenting with that medium, choreographing famous dancers, such as Rudolf Nureyev, the former star of the Russian Kirov ballet. Nureyev was interested in working with her partly because she had learned how to interpret the relatively restricted spaces available to the television camera and partly because her vocabulary of movements is very different from that of classical ballet. He welcomed a new dance challenge. Tharp choreographed *The Sinatra Suite,* a duet with Nureyev and Elaine Kudo, set to a group of songs sung by Frank Sinatra. The sultry style that Nureyev brought to this American music and choreography was striking. Nureyev again showed his versatility by dancing in Tharp's *Push Comes to Shove,* set to ragtime music interwoven with selections from Haydn symphonies. These dances have no explicit pretext.

PERCEPTION KEY   Dance and Television

The dance is becoming more available through television. Take advantage of these performances and keep asking yourself—after participation—four basic questions:

1. Did the movements of the dancers follow closely the rhythms of the music?
2. What was the subject matter?
3. Did the form give you insight into the subject matter?
4. If so, in what ways? Discuss what you think was revealed.

Having a mental set of such questions should help focus your attention for the next performance and lead to more intense participations.

Summary

Through the medium of the moving human body, the form of dance can reveal visual patterns or feelings or states of mind or narrative or, more probably, some combination. The first step in learning to participate with the dance is to learn the nature of its movements. The second is to be aware of its different kinds of subject matter. The content of dance gives us insights about our inner life, especially states of mind, that supplement the insights of music. Dance has the capacity to transform a pretext, the narrative which it enacts, whether the pretext is a story or a state of mind or a feeling. Our attention should be drawn into participation with this transformation. The insight we get from the dance experience is dependent on our awareness of this transformation.

Bibliography

Cohen, Selma Jean. *Dance as a Theatre Art*. New York: Dodd, Mead, 1974.

Copeland, Roger, and Marshall Cohen, eds. *What Is Dance?* New York: Oxford University Press, 1983.

DeMille, Agnes. *Dance to the Piper*. Boston: Houghton Mifflin, 1952.

Duncan, Isadora. *Art of the Dance*, 2d ed. New York: Theatre Arts, 1977.

Emery, Lynne Fauley. *Black Dance in the U.S. from 1619 to Today*, 2d ed. Salem, New Hampshire: Ayer, 1988.

Fergusson, Erna. *Dancing Gods: Indian Ceremonials of New Mexico and Arizona*. Albuquerque: University of New Mexico Press, 1966.

Friedman, James Michael. *Dancer and Spectator: An Aesthetic Distance*. San Francisco: Balletmonographs, 1976.

Humphrey, Doris. *The Art of Making Dances*. Edited by Barbara Pollack. New York: Grove Press, 1959.

Jowitt, Deborah. *Time and the Dancing Image*. New York: William Morrow, 1988.

Magriel, Paul, ed. *Nijinsky, Pavlova, Duncan*. New York: Da Capo, 1977.

Migel, Parmenia. *The Ballerinas*. New York: Macmillan, 1972.

Nadel, Myron, and Constance Miller, eds. *The Dance Experience*. New York: Universe Books, 1978.

Percival, John. *Modern Ballet*. New York: Dutton, 1970.

Reynolds, Nancy. *In Performance: A Companion to the Classics of the Dance*. New York: Harmony Books, 1980.

Sachs, Curt. *World History of the Dance*. New York: Norton, 1965.

Sparshott, Francis. *Off the Ground: First Steps to a Philosophical Consideration of the Dance*. Princeton, N.J.: Princeton University Press, 1988.

Stearns, Marshall. *Jazz Dance: The Story of American Vernacular Dance*. New York: Macmillan, 1968.

Stuart, Muriel. *The Classic Ballet*. New York: Knopf, 1969.

Note: The Index to 16mm Educational Films (National Information Center for Educational Media, 1984) lists dance films and sources. For *Dance in America* and other series, contact the local PBS TV station. Some of the dances mentioned in this chapter are available on VHS or DVD from Kultur International Films, 1-800-573-3782 or www.kultur.com. Among them are *Swan Lake* (catalog #1162), Alvin Ailey's *Revelations* (included on *Four By Ailey*, #0075), and *Martha Graham: An American Original in Performance* (#1177). For additional dance films and their distributors, search the database at www.dancefilmsassn.org/search.

Internet Resources

ALVIN AILEY AMERICAN DANCE THEATRE

http://www.alvinailey.org/

AMERICAN BALLET THEATER

http://www.abt.org/

CONTEMPORARY AND MODERN DANCE COMPANIES

http://www.dancer.com/dance-links/modern.htm

DANCE LINKS

http://www.dancer.com/dance-links/

DANCE MAGAZINE

http://www.dancemagazine.com/

HISTORY OF GREEK DANCE

http://www.annaswebart.com/culture/dancehistory/

MARK MORRIS DANCE COMPANY

http://www.culturevulture.net/Dance/markmorris.htm

MERCE CUNNINGHAM DANCE COMPANY

http://www.merce.org/

SAPPHIRE SWAN DANCE DIRECTORY (NUMEROUS VALUABLE LINKS)

http://www.sapphireswan.com/dance/

TWYLA THARP DANCE COMPANY

http://www.twylatharp.org/

CHAPTER 11

Film

Most of the discussion that follows can be considered descriptive criticism, although in the area of film what most of us practice most of the time is evaluative criticism. Most of us decide a film is good or bad, satisfying or unsatisfying, and we do so in a public way, sharing our evaluation readily with our friends. The basis on which we make evaluative judgments of films is, to a large extent, also the subject of this chapter. Our concerns are to point to cinematic excellence in several areas: cinematography, the care with which a film is photographed; the completeness and excellence of the script or story line; acting and character development; editing, the care with which separate shots are joined together to achieve a satisfying structure for the film; music, the way in which sound evokes emotion or establishes mood.

When we evaluate a film, all or most of these factors are likely to come into play. It is also true that many of the features discussed in Chapter 8 on drama apply to most films, since most films are forms of dramatic literature. This chapter examines each of these components in enough depth to make us aware of their contributions to film. Most films handle all these factors in a serviceable fashion—only a few will handle any of them badly enough for us to notice. However, it is also true that only a few—such as *Casablanca, Jules and Jim, Citizen Kane, A Wonderful Life,* or *The Searchers*—handle them well enough for us to think of them as classics. Most of the films we discuss are in or close to this category of achievement.

The Subject Matter of Film

Within a century, the film has become the most popular art form around the world, mainly because of its realism. Film is never completely lifelike, of course, but it is more so than any other medium. From the beginning, film borrowed principles of visual organization from painting. Even today, as films are planned, a storyboard is often created with drawings of scenes that are realized on film very close to the way they were designed. But unlike the image of painting, the images of film move, projected on a screen at twenty-four frames per second, and the eye merges them as if they were continuous action. The indebtedness of film to drama and literature is also great, since virtually all films have a narrative structure the characters follow. When films were young and silent, a pianist provided mood music to intensify visual scenes. After 1926, many films incorporated a soundtrack not only with the dialogue, but also with background music that has now become virtually indispensable. Because the film is relatively inexpensive to see, it reaches millions, providing them with what may be their primary experience of art and, by extension, their primary experience of the arts which the film borrows from.

Except in its most reductionist form, the subject matter of most great films is very difficult to isolate and restate in words. You could say that death is the subject matter of Bergman's *The Seventh Seal* (see Figure 11-2). But you would also need to observe that the knight's sacrifice to save the lives of others—which he accomplishes by playing chess with Death—is also part of the subject matter of the film. As David Cook explains in *A History of Narrative Film*, there is a complexity of subject matter in film that is rivaled only by literature.

It may be that the very popularity of film and the ease with which we can access it lead us to ignore the form and the insights form offers into subject matter. For example, is it really possible to catch the subtleties of form of a great film in one viewing? Yet, how many of us see a great film more than once? Audiences generally enjoy, but rarely analyze, films. Some of the analysis that follows may help your enjoyment as well as your analyses.

Except perhaps for opera, film more than any of the other arts involves collaborative effort. Most films are written by a scriptwriter, then planned by a director who may make many changes. However, even if the director is also the scriptwriter, the film needs a producer, camera operators, an editor, designers, researchers, costumers, actors, and actresses. Auteur criticism regards the director as equivalent to the *auteur*, or author, of the film. For most moviegoers, the most important persons involved with the film will almost surely be not the director, but the stars who appear in the film. Meryl Streep, Judi Dench, Anthony Hopkins, and Morgan Freeman are more famous than such directors of stature as Ingmar Bergman, Federico Fellini, Lina Wertmuller, Akira Kurosawa, Jane Campion, or Krzyzstof Kieslowski.

Directing and Editing

The two dominant figures in early films were directors who did their own *editing:* D. W. Griffith and Sergei Eisenstein, unquestionably the great early geniuses of filmmaking. They managed to gain control over the production of their works so that they could craft their films into a distinctive art. Some of their films are still considered among the finest ever made. *Birth of a Nation* (1916) and *Intolerance* (1918) by Griffith and *Potemkin* (1925) and *Ivan the Terrible* (1941–1946) by Eisenstein are still being shown and are still influencing contemporary filmmakers. These men were more than just directors. With many of their films they were responsible for almost everything: writing, casting, choosing locations, handling the camera, directing, editing, and financing.

Directing and editing are probably the most crucial phases of filmmaking. Today most directors control the acting and supervise the photography, carried out by skilled technicians who work with such problems as lighting, camera angles, and focusing, as well as the motion of the camera itself (some sequences use a highly mobile camera, while others use a fixed camera). Among the resources available to directors making choices about the use of the camera are the kinds of shots that may eventually be edited together. A *shot* is a continuous length of film exposed in the camera without a break. Some of the most important kinds of shots follow:

Establishing shot: Usually a distant shot establishes important locations or figures in the action.

Close-up: An important object, such as the face of a character, fills the screen.

Long shot: The camera is far distant from the most important characters, objects, or scenes.

Medium shot: What the camera focuses on is neither up close nor far distant. There can be medium close-ups and medium long shots too.

Following shot: The camera keeps a moving figure in the frame, usually keeping pace with the figure.

Point-of-view shot: The camera records what the character must be seeing; when the camera moves, it implies that the character's gaze moves.

Tracking shot: A shot in which the camera moves forward, backward, or sidewise.

Crane shot: The camera is on a crane or movable platform and moves upward or downward.

Hand-held shot: The camera is carried, sometimes on a special harness, by the camera operator.

If you watch television or see films, you have seen all these shots hundreds of times. Add to these specific kinds of shots the variables of camera angles, types of camera lenses, variations in lighting, variations in approach to sound, and you can see that the technical resources of the director are enormous. The addition of script and actors enriches the director's range of choices so that they become almost dizzying.

The editor, almost always under the control of the director, puts the shots in order after the filming is finished. This selective process is highly complex and of supreme importance, for the structuring of the shots forms the film. The alternatives are often vast, and if the film is to achieve an artistic goal—insight into its subject matter—the shot succession must be creatively accomplished. The editor trims the shots to an appropriate length, then joins them with other shots to create the final film. Edited sequences sometimes shot far apart in time and place are organized into a unity. Films are rarely shot sequentially, and only a part of the total footage is shown in a film. The old saying of the bit-part actor — "I was lost on the cutting-room floor" — attests to the fact that sometimes interesting footage is omitted. Often some of the most bitter arguments in filmmaking are between the director and the editor, who can frequently disagree on how to edit a film. Sometimes, especially in video stores, you will see the term "Director's Cut" on a film, meaning that the director edited the film to please his or her vision — often adding sequences originally omitted to conform to the perceived needs of the exhibiting theaters.

It helps to know the resources of the editor, who cuts the film to create certain relationships between takes. These relationships, or cuts, are often at the core of the director's distinctive style. Some of the most familiar of the director's and editor's choices follow:

Continuity cut: shots edited to produce a sense of narrative continuity, following the action stage by stage. The editor can also use a discontinuity cut to break up the narrative continuity for effect.

Jump cut: sometimes just called a cut; moves abruptly from one shot to the next, with no preparation and often with a shock.

Cut-in: an immediate move from a wide shot to a very close shot of the same scene; the editor may cut out, as well.

Cross-cutting: alternating shots of two or more distinct actions occurring in different places (but often at the same time).

Dissolve: one scene disappearing slowly while the next scene appears as if beneath it.

Fade: includes fade-in (a dark screen growing brighter to reveal the shot) and fade-out (the screen darkens, effectively ending the shot).

Wipe: transition between shots, with a line moving across or through the screen separating one shot from the next.

Graphic match: joining two shots that have similar composition, color, or scene.

Montage sequence: a sequence of images dramatically connected but physically disconnected.

Shot, reverse shot: a pair of shots where the first shot shows a character looking at something; reverse shot shows what the character sees.

Our responses to film depend on the choices that directors and editors make regarding shots and editing almost as much as they do on the nature of the narrative and the appeal of the actors. In a relatively short time film editing has become almost a kind of language—a language of imagery with close to universal significance.

When the editing is handled well, it can be profoundly effective, because it is impossible in real-life experience to achieve what the editor achieves. By eliminating the irrelevant, good editing accents the relevant. We cannot go instantly from the Los Angeles airport, where we are watching a hired assassin from Chicago land, to the office of the political candidate he has come to kill. Film can do this with ease. The *montage*—dramatically connected but physically disconnected images—can be made without a word of dialogue. You undoubtedly can recall innumerable instances of this kind of editing. When done well, this tying together of images that could not possibly occur together in life enhances the meaning of the images we see.

PERCEPTION KEY   Techniques of Directing and Editing

1. Study a film and record the kinds of shots and cuts you see. How many of those listed above are used?
2. Keep track of the length of time spent in any given shot in seconds and minutes. Is there a major difference between the length of shots in older films and in newer films? In action films and romantic films? In tragic films and comedies? In horror films and cartoon films? Which kinds of cuts seem preferred in each kind of film?
3. What is the emotional effect of the various cuts available to editors? Does one kind of cut affect your response more than another?
4. Do certain choices in shots or cuts produce predictable emotional reactions?

The Participative Experience and Film

Our participation with film is often virtually involuntary. For one thing, most of us know exactly what it means to lose our sense of place and time in a movie. This loss seems to be achieved rapidly in all but the most awkwardly conceived films. In a film like *Black Orpheus* (1958), shot in Rio, the intensity of tropical colors, Latin American music, and the dynamics of the carnival produce an imaginary or virtual reality so intense and vital that actual reality seems dull by comparison. But then there are other films that create the illusion of life itself. Aristotle analyzed the ways in which drama imitates life and the ways in which an audience identifies with some of the actors on the stage (Chapter 8). Yet, the film seems to have these powers to an even greater degree than the stage.

Cinematic realism makes it easy for us to identify with actors who represent our values (a kind of participation). For instance, in *Forrest Gump* (1994), Tom Hanks plays what seems to be, on the surface, a mentally defective person. But Gump is not just dumb—he is good at heart and positive in his thinking. He is a character in whom cunning—not just intelligence—has been removed, and in him the audience sees their lost innocence. It would be very doubtful that anyone in the audience consciously identified with Gump, but it was clear from the reception of the film that something in him touched a nerve in the audience and was, in the final analysis, both appealing and cheering. Gump is an unlikely hero primarily because he is trusting, innocent, and good-hearted. When the audience participates with that film, it is in part because the audience sees in Gump what it would like to see in itself.

Film, Drama, Television, and Participation

1. Observe people coming out of a movie theater. Can you usually tell by their behavior whether the film was a western, comedy, tragedy, melodrama, or something else?
2. Does it make a significant difference whether you experience a film in an empty or a packed theater? Is laughter somehow enhanced in a crowd? Is the humor of a comic film significantly weakened if you see it alone?
3. Compare your experiences of the same film in the theater and on television. Which presentation engages your participation more intensely? Is the difference in the sizes of the screens mainly responsible for any difference in the intensity of participation? Or is it, perhaps, the stronger darkness that usually surrounds you in the theater? What other factors might be involved? The film director David Lynch "likens seeing his movies on video to looking at a bad reproduction of a painting." Do you agree?
4. Do you think it would be easier to make a television film or a theater film? What would the basic differences be?

Other forms of identification happen in films all the time. In the *Rambo* films of the 1970s and 1980s, America seemed to identify with Sylvester Stallone, who did single-handedly what the nation could not: win the Vietnam War. It may be that we naturally identify with heroes in films, as we do in books. The characters played by extremely charismatic actors, like Julia Roberts or Paul Newman, almost always appeal to some aspect of our personality, even if sometimes that aspect is frightening. Such may be the source, for instance, of the appeal of Hannibal Lector in *The Silence of the Lambs* (1992), in which Anthony Hopkins not only appears as a cannibal, but actually gets away with it, identifying his former doctor as his next victim, whose liver he plans to eat with some "fava beans and a nice Chianti."

There are problems with this kind of loss of self, which is often a veiled appeal to the worship of self. Film can inform us about ourselves, or it can cause a short circuit of self-awareness: We simply indulge in hero worship with ourselves as the hero. Other arts may also cause this short circuit, of course, but the temptation seems most likely with film.

There are two kinds of participative experiences with film. One is not principally filmic in nature and is represented by a kind of self-indulgence that depends upon self-justifying fantasies. We imagine ourselves as James Bond, for example, and ignore the interrelationship of the major elements of the film. The other kind of participation evolves from an acute awareness of the details and their interrelationships. This second kind of participative experience means much more to us ultimately because it is significantly informative: We understand the content by means of the form.

Just a word more about the first kind of participation. It is usually referred to as "escapism." Escape films give us the chance to see ourselves complimented in a movie, thus satisfying our desire for self-importance. Unhappily, escape films often help us avoid doing anything about achieving something that would really make us more important to ourselves. In some ways these films help rob people of the chance to be something in their own right. Most television dramas depend on this effect for their success.

Perhaps it is true that large masses of people need this kind of entertainment in order to avoid the despair that would set in if they had to face up to the reality of their lives. It may be cynical to think so, yet it is highly possible that many people who make motion pictures believe this to be a justification for what they are doing.

The fact that film may cause such an intense participation of the wrong kind prevents us from perceiving the content of the film. We can see a film and know nothing about the finer points of its form and meaning — the nuances that make a film worth experiencing and then pondering over because of its impact on us. Most films, unfortunately, are hardly worth seeing more than once (or even once), while there are a few that are rightly called classics because of their humanizing achievement through structural excellence. We want to get a sense of how to appreciate a film that is a classic. Questions of criticism, as we established in Chapter 3, are always implicitly operative when we view a film or any work of art.

The Film Image

The starting point of film is the moving image. Just as still photographs and paintings can move us profoundly by their organization of visual experience, so can such images when they are set to motion. Indeed, many experts insist that no artistic medium ever created has the power to move us as deeply as the medium of moving images. They base their claim not just on the mass audiences who have been profoundly stirred but also on the fact that the moving images of the film are similar to the moving images we perceive in life. We rarely perceive static images except when viewing such things as paintings or photographs. Watching a film closely can help us perceive much more intensely the visual worth of many of the images we experience outside film. We see, for example, someone walking in a jaunty, jumpy fashion with his feet turned out. Our visual interest is immediately enhanced if we remember Charlie Chaplin, and almost always we will remember if we have participated with a Chaplin film. There is a very long tracking shot in *Weekend*, by Jean-Luc Godard, of a road piled up with wrecked or stalled cars. The camera glides along nervelessly imaging the gridlock with fires and smoke and seemingly endless corpses scattered here and there along the roadsides — unattended. The stalled and living motorists are obsessed with getting to their vacation resorts. The horns honk and honk. The unbelievable elongation of the procession and the utter grotesqueness of the scenes evoke black humor at its extreme. If in reality we have to face anything even remotely similar, the intensity of our vision inevitably will be heightened if we have seen *Weekend*.

PERCEPTION KEY Godard's *Weekend*

Assuming that the analysis above is accurate, would you rather not have seen *Weekend* if you someday are confronted with a bad car accident? If so, why? If not, why?

FIGURE 11-1
From Jean Renoir's *The Grand Illusion* (1936) with Erich von Stroheim, Jean Gabin, and Marcel Dalio. (A Continental Distributing, Inc., release, National Film Archive)

Many early filmmakers composed their films by adding single photographs to each other, frame by frame. Movement in motion pictures is caused by the physiological limitations of the eye. It cannot perceive the black line between frames when the film strip is moved rapidly. All it sees is the succession of frames minus the lines that divide them, for the eye cannot perceive separate images or frames that move faster than one-thirtieth of a second. This is to use the language of the camera, which can take a picture in much less time than that. Motion picture film is usually projected at a speed of twenty-four frames per second, and the persistence of vision merges the images.

Because of this, many filmmakers, both early and contemporary, attempt to design each individual frame as carefully as they might a photograph. (See "Photography and Painting: The Pictorialists" in Chapter 12). Jean Renoir, the famous French filmmaker and son of painter Pierre-Auguste, sometimes composed frames like a tightly unified painting, as in the *Grand Illusion* (1936) (Figure 11-1) and *The Rules of the Game* (1939). Sergei Eisenstein also framed many of his images especially carefully, notably in *Potemkin* (1925). David Lean, who directed *Brief Encounter* (1945), *Bridge Over the River Kwai* (1957), *Lawrence of Arabia* (1962, re-released 1988), *Dr. Zhivago* (1965), and *Ryan's Daughter* (1970), also paid very close attention to the composition of individual frames.

FIGURE 11-2
From Ingmar Bergman's *Seventh Seal* (1957). (© Svensk Film Industry, Stockholm. National Film Archive)

FIGURE 11-3
Gianni di Venanzo's powerful recessional shot for Federico Fellini's *8½*. Guido (Marcello Mastroianni) greets his mistress Carla (Sandra Milo) at the spa train station. (© 1963 Embassy Pictures Corp. The Museum of Modern Art Film Stills Archive)

FIGURE 11-4
From *Citizen Kane* (1941)
with Orson Welles and
Dorothy Comingore, directed
by Orson Welles. (The
Museum of Modern Art Film
Stills Archive)

PERCEPTION KEY   Still Frames and Photography

Study Figures 11-1,11-2, 11-3, and 11-4.

1. How would you evaluate these stills with reference to tightness of composition? For example, do the details and parts interrelate so that any change would disrupt the unity of the totality? Compare with Figure 2-2 and discuss.
2. Compare the stills with Figures 12-12, 12-20, and 12-21. Are the stills as tightly organized as the photographs? Discuss.

For some directors, the still moments of the film must be as exactly composed as a painting. The theory is that if the individual moments of the film are each as perfect as can be, the total film will be a cumulative perfection. This seems to be the case only for some films. In films that have long meditative sequences, such as Orson Welles' *Citizen Kane* (1941) (Figure 11-4) or Bergman's *Cries and Whispers* (1972), or sequences in which characters or images are relatively unmoving for significant periods of time, such as Robert Redford's *A River Runs Through It* (1994), the carefully composed still image may be of real significance. Nevertheless, no matter how powerful, most stills from fine films will reveal very little of the significance of the entire film all by themselves: It is their sequential movement that brings out their effectiveness.

FIGURE 11-5
Storyboard images from
Kevin Costner's *Dances with
Wolves* (1990), by Steve Burg
and Leonard Morganti.
(From *Dances with Wolves:
The Illustrated Story of the
Epic Film*, Kevin Costner,
Michael Blake, and Jim Wilson. Compilation and design
© 1990 by Newmarket Press,
New York)

The still frame and the individual shot are the building blocks of film. Controlling the techniques that produce and interrelate these blocks is the first job of the film artist. We can see from the storyboard sketches by Steve Burg and Leonard Morganti from Kevin Costner's *Dances with Wolves* (1990) (Figure 11-5) that planning individual images before shooting begins can be an important part of making a film.

Camera Point of View

Obviously the motion in the motion picture can come from numerous sources. The actors can move toward, away from, or across the field of camera vision. When something moves toward the camera it moves with astonishing speed, as we all know from watching the images of a moving locomotive (the favorite vehicle for this technique so far) rush at us and then "catapult over our heads." The effect of the catapult is noteworthy because it is characteristic of the film medium.

People move before us the way they move before the camera, but the camera (or cameras) can achieve visual things that our unaided eye cannot: showing the same moving action from a number of points of view simultaneously, for instance, or showing it from a camera angle the eye cannot achieve. The realistic qualities of a film can be threatened, however, by being too sensational, with a profusion of shots that would be impossible in a real-life situation. Although such virtuoso effects can dazzle us at first, the feeling of being dazzled can degenerate into being dazed.

Another way the film portrays motion is by the movement or tracking of the camera. In a sequence in John Huston's *The Misfits* (1961), cowboys are rounding up wild mustang horses to sell for dog food, and some amazing scenes were filmed with the camera mounted on a pickup truck chasing fast-running horses. The motion in these scenes is overwhelming because Huston combines two kinds of rapid motion—of trucks and of horses. Moreover, the motion is further increased because of the narrow focus of the camera and the limited boundary of the screen. The recorded action excludes vision that might tend to distract or dilute the motion we are permitted to see. Much the same effect was achieved in the buffalo run in *Dances with Wolves* thirty years later. The screen in motion pictures always constrains our vision, even when we imagine the space beyond the screen that we do not see, as when a character moves off the filmed space. Eliminating the space beyond the images recorded by the camera circumscribes and fixes our attention. And such attention is bound to enhance the rapidity and intensity of the moving images.

A final basic way film can achieve motion is by means of the camera lens. Even when the camera is fixed in place, a lens that affords a much wider, narrower, larger, or smaller field of vision than the eye normally supplies will give the illusion of motion, since we instinctively feel the urge to be in the physical position that would supply that field of vision. Zoom lenses, which change their focal length along a smooth range—thus bringing images gradually closer or farther away—are even more effective for suggesting motion, especially for small-screen viewing of movies on television. One

FIGURE 11-6
From Stanley Kubrik's MGM release *2001: A Space Odyssey.* Dr. Floyd (William Sylvester), one of the scientists from the Clavius moon base, descends the ramp into the TMAi excavation and, for the first time, the visiting scientist from Earth has a close look at the strange object, which has been hidden beneath the lunar surface for millions of years. (© 1968 Warner Brothers. All rights reserved)

PERCEPTION KEY   Camera Vision

Make a mask with two small cutout rectangles, approximately ⅜ inch long × ½ inch wide, as shown:

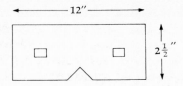

Place the mask so that you can see only out of the slits. This experiment can be conducted almost as effectively by using simple pinholes in place of cutout rectangles. In fact, for those who wear glasses it may be more effective, because the pinholes are actually "lenses" and may permit some people with defective vision to see fairly clearly without their glasses.

1. Does the "framing" of the cutouts make you unusually sensitive to the way things look?
2. What effect does moving your head have on the composition of the things you see?
3. What are some of the differences between using one eye, then both eyes? Which is more the way the camera sees? What do you learn from viewing a scene first with one eye, then the other?
4. An important feature of this experiment is the analogy with the motion of the camera. Be sure you get a sense of what happens to your visual field when you move your head in the fashion a camera would move. Are you capable of any motion that is impossible for the camera?
5. If the camera is the principal tool of filmmaking, do directors give up artistic control when they have photographers operate the machines? Does your experimenting in the questions above suggest there may be a camera "language" that directors should be controlling themselves? Given your experience with film and cameras, how might camera language be defined?

FIGURE 11-7
From *Star Wars* (1977).
(Everett Collection)

of the favorite shots on television is that of a figure walking or moving in some fashion, which looks, at first, as if it were a medium shot but which is actually revealed as a long shot when the zoom is reversed. Since our own eye cannot imitate the action of the zoom lens, the effect the lens has can be quite dramatic when used creatively. It is something like the effect that slow motion or stop motion has on us. It interrupts our perceptions of something—something that had seemed perfectly natural—in a way that makes us aware of the film medium itself. On the other hand, with many people experimenting with 8× zooms on video cameras, it is clear that zoom shots are quick to become very tedious.

Sometimes technique can take over a film by becoming the most interesting aspect of the cinematic experience. The Academy Award winner *2001: A Space Odyssey* (1968) (Figure 11-6), *Star Wars* (1977), *Close Encounters of the Third Kind* (1977), and the seven Star Trek films of the 1970s and 1980s have similar themes, concentrating on space, the future, and fantastic situations. All include shots of marvelous technical achievements, such as the images of the computer-guided cameras that follow the space vehicles of Luke Skywalker and Han Solo in the dramatic conclusion of *Star Wars* (Figure 11-7). But some critics have argued that these technical achievements were ends rather than means to artistic revelation.

PERCEPTION KEY   Technique and Film

1. Are the technical triumphs of films such as *Star Wars* used as means or ends? If they are the ends, then are they the subject matter? What kind of problem does such a possibility raise for our appreciation of the film?
2. In *Tom Jones* (1963) a technique called the "double take" was introduced. After searching for his wallet everywhere, Tom turns and looks at the audience and asks whether we have seen his wallet. Is this technique a gimmick or artistically justifiable? Could you make a defensible judgment about this without seeing the film?

3. Recently old black-and-white films have been "colorized," a technique espoused by Ted Turner. In the case of *It's a Wonderful Life*, James Stewart protested vigorously before a congressional committee, and Frank Capra, the director, issued a passionate sickbed plea. Do you agree with Turner or with Stewart and Capra? Why? Try to see a colorized version of *Casablanca* and compare it with the original. Which do you prefer? Why?

Audience Response to Film

Because it is so easy to shoot a scene in various ways, a good director is constantly choosing the shot that he or she hopes has the most meaning within the total structure. When Luis Buñuel briefly shows us the razoring of a woman's open eyeball in *Un Chien Andalou* (1928) (it is really a slaughtered cow's eyeball), he is counting on our personal horror at actually seeing such an act, but the scene is artistically justifiable because Buñuel carefully integrated the scene into the total structure of the film. Unfortunately, many films show sheer violence without any attempt to inform — for example, *Halloween* (1979), *Friday the 13th* (1979) and its many sequels, and *Nightmare on Elm Street* (1985) and its many sequels. The violence is used strictly for shock value, but it is so overdone that the audience is rarely moved by it. A curious phenomenon about experiencing film as well as drama is that the imagination of the audience is often a much more reliable instrument for the interpretation of horror than the fully realized visual scene.

Clever directors can easily shock their audiences. But the more complex responses, some of which are as difficult to control as they are to attain, are the aim of the enduring filmmakers. When Ingmar Bergman shows us the rape scene in *The Virgin Spring* (1959), he does not saturate us with horror. And the murder of the rapists by the girl's father is preceded by an elaborate purification ritual that relates the violence and horror to profound meaning. In any art, control of audience response is vital. We can become emotionally saturated just as easily as we can become bored. The result is indifference.

Sound

Al Jolson's *Jazz Singer* (1927) introduced sound, although it was not welcomed by everyone. Sergei Eisenstein feared, as did many others, that sound might kill the artistic integrity of film. He was afraid that with sound no one would work with the images that create a film language and that film would once again become subservient to drama. Eisenstein knew that images in motion could sustain the kind of dramatic tension that was once thought limited to the dramatic stage. This is a point of consummate importance. First of all, a film is images in motion. Great filmmakers may exploit sound and other elements, but they will never make them the basic

FIGURE 11-8
Religious services held in the field while a tank flame-thrower destroys crops in the background in *Apocalypse Now*. (© 1979 United Artists Corp. The Museum of Modern Art The Film Stills Archive)

ingredients of the film. On the other hand, less creative filmmakers will rely on the dialogue of the film almost exclusively, using the camera to do little more than visually record people talking to one another.

Sound in film may involve much more than the addition of dialogue to the visual track. Music had long been a supplement of the silent films, and special portfolios of piano and organ music were available to the accompanist who played in the local theater while coordinating the music with the film. They indicated the kind of feelings that could be produced by merging special music with chase, love, or suspense scenes. D. W. Griffith's *Birth of a Nation* (1916) features a "rescue" charge by the Ku Klux Klan, which was cut to the dynamics of Richard Wagner's *Die Walküre*. Francis Ford Coppola may have had that in mind when he made the incredible helicopter battle scene in *Apocalypse Now* (1979) (Figure 11-8) to Wagner's "Ride of the Valkyries." *Apocalypse Now*, a film about the Vietnam War, used sound in exceptionally effective ways, especially in scenes such as the skyrocket fireworks battle deep in the jungle. But perhaps the most powerful cinematic sound produced so far occurs in the opening scenes of *Saving Private Ryan* (1999, directed by Steven Spielberg)—the storming of the Normandy beach on D day, June 6, 1944.

Sound may intensify our experience of film. Not only do we expect to hear dialogue, but we also expect to hear the sounds we associate with the action on screen, whether it is the quiet chirping of crickets in a country scene in *Sounder* (1972) or the dropping of bombs from a low-flying Japanese Zero in *Empire of the Sun* (1987). Subtle uses of sound sometimes prepare us for action that is yet to come, such as when in *Rain Man* (1989) we see Dustin Hoffman and Tom Cruise walking toward a convertible, but we hear the dialogue and road sounds from the next shot, when they are driving down the highway. That editing technique might have been very unsettling in the 1930s, but filmmakers have had sixty years to get our sensibilities accustomed to such disjunctions.

A very famous disjunction occurs in the beginning of *2001: A Space Odyssey* when, watching images of one tribe of apes warring with another tribe of apes in prehistoric times, we hear the rich modern harmonies of Richard Strauss's dramatic tone poem *Also Sprach Zarathustra*. The music suggests one very sophisticated mode of development inherent in the future of these primates—whom we see in the first phases of discovering how to use tools. They already show potential for creating high art. Eventually the sound and imagery coincide when the scene changes to 2001, with scientists on the moon discovering a monolithic structure identical to one the apes had found on earth.

PERCEPTION KEY   Sight and Sound

1. Analyze carefully the next film you see on television. Examine the frames for their power as individual compositions, recalling some of the points made in the chapters on painting and sculpture. How strong is the film in this respect?
2. Do the size and shape of the television screen inhibit intense visual experience? Is your participation with film stronger with television or in the theater? Why?
3. Turn off the sound entirely. Can you follow clearly what is going on? Is much of importance lost?
4. Block out the video portion of the program and listen to the sound only. Can you follow clearly what is going on? Is much of importance lost? When you come right down to it, you may find that in second-rate films not terribly much is lost when the images are eliminated.

Image and Action

These experiments probably indicate that most contemporary film is a marriage of sight and sound. Yet we must not forget that film is a medium in which the moving image—the action—is preeminent, as in Federico Fellini's *8½* (1963). The title refers to Fellini's own career, ostensibly about himself and his making a new film after seven and a half previous films. *8½* is about the artistic process. Guido, played by Marcello Mastroianni (Figure 11-3), brings a group of people to a location to make a film. But from the first shot of his having a nervous breakdown in a car in heavy Rome traffic, cross-cut with a large statue of Christ being flown by a helicopter over

Rome, the action points inward to Guido's mind. His visual confusion, combined with the claustrophobia produced by the intense sound, reveals something of his inner state.

What follows centers on Guido's loss of creative direction, his psychological problems related to religion, sex, and his need to dominate women. As he convalesces from his breakdown, he brings people together to make a film, but he has no clear sense of what he wants to do, no coherent story to tell. *8½* seems to mimic Fellini's situation so carefully that it is difficult to know whether Fellini planned out the film or not. He has said "I appeared to have it all worked out in my head, but it was not like that. For three months I continued working on the basis of a complete production, in the hope that meanwhile my ideas would sort themselves out. Fifty times I nearly gave up."[1] And yet, most of the film is described in a single letter to Brunello Rondi (a writer of the screenplay), written long before the start of production.

The film is episodic, with memorable dream and nightmare sequences, some of which are almost hallucinatory. Such scenes focus on the inward quest of the film: Guido's search for the cause of his creative block so that he can resolve it. By putting himself in the center of an artistic tempest, he mirrors his own psychological confusion in order to bring it under control. Indeed, he seems intent on creating artistic tension by bringing both his wife and mistress to the location of the film.

The film abandons continuous narrative structure in favor of episodic streams of consciousness in the sequences that reveal the inner workings of Guido's mind. In a way they may also reveal the inner workings of the creative mind if we assume that Fellini projected his own anxieties into the film. *8½* is revelatory of the psychic turmoil of creativity.

Film Structure

Michael Cimino's portrayal of three hometown men who fight together in Vietnam, *The Deer Hunter* (1979) (Figure 11-9), has serious structural problems because the film takes place in three radically different environments, and it is not always clear how they are related. Yet, it won several Academy Awards and has been proclaimed one of the great antiwar films. Cimino took great risks by dividing the film into three large sections: sequences of life in Clairton, Pennsylvania, with a Russian Orthodox wedding and a last hunting expedition for deer; sequences of war prisoners and fighting in Vietnam; sequences afterward in Clairton, where only one of the three men, Mike, played by Robert DeNiro, is able to live effectively. Mike finally sets out to get Steven to return from the wheelchair ward of the VA hospital to his wife. Then he sets out to find his best friend, Nick, a heroin addict still in Saigon, playing Russian roulette for hardened Vietnamese gamblers. Russian roulette was not an actual part of the Vietnam experience, but Cimino made it a metaphor for the senselessness of war.

[1]John Kobal, *The Top 100 Movies* (New York: New American Library, 1988).

FIGURE 11-9
John Savage in a scene from
The Deer Hunter (1979).
(EMI/Columbia/Warners/
The Kobal Collection)

Cimino relied in part on the model of Dante's *Divine Comedy*, also divided into three sections — Hell, Purgatory, and Paradise. In *The Deer Hunter* the rivers of molten metal in the steel mills and, more obviously, the war scenes suggest the ghastliness of Hell. The extensive and ecstatic scenes in the Russian Orthodox church suggest Paradise, while life in Clairton represents an in-between, a kind of Purgatory. In one of the most stirring episodes, when he is back in Saigon during the American evacuation looking for Nick, Mike is shown standing up in a small boat negotiating his way through the canals. The scene is a visual echo of Eugene Delacroix's *Dante and Virgil in Hell*, a famous nineteenth-century painting. For anyone who recognizes the allusion to Dante, Cimino's structural techniques become clearer, as do his views of war in general and of the Vietnam War in particular.

The function of photography in films such as *8½* and *The Deer Hunter* is sometimes difficult to assess. If we agree that the power of the moving image is central to the ultimate meaning of the motion picture, we can see that the most important structural qualities of any good film develop from the choices made in the editing stage. Sometimes different versions of a single action will be filmed, the director and the editor deciding which will be in the final mix after testing each version in relation to the overall structure.

The episodic structure of Ridley Scott's *Thelma and Louise* (1991) (Figure 11-10) lends itself to contrasting the interiors of a seamy Arkansas nightclub and a cheap motel with the magnificent open road and dramatic landscape of the Southwest. Louise, played by Susan Sarandon, and Thelma, played by Geena Davis, are on the run in Louise's 1956 Thunderbird con-

FIGURE 11-10
Susan Sarandon and Geena
Davis in *Thelma & Louise*
(1991). (MGM/Pathe/The
Kobal Collection)

vertible after Louise shoots and kills Harlan, who has attempted to rape
Thelma. Knowing their story will not be believed, they head for Mexico and
freedom, but never get there. Callie Khouri wrote the script for this femi-
nist film and cast the women as deeply sympathetic outcasts and despera-
does—roles traditionally reserved for men. In one memorable scene, a
truck driver hauling a gasoline rig makes lecherous faces at the women and
generally harasses them. The cross-cutting builds considerable tension
which is relieved, at first, when the women pull over as if they were interested in him. As the driver leaves his truck to walk toward them, they shoot
his rig and it explodes like an inferno. The editing in this film is quite conventional, but everyone who has seen it is very likely to remember this
scene, whose exceptional power depends on the use of cross-cutting.

The editor's work gives meaning to the film just as surely as the
scriptwriter's and the photographer's. Observe, for instance, the final scenes
in Eisenstein's *Potemkin*. The battleship *Potemkin* is steaming to a confrontation with the Russian fleet. Eisenstein rapidly cuts from inside the
ship to outside: showing a view of powerfully moving engine pistons, then
the ship cutting deeply into the water, then rapidly back and forth, showing
anxiety-ridden faces, all designed to raise the emotional pitch of anyone
watching the movie. This kind of cutting or montage was used by Alfred
Hitchcock in the shower murder scene of the 1960 horror thriller *Psycho*.
He demonstrated that the technique could be used to increase tension and
terror, even though no explicit murderous actions were shown on screen.
Ironically, the scene was so powerful that its star, Janet Leigh, avoids show-
ers as much as possible, always preferring the bath.

Filmic Meanings

We cannot completely translate filmic meaning into language. We can only approximate a translation by describing the connections—emotional, narrative, symbolic, or whatever—implied by the sequence of images. When we watch the overturning coffin in Bergman's *Wild Strawberries* (1957), for example, we are surprised to find that the figure in the coffin has the same face as Professor Borg, the protagonist, who is himself a witness to what we see. Borg is face to face with his own death. That this scene has special meaning seems clear, yet we cannot completely articulate its significance. The meaning is embodied in the moving images. The scene has a strong tension and impact, and yet it is apparent that the full meaning depends on the context of the whole film in which it appears. The relation of detail to structure exists in every art, of course, but that relation in its nuances often may more easily be missed in our experiences of the film. For one thing, we are not accustomed to permitting images to build their own meanings apart from the meanings we already associate with them. Second, we do not always observe the way one movement or gesture will mean one thing in one context and an entirely different thing in another context. Third, moving images generally are more difficult to remember than still images, as in painting, and thus it is more difficult to become aware of their connections.

The filmmaker must control contexts, especially with reference to the gesture. In Eric Rohmer's film *Claire's Knee* (1970), a totally absurd gesture, the caressing of an indifferent and relatively insensitive young woman's knee, becomes the fundamental focus of the film. This gesture is loaded with meaning throughout the entire film, but loaded only for the main masculine character and us. The young woman is unaware that her knee holds such power over the man. Although the gesture is absurd, in a way it is plausible, for such fixations can occur to anyone. But this film is not concerned solely with plausibility; it is mainly concerned with the gesture in a context that reveals what is unclear in real-life experience—the complexities of some kinds of obsessions. And this is done primarily through skillful photography and editing rather than through spoken narrative.

PERCEPTION KEY   Gesture

1. Watch a silent film with Charlie Chaplin or Buster Keaton. Enumerate the most important gestures. If a gesture is repeated, does it accumulate significance? If so, why? Does the absence of sound increase the importance of gesture? Suppose speech were inserted into this film. Would this decrease the importance of the gesture?

2. Examine a few recent films for their use of gesture. Are the gestures used in any way to tie the images together, making them more coherent? Be specific. Did you find any film in which gesture played no significant role?

3. Compare the gestures in film with the gestures of sculpture. How do they differ? Do you see film sometimes borrowing familiar gestures, such as the posture of Michelangelo's *David* (Figure 5-10)?

4. To what extent are the films you have watched meaningful because of their relationship to the world we inhabit?

The Context of Film History

All meanings, linguistic or nonlinguistic, exist within some kind of context. Most first-rate films exist in many contexts simultaneously, and it is our job as sensitive viewers to be able to decide which are the most important. Film, like every art, has a history, and this history is one of the more significant contexts in which every film takes place. In order to make that historical context fruitful in our filmic experiences, we must do more than just read about that history. We must accumulate a historical sense of film by seeing films that have been important in the development of the medium. Most of us have a very rich personal backlog in film; we have seen a great many films, some of which are memorable and many of which have been influenced by landmark films.

Furthermore, film exists in a context that is meaningful for the life work of a director and, in turn, for us. When we talk about the films of Orson Welles, Bergman, or Fellini, we are talking about the achievements of artists just as much as when we talk about the achievements of Rembrandt, Vermeer, or Van Gogh. Today we watch carefully for films by Steven Spielberg, Francis Coppola, Michelangelo Antonioni, Michael Cimino, Woody Allen, Robert Altman, Martin Scorsese, Spike Lee, Jane Campion, Quentin Tarantino, and Lina Wertmuller — to name only a few of the most active current directors — because their work has shown a steady development and because they, in relation to the history of the film, have shown themselves in possession of a vision that is transforming the medium. In other words, they are altering the history of film in significant ways. In turn, we should be interested in knowing what they are doing because they are providing new contexts for increasing our understanding of film.

But these are only a few contexts in which films exist. Every film exists in a social context, in relation to the social system it springs from and portrays or idealizes or criticizes. We do not usually judge films specifically on the basis of their ability to make social comment, but if we lived in China we would probably judge a film on the basis of its ability to make a positive contribution to the building of a new society. Obviously, the context of the society would then outweigh the context of internal parts — the relation of detail to structure.

Our concerns in this book have not been exclusively with one or another kind of context, although we have assumed that the internal context of a work of art is necessarily of first importance to begin with. But no work can be properly understood without resorting to some external contextual examination. To understand the content of a work of art we must understand something about the subject matter, and the subject matter is always embedded in some external context. Even such a simple act as a gesture may need explanation. For example, in Greece to put the palm of your hand in the face of someone is considered insulting. If we do not know that and are watching a film involving Greece which involves that gesture, we may be completely misled. A visual image, a contemporary gesture, even a colloquial expression will sometimes show up in a film and need explication in order to be fully understood. Just as we sometimes have to look up a word in a dictionary — which exists outside a poem, for instance — we sometimes have to look outside a film for explanations. Even Terence Young's James Bond thriller movies need such explication, although we rarely think about that. If we failed to understand the political assumptions underlying such films, we would not fully understand what was going on.

Francis Ford Coppola's *The Godfather*

Coppola's *The Godfather* (Figures 11-11 and 11-12), produced in 1972, was based on Mario Puzo's novel about an Italian immigrant fleeing from Sicilian Mafia violence. He eventually became a Don of a huge crime family in New York City. The film details the gradual involvement of Michael Corleone, played by Al Pacino, in his father's criminal activities during the years from 1945 to 1959. His father Vito, played by Marlon Brando, suffers the loss of Sonny, an older son, and barely survives an assassination attempt. As Michael becomes more and more a central figure in his family's "business," he grows more frightening and more alienated from those around him until, as Godfather, he becomes, it seems, totally evil.

Although some critics complained that the film glorified the Mafia, almost all have praised its technical mastery. A sequel, *The Godfather: Part II*, was produced in 1974 and, while not as tightly constructed as the first film, it fleshes out the experience of Michael as he slowly develops into a criminal. Both films center on the ambiguities involved in the conversion of the poverty-ridden Vito into a wealthy and successful gangster and Michael's conversion from innocence to heartless criminality.

The Godfather films both engage our sympathy with Michael and yet increasingly horrify us with many of his actions. We admire Michael's personal valor and his respect for father, family, and friends. But we also see the corruption and violence that are the bases of his power. Inevitably, we have to work out for ourselves the ambiguities that Coppola sets out.

THE NARRATIVE STRUCTURE OF *THE GODFATHER, PARTS I AND II*

The narrative structure of most films supplies the framework on which the filmmaker builds the artistry of the shots and sound. An overemphasis on the artistry, however, can distract a viewer from the narrative, whereas a great film avoids allowing technique to dominate a story. Such is the case with *The Godfather* and *The Godfather: Part II*, we believe, because the artistry produces a cinematic lushness that helps tell the story.

The first film begins with Michael Corleone, as a returning war hero in 1945, refusing to be part of his father's criminal empire. The immediate family enjoys the spoils of criminal life—big cars, a large house in a guarded compound, family celebrations, and lavish weddings. Although Michael's brothers are active members of the crime family, they respect his wishes to remain apart.

FIGURE 11-11
Don Vito Corleone, the God-father (Marlon Brando), con-fers with a wedding guest who requests an important favor in *The Godfather*. (© 1972 Paramount Pictures Corporation/Photofest)

FIGURE 11-12
Michael Corleone (Al Pacino), with his father dead, is now the Godfather, reflecting on the world he has created for himself. (© 1972 Paramount Pictures Corporation/The Kobal Collection)

In a dispute over whether to add drug-running to the business of gambling, prostitution, extortion, and labor racketeering, Vito is gunned down, but not killed. Michael comes to the aid of his father and so begins his career in the Mafia. It takes him only a short time to rise to the position of Godfather when Vito is too infirm to continue. When he marries Kay, played by Diane Keaton, Michael explains that the family will be totally legitimate in five years. She believes him, but the audience already knows better. It is no surprise that seven years later, the family is more powerful and ruthless than ever.

In a disturbing and deeply ironic sequence, Michael acts as godfather in the church baptism of his nephew, while at the same time his lieutenants are murdering the heads of the five rival crime families. Coppola jump-cuts back and forth from shots of Michael in the church promising to renounce the work of the devil to shots of his men turning the streets of New York into a bloodbath. This perversion of the sacrament of baptism illustrates the depths to which Michael has sunk.

In the second film, as the family grows in power, Michael moves to Tahoe, gaining control of casino gambling in Nevada. He corrupts a senator, who even while demanding kickbacks expresses contempt for Italians. However, when the senator is compromised by killing a prostitute, he cooperates fully with the Corleones. The point is made again and again that without such corrupt officials, the Mafia would be significantly less powerful.

Michael survives an assassination attempt made possible by his brother Fredo's collusion with another gangster who is Michael's nemesis. At first he does nothing but refuse to talk to Fredo, but when their mother dies, Michael has Fredo murdered. Meanwhile, Kay has left him, and those who were close to him, except his stepbrother Tom Hagen (Robert Duvall), have been driven away or murdered. The last images we have of Michael show him alone in his compound staring into a darkened room. We see how far he has fallen since his early idealism.

COPPOLA'S IMAGES

Coppola chooses his frames with great care, and many would make an interesting still photograph. He balances his figures carefully, especially in the quieter scenes, subtly using asymmetry to accent movement. Sometimes he uses harsh lighting that radiates from the center of the shot, focusing attention and creating tension. He rarely cuts rapidly from one shot to another but depends on conventional establishing shots — such as showing a car arriving at a church, a hospital, a home — before showing us shots of their interiors. This conventionality intensifies our sense of the period of the 1940s and 1950s, since most films of that period relied on just such techniques.

Darkness dominates, and interiors often have a tunnel-like quality, suggesting passages to the underworld. Rooms in which Michael and others conduct their business usually have only one source of light, and the resulting high contrast is disorienting. Bright outdoor scenes are often marked by barren snow or winds driving fallen leaves. The seasons of fall and winter predominate, suggesting loneliness and death.

The music in *The Godfather* helps Coppola evoke the mood of the time the film covers. Coppola used his own father, Carmine Coppola, as a composer of some of the music. There are some snatches of Italian hill music from small villages near Amalfi, but sentimental dance music from the big band period of the 1940s and 1950s predominates.

An ingenious and effective use of sound occurs in the baptism/murder scene discussed earlier. Coppola keeps the sounds of the church scene—the priest reciting the Latin liturgy, the organ music, the baby crying—on the soundtrack even when he cuts to the murders being carried out. This accomplishes two important functions—it reinforces the idea that these two scenes are actually occurring simultaneously, and it underscores the hypocrisy of Michael's pious behavior in church. Because such techniques are used sparingly, this instance works with great power.

THE POWER OF *THE GODFATHER*

Those critics who felt the film glorified the Mafia seem not to have taken into account the fated quality of Michael. He begins like Oedipus—running away from his fate. He does not want to join the Mafia, but when his father is almost killed, his instincts push him toward assuming the role of Godfather. The process of self-destruction consumes him as if it were completely out of his control. Moreover, despite their power and wealth, Michael and the Corleones seem to have a good time only at weddings, and even then the Godfather is doing business in the back room. Everyone in the family suffers. No one can come and go in freedom. Everyone lives in an armed camp. All the elements of the film reinforce that view. The houses are opulent, but vulnerable to machine guns. The cars are expensive, but they blow up. Surely such a life is not a glory.

In shaping the film in a way that helps us see Mafia life as neither glamorous nor desirable, Coppola forces us to examine our popular culture—one that seems often to venerate criminals like Bonnie and Clyde, Jesse James, Billy the Kid, and John Dillinger. At the same time Coppola's refusal to treat his characters as simply loathsome, his acknowledgment that they are in some sense victims as well as victimizers, creates an ambiguity that makes his film an impressive achievement.

James Cameron's *Titanic*

On April 15, 1912, the greatest ship of its time, on its maiden voyage from England to America, struck an iceberg and sank; 1,500 people drowned. As James Cameron's film opens, a character says, "So this is the ship they say is unsinkable." Few historical events—outside the Holocaust, September 11, and wars—have been so unbelievable and so traumatic. The subject matter is epochal.

FIGURE 11-13
Jack (Leonardo diCaprio) and Rose (Kate Winslet) on the prow of the ship in *Titanic* (1997). (*Titanic* © 1997 Paramount Pictures Corporation and Twentieth Century Fox. All rights reserved. Photo courtesy Everett Collection.)

FIGURE 11-14
The ship sinking. (*Titanic* © 1997 Paramount Pictures Corporation and Twentieth Century Fox. All rights reserved. Photo courtesy Everett Collection.)

If ever a major production was called for, this was it. And Cameron delivered (Figures 11-13 and 11-14). The profits ran over a billion dollars and the film won eleven Academy Awards, including Best Film and Best Director.

Titanic

See the film before proceeding with the following questions. Then if possible obtain a video in order to stop and go for analysis. Discuss with others.

1. Does your foreknowledge of the doom of the *Titanic* help make more plausible the many extraordinary coincidences? For example, Rose and Jack always seem to meet at the prow of the ship, usually without any planning; and on the last night with a beautiful sunset they possess that prow alone, with 2,200 other passengers totally out of view. (Notice at the beginning of the film how the underwater shots focus on the prow.) Are there such extraordinary coincidences in *The Godfather*?

2. Are there scenes in which too much is asked of our credibility? For example, Rose's smashing ax cut on Jack's chains with her eyes closed? Aristotle praised plausibility in the action of a drama. Do you think he would negatively criticize this scene?

3. The movie time of the sinking is close to the actual time, a little over an hour. Some critics have complained that this historical accuracy is unwarranted and the last hour should have been condensed. Do you agree?

4. Compare the pace of the shots before the iceberg is struck with the pace after. Once the ship goes down, what happens to the pace with the scenes of the lifeboats and Rose and Jack? Why?

5. The visual imagery is powerful and compelling. Is it overdone? Would the two main plots—the story of the ship and the story of Rose and Jack—interweave successfully without this extraordinary imagery?

6. Rose's memory coming into visual play is introduced at one point with the fading of her old eye into her young eye. Is this an effective device? Or too tricky?

7. The name Rose DeWitt Bukater suggests aristocracy, pomp, wealth. The name Jack Dawson suggests the ordinary. Rose rarely speaks to Jack without saying "Jack." And Jack rarely speaks to Rose without saying "Rose." Why?

8. Suppose the story of the greedy treasure-hunting crew and the shots of the present-day sunken ship had been edited out, including the humorous scenes of Rose's transportation to the salvage ship. Would a more direct narrative with Rose simply telling her story have been more compelling? If that were done, the subplot about the jewel that Rose drops into the ocean at the end—back to Jack—would have had to be eliminated. Would this have helped avoid some of the soap-opera aura that a number of critics have sneeringly noted? Would you have edited out the jewel story? If so, why?

9. On the last night Rose and Jack make love. The scene recalls *Romeo and Juliet* as well as Freud's theory of the close connection of sex with death. Earlier in the film Rose even mentioned Freud in a sarcastic reference to male dominance, followed by the seriously meant remark of one of the

males: "Freud? Who is he? Is he a passenger?" Is this effective dialogue? And is the dialogue in general effective? Do you ever find places where the film is too talky? If so, where?

10. On the prow with Jack, Rose exclaims: "I'm flying, Jack!" The camera sweeps the far horizon, and a world is opened with unknown endless possibilities. Rose has cut loose from the snobbery, the prejudice, the stifling narrowness of her class, which made women the servants of men. Do you think the story of Rose could be read as symbolic of female liberation? Or is this overreading? Her character in any case is transformed. Are there any other such transformations? If not, does this strengthen the role of Rose as perhaps archetypal?

11. Are the sound effects emotional intensifiers? Does the sound sometimes help give the illusion of depth to the moving images? Is the silence among the floating dead more effective because of its contrast with the preceding horrendous clamor?

12. What do you think about the music by James Horner? Does Rose's theme have a rightness about it?

13. Do you think Cameron's decision to have the orchestra play on while the ship sinks is dramatically right? Consider the device of contrast here—the chaos and the hymn.

14. Only four first-class female passengers drowned (three voluntarily chose to stay). Fifteen of ninety-three women in second-class accommodations drowned. Fifty-one out of 179 females from the third-class section drowned. Class distinctions were sharply emphasized throughout the film. How successfully was this topic interwoven with the other plots?

15. Identify examples of the following (a stop-and-go video would be most helpful): musical crescendoes that bridge scene changes; strong tonal contrasts such as warm browns to cold blues; slow matching dissolves (the fading of one scene into another) versus fast cuts without transition; close camera work versus distanced observation.

16. Earlier in this chapter is a list of types of shots and cuts. Try to identify as many of these as you can and determine why they were used.

17. What do you think of the final scenes, the dissolve from the sunken ship to the sequence that has Rose greeted by a throng of passengers as she climbs the great stairway to kiss Jack, and then the fading into black? Would you edit it out? If so, why?

18. Does the film bring you into participation? That is the ultimate standard for evaluation. Try to see the film again. Is your experience more participatory because of the analysis of this Perception Key? Remember—participation and analysis should be two separate experiences! Try to see some other "big-storied" movies, such as Spielberg's *Saving Private Ryan*. Think about the same kind of questions that have been set out here.

19. Finally, compare *Titanic* with *The Godfather*. Do you think one or both or neither will become a classic? Why?

Experimentation

In the early days of film, complex technical problems were at the forefront—lighting, zooming, montage, and the like. Most of these problems now have answers, thanks especially to early filmmakers such as Griffith and Eisenstein. Today the problems center on what to do with these answers. For example, Andy Warhol, primarily a painter and sculptor, did some interesting work in raising questions about film, especially about the limits of realism, for realism is often praised in films. But when Warhol puts a figure in front of a camera to sleep for a full eight hours, we get the message: We want a transformation of reality that gives us insight into reality, not reality itself. The difference is important because it is the difference between reality and art. Except when unconscious or dreaming, we have reality in front of us all of the time. We have art much less frequently. Realistic art is a selection of elements that convey the illusion of reality. When we see Warhol's almost direct transcription of reality on film, we understand that selecting — through directing and editing — is crucial to film art. The power of most striking films is often their ability to condense experience, to take a year, for example, and portray it in ninety minutes. This condensation is what Marcel Proust, one of the greatest of novelists, expected from the novel:

> Every emotion is multiplied ten-fold, into which this book comes to disturb us as might a dream, but a dream more lucid, and of a more lasting impression, than those which come to us in sleep; why, then, for a space of an hour he sets free within us all the joys and sorrows in the world, a few of which, only, we should have to spend years of our actual life in getting to know, and the keenest, the most intense of which would never have been revealed to us because the slow course of their development stops our perception of them. It is the same in life; the heart changes . . . but we learn of it only from reading or by imagination; in reality its alteration . . . is so gradual that . . . we are still spared the actual sensation of change.[2]

Some films address the question of the portrayal of reality. Antonioni's *Blow Up* (1966), for example, had the thread of a narrative holding it together: a possible murder and the efforts of a magazine photographer, through the medium of his own enlargements, to confirm the reality of that murder. But anyone who saw the film might assume that the continuity of the narrative was not necessarily the most important part of the film. Much of the meaning seems to come out of what were essentially disconnected moments: an odd party, some strange driving around London, and some extraordinary tennis played without a ball. What seemed most important, perhaps, was the role of the film itself in suggesting certain realities. In a sense the murder was a reality only after the film uncovered it. Is it possible that Antonioni is saying something similar about the reality that surrounds the very film he is creating? There is a reality, but where? Is *Blow Up* more concerned with the film images as reality than it is with reality outside the film? If you have a chance to see this fascinating film, be sure you ask that puzzling question.

Some more extreme experimenters remove the narrative entirely and simply present successions of images, almost in the manner of a nightmare or a drug experience. Sometimes the images are abstract, nothing more than visual patterns, as with abstract painting. Some use familiar images,

---

[2]Marcel Proust, *Swann's Way*, trans. C. K. Scott Moncrieff (New York: Modern Library, 1928), p. 119.

but modify them with unexpected time-lapse photography and distortions of color and sound. Among the more successful films of this kind are *Koyaanisqatsi* (1983) and *Brooklyn Bridge* (1994). The fact that we have very little abstract film may have several explanations. Part of the power of abstract painting seems to depend on its "all-at-onceness" (see Abstract Painting, Chapter 4), precisely what is missing from film. Another reason may be tied in, again, with the popular nature of the medium—the masses simply do not prefer abstraction.

The public generally is convinced that film, like literature and drama, must have plots and characters. Thus even filmic cartoons are rarely abstract, although they are not photographs but drawings. Such animated films as *Pinocchio* (1940), *Fantasia* (1940), and *Dumbo* (1941) have yielded to enormously successful later films such as *The Yellow Submarine* (1968), *Beauty and the Beast* (1993), *The Lion King* (1994), *Toy Story* (1995), and *Pocahontas* (1995). It may be unreasonable to consider animated films as experimental, and it is certainly unreasonable to think of them as children's films, since adult audiences have made them successful. What they seem to offer an audience is a realistic approach to fantasy that has all the elements of the traditional narrative film. This may also be true of animated films using clay figures and puppets for actors. These have had a narrower audience than cartoon and computer animations and have been restricted to film festivals, which is where most experimental films are presented.

PERCEPTION KEY   Make a Film

The easy availability of video recorders makes it possible for you to make a film (actually a video). You may also have access to an 8mm film camera and projector. With a video camera, you may need to rerecord on a VCR, reorganizing your visual material to take advantage of the various shot and editing techniques.

1. Develop a short narrative plan for your shots. After shooting, edit your shots into a meaningful sequence.

2. Instead of a narrative plan, choose a musical composition that is especially interesting to you, and then fuse moving images with the music.

3. Short of making a film, try some editing by finding and clipping from twenty to thirty "stills" from magazines, brochures, newspapers, or other sources. Choose stills you believe may have some coherence, and then arrange them in such a way as to make a meaningful sequence. How are your stills affected by rearrangement? This project might be more interesting if you use or make slides for viewing. Then add a soundtrack to heighten interest by clarifying the meaning of the sequence.

Summary

The making of film is exceptionally complex because of the necessary and often difficult collaboration required among many people, especially the director, scriptwriter, actors, photographer, and editor. The range of possible subject matters is exceptionally extensive for film. The resources of the director in choosing shots and the imagination of the editor in joining shots provide the primary control over the material. Such choices translate into evoking emotional responses from the audience. The point of view that can be achieved with the camera is similar to that of the unaided human eye, but because of technical refinements, such as the wide-angle zoom lens and moving multiple cameras, the dramatic effect of vision can be greatly intensified. Because it is easy to block out everything irrelevant to the film in a dark theater, our participative experiences with film tend to be especially strong and much longer, of course, than with other visual arts. The temptation to identify with a given actor or situation in a film may distort the participative experience by blocking our perception of the form of the film, thus causing us to miss the content. The combination of sound, both dialogue and music (or sound effects), with the moving image helps engage our participation. The film is clearly the most popular of our modern arts.

Bibliography

Allen, Richard, and Murray Smith, eds. *Film Theory and Philosophy*. New York: Oxford University Press, 1997.

Allen, Robert C. *Film History: Theory and Practice*. New York: Random House, 1985.

Andrew, Dudley. *Concepts of Film Theory*. New York: Oxford University Press, 1984.

Arnheim, Rudolf. *Film as Art*. London: Faber and Faber, 1983.

Bazin, André. *What Is Cinema?* Berkeley: University of California Press, 1974.

Bobker, Lee R. *Elements of Film*, 3rd ed. New York: Harcourt Brace Jovanovich, 1981.

Bordwell, David. *Narration in the Fiction Film*. Madison: University of Wisconsin Press, 1985.

Branigan, Edward. *Point of View in the Cinema*. Berlin: Mouton, 1984.

Braudy, Leo, and Marshall Cohen, eds. *Film Theory and Criticism: Introductory Readings*, 5th ed. New York: Oxford University Press, 1999.

Cavell, Stanley. *World Viewed*. Cambridge, Mass.: Harvard University Press, 1979.

Cook, David A. *A History of Narrative Film*. New York: Norton, 1996.

Eisenstein, Sergei. *Film, Form and Film Sense*. Translated by Jay Leyda. New York: Harcourt Brace Jovanovich, n.d.

Giannetti, Louis. *Understanding Movies*, 7th ed. Upper Saddle River, N.J.: Prentice-Hall, 1996.

Huss, Roy, and Norman Silverstein. *The Film Experience*. New York: Dell, 1969.

Jacobs, Lewis. *The Emergence of Film Art*, 2d ed. New York: Norton, 1979.

Kracauer, Siegfried. *Theory of Film*. New York: Oxford University Press, 1960.

Lehman, Peter, ed. *Close Viewings: An Anthology of New Film Criticism*. Tallahassee: Florida State University Press, 1990.

Lubin, David M. *Titanic*. Bloomington: Indiana University Press, 2000.

MacDonald, Scott. *Avant-Garde Film*. New York: Cambridge University Press, 1993.

Monaco, James. *How to Read a Film*. New York: Oxford University Press, 1981.

Ponech, Trevor. *What Is Non-Fiction Cinema?* Boulder, Colo.: Westview, 1999.

Pudovkin, V. I. *Film Technique and Film Acting*. Edited and translated by I. Montagu. New York: Grove Press, 1960.

Rothman, William. *The "I" of the Camera: Essays in Film Criticism, History, and Aesthetics*. New York: Cambridge University Press, 1989.

Weis, Elizabeth, and John Belton, eds. *Film Sound: Theory and Practice*. New York: Columbia University Press, 1985.

AFRICAN DIASPORA FILM FESTIVAL
http://www.africanfilm.com/festival/

CANNES FILM FESTIVAL
http://www.festival-cannes.fr/

CINEMA HISTORY
http://www.gen.umn.edu/faculty_staff/yahnke/film/cinema.htm

CINEMA JOURNAL
http://www.cinemastudies.org/cj.htm

COMPUTERS AND FILM
http://128.174.194.59/cybercinema/

EARLY CINEMA
http://www.earlycinema.com/

FILM HISTORY RESEARCH GUIDE
http://www.tweedlebop.com/kendra/film/

THE GODFATHER
http://www.filmsite.org/godf.html
http://www.jgeoff.com/godfather/

INFLOW'S SCREENPLAY REPOSITORY (MANY CURRENT SCREENPLAYS, IN-
CLUDING *THE GODFATHER*)
http://corky.net/scripts/

THE ROSEBUD PROJECT: DIGITAL RESOURCE FOR FILM STUDIES
http://www.inform.umd.edu/rosebud/

CHAPTER 12

Photography

The Camera before Photography

Before the invention of film and light-sensitive paper, painters as early as the sixteenth century sometimes used a camera obscura to help achieve realistic representations of space and depth. The camera obscura was a box with a small hole on one side, usually fitted with a lens, through which light from a well-lit scene entered to produce an inverted image on a screen placed opposite to the hole (Figure 12-1). A mirror reflects the image, right side up, on a drawing surface where its outlines can be traced. Thus, a three-dimensional scene could be accurately translated to a two-dimensional surface. The camera obscura was the direct precursor of the camera.

The Power of Representation

Louis J. M. Daguerre (1789–1851) invented the first practical system for producing permanent photographic prints in 1839. Daguerre had originally used a camera obscura to help him paint gigantic backdrops for opera, which in turn led him to experiment with photography.

In addition to its capacity to produce accurate perspective and great detail, the camera lens "crops" (restricts) the visual field before it. When the photograph became widely available in the 1840s and 1850s, the images printed on paper were in black-and-white or sepia (brown-and-white). Monochrome images transform their subject in complex ways, but modern color prints produce such faithful renditions of the scene that it is difficult for some viewers to perceive the image as something other than what it represents. For that reason contemporary photographers constantly search for new means of transformation in order to expand the resources of photography as art.

The success of photography in reproducing realistic scenes and people had an instant impact on painting. Paul Delaroche, a French academic painter (1795–1856), was widely admired for his realistic technique, as in

FIGURE 12-1
Camera obscura: The image focused by a lens is imprinted on a drawing surface and then traced. (Culver Pictures)

his *Execution of Lady Jane Grey* (1834) (Figure 12-2), a massive painting (97 × 117 inches). When he saw the daguerreotype process first demonstrated in 1839, he declared, "From today painting is dead." He was quite wrong, but he was responding to the realistic detail Daguerre's almost instant process (like the modern Polaroid) could extract from reality. Even today realism remains among the most important resources of the photographic medium.

PERCEPTION KEY   *Execution of Lady Jane Grey*

1. What aspects of Delaroche's style of painting would have made him think of photography as a threat? In what ways is this painting similar to a photograph?
2. Is it surprising to learn that this painting was exhibited five years before Delaroche saw a photograph — actually before the invention of photography?
3. Like some painters before him, Delaroche may have used the camera obscura to compose his figures and render them exactly as they appeared. Does this painting become less a work of art if in fact Delaroche used such an instrument to assist him?

The capacity of the camera to capture and control details is exhibited in many early photographs — for example, Robert Howlett's portrait of Isambard Kingdom Brunel (1857), a builder of steamships (Figure 12-3). Howlett widened the aperture of the lens (letting in more light) and exposed the picture for a shorter time (thus affecting the depth of the field at which objects are in focus). As a result, only Brunel's body is in focus. The wood pilings in the lower right are in soft focus because they are just out of that depth of field. The pile of anchor chains, which serves as background, is even farther out of focus, thus softening their massive, fascinating pattern. By being out of focus, the chains are rendered subservient to Brunel and help establish his mastery as a famous designer of great steamships. The huge chains make this image haunting, whereas rendering them sharply (which Howlett could easily have done) would have weakened the effect. In *Execution of Lady Jane Grey* most everything is in sharp focus, which may simply mean that Howlett's style of selective focus was not part of

Delaroche's repertoire. It's difficult to imagine Howlett's photograph in color, although if Delaroche had painted it, the gold watch chain and fob surely would have been made prominent.

Brunel's posture is typical of photographs of the period. We have many examples of men lounging with hands in pockets and cigar in mouth, but few paintings portray men this way. Few photographs of any age show us a face quite like Brunel's. It is relaxed, as much as Brunel could relax, but it is also impatient, "bearing with" the photographer. And the eyes are sharp, businessman's eyes. The details of the rumpled clothing and jewelry do not compete with the sharply rendered face and the expression of control and power. Howlett has done, by simple devices such as varying the focus, what many portrait painters do by much more complex means — reveal something of the character of the model.

FIGURE 12-3
Robert Howlett, *Isambard Kingdom Brunel.* 1857. (International Museum of Photography at the George Eastman House, Rochester)

Julia Margaret Cameron's portrait of Sir John Herschel (1867) (Figure 12-4), and Étienne Carjat's portrait of the French poet Charles Baudelaire (1870) (Figure 12-5), unlike Howlett's portrait, ignore details in the background. But their approaches are also different from each other. Cameron, who reported being interested in the way her lens could soften detail, isolates Herschel's face and hair. She drapes his shoulders with a black velvet shawl so that his clothing will not tell us anything about him or distract us from his face. Cameron catches the stubble on his chin and permits his hair to "burn out," so we perceive it as a luminous halo. The huge eyes, soft and bulbous with their deep curves of surrounding flesh, and the downward curve of the mouth are depicted fully in the harsh lighting. While we do not know what he was thinking, the form of this photograph reveals him as a thinker of deep ruminations. He was the chemist who first learned how to permanently fix a photograph.

The portrait of Baudelaire, on the other hand, includes simple, severe clothing, except for the poet's foulard, tied in a dashing bow. The studio backdrop is set far out of focus so it cannot compete with the face for our attention. Baudelaire's intensity creates the illusion that he is looking at us. Carjat's lens was set for a depth of field of only a few inches. Thus, Baudelaire's head is in focus, but not his shoulders. What Carjat could not control, except by waiting for the right moment to uncover the lens (at this time there was no shutter because there was no "fast" film), was the exact expression he could catch.

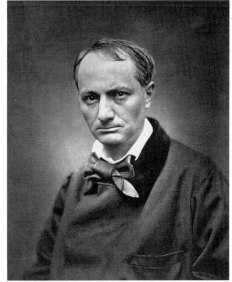

FIGURE 12-4 *(left)*
Julia Margaret Cameron, *Sir John Herschel.* 1867. (International Museum of Photography at the George Eastman House, Rochester)

FIGURE 12-5 *(right)*
Étienne Carjat, *Charles Baudelaire.* 1870. (International Museum of Photography at the George Eastman House, Rochester)

One irony of the Carjat portrait is that Baudelaire, in 1859, had condemned the influence of photography on art, declaring it "art's most mortal enemy." He thought that photography was adequate for preserving visual records of perishing things, but that it could not reach into "anything whose value depends solely upon the addition of something of a man's soul." Baudelaire was a champion of imagination and an opponent of realistic art: "Each day art further diminishes its self-respect by bowing down before external reality; each day the painter becomes more and more given to painting not what he dreams but what he sees."[1] Some critics and philosophers of art argue that photography is not an art—or at least not a major art—on grounds different from Baudelaire's. Images can be selected and controlled, of course, but after their "taking" what can be done with them is very restricted. Therefore the photographer's ability to transform subject matter is also very restricted. Painters, on the other hand, create their images and in doing so have much greater flexibility in organizing their media—color, line, and texture. Perhaps this argument falters somewhat today because of the capacity of the computer to alter, distort, and transform the image of the camera. But even without the magical powers of the computer, the photograph can be richly informative. It is not restricted only to recording slices of life.

PERCEPTION KEY   Photography and Art

1. Do you agree with Baudelaire that photography is "art's most mortal enemy"? What reasons might lead Baudelaire to express such a view?

---

[1]*The Mirror of Art* (London, Phaidon, 1955), p. 230.

2. Baudelaire's writings suggested that he believed art depended on imagination and that realistic art was the opponent of imagination. Why would he hold such an opinion? Is it one that you hold yourself?

3. Read a poem from Baudelaire's most celebrated volume—*The Flowers of Evil.* You might choose "Twilight: Evening" from a group he called "Parisian Scenes." In what ways is his poem unlike a photograph? (Consider the questions of literary representation of visual imagery and allusion.)

4. Considering his attitude toward photography, why would he have sat for a portrait such as Carjat's? Would you classify this portrait as a work of art?

Compare Carjat's and Cameron's portraits with Rembrandt's *Self-Portrait* (Figure 4-15). Both photographers were familiar with Rembrandt's stylistic choices about lighting and background. Neither photograph has imitated Rembrandt's pose, but the use of a rich dark background in Cameron's photograph and the direct, frank stare of Carjat's subject demonstrate an awareness of style and a carefulness of expression that parallel Rembrandt's. Indeed, the photographs and the painting seem to have a similar purpose—to reveal the personality of the subject. They all share a sense of dramatic purpose, as if each subject were caught in an instant of time at a moment of meditation. And all of them exhibit superb lighting.

An impressive example of the capacity of the photographic representation is Timothy O'Sullivan's masterpiece, *Canyon de Chelley, Arizona,* made in 1873 (Figure 12-6). Many photographers have gone back to this scene, but none have treated it quite the way O'Sullivan did, although most, like Ansel Adams (see Figure 12-11), pay homage. O'Sullivan chose a moment of intense sidelighting, which falls on the rock wall but not on the nearest group of buildings. He waited for that moment when the great rock striations and planes would be most clearly etched by the sun. The closer group of buildings is marked by strong shadow. Comparing it to the more distant group shows a remarkable negative-positive relationship. The groups of buildings are purposely contrasted in this special photographic way. One question you might ask about this photograph is whether it reveals the "stoniness" of this rock wall in a manner similar to the way Cézanne's *Mont Sainte-Victoire* (Figure 2-4) reveals the "mountainness" of the mountain.

The most detailed portions of the photograph are the striations of the rock face, whose tactile qualities are emphasized by the strong sidelighting. The stone buildings in the distance have smoother textures, particularly as they show up against the blackness of the cave. That the buildings are only twelve to fifteen feet high is indicated by comparison with the height of the barely visible men standing in the ruins. Thus nature dwarfs the work of humans. By framing the canyon wall, and by waiting for the right light, O'Sullivan has done more than create an ordinary "record" photograph. He has concentrated on the subject matter of the puniness and softness of humans, in contrast with the grandness and hardness of the canyon. The content centers on the extraordinary sense of stoniness—symbolic of permanence—as opposed to the transience of humanity, made possible by the capacity of the camera to transform realistic detail.

FIGURE 12-6
Timothy O'Sullivan, *Canyon de Chelley, Arizona.* 1873. (International Museum of Photography at the George Eastman House, Rochester)

Photography and Painting: The Pictorialists

Pictorialists are photographers who use the achievements of painting, particularly realistic painting, in their effort to realize the potential of photography as art. The early pictorialists tried to avoid the head-on directness of Howlett and Carjat, just as they tried to avoid the amateur's mistakes in composition, such as including distracting details and unbalanced compositions. The pictorialists controlled details by subordinating them to structure. They produced compositions that usually relied on the same underlying structures found in most nineteenth-century paintings until the dominance of the Impressionists around the 1880s. Normally the most important part of the subject matter was centered in the frame. Pictorial lighting, also borrowed from painting, often was sharp and clearly directed, as in Alfred Stieglitz's *Paula* (Figure 12-7) and Sally Mann's *The Last Time Emmett Modeled Nude* (Figure 12-8). The subject matter of pictorial photography is usually dramatic.

Generally, the pictorialist photograph was soft in focus, Rembrandt-like (Figure 4-15), centrally weighted, and carefully balanced symmetrically. By relying on the formalist characteristics of early and mid-nineteenth-century paintings, pictorialist photographers often evoked emotions that bordered on the sentimental. Indeed, one of the complaints modern commentators have about the development of pictorialism is that it was emotionally shallow.

FIGURE 12-7
Alfred Stieglitz, *Paula.* 1889.
(International Museum of
Photography at the George
Eastman House, Rochester)

Rarely criticized for sentimentalism, Alfred Stieglitz was, in his early work, a master of the pictorial style. His *Paula,* done in 1889, places his subject at the center in the act of writing. The top and bottom of the scene are printed in deep black. The light, streaking through the venetian blinds and creating lovely strip patterns, centers on Paula. Her profile is strong against the dark background partly because Stieglitz has removed in the act of printing one of the strips that would have fallen on her lower face. The candle, ordinarily useless in daylight, is a beacon of light because of its position. The strong vertical lines of the window frames reinforce the verticality of the candle and echo the back of the chair.

A specifically photographic touch is present in the illustrations on the wall: photographs arranged symmetrically in a triangle (use a magnifying glass). Two prints of the same lake-skyscape are on each side of a woman in a white dress and hat. The same photograph of this woman is on the writing table in an oval frame. Is it Paula? The light in the room echoes the light in the oval portrait. The three hearts in the arrangement of photographs are balanced; one heart touches the portrait of a young man. We wonder if Paula is writing to him. The cage on the wall has dominant vertical lines, crossing the light lines cast by the venetian blind. Stieglitz may be suggesting that Paula, despite the open window, may be in a cage of her own.

FIGURE 12-8
Sally Mann, *The Last Time Emmett Modeled Nude*. 1987. (© Sally Mann, courtesy Houk Friedman, New York)

Stieglitz has kept most of the photograph in sharp focus because most of the details have something to tell us. If this were a painting of the early nineteenth century, for example one by Delaroche, we would expect much the same style. We see Paula in a dramatic moment, with dramatic light, and with an implied narrative suggested by the artifacts surrounding her. It is up to the viewer to decide what, if anything, the drama implies.

Pictorialism is still an ideal of many good photographers, although we associate it mainly with those working at the beginning of the twentieth century. One of the most controversial of contemporary photographers, Sally Mann, has produced an interesting body of work using her children as her models. Not all of her work would fit the pictorialist ideal, but *The Last Time Emmett Modeled Nude* (Figure 12-8) provides us with a visual drama: What is this nude child doing? And why is his countenance so disturbed? The darkness of the water and shoreline, with the lyrical nimbus of light to the left of the child, suggests a foreboding, perhaps threatening moment. But however one interprets the composition, Mann presents a dramatic moment. Something is about to happen. Her isolation of the figure and the drama of the setting produce something like the mystery of a dream. Is anything archetypal suggested? Note, incidentally, the way the hands stand out like claws.

PERCEPTION KEY Pictorialism and Sentimentality

1. Pictorialists are often condemned for their sentimentality. Write down your definition of sentimentality.
2. Are *Paula* and *The Last Time Emmett Modeled Nude* sentimental? Is their subject matter sentimental, or does their formal treatment make a neutral subject matter sentimental?
3. Is Delaroche's *Execution of Lady Jane Grey* sentimental? Does its sharpness of detail contribute to sentimentality? Would softening the lines and textures make the painting more or less sentimental? Why?
4. Is sentimentality desirable in paintings, photographs, or any art form?

Both paintings and photographs, of course, can be sentimental in subject matter. The severest critics of such works complain about their *sentimentality:* the falsifying of feelings by demanding responses that are cheap or easy to come by. Sentimentality is usually an oversimplification of complex emotional issues. It also tends to be mawkish and self-indulgent. The case of photography is special because we are accustomed to the harshness of the camera. Thus, when the pictorialist finds tenderness, romance, and beauty in everyday occurrences, we become suspicious. We may be more tolerant of painting doing those things, but in fact we should be wary of any such emotional "coloration" in any medium if it is not restricted to the subject matter.

The pictorialist approach, when not guilty of sentimentalism, has great strengths. The use of lighting that selectively emphasizes the most important features of the subject matter often helps in creating meaning. Borrowing from the formal structures of painting also may help clarify subject matter. Structural harmony of the kind we generally look for in representational painting is possible in photography. Although it is by no means limited to the pictorialist approach, it is clearly fundamental to that approach.

Straight Photography

In his later work, beginning around 1905, Alfred Stieglitz pioneered the movement of *straight photography,* a reaction against pictorialism. *The F/64 Group,* working in the 1930s, and a second school, the *Documentarists,* continue the tradition. Straight photographers took the position that, as Aaron Siskind said later, "Pictorialism is a kind of dead end making everything look beautiful." The straight photographer wanted things to look essentially as they do, even if they are ugly.

Straight photography aimed toward excellence in photographic techniques, independent of painting. Susan Sontag summarizes: "For a brief time—say, from Stieglitz through the reign of Weston—it appeared that a solid point of view had been erected with which to evaluate photographs: impeccable lighting, skill of composition, clarity of subject, precision of focus, perfection of print quality."[2] Some of these qualities are shared by

---

[2]*On Photography* (New York: Farrar, Straus, and Giroux, 1977), p. 136.

FIGURE 12-9
Alfred Stieglitz, *The Steerage*.
1907. Photogravure (artist's
proof), 12⅝ × 10⅚ inches.
The Museum of Modern Art,
New York. Provenance
unknown. (Digital image ©
The Museum of Modern Art,
New York/Licensed by Scala/
Art Resource, New York)

pictorialists, but new principles of composition—not derived from paint-ing—and new attitudes toward subject matter helped straight photography reveal the world straight, as it really is.

STIEGLITZ: PIONEER OF STRAIGHT PHOTOGRAPHY

One of the most famous straight photographs leading to the F/64 Group was Stieglitz's *The Steerage* of 1907 (Figure 12-9). It was taken under condi-tions that demanded quick action.

PERCEPTION KEY   *The Steerage*

1. How many of the qualities Susan Sontag lists above can be found in this photograph?
2. What compositional qualities make this photograph different from the pic-torialist examples we have discussed? How does the structural organization control the details of the photograph?
3. What is the subject matter of the photograph? Is the subject matter made to seem beautiful? Should it be?
4. Does the framing cut off important figural elements of the photograph? If so, is this effective?
5. Does the photograph have content? If so, how does the form achieve it? And what is the content?

The Steerage portrays poor travelers huddled in the "budget" quarters of the *Kaiser Wilhelm II*, which is taking this group of immigrants, disappointed because of economic hardship, back to their native lands. Ironically, the New York Public Library uses his photograph to celebrate the arrival of immigrants in America. Stieglitz wrote that while strolling on deck he was struck by a

> round straw hat, the funnel leaning left, the stairway leaning right, the white drawbridge with its railing made of circular chains, white suspenders crossing on the back of a man in the steerage below, round shapes of iron machinery, a mast cutting into the sky, making a triangular shape. . . . I saw a picture of shapes and underlying that the feeling I had about life.[3]

The Steerage shares much with the pictorialist approach: dramatic lighting and soft focus. But there is much that the pictorialist would probably avoid. For one thing, the *framing* omits important parts of the funnel, the drawbridge, and the nearest people in the lower-right quadrant. Moreover, the very clutter of people—part of the subject matter of the photograph—would be difficult for the pictorialist to tolerate. And the pictorialist certainly would be unhappy with the failure to use the center of the photograph as the primary region of interest. Certain focal points have been used by Stieglitz to stabilize the composition: the straw hat attracts our eye, but so too does the white shawl of the woman below. The bold slicing of the composition by the drawbridge sharpens the idea of the separation between the well-to-do and the poor. On the other hand, the leaning funnel, the angled drawbridge and chains, the angled ladder on the right, and the horizontal boom at the top of the photograph are rhythmically interrelated. This rhythm is peculiarly mechanical and modern. The stark metal structures are in opposition to the softer, more random assortment of the people. Photographs like this can help teach us how to see and appreciate formal organizations.

THE F/64 GROUP

The name of the group derives from the small aperture, F/64, which ensures that the foreground, middle ground, and background will all be in sharp focus. The group declared its principles through manifestos and shows by Edward Weston, Ansel Adams, Imogen Cunningham, and others. It continued the reaction against pictorialism, adding the kind of nonsentimental subject matter that interested the later Stieglitz. Edward Weston, whose early work was in the soft focus school, developed a special interest in formal organizations. He is famous for his nudes and his portraits of vegetables, such as artichokes, eggplants, and green peppers. His nudes rarely

---

[3]Quoted in Beaumont Newhall, *The History of Photography* (New York: Museum of Modern Art, 1964), p. 111.

FIGURE 12-10
Edward Weston, *Nude*. 1936.
(© 1981 Center for Creative
Photography, Arizona Board
of Regents, Used by
permission)

show the face, not because of modesty, but because the question of the identity of the model can distract us from contemplating the formal relationships of the human body.

Weston's *Nude* (Figure 12-10) shows many of the characteristics of the F/64 Group. The figure is isolated and presented for its own sake, the sand being equivalent to a photographer's backdrop. The figure is presented not as a portrait of a given woman, but rather as a formal study. Weston wanted us to see the relationship between legs and torso, to respond to the rhythms of line in the extended body, and to appreciate the counterpoint of the round, dark head against the long, light linearity of the body. Weston enjoys some notoriety for his studies of peppers, because his approach to vegetables was similar to his approach to nudes. We are to appreciate the sensual curve, the counterpoints of line, the reflectivity of skin, the harmonious proportions of parts.

Weston demanded objectivity in his photographs. "I do not wish to impose my personality upon nature (any of life's manifestations), but without prejudice or falsification to become identified with nature, to know things in their very essence, so that what I record is not an interpretation—my ideas of what nature should be—but a revelation."[4] One of Weston's ideals was to capitalize on the capacity of the camera to be objective and impersonal, an ideal that the pictorialists usually rejected.

---

[4]*The Daybooks of Edward Weston*, ed. Nancy Newhall, 2 vols. (New York: Aperture, 1966), vol. 2, p. 241.

FIGURE 12-11
Ansel Adams, *Antelope House Ruin*. Canyon de Chelley National Monument, Arizona. 1942. (Photograph by Ansel Adams. © 1995 by the Trustees of the Ansel Adams Publishing Rights Trust. All Rights Reserved.)

The work of Ansel Adams establishes another ideal of the F/64 Group: the fine print. Even some of the best early photographers were relatively casual in the act of printing their negatives. Adams spent a great deal of energy and skill in producing the finest print the negative would permit, sometimes spending days to print one photograph. He developed a special system (the Zone System) to measure tonalities in specific regions of the negative so as to control the final print, keeping careful records so that he could duplicate the print at a later time. In even the best of reproductions it is difficult to point to the qualities of tonal gradation that constitute the fine print. Only the original can yield the beauties that gradations of silver or platinum can produce. In his *Antelope House Ruin* (Figure 12-11), Adams aimed for a print of textural subtleties. Unlike O'Sullivan (Figure 12-6), Adams did not stress the contrast between the rock and the houses. He chose a canyon face and a lighting that emphasized the textural gradations that would yield a print of tonal brilliance. O'Sullivan revealed the substance of rock and ruin. Adams revealed their textures.

| PERCEPTION KEY | O'Sullivan and Adams |

1. Compare O'Sullivan's photograph (Figure 12-6) with Adams's version. Is the subject matter the same in both photographs? Explain.

FIGURE 12-12
Eugène Atget, *Balcon, 17 rue du Petit-Pont*. 1913. AP:6014. Albumen-silver print from a glass negative, 8⅝ × 7 inches (22 × 17.9 cm). The Museum of Modern Art, New York. Abbott-Levy Collection. Partial gift of Shirley C. Burden. (1.1969.1947) (Digital image © The Museum of Modern Art, New York/Licensed by Scala/Art Resource, New York)

2. How do the formal organizations of the photographs differ? What does their organization emphasize in each case?
3. To what extent is the content of both photographs similar, assuming there is content? To what extent is it different?

The Documentarists

Time is critical to the Documentarist, who portrays a world that is disappearing so quickly we cannot see it go. Henri Cartier-Bresson used the phrase "the decisive moment" to define that crucial interaction of shapes and spaces, formed by people and things, that tells him when to snap his shutter. Not all his photographs are decisive; they do not all catch the action at its most intense point. But those that do are pure Cartier-Bresson.

Many Documentarists agree with Stieglitz's description (earlier in this chapter) of the effect of shapes on his own feelings, as when he took *The Steerage*. Few contemporary Documentarists, however, who are often journalists like Cartier-Bresson, can compose the way Stieglitz could. But the best develop an instinct—usually nurtured by years of visual education—for the powerful formal statement even in the midst of disaster, as one can see in Adams's *Execution in Saigon* (Figure 2-2).

Eugène Atget spent much of his time photographing in Paris in the early morning when no one would bother him. The balcony and storefront in Figure 12-12 are shot from a sharp angle, to avoid reflecting himself in the

FIGURE 12-13
James Van Der Zee, *Couple in Raccoon Coats*, 1932. (© 1997 All rights reserved by Donna Van Der Zee)

glass. Everything is in sharp focus. The importance of this photograph is not in the way the shapes are organized (Stieglitz), nor its objectivity (Weston), but, as Beaumont Newhall has said, in the way this "work has no reference to any graphic medium other than photography."[5] The innocence of this photograph links Atget with the contemporary photographer Gary Winogrand, who said, "I photograph to see what something will look like photographed." Atget seems to have felt that way in early twentieth-century France. His work has been inspiring to many photographers trying to break away from the grip of pictorialism. Atget's work did not refer to painting: It created its own photographic reference. We see a photograph, not just a thing photographed.

James Van Der Zee worked in a somewhat different tradition from Atget. His studio in Harlem was so prominent that many important African American citizens felt it essential that he take their portrait. Like Atget, he was fascinated with his community, photographing public events and activities from the turn of the century into the 1930s. *Couple in Raccoon Coats* (Figure 12-13) is reminiscent of Howlett as well as of Atget. As with Howlett's photographs, there is the contrast of soft focus for the background and sharp focus for the foreground. Thus, the couple and their new car stand out brilliantly. Additionally, the interaction of formal elements is so complex that it reminds us of Atget: There has been no reduction of

---

[5]Newhall, *History of Photography*, p. 137.

FIGURE 12-14
Henri Cartier-Bresson,
Lisbon. 1955. (© Henri
Cartier-Bresson/Magnum
Photos)

shapes to a simpler geometry. However, the car with its strong horizontals helps accent the verticals of the couple, accented further by the verticals of the buildings. The style and elegance of the couple are what Van Der Zee was anxious to capture. Our familiarity with the chief elements in the photograph — brownstones, car, and fur-coated people — help make it possible for him to avoid the soothing formal order the pictorialist might have used. If anything, Van Der Zee is moving toward the snapshot aesthetic that was another generation in the making. His directness of approach puts him in the documentary tradition.

Unlike Atget and Van Der Zee, who used large cameras, Cartier-Bresson used the 35-mm Leica and specialized in photographing people. He preset his camera in order to work fast and instinctively. His *Lisbon* (Figure 12-14) shows his instinct for tight formal organization, with the sharp diagonal of the cannon meeting the diagonal formed by the three aligned men. The umbrella and the left arm of the man holding it are poised at the right place to cap this arrangement. The angle of the wall echoes this triangulation, establishing a clear relationship among the basic elements of the composition. The men have been caught in a moment of reflection, as if they, like the defunct cannon, are parts of the ancient history of Lisbon. The formal relationship of elements in a photograph can produce various kinds of significance or apparent lack of significance. The best documentarists search for the strongest coherency of elements while also searching for the decisive moment. That moment is the split-second peak of intensity, and it is defined especially with reference to light, spatial relationships, and expression.

FIGURE 12-15
Dorothea Lange, *Migrant Mother.* 1936. (© Dorothea Lange Collection, The Oakland Museum of California, The City of Oakland. Gift of Paul Taylor)

PERCEPTION KEY The Documentary Photographers

1. Are any of these documentary photographs (Figures 12-12 through 12-16) sentimental?
2. Some critics assert that these photographers have made interesting social documents, but not works of art. What arguments might support their views? What arguments might contest their views?
3. Contemporary photographers and critics often highly value the work of Atget because it is "liberated" from the influence of painting. What does it mean to say that his work is more photographic than it is painterly?
4. What is the subject matter of each photograph? What is the content of each photograph, if any?

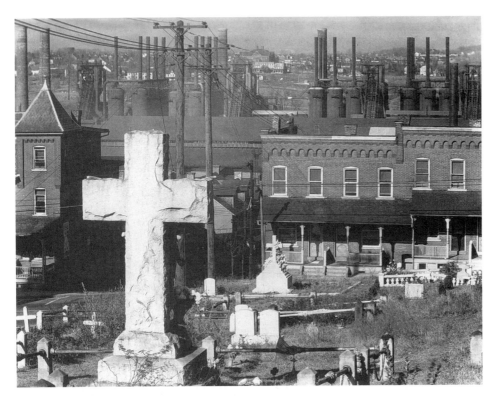

FIGURE 12-16
Walker Evans, *A Graveyard and Steel Mill in Bethlehem, Pennsylvania.* 1935. Gelatin-silver print, 7⅞ × 9⅝ inches. The Museum of Modern Art, New York. Gift of the Farm Security Administration. (569.1953) (Digital image © The Museum of Modern Art, New York/Scala/Art Resource, New York)

Dorothea Lange and Walker Evans were Documentarists who took part in a federal program to give work to photographers during the Depression of the 1930s. Both created careful formal organizations. Lange (Figure 12-15) stresses centrality and balance by placing the children's heads next to the mother's face, which is all the more compelling because the children's faces do not compete for our attention. The mother's arm leads upward to her face, emphasizing the other triangularities of the photograph. Within ten minutes, Lange took four other photographs of this woman and her children, but none could achieve the power of this photograph. Lange caught the exact moment when the children's faces turned and the mother's anxiety comes forth with utter clarity, although the lens mercifully softens its focus on her face, while leaving her shabby clothes in sharp focus. This softness helps humanize our relationship with the woman. Lange gives us an unforgettable image that brutally and yet sympathetically gives us a deeper understanding of what the Depression was for many.

Evans's photograph (Figure 12-16) shows us a view of Bethlehem, Pennsylvania, and the off-center white cross reminds us of what has become the message of Christ. The vertical lines are accentuated in the cemetery stones, repeated in the telephone lines, porch posts, and finally in the steel-mill smokestacks. The aspirations of the dominating verticals, however, are dampened by the strong horizontals, which, because of the low angle of the shot, tend to merge from the cross to the roofs. Evans equalizes focus, which helps compress the space so that we see the cemetery on top of the living space, which is immediately adjacent to the steel

FIGURE 12-17
Diane Arbus, *A Jewish Giant at Home with His Parents in the Bronx, N.Y.* (© 1971 by the estate of Diane Arbus. Photograph courtesy Robert Miller Gallery)

mills where some of the people who live in the tenements work and where some of those now in the cemetery died. This compression of space suggests the closeness of life, work, and death. We see a special kind of sadness in this steel town—and others like it—that we may never have seen before. Evans caught the right moment for the light, which intensifies the white cross, and he aligned the verticals and horizontals for their best effect.

The Snapshot

Photography in recent years has gone in so many directions that classifications tend to be misleading. The snapshot style, however, has become somewhat identifiable, a kind of rebellion against the earlier movements, especially the pictorial. Janet Malcolm claims, "Photography went modernist not, as has been supposed, when it began to imitate modern abstract art but when it began to study snapshots."[6] John Szarkowski of the Museum of Modern Art in New York has praised the snapshot as one of the great resources of the medium. The snapshot appears to have low technical demands, allows for cluttered composition, and "snaps" reality presumably just as it is. No school of photography has established a snapshot canon. It seems to be a product of amateurs, a kind of folk photography. The snapshot appears primitive, spontaneous, and accidental. But the snapshot may

---

[6]*Diana and Nikon: Essays on the Aesthetics of Photography* (Boston: David Godine, 1980), p. 113.

FIGURE 12-18
Robert Frank, *Gallup, New Mexico*. 1955–1956. (© Robert Frank, courtesy Pace/MacGill Gallery, New York)

not be unplanned and accidental, as is evidenced, for instance, in the powerful work of Diane Arbus and Robert Frank. The folk or amateur feel of their photographs is usually only a veneer. The basic difference between the snapshot and the documentary is that veneer.

Diane Arbus was drawn to people who were outcasts, and her personality permitted her to establish a liaison that produced frank and remarkable images. Her photograph of the Jewish giant with his parents (Figure 12-17) is striking primarily because of the strangeness of the subject matter. Arbus has organized the details carefully. The giant is standing, bent over against the ceiling. His parents stand beside him looking up in wonderment. The simplicity and ordinariness of this room are significant when we think of how unordinary this scene is. In one way, Arbus is feeding our curiosity for looking at freaks, but in another way she is showing us that freaks are like us. We know this, of course, but Arbus's images make us feel its truth. Arbus brought exceptional sensitivity to her work and great sympathy for her subjects.

Robert Frank, a Swiss photographer famous for his study of America in 1958, specializes in unusual camera angles. His *Gallup, New Mexico* (Figure

12-18) gives the impression of being unplanned, with little attention to the Weston dogma concerning the fine print (the book it appeared in was wretchedly printed). However, despite its unconventional composition, it may achieve content. Judge for yourself. The light is brutal, befitting a tough, male-dominated environment. The sharp angle of presentation is unsettling and contributes to our lack of ease. The main figure, posed with his hands in his pockets, seems at home in this environment, while the menacing black forms of the men in the foreground shadow us from the scene. We cannot tell what is going on, but we are given a feel of the place. One of Weston's concerns — rendering the essence of the scene — perhaps is satisfied. However, Weston's concern for objectivity, the impersonal rendering of the subject matter, is partially ignored. We are presented with a scene where violence lurks just beneath the surface, and this seems an objective representation; but we also sense Frank's personal statement in the exceptionally low camera angle and the unusual framing.

When he died of AIDS in 1989 at age 42, Robert Mapplethorpe was arguably the best-known young photographer in America. Six months after his death he became even better known to the public because an exhibit of his work, supported by a grant from the National Endowment for the Arts, caused Senator Jesse Helms (R-NC) to add an amendment to an important appropriations bill that would make it almost impossible for the NEA to fund exhibitions of the work of artists like Mapplethorpe. The amendment reads:

> None of the funds authorized to be appropriated pursuant to the Act may be used to promote, disseminate, or produce — (1) obscene or indecent materials, including but not limited to depictions of sadomasochism, homo-eroticism, the exploitation of children, or individuals engaged in sex acts; or (2) material which denigrates the objects or beliefs of the adherents of a particular religion or non-religion; or (3) material which denigrates, debases, or reviles a person, group, or class of citizens on the basis of race, creed, sex, handicap, age, or national origin.

The provisions of this bill — which was defeated — would essentially apply to every federal granting or exhibition agency, including the National Gallery of Art. The exhibit that triggered this response included Mapplethorpe's photographs of the homosexual community of New York to which he belonged. Some of his work portrays bondage, sadomasochistic accoutrements, and nudity. Such works so angered Senator Helms apparently that his proposed law would make it difficult, if not impossible, for photographers such as Mapplethorpe to get the kind of government support that artists of all kinds have been given since World War II. The decision to withhold support would not be made by experts in the arts, but by government functionaries.

Despite the defeat of the bill, federal support to public radio, public television, public institutions such as the most prominent museums in the United States, and all the public programs designed to support the arts has been curtailed so profoundly as to jeopardize the careers of dancers, composers, symphony orchestras, and virtually all arts organizations. Interestingly, similar pressure was put on the arts by the governments of

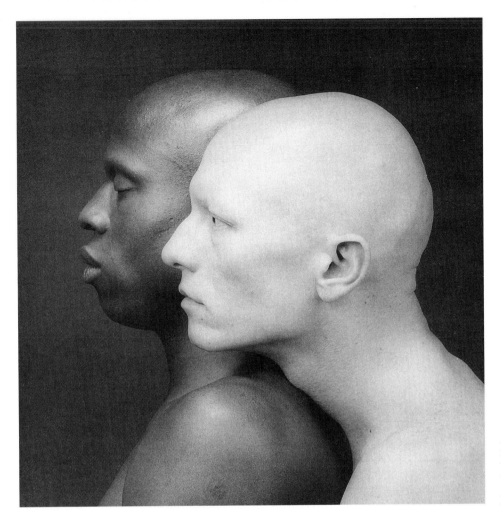

FIGURE 12-19
Robert Mapplethorpe, *Ken Moody and Robert Sherman, 1984.* (© 1984 The Estate of Robert Mapplethorpe)

Franco, Stalin, Hitler, and Mao. The outcome of political control in the United States over the arts is very much in doubt. We will consider this issue briefly in Chapter 14.

Mapplethorpe's double portrait (Figure 12-19) might well be considered controversial in the light of Helms's amendment. Who is to say that this is not a homosexual portrait? Are there racial implications to this photograph? These are questions that may impinge on the photographic values of the portrait. Mapplethorpe has interpreted these heads almost as if they were sculptured busts. There is no hair. The surfaces are cool, almost stone-like. The tonal range of darks and lights is a marvel, and one of the most important challenges of this photograph was in making the print manifest the range of the paper from the brightest white to the darkest black. Mapplethorpe portrayed the coolness and detachment of his subjects. Instead of revealing their personality, Mapplethorpe seems to aim at revealing their physical qualities by inviting us to compare them not only with each other, but also with the images we have in our minds of conventional portrait busts.

PERCEPTION KEY   Art and Censorship

1. Should government support the arts as a means of improving the life of the public? The government supports education; is art a form of education?
2. Would you vote for the Helms amendment? Are there works in this book that you believe would fall under one of the three categories that it restricts from support? Is it right for the government of the United States to restrict support of art, however presumably obscene, sacrilegious, or immoral? If a work of art enlightens, then are not obscenity, the sacrilegious, and the immoral transformed? If so, then would you agree that these undesirables may be the subject matter of a work of art but never the content?
3. Why would artists feel it appropriate to shock the public rather than to pander to its tastes? Is it possible that artists who pander to public taste ought to be censored on the basis that they are unoriginal, greedy, and socially destructive?
4. If the U.S. government has the right to reject art that offends, should it not also imprison the offending artist (as was done in the Soviet Union, Germany, and China)?
5. What are the alternatives to censorship of the arts?

Color Photography

Color photographers often choose apparently inconsequential subject matter in order to release the viewer from the tyranny of the scene, thereby permitting the viewer to concentrate on nuances of lighting and texture and structure. These are expressly photographic values. In a sense such photographers follow Atget's lead (Figure 12-12).

An example of the opposite approach is the pictorialism of the typical journalistic photograph, such as those seen in *National Geographic,* a publication whose color photographs are celebrated, but almost always because they are excellent records of picturesque subjects. In the color photographs of Joel Meyerowitz and Cindy Sherman, we are in worlds far removed from journalism.

Meyerowitz sometimes makes the pictured scene secondary to color harmonies and light, so that the subject matter of *Red Interior, Provincetown* (1977) (Figure 12-20) is almost as much about the play of the red and white and blues as it is about the moon, cars, and cottages. Yet those objects are there, and the complex interrelationship between them and Meyerowitz's hymn to color and light makes this photograph a fascinating study in lyric sensuality.

Cindy Sherman is one of the few American photographers to have had a one-woman show at the prestigious Whitney Museum in New York City. Her work has annoyed, confounded, and alarmed many people both ignorant and well informed about photography as an art. For many years she photographed herself in various costumes, with makeup and guises that showed her almost limitless capacity to interpret her personality. Those color photographs often had a snapshot quality and probably were most interesting when seen as a group rather than individually.

FIGURE 12-20
Joel Meyerowitz, *Red Interior, Provincetown.* 1977. (© Joel Meyerowitz/Courtesy of Ariel Meyerowitz Gallery, New York)

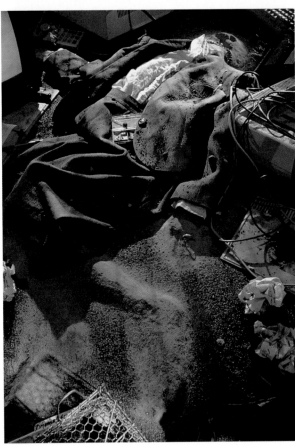

FIGURE 12-21
Cindy Sherman, *Untitled.* 1987. Color photograph, 86⅛ × 61⅛ inches. (Metro Pictures)

Some of Sherman's work is often condemned because it seems designed to gross out the audience with images of garbage, offal, vomit, and body parts. The crumpled suit and assorted garbage in *Untitled* (Figure 12-21) seems to be the residue of a life. In the middle of the carpet is a small pile of ashes that may suggest the remains of a cremated person (Cindy Sherman?). This photograph should not be read only in terms of its objects. Color is also part of the subject matter, as it is in *Red Interior, Provincetown,* and can be appreciated somewhat the way one appreciates the color of a Rothko (Figure 4-11). The objects she photographed have been purposely simplified and relocated. This is not the kind of photograph about which anyone would ask, "Where was this taken?"

PERCEPTION KEY   The Modern Eye

1. Which of the black-and-white photographs in this chapter is least like a snapshot?
2. Compare the photographic values of Mapplethorpe's *Ken Moody and Robert Sherman* with those of Arbus's *A Jewish Giant*. In which are the gradations of tone from light to dark more carefully modulated? In which is the selectivity of the framing more consciously and apparently artistic? In which is the subject matter more obviously transformed by the photographic image?
3. Which of the color photographs best combines the colors with the objects they presumably help interpret? What do the colors suggest about those objects?
4. Photocopy one of the color photographs to produce a black-and-white image. What has been lost? Is the color essential to the success of the photograph?
5. We have suggested that both the Meyerowitz and the Sherman photographs could be read as abstract rather than as representational, as we also suggested with regard to Parmigianino's *The Madonna with the Long Neck* (Figure 4-4) and Frankenthaler's *Flood* (Figure 4-7). These are controversial questions and especially with regard to photography, for the photograph would seem to be inherently representational. What do you think?

Summary

The capacity of photography to record reality faithfully is both a virtue and a fault. It makes many viewers of photographs concerned only with what is presented (the subject matter) and leaves them unaware of the way it has been represented (the form). Because of its fidelity of presentation, photography seems to some to have no transformation of subject matter. This did not bother early photographers, who were delighted at the ease with which they could present their subject matter. The pictorialists, on the other hand, relied on nineteenth-century representational painting to guide them in their approach to form. Their carefully composed images are still valued by many photographers. But the reaction of the straight photographers, who wished to shake off any dependence on painting and disdained sentimental subject matter, began a revolution that emphasized the special qualities of the medium: especially the tonal range of the silver or platinum print (and now color print), the impersonality of the sharply defined object (and consequent lack of sentimentality), spatial compression, and selective framing. The revolution has not stopped there, but has pushed on into unexpected areas, such as the exploration of the snapshot and the rejection of the technical standards of the straight photographers. Many contemporary photographers are searching for new ways of photographic seeing based on the capacity of the computer to transform and manipulate images. This is a very exciting prospect.

Bibliography

Barthes, Roland. *Camera Lucida.* New York: Hill and Wang, 1981.

Bayer, Jonathan. *Reading Photographs: Understanding the Aesthetics of Photography.* New York: Pantheon, 1977.

Berger, John, and Jean Mohr. *Another Way of Telling.* New York: Pantheon, 1982.

Danto, Arthur. *Playing with the Edge: The Photographic Achievement of Robert Mapplethorpe.* Berkeley University of California Press, 1995.

Doty, Robert. *Photo-Secession.* New York: Dover, 1978.

Evans, Jessica, ed. *The Camera Work Essays: Context and Meaning in Photography.* New York: New York University Press, 1997.

Hambourg, Maria Morris, et al., eds. *The Waking Dream: Photography's First Century.* New York: Metropolitan Museum of Art, 1993.

Jeffrey, Ian. *Photography.* London: Thames and Hudson, 1985; 1991.

Lyons, Nathan. *Photographers on Photography.* Englewood Cliffs, N.J.: Prentice-Hall, 1966.

Malcolm, Janet. *Diana and Nikon: Essays on the Aesthetics of Photography.* Boston: David Godine, 1980.

Maynard, Patrick. *The Engine of Visualization: Thinking through Photography.* Ithaca, N.Y.: Cornell University Press, 1997.

Newhall, Beaumont. *The History of Photography,* 5th ed. New York: Museum of Modern Art, 1994.

Newhall, Beaumont, ed. *Photography: Essays and Images.* New York: Museum of Modern Art, 1980.

Petruck, Peninah R., ed. *The Camera Viewed.* 2 vols. New York: Dutton, 1979.

Rosenberg, Harold. *The Tradition of the New.* New York: McGraw-Hill, 1965.

Sandler, Martin W. *The Story of American Photography.* Boston: Little, Brown, 1979.

Sontag, Susan. *On Photography.* New York: Farrar, Straus, and Giroux, 1977.

Internet Resources

DIANE ARBUS

http://www.temple.edu/photo/photographers/arbus/arbus.htm

HENRI CARTIER-BRESSON

http://www.temple.edu/photo/photographers/cartier_bresson/thumbdex.htm

CALIFORNIA MUSEUM OF PHOTOGRAPHY

http://www.cmp.ucr.edu/

THE CIVIL WAR COLLECTION (FROM THE LIBRARY OF CONGRESS)

http://memory.loc.gov/ammem/cwphtml/cwphome.html

EDWARD CURTIS: IMAGES OF THE NORTH AMERICAN INDIAN
http://memory.loc.gov/ammem/award98/ienhtml/curthome.html

GEORGE EASTMAN HOUSE (CLASSIC PHOTOS, EXHIBITIONS)
http://www.eastman.org/

LIBRARY OF CONGRESS PRINTS AND PHOTOGRAPHS
http://lcweb.loc.gov/rr/print/catalog.html

MASTERS OF PHOTOGRAPHY (IMAGES BY GREAT PHOTOGRAPHERS)
http://www.masters-of-photography.com/

WOMEN IN PHOTOGRAPHY INTERNATIONAL
http://www.womeninphotography.org

PART III
Interrelationships

CHAPTER 13

The Interrelationships of the Arts

We shall outline and classify only the most important interrelationships of the arts. Understanding something about the ways the arts mix should help sharpen our perceptions and deepen our participation.

The close ties among the arts occur because artists share a special purpose: the revelation of values. Furthermore, every artist must use some medium, some kind of "stuff" that can be formed to communicate that revelation (content) about something (subject matter). All artists share some elements of media, and this sharing encourages their interaction. For example, painters, sculptors, and architects use color, line, and texture. Sculptors and architects work with the density of materials. Rhythm is basic to the composer, choreographer, and poet. Words are elemental for the poet, novelist, dramatist, and composer of songs and operas. Images are basic to the painter, filmmaker, and photographer. Artists constitute a commonwealth—they share the same end and similar means.

The interrelationships among the arts are enormously complex. We hope the following classification of *appropriation, synthesis,* and *interpretation* will clear some paths through the maze.

Appropriation

Artistic *appropriation* occurs when (1) artists combine their basic medium with the medium of another art or arts, but (2) keep their basic medium clearly dominant. For example, music is the basic medium for composers of opera. The staging may include architecture, painting, and sculpture. The language of the drama may include poetry. The dance, so dependent on music, is often incorporated in opera, and sometimes in contemporary opera so are photography and even film. Yet, music almost always dominates in opera. We may listen to Beethoven's *Fidelio* or Bizet's *Carmen* on a

383

CD time after time. Yet, it is hard to imagine anyone reading the *librettos* over and over again. Although essential to opera, the drama, along with the staging, rarely dominates the music. Often the librettos by themselves are downright silly. Nevertheless, drama and the other appropriated arts generally enhance the feelings interpreted by the music.

PERCEPTION KEY   Opera

Attend an opera or use a video of an opera by Puccini, perhaps *La Bohème*.

1. Compare your experience of seeing the opera with just listening. Is your enjoyment greatly diminished if you only listen? If so, why?
2. Watch a video of the opera for a short time without the sound. Your enjoyment presumably will be greatly diminished. Why?
3. Read the libretto. Is it interesting enough to achieve participation, as with a good poem or novel? Would you want to read it again?
4. Have you experienced any opera in which the drama dominates the music? Wagner claimed that in *The Ring* he wedded music and drama (and other arts as well) so closely that neither dominates the *Gesamtkunstwerk* (the complete artwork). Read the libretto of one of the four operas that constitute *The Ring*, and then go to or listen to the opera. Do you agree with Wagner's claim?
5. Go to Verdi's *Otello*, one of his last operas, or use a video. Shakespeare's drama is of the highest order, although much of it is lost not only in the very condensed libretto, but also in the translation into Italian. Does either the music or the drama dominate? Or is there a synthesis?

Except for opera, architecture is the art that appropriates the most. Its centering of space makes room for the placement of sculpture, painting, and photography; the reading of poetry; and the performance of drama, music, and dance. The sheer size of architecture tends to make it prevail over any of the incorporated arts, the container prevailing over the contents. The obvious exceptions occur when the architecture functions mainly as a place to show painting or sculpture. For example, Leonardo's fresco of the *Last Supper* (Figure 3-1) in the refectory of Santa Maria delle Grazie in Milan fits into the wall opposite the entrance. The beauty and power of the painting completely subordinate the room, helping to make it nondescript. Leonardo even harmonized the lines of the side walls and ceiling of the refectory with the lines of the painting that recede to a vanishing point behind the head of Christ.

The architecture of Gaudí's Sagrada Familia (Figures 6-20 to 6-22), on the other hand, is certainly not nondescript. Yet, despite its great size and powerful vertical stretches—surely a sky-oriented building—a good case can be made, perhaps, that the sculpture is just as compelling.

Architecture

1. Review the photographs of buildings in Chapter 6. Are there any in which it would appear that any of the included arts dominate the architecture?

2. Try to visit Wright's Guggenheim Museum (Figures 6-9 and 6-10) or study more photographs of the interior. Does the architecture tend to dominate the exhibited paintings and sculpture? If so, is that a proper function for the architecture of a museum? Note that as you walk on the ramps you view the paintings and sculptures from a slanted position. Note also that often you can easily view the paintings and sculptures that are both near and far across the whirling space.

3. Do you know of any works of architecture that are completely free of the other arts and would seem to resist the incorporation of the other arts? Any buildings that are pure, so to speak? What about Mies van der Rohe's Farnsworth residence (Figure 6-27)? What about Mies's Seagram Building (Figure 6-8). One critic has described the Seagram as glassy-eyed and expressionless. What about some opulent sculptural trim? Discuss.

Synthesis

By *synthesis,* we mean relatively equal combining of the media of one or more arts—for example, architecture and sculpture in Gaudí's church. Perhaps the most obvious synthesis occurs with dance and music. Very few dances work without music. And many times music is just as important as the dance. Stravinsky's music for the *Firebird, Petrouchka,* and *The Rite of Spring* offers marvelous revelations of feelings and states of mind, but so do the dances. The music supports the dance and vice versa. On the other hand, the pretexts of the narratives are not very interesting, more appropriated than synthesized.

Cage, Cunningham, and Rauschenberg

A 1987 video called *The Collaborators* recorded a dialogue among Cage, the composer; Cunningham, the choreographer; and Rauschenberg, the painter. It is a fascinating and humorous record of how artists with different media sometimes work together. Try to see this video. It concludes with a complete showing of *Coast Zone,* a famous instance of collaboration between Cage and Cunningham, filmed in the Cathedral of St. John the Divine in New York City in 1981.

1. Both artists claim that they worked independently of each other. Cunningham states that his dance is for the eye and Cage's music is for the ear. The dance and the music were performed together, sharing the same space and time. Yet, somehow we are supposed to perceive the dance and the music independently. No attempt, they claim, was made to unify the dance and the music. Do you find the resulting lack of coherence irritating? Do you find Cage's humming and mumbling distracting as you watch the dance? And what about the predictably unpredictable noises and tones? Do you find them nerve-wracking? If so, what do you think Cage and Cunningham would say about your reactions?

2. Do you find yourself trying to unify the music with the dance? Do you suppose that Cage and Cunningham might be challenging you to make their works coherent in your participation with them, making you also a collaborator?
3. Mark Morris combined a lyric poem by John Milton with the music of Handel in one of his dances. If you can see this dance or can get a video, ask yourself whether the dance appropriates these other arts or synthesizes with them. Since at least two of the three artists are among the great, the question should be especially interesting.

Music and poetry sometimes are combined synthetically. The old Cathedral of Coventry, destroyed in World War II, was redesigned, rebuilt, and dedicated in 1959. For that dedication Benjamin Britten composed the famous *War Requiem*, basing his music on the bitterly sad poems of Wilfred Owens, killed in the trenches just before the ending of World War I. The music and poems, we think, are inextricably melded.

PERCEPTION KEY   Music and Poetry

1. Listen to Britten's *War Requiem*. Do you agree that the music and the poetry are a synthesis? Discuss.
2. Listen to Britten's *Serenade for Tenor, Horn, and Strings* that includes Blake's *The Sick Rose* (pages 223–224). Does Britten appropriate the poem, or is there a synthesis?
3. Do you find a synthesis of music and words in any of the songs where Franz Schubert uses the poems of Goethe? If so, is our participation all the stronger because of that?
4. See if you can find a synthesis of music and words in any of the species of popular music, such as folk, jazz, soul, rock, rap, and country.
5. With the rap music of Eminem, do you find the lyrics—often offensive to the traditional listener—and music generally a synthesis? Discuss.
6. Do you think that music could be synthesized with Shakespeare's Sonnet 73 (pages 220–221)? Or does the linguistic power and intricacy of the sonnet repel either appropriation or synthesis? Is the poem so wonderful it should be left alone?

The last question of the Perception Key may imply that literature, especially of high quality, tends to resist mixing with other arts. The novelist and poet, it seems, rarely needs the help of other arts. The extraordinary complexity and flexibility of language gives most literary artists all they need to express their meaning. Do you agree? Discuss.

PERCEPTION KEY   Literature

Examine the poems in Chapter 7.

1. Would any be enriched by the inclusion of other arts? For example, do any of the poems lend themselves to song? If so, would such mixing be more of an appropriation or a synthesis? Explain.

2. Lawrence's "Piano" (pages 206–207) would seem to be a good candidate for a song. Or do you think musical accompaniment would distract from the power of the poem? Explain.

Painting and sculpture have been combined more and more in recent years. Synthesis, however, seems to be rarely achieved. Despite the sharing of line, color, and texture, the imaginary space created by painters tends to resist equal mixing with the enlivening of real space created by sculptors. Thus there is a strong tendency toward appropriation by either art. Despite the use of the lovely white in Hepworth's *Pelagos* (Figure 5-16), it would be strange to describe the work as a painting. The grain and density of the wood and the push and pull of curved "real space" subordinate any suggestion of "imaginary space." And this would seem to remain true even if Hepworth had painted a beautiful landscape on the white.

PERCEPTION KEY   Painting and Sculpture

Does painting or sculpture dominate in Robert Rauschenberg's *Winter Pool* (Figure 13-1)? Rauschenberg called this kind of work a "combine-painting." Does that description tend to influence your decision in any way? If so, why?

Perhaps there is a synthesis of two kinds of experience with this work of Rauschenberg, one of the most experimental of visual artists. We may participate with it as sculpture and then participate with it as painting. Or vice versa. Either experience leads to the other, a dialectical balance, the participations resonating with each other. If we treasure painting more than sculpture, we probably will begin with pictorial dominance. If we treasure sculpture more than painting, we probably will begin with sculptural dominance. But, in any case, *Winter Pool* may lead to an oscillation of participations that is a kind of synthesis.

The photographer's media—light, line, texture, shapes, and recently color—are close to the painter's. And the interaction between these two arts also is close. For example, the pictorial tradition in photography was directly influenced by painting, and painting was directly influenced by the realistic detail produced by photography (see Chapter 12). But the most useful and widespread interaction of photography with the other arts is its practical role as a recorder. Without photographs, this book, for better or worse, would be impossible. Photography, along with film, now provides us with a museum without walls. Photography can record the "still moments"—the painting, for instance. Film can record the "moving moments"—the dance, for instance. Both film and photography tend to be the arts best suited to use other arts as their subject matter. For example, a recent film of the life of Jackson Pollock may help us understand his paintings.

FIGURE 13-1
Robert Rauschenberg, *Winter Pool*. 1959. Mixed media, 229 × 151 × 10 inches. (Photo © Geoffrey Clements/ Corbis. Art © Robert Rauschenberg/Licensed by VAGA, New York, NY)

Interpretation

When a work of art takes another work of art as its subject matter, the former is an *interpretation* of the latter. Thus Zeffirelli's film—*Romeo and Juliet*—takes Shakespeare's drama for its subject matter. The film interprets the play. It is fascinating to observe how the contents—the meanings—differ because of the different media. We will analyze a few interesting examples. Bring to mind other examples as you read the text.

FILM INTERPRETS LITERATURE: *HOWARDS END*

E. M. Forster's novel *Howards End* (1910) was made into a remarkable film in 1992 (Figures 13-2 and 13-3) by producer Ismail Merchant and director James Ivory. Ruth Prawer Jhabvala wrote the screenplay. The film starred Anthony Hopkins and Emma Thompson who, along with Jhabvala, won an Academy Award. The film itself was nominated as best picture, and its third Academy Award went to the design direction of Luciana Arrighi and Ian Whittaker .

FIGURE 13-2
Anthony Hopkins and Emma
Thompson in *Howards End.*
(© 1992 Merchant-Ivory
Productions)

FIGURE 13-3
Emma Thompson and
Helena Bonham Carter in
Howards End. (© 1992
Merchant-Ivory Productions)

The team of Merchant-Ivory, producer–director, has become distinguished for period films set in the late nineteenth century and early twentieth century. Part of the reputation won by Merchant-Ivory films is due to
their detailed designs. Thus, in a Merchant-Ivory film one expects to see

Edwardian costumes meticulously reproduced, period interiors with prints and paintings, authentic architecture, both interior and exterior, and details sumptuously photographed so that the colors are rich and saturated and the atmosphere appropriately reflecting the era just before and after 1900.

All of that is true of the production of *Howards End*. But the subtlety of the interplay of the arts in the film is intensified because of the subtlety of the interplay of the arts in the novel. Forster wrote his novel in a way that emulates contemporary drama, at least in part. His scenes are dramatically conceived, with characters acting in carefully described settings, speaking in ways that suggest the stage. Moreover, Forster's special interest in music and the role culture in general plays in the lives of his characters makes the novel especially challenging for interpretation by moving images.

The film follows Forster's story faithfully. Three families at the center of the story stand in contrast: the Schlegel sisters, Margaret and Helen; a rich businessman Henry Wilcox, his frail wife Ruth, and their superficial, conventional children; and a poor, young, unhappily married bank clerk, Leonard Bast, whom the Schlegel sisters befriend. Margaret and Helen are idealistic and cultured. The Wilcoxes, except for Ruth, are uncultured snobs. When Ruth dies, Henry proposes to and is accepted by Margaret. Her sister Helen, who detests Henry, is devastated by this marriage, and turns to Leonard Bast. The story becomes a tangle of opposites and, because of the stupidity of Henry's son Charles, turns tragic. In the end, thanks to the moral strength of Margaret, reconciliation becomes possible.

Read the novel first, and then see the film. In one scene early in the novel, some of the protagonists are in Queen's Hall in London listening to Beethoven's Fifth Symphony. Here is Forster's wonderful description:

> It will be generally admitted that Beethoven's *Fifth Symphony* is the most sublime noise that has ever penetrated into the ear of man. All sorts and conditions are satisfied by it. Whether you are like Mrs. Munt, and tap surreptitiously when the tunes come—of course, not so as to disturb the others; or like Helen, who can see heroes and shipwrecks in the music's flood; or like Margaret, who can only see the music; or like Tibby, who is profoundly versed in counterpoint, and holds the full score open on his knee; or like their cousin, Fräulein Mosebach, who remembers all the time that Beethoven is "echt Deutsch" [pure German]; or like Fräulein Mosebach's young man, who can remember nothing but Fräulein Mosebach: in any case, the passion of your life becomes more vivid, and you are bound to admit that such a noise is cheap at two shillings.

Now that is a passage surely worth recording. But how could you get it into a film unless by a "voiceover," an awkward technique in this context. Observe how this scene is portrayed in the film. Also observe in the film the awkward drawn-out scenes of Leonard Bast pursuing Helen in the rain (she inadvertently had taken his umbrella when leaving the concert hall). One keeps wondering why the soaking Leonard does not simply run and catch up with Helen. In the novel these events are much more smoothly handled. In such portrayals, written language has the advantage.

Conversely, the film captures something in 1992 that the novel could not have achieved in its own time—the sense of loss for an elegant way of life in the period before World War I. The moving images create nostalgia for a past totally unrecoverable. Nostalgia for that past is, of course, also created by Forster's fine prose, but not with the power of moving images. Coming back to the novel after its interpretation by the film surely makes our participation more complete.

PERCEPTION KEY   *Howards End*

1. Do the filmic presentations of Margaret Schlegel and Henry Wilcox "ring true" to Forster's characterizations? If not, what are the deficiencies?
2. Is the background music effective?
3. What kind or kinds of cuts are used in the film (page 323)? Are they effectively used? Explain.
4. In which work, the novel or the film, are the social issues of greater importance? Which puts more stress on the class distinctions between the Basts and both the Schlegels and the Wilcoxes? Which seems to have a stronger social message?
5. How does the film — by supplying the images your imagination can only invent in reading the novel — affect your understanding of the lives of the Schlegels, Wilcoxes, and Basts?
6. Can you return to the novel after seeing the film and read the novel with basically the same understanding?

MUSIC INTERPRETS DRAMA: *THE MARRIAGE OF FIGARO*

Perhaps in the age of Wolfgang Amadeus Mozart (1756–1791) the opera performed a function for literature somewhat equivalent to what the film does today. Opera — in combining music, drama, sets, and sometimes dance — was held in highest esteem in Europe in the eighteenth century. And despite the increasing competition from film and musical comedy, opera is still performed to large audiences in theaters and larger audiences on television. Among the world's greatest operas, few are more popular than Mozart's *The Marriage of Figaro* (1786), written when Mozart was only thirty.

Mozart's play interprets the French play *The Marriage of Figaro* (1784), by Pierre Augustin de Beaumarchais, a highly successful playwright friendly with Mme. Pompadour, mistress of Louis XVI at the time of the American Revolution. Beaumarchais began as an ordinary citizen, bought his way into the aristocracy, survived the French Revolution, went into exile, and later died back in France. His plays were the product of, yet comically critical of, the aristocracy. *The Marriage of Figaro*, written in 1780, was held back by censors as an attack on the government. Eventually produced to great acclaim, it was seditious enough for later commentators to claim that it was an essential ingredient in fomenting the French Revolution of 1789.

Mozart, with Lorenzo Da Ponte, who wrote the libretto, remained generally faithful to the play, although changing some names and the occupations of some characters. They reduced the opera to four acts from Beaumarchais' five, although the entire opera is three hours long.

In brief, it is the story of Figaro, servant to Count Almaviva, and his intention of marrying the countess's maid Susanna. The count has given up the feudal tradition, which would have permitted him to sleep with Susanna first, before her husband. However, he regrets his decision because he has fallen in love with Susanna and now tries to seduce her. When his wife, the countess, young and still in love with him, discovers his plans, she throws in with Figaro and Susanna to thwart him. Cherubino, a very young man—sung by a female soprano—feels the first stirrings of love and desires both the countess and Susanna in turn. He is a page in the count's employ and when his intentions are discovered, he is sent into the army. One of the greatest *arias* in the opera is "Non più andrai," "From now on," which Figaro sings to Cherubino, telling him that his amorous escapades are now over. The nine-page aria is derived from part of a single speech of Beaumarchais' Figaro:

> No more hanging around all day with the girls, no more cream buns and custard tarts, no more charades and blind-man's-bluff; just good soldiers, by God: weatherbeaten and ragged-assed, weighed down with their muskets, right face, left face, forward march.[1]

Mozart's treatment of the speech demonstrates one of the resources of opera as opposed to straight drama. In the drama, it would be very difficult to expand Figaro's speech to intensify its emotional content, but in the opera the speech or parts of it can be repeated frequently and with pleasure, since the music that underpins the words is delightful to hear and rehear. Mozart's opera changes the emotional content of the play because it intensifies feelings associated with key moments in the action.

The aria contains a very simple musical figure that has nonetheless great power in the listening. Just as Mozart is able to repeat parts of dialogue, he is able to repeat notes, passages, and patterns. The pattern repeated most conspicuously is that of the arpeggio, a chord whose notes are played in quick succession instead of simultaneously. The passage of three chords in the key of C expresses a lifting feeling of exuberance (Figure 13-4). Mozart's genius was marked by a way of finding the simplest, yet most unexpected, solutions to musical problems. The arpeggio is practiced by almost every student of a musical instrument, yet it is thought of as something appropriate to practice rather than performance. Thus, Mozart's usage comes as a surprise.

FIGURE 13-4
Arpeggio from "Non più andrai," *The Marriage of Figaro.*

[1]Beaumarchais, *The Marriage of Figaro,* tr. Bernard Sahlins. Copyright 1994. Chicago: Ivan R. Dee, 1332 North Halsted Street, Chicago 60622, p. 29.

The very essence of the arpeggio in the eighteenth century was constant repetition, and in using that pattern Mozart finds yet another way to repeat elements to intensify the emotional effects of the music. The listener hears the passage, is captured, yet hardly knows in any conscious way why it is as impressive and as memorable as it is. There are ways of doing similar things in drama — repeating gestures, for example — but there are very few ways of repeating elements in such close proximity as the arpeggio without risking boredom.

The plot of the opera, like that of the play, is based on thwarting the plans of the count with the use of disguise and mix-ups. Characters are hidden in bedrooms, thus overhearing conversations they ought not hear. They leap from bedroom windows, hide in closets, and generally create a comic confusion. The much older Marcellina and her lawyer Bartolo introduce the complication of a breach of promise suit between her and Figaro just as Figaro is about to marry. The count uses it to his advantage while he can, but the difficulty is resolved in a marvelously comic way: Marcellina sees a birthmark on Figaro and realizes he is her son and the son of Bartolo, with whom she had an affair. That finally clears the way for Figaro and Susanna, who, once they have shamed the count into attending to the countess, can marry.

Mozart's musical resources include techniques that cannot easily be duplicated in straight drama. For example, his extended use of duets, quartets, and sextets, in which characters interact and sing together, would be impossible in the original drama. The libretto gave Mozart a chance to have one character sing a passage while another filled in with an aside. Thus, there are moments when one character sings what he expects others want him to say, while another character sings his or her inner thoughts, specifically designed for the audience to hear. Mozart reveals the duplicity of characters by having them sing one passage "publicly" while revealing their secret motives "privately."

The force of the quartets and the sextets in *The Marriage of Figaro* is enormous, adding wonderfully to the comic effect that this opera always achieves. Their musical force, in terms of sheer beauty and subtle complexity, is one of the hallmarks of the opera. In the play it would be impossible to have six characters speaking simultaneously, but with the characters singing, such a situation becomes quite possible.

The resources that Mozart had in orchestration helped him achieve effects that the stage could not produce. The horns, for example, are sometimes used for the purposes of poking fun at the pretentious count, who is a hunter. The discords found in some of the early arias resolve themselves in later arias when the countess smooths them out, as in the opening aria in Act II: *Porgi Amor* (Pour forth, O Love). The capacity of the music to emulate the emotional condition of the characters is a further resource that permits Mozart to emphasize tension, as when, for example, dissonant chords seem to stab the air to reflect the anxiety of the count. Further, the capacity to bring the music quite low (pianissimo) and then contrast it with brilliant loud passages (fortissimo) adds a dimension of feeling that the play can barely even suggest.

Mozart's *The Marriage of Figaro* also has been successful because of its political message, which is essentially democratic. The opera presents us with a delightful character, Figaro, a barber become a servant, who is level-headed, somewhat innocent of the evil ways of the world, and a smart man when he needs to be. He loves Susanna, who is much more worldly-wise than he, but who is also a thoughtful, intelligent young woman. In contrast, the count is an unsympathetic man who resents the fact that his servant Figaro can have what he wants but cannot possess. The count is outwitted by his servant and his wife at almost every turn. The countess is a sympathetic character. She loves her husband, knows he wants to be unfaithful, but plays along with Susanna and Figaro in a scheme involving assignations and disguises in order to shame him into doing the right thing. The audiences of the age loved the play because they reveled in the amusing way that Figaro manipulates his aristocratic master. Beaumarchais' play was as clear about this as the opera. Mozart's interpretation of the play (his subject matter) reveals such a breadth and depth of feeling that now the opera is far more appreciated than the play.

PERCEPTION KEY Beaumarchais' and Mozart's *The Marriage of Figaro*

Read Beaumarchais' play and Da Ponte's libretto, and see or listen to Mozart's opera. Unfortunately, there is no video available of the Beaumarchais play, but there are several videos of the opera. The Deutsche Grammophone version, with Dietrich Fisher-Dieskau as the count, is excellent and has English subtitles. Listening to the opera while following the libretto is also of great value. Listen for the use of individual instruments, such as the clarinets on the offbeat, the power of horns and drums, and the repetition of phrases. Pay attention especially to the finale, with its power, simplicity, and matchless humor.

1. Compare the clarity of the development of character in both play and opera. What differences in feeling do the respective works produce?
2. Is character or plot foremost in Beaumarchais' work? Which is foremost in Mozart's?
3. Suppose you know nothing about the drama and listen only to the music. Would your participation be significantly weakened? Discuss.

POETRY INTERPRETS PAINTING: *THE STARRY NIGHT*

Poets often use paintings, especially famous ones, for their subject matter. Since paintings are wordless, they tend to invite commentary. Vincent van Gogh was a tormented man whose slide into insanity has been chronicled in letters, biographies, romantic novels, and films. His painting *The Starry Night* (Figure 13-5) is an eloquent, tortured image filled with dynamic swirls and rich colors, portraying a night that is intensely threatening.

The first poem, by Robert Fagles (b. 1933), speaks from the point of view of van Gogh, imagining a psychic pain that has somehow been relieved by the act of painting:

FIGURE 13-5
Vincent van Gogh, *The Starry Night.* 1889. Oil on canvas, 29 × 36¼ inches (73.7 × 92.1 cm). The Museum of Modern Art, New York. Acquired through the Lillie P. Bliss Bequest. (Digital image © The Museum of Modern Art, New York/Licensed by Scala/ Art Resource, New York)

THE STARRY NIGHT

Long as I paint
I feel myself
less mad
the brush in my hand
a lightning rod to madness

But never ground that madness
execute it ride the lightning up
from these benighted streets and steeple up
with the cypress look its black is burning green

I am that I am it cries
it lifts me up the nightfall up
the cloudrack coiling like a dragon's flanks
a third of the stars of heaven wheeling in its wake
wheels in wheels around the moon that cradles round the sun

and if I can only trail these whirling eternal stars
with one sweep of the brush like Michael's sword if I can
cut the life out of the beast—safeguard the mother and the son
all heaven will hymn in conflagration blazing down
    the night the mountain ranges down
    the claustrophobic valleys of the mad

is what I have instead of heaven
God deliver me — help me now deliver
all this frenzy back into your hands
our brushstrokes burning clearer into dawn

Anne Sexton (1928–1975) was one of America's most powerful poets, but her brief life was cut short by insanity and then suicide. She may have seen the painting as an emblem of madness from a perspective that most sane people cannot. In light of her personal journey, it is especially fascinating to see how she interprets the painting:

THE STARRY NIGHT

That does not keep me from having a terrible need of — shall I say the word — religion. Then I go out at night to paint the stars.

Vincent van Gogh in a letter to his brother Theo.

The town does not exist
except where one black-haired tree slips
up like a drowned woman into the hot sky.
The town is silent. The night boils with eleven stars
Oh starry starry night! This is how
I want to die.

It moves. They are all alive.
Even the moon bulges in its orange irons
to push children, like a god, from its eye.
The old unseen serpent swallows up the stars.
Oh starry starry night! This is how
I want to die:

into that rushing beast of the night,
sucked up by that great dragon, to split
from my life with no flag,
no belly,
no cry.

Both poets offer only the briefest description of the painting. If one had not seen it, no reader could know quite what the painting looks like. Yet, both poets move directly to the emotional core of the painting, its connection with madness and psychic pain. For Fagles, the effort was intensely imaginative. For Sexton, perhaps, less so. Shortly before she wrote her poem her father had died and she had an illegal abortion because she feared the baby she was about to have was not fathered by her husband. Her personal life was terribly tormented for several months before she wrote the poem, but she continued to write all the time, producing her most widely read volume, *All My Pretty Ones*, which, for a book of modern poetry, had extraordinary sales and a great popularity. Interestingly, both poets see in the painting the form of a dragon, the biblical beast that hounded humanity to make a hell of life.

| PERCEPTION KEY | Fagles' and Sexton's "The Starry Night" |

1. How relevant is the imagery of the beast in the poems to an understanding of the content of the painting?
2. Do the poems help you interpret the imagery of the painting in ways that are richer than before you read the poems? Or do the poems distract you from the painting?
3. How effective would the poems be if there were no painting for their subject matter? Could they stand on their own, or must they always be referenced to the painting?
4. Do you understand the painting better because of these poems?
5. Write your own poems about this painting. Or choose another painting reproduced in this book.

SCULPTURE INTERPRETS POETRY:
APOLLO AND DAPHNE

The Roman poet Ovid (43 B.C.–A.D. 17) has inspired artists even into modern times. His masterpiece, *The Metamorphoses,* includes a large number of myths that were of interest to his own time and that have inspired readers of all ages. The title implies changes, virtually all kinds of changes imaginable in the natural and divine world. The sense that the world of Roman deities intersected with humankind had its Greek counterpart in Homer, whose heroes often had to deal with the interference of the gods in their lives. Ovid inspired Shakespeare in literature, Botticelli in painting, and, perhaps most impressively, the sculptor Gian Lorenzo Bernini (1598–1680).

Bernini's technique as a sculptor was without peer in his age. His purposes were quite different from those of most modern sculptors in that he was not particularly interested in "truth to materials" (pages 133–135). If anything, he was more interested in showing how he could defy his materials and make marble appear to be flesh in motion.

Apollo and Daphne (1622–1625) represents a section of *The Metamorphoses* in which the god Apollo falls in love with the nymph Daphne (Figure 13-6). Cupid had previously hit Apollo's heart with an arrow to inflame him, while he hit Daphne with an arrow designed to make her reject love entirely. Cupid did this in revenge for Apollo's having killed the python with a bow and arrow. Apollo woos Daphne fruitlessly, she resists, and he attempts to rape her. As she flees from him she pleads with her father, the river god, Peneius, to rescue her, and he turns her into a laurel tree just as Apollo reaches his prey. Here is the moment in Ovid:

> The god by grace of hope, the girl, despair,
> Still kept their increasing pace until his lips
> Breathed at her shoulder; and almost spent,
> The girl saw waves of a familiar river,
> Her father's home, and in a trembling voice
> Called, "Father, if your waters still hold charms
> To save your daughter, cover with green earth
> This body I wear too well," and as she spoke

FIGURE 13-6
Gian Lorenzo Bernini, *Apollo and Daphne*. 1622–1625. Marble, 8 feet high. Galleria Borghese, Rome. (© Scala/Art Resource, New York)

A soaring drowsiness possessed her; growing
In earth she stood, white thighs embraced by climbing
Bark, her white arms branches, her fair head swaying
In a cloud of leaves; all that was Daphne bowed
In the stirring of the wind, the glittering green
Leaf twined within her hair and she was laurel.

Ovid portrays the moment of metamorphosis as a moment of drowsiness as Daphne becomes rooted and sprouts leaves. It is this instant that Bernini has chosen, an instant during which we can see the normal human form of Apollo, while Daphne's thighs are almost enclosed in bark, her hair and hands growing leaves. The details of this sculpture, whose figures are life-size, are extraordinary. In the Borghese Gallery in Rome, one can walk around the sculpture and examine it up close. The moment of change is so astonishingly wrought that one virtually forgets that it is a sculpture. Bernini has converted the poem into a moment of drama through the medium of sculpture.

Certainly Bernini's sculpture is an "illustration" of a specific moment in *The Metamorphoses,* but it goes beyond illustration. Bernini has brought the moment into a three-dimensional space, with the illusion of the wind blow-ing Apollo's garments and with the pattern of swooping lines producing a sense of motion. From almost any angle, this is an arresting interpretation, even for those who do not recognize the reference to Ovid.

PERCEPTION KEY   Ovid's *The Metamorphoses* and Bernini's *Apollo and Daphne*

1. Bernini's sculpture is famous for its virtuoso perfection of carving. Yet in this work "truth to materials" is largely bypassed. (Compare Michelangelo's *Pietà*, Figure 5-5). Does this diminish the effectiveness of the work? Discuss.
2. Bernini assumed that his audience would realize he was interpreting Ovid's story. Did Bernini choose the right moment for conveying the full power of Ovid's passage on Apollo and Daphne? Is there any other moment that might be of equal interest?
3. If you did not know Ovid's *Metamorphoses,* what would you believe to be the subject matter of the sculpture?
4. Do you believe it is a less interesting work if you do not know Ovid?

PAINTING INTERPRETS DANCE AND MUSIC: *THE DANCE* AND *MUSIC*

Henri Matisse (1869–1954) was commissioned to paint *The Dance* and *Music* (both 1910) by Sergey Shchukin, a wealthy Russian businessman in Moscow who had been a long-time patron. The works were murals for a monumental staircase and, since the Russian Revolution of 1917, have been at the Hermitage in Saint Petersburg (Leningrad). In Matisse's time Shchukin entertained lavishly and his guests were sophisticated, well-traveled, beautifully clothed patrons of the arts who went regularly to the ballet, opera, and lavish orchestral concerts. Matisse made his work stand in stark contrast to the aristocratic world of his potential viewers.

According to Matisse, *The Dance* (Figure 13-7) derived originally from observation of local men and women dancing on the beach in a fishing village in southern France where Matisse lived for a short time. Their *sardana* was a stylized traditional circle dance, but in the Matisse the energy and joy are wild. *The Dance* interprets the idea of dance rather than any particular dance. Moreover, it is clear that Matisse reaches into the earliest history of dance, portraying naked women and a man dancing with abandon on a green mound against a dark blue sky. Their sense of movement is implied in the gesture of each leg, the posture of each figure, and the instability of pose. The figures have been described as primitive, but their hairdos suggest that they might be contemporary dancers returning to nature and dancing in accord with an instinctual sense of motion.

Music is similarly primitive, with a fiddler and pipes player (who look as if they were borrowed from a Picasso painting) and three singers sitting on a mound of earth against a dark blue sky (Figure 13-8). They are painted in the same flat reddish tones as the dancers, and it seems as if they are playing and singing the music that the dancers are themselves hearing. Again, the approach to the art of music is as basic as the approach to the art of dance, except that a violin, of course, would not exist in a primitive society.

FIGURE 13-7
Matisse, *The Dance*. 1910.
Decorative panel, oil on canvas, 102¼ × 125½ inches. The Hermitage, St. Petersburg.
(Photo © Scala/Art Resource, New York. Art © 2003 Succession H. Matisse, Paris/ Artists Rights Society [ARS], New York)

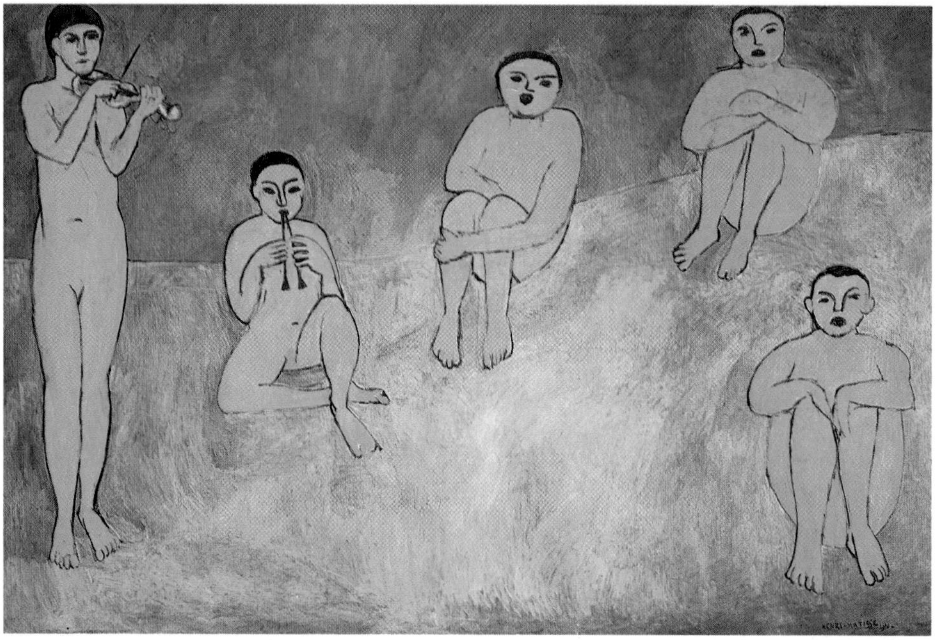

FIGURE 13-8
Matisse, *Music*. 1910. Decorative panel, oil on canvas, 102¼ × 153 inches. The Hermitage, St. Petersburg.
(Photo © Scala/Art Resource, New York. Art © 2003 Succession H. Matisse, Paris/ Artists Rights Society [ARS], New York)

The violin represents the strings and the pipes the woodwind of the modern orchestra, whereas the other musicians use the most basic of instruments, the human voice. The figures are placed linearly as if they were notes on a staff, a musical phrase with three rising tones and one falling tone. Music is interpreted as belonging to a later period than the dance.

The two panels, *The Dance* and *Music,* seem designed to work together to imply an ideal for each art. Instead of interpreting a specific artistic moment, Matisse appears to be striving to interpret the essential nature of both arts.

PERCEPTION KEY   Painting and the Interpretation of *The Dance* and *Music*

1. Must these paintings (Figures 13-7 and 13-8) be hung near each other for both to achieve their complete effect? If they are hung next to one another, would they need to have their titles evident for the viewer to respond fully to them?
2. What qualities of *The Dance* make you feel that kinetic motion is somehow present in the painting? What is dancelike here?
3. What does Matisse do to make *Music* somehow congruent with our ideas of music? Which shapes within the painting most suggest music?
4. Suppose the figures and the setting were painted more realistically. How would that stylistic change affect our perception of the essential nature of dance and music?
5. Does participating with these paintings and reflecting on their achievement help you respond better to dance and music?

It is fitting to close this chapter with questions arising from a film and an opera that take as their subject matter the same source: Thomas Mann's novella *Death in Venice,* published in 1911. Luchino Visconti's 1971 film interprets the story in one way; Benjamin Britten's 1973 opera interprets the story in a significantly different way. Both, however, are faithful to the story. The difference in media has much to do with why the two interpretations of Mann's story are so different despite their basically common subject matter.

PERCEPTION KEY   *Death in Venice:* Three Versions

Read Thomas Mann's novella *Death in Venice* published in 1911. This is a haunting tale—one of the greatest short stories of the twentieth century—of a very disciplined, famous writer who, in his fifties, is physically and mentally exhausted. Gustav von Aschenbach seeks rest by means of a vacation, eventually coming to Venice. On the beach there, he becomes obsessed with the beauty of a boy. Despite Aschenbach's knowledge of a developing epidemic of cholera, he remains, and being afraid the boy will be taken away, withholds information about the epidemic from the boy's mother. Casting aside restraint and shame, Aschenbach even attempts, with the help of a barber, to appear youthful again. Yet Aschenbach, a master of language, never speaks to the boy nor can he find words to articulate the origins of his obsession and love. Collapsing in his chair with a heart attack, he dies as he watches the boy walking off into the sea. Try to see Visconti's film, starring Dirk Bogarde. And listen to Britten's opera with the libretto by Myfanwy Piper, as recorded by London Records, New York City, and starring Peter Pears.

1. Which of these three versions do you find most interesting? Why?
2. Does the film reveal insights about Aschenbach (and ourselves) that are missed in the novella? Does the opera reveal insights that escape both the novella and the film? Be specific. What are the special powers and limitations of these three media?

3. In both the novella and the opera the opening scene has Aschenbach walking by a cemetery in a suburb of Munich. The film opens, however, with shots of Aschenbach coming into Venice in a gondola. Why do you think Visconti did not use Mann's opening? Why, on the other hand, did Britten use Mann's opening?

4. In the film, Aschenbach is portrayed as a composer rather than a writer. Why?

5. In the opera, unlike the film, the dance plays a major role. Why?

6. The hold of a boy over a mature, sophisticated man such as Aschenbach may seem at first highly improbable and contrived. How does Mann make this improbability seem plausible? Visconti? Britten?

7. Is Britten able to articulate the hidden deeper feelings of Aschenbach more vividly than Mann or Visconti? If so, how? What can music do that these other two arts cannot do in this respect? Note Aschenbach's thought in the novella: "Language could but extol, not reproduce, the beauties of the sense." Note also that Visconti often uses the music of Gustav Mahler to help give us insight into the depths of Aschenbach's character. Does this music, as it meshes with the moving images, do so as effectively as Britten's music?

8. Do you think that seeing Britten's opera performed would add significantly to your participation? Note that some opera lovers prefer to hear only the music and shut their eyes most of the time in the opera house.

9. Do these three works complement each other? After seeing the film or listening to the opera, does the novella become richer for you? If so, how is this to be explained?

10. In the novella, Socrates tells Phaedrus, "For beauty, my Phaedrus, beauty alone, is lovely and visible at once. For, mark you, it is the sole aspect of the spiritual which we can perceive through our senses, or bear so to perceive." But in the opera, Socrates asks, "Does beauty lead to wisdom, Phaedrus?" Socrates answers his own question: "Yes, but through the senses . . . and senses lead to passion . . . and passion to the abyss." Why do you think Britten made such a drastic change in emphasis?

11. What insights into our lives are brought to us by these works? For example, do you have a better understanding of the tragedy of beauty and of the connection between beauty and death? Again, do we have an archetype?

Summary

The arts closely interrelate because artists have the same purpose: the revelation of values. They also must use some medium that can be formed to communicate that revelation, and all artists generally share some elements of media. Furthermore, in the forming of their media, artists use the same principles of composition. Thus interaction among the arts is easily accomplished. The arts mix in many ways. *Appropriation* occurs when artists combine their medium with the medium of another art or arts but keep their basic medium clearly dominant. *Synthesis* occurs when artists combine their medium in more or less of a balance with the medium of another art or arts. *Interpretation* occurs when artists use another work of art as their subject matter. Artists constitute a commonwealth—sharing the same end and using similar means.

Bibliography

Beaumarchais, Pierre Augustin de. *The Marriage of Figaro*. Translated by Bernard Sahlins. Chicago: Ivan Dee, 1994.

Biancolli, Louis. *The Mozart Handbook*. New York: Grosset and Dunlap, 1954.

Butler, Christopher. *Early Modernism*. Oxford, England: Clarendon Press, 1994.

Dizikes, John. *Opera in America: A Cultural History*. New Haven, Conn.: Yale University Press, 1993.

Feldman, Edmund Burke. *Varieties of Visual Experience*. New York: Abrams, n.d.

Fleming, William. *Concerts of the Arts: Their Interplay and Modes of Relationship*. Pensacola: University of West Florida Press, 1990.

Horst, Louis. *Modern Dance Forms in Relation to the Other Modern Arts*. New York: Dance Horizons, 1961.

Hunt, John Dixon. *Poetry, Painting, and Gardening during the Eighteenth Century*. Baltimore: Johns Hopkins University Press, 1976.

Lange, Art, and Nathaniel Mackey, eds. *Moment's Notice: Jazz in Poetry and Prose*. Minneapolis: Coffee House Press, 1993.

Meyer, Leonard B. *Music, the Arts, and Ideas*. Chicago: University of Chicago Press, 1994.

Motherwell, Robert, ed. *The Dada Painters and Poets: An Anthology*, 2d ed. Cambridge, Mass: Belknap Press, 1989.

Mozart, Wolfgang Amadeus. *The Marriage of Figaro*. London: John Calder, 1983.

Nakamura, Ako. *The Interface between Art and Music*. New Haven, Conn.: Yale University Press, 1990.

North, Michael. *The Final Sculpture: Public Monuments and Modern Poets*. Ithaca, N.Y.: Cornell University Press, 1985.

Pevsner, Nikolaus. *Academies of Art*. New York: Cambridge University Press, 1940.

Sachs, Curt. *The Commonwealth of Art*. New York: Norton, 1946.

Scharf, Aaron. *Art and Photography*. New York: Penguin, 1974.

Walters, Thomas A. *The Arts: A Comparative Approach to the Arts of Painting, Sculpture, Architecture, Music, and Drama*. Lanham, Md.: University Press of America, 2000.

Internet Resources

CLASSICAL MYTH AND ART

http://www.humanities-interactive.org/ancient/myth/
http://www-lib.haifa.ac.il/www/art/mythology_westart.html
http://www.webcom.com/shownet/medea/grklink.html

LITERATURE AND FILM

http://www.nv.cc.va.us/home/bpool/dogwood/filmdefault.htm
http://www.cocc.edu/humanities/HIR/film/filmadaptation.htm

NATIVE AMERICAN DANCE AND MYTH

http://www.csulb.edu/~d49er/fall98/v5n51-indians.html

OPERA

http://rick.stanford.edu/opera/main.html

POETRY, ART, AND MUSIC

http://easyweb.easynet.co.uk/~c.english/
http://www.recmusic.org/lieder/

ZARZUELA OPERA

http://www.nashwan.demon.co.uk/zarzuela.htm

CHAPTER 14

Is It Art or Something Like It?

Our world is filled with works that obviously are not art. To a much lesser extent there are works that appear to be "almost art," possessing "artlike" characterisics, sharing some of the significant features of works of art. There are "family resemblances." O'Keeffe's *Ghost Ranch Cliffs* (Figure 4-13), universally accepted as a work of art, is described as beautiful, and so are many wallpapers. Cézanne's *Mont Sainte-Victoire* (Figure 2-4) has a balanced structure, and so does Alexei Vasilev's *They Are Talking about Us in Pravda* (see Figure 14-11). Picasso's *Guernica* (Figure 1-4) is shocking and ugly, and so is *ATM Piece* (see Figure 14-23). The traditional distinctions often made between "fine art" and "popular art," "highbrow art" and "lowbrow art," are misleading. We will use a more precise terminology: art and the *artlike*.

In Chapter 2 we argued that a work of art is a form-content. The form of a work of art is more than just an organization of media. Artistic form clarifies, give us insight into some subject matter (something important in our world). A work of art is revelatory of values. Conversely, an artlike work is not revelatory. It has form but lacks a form-content. But what is revelatory to one person might not be to another. What is revelatory to one culture might not be to another. As time passes, a work that was originally not understood as art may become art for both critics and the public — cave paintings are an example (Figure 1-1). It is highly unlikely that the cave painters and their society thought of their works as art. If one argues that art is entirely in the eyes of the beholder, then it is useless to try to distinguish art from the artlike. But we do not agree that art is *entirely* in the eye of the beholder. And we think it is of paramount importance to be able to distinguish art from the artlike. To fail to do so leaves us in chaotic confusion, without any standards. Anything goes. Joyce Kilmer's poetry is just as good as Shakespeare's; Norman Rockwell's painting (see Figure 14-9) is just as good as Raphael's (see Figure 14-14).

However, it is surely important to keep the boundaries between art and the artlike flexible, and the artlike should not be blindly disparaged. Undoubtedly, there are many artlike works — much propaganda, *pornography,* and *shock art,* for example — that may deserve condemnation. But to

General Guidelines for Types of "Artlike" Creations

Traditional   Avant-Garde

I Illustration (Realism)	II Decoration	III Craftwork	IV Design	V Idea Art	VI Performance Art	VII Shock Art	VIII Virtual Art
Advertisement				Dada Duchampism Conceptual Art			
Folk							
Popular							
Propaganda							
Kitsch **C**		**R**		**A**	**F**		**T**

Differences

Works closed	Works open
Establishment	Anti-establishment
Craft emphasized	Craft de- emphasized
Chance avoided	Chance invited
Makers separate from media	Makers may be part of media
Audience separate from work	Audience may be part of work

denigrate the artlike in order to praise art is critical snobbery. For the most part, the artlike plays a very civilizing role — as does, for instance, the often marvelous beauty of crafts. To be unaware, however, of the differences between art and the artlike or to be confused about them weakens our perceptive abilities. This is especially true in our time, for we are inundated with myriads of works that are labeled art, often on no better grounds than that the maker says so. Concepts (beliefs) govern percepts to some extent. Confused concepts lead to confused perceptions. The fundamental and common feature that is shared by art and the artlike is the crafting — the skilled structuring of some medium. The fundamental feature that separates art from the artlike is the revelatory power of that crafting, the form-content (pages 59–62), the clarification of some subject matter. But we may disagree about whether a particular work has revelatory power. The borderline between art and the artlike can be very tenuous. In any case, our judgments should always be understood as debatable.

We shall classify and briefly describe some of the basic types of the artlike. We will use examples mainly from the visual field, not only because that field usually cannot be shut out, but also because that field is the most saturated with what appears to be art. Our classifications will not be exhaustive, for the various manifestations of the artlike, especially in recent years, appear endless. Nor will our classifications be exclusive, for many kinds of the artlike mix with others. For example, folk art always is craftwork, may be decoration, and usually is a popular art.

We shall briefly analyze eight fundamental types of works that often are on or near the boundary of art: illustration, decoration, craftwork, design, idea art, performance art, shock art, and virtual art (see the chart "General Guidelines for Types of 'Artlike' Creations"). This schema omits, especially with respect to the avant-garde, other types and many species. However, we hope that it provides a semblance of organization to a very broad and confusing range of phenomena that rarely have been addressed. The schema, furthermore, should highlight the most important issues. The division between the traditional and the avant-garde points up the powerful shift in the "new art" trends beginning with Dada during World War I. The avant-garde seems to exist in every art tradition, but never has it been so radicalized as in the twentieth century. That is one of the reasons why the art of our time is so extraordinarily interesting from a theoretical perspective. We flock to exhibitions and hear, "What is going on here? This is art? You've got to be kidding." In this chapter, we can only begin to do justice to the controversy and excitement the avant-garde continues to produce. This should be an engaging chapter. Those who are conservative in approaching the avant-garde should remember this caution by the late Jean Dubuffet, the painter-sculptor: "The characteristic property of an inventive art is that it bears no resemblance to art as it is generally recognized and in consequence . . . does not seem like art at all."

The four types placed under "Traditional" on the chart belong fairly clearly under the artlike. Many centuries of professional criticism have made possible something of an objective perspective for such classification. On the other hand, with the four types placed under "Avant-Garde," there has been much less time to develop an objective perspective. Because of the natural instinct that shuns the new, there is a tendency to place all or most of the works of the avant-garde automatically under the artlike. This is surely a mistake. Avant-garde works can be revelatory—they can be art. They do it, however, in different ways from traditional art, as is indicated by the listing under "Differences" on the chart. The key: Does the work give us insight? This eightfold typology is one way of classifying works that are not revelatory, but that does not mean that they cannot have very useful and distinctive functions. The basic function of decoration, for example, is the enhancement of something else. The basic function of idea art is to make us think about art. Every work should be judged by its unique merits. We should be in a much better position now than before the study of this text to make distinctions, however tentative, between art and the artlike.

PERCEPTION KEY   Theories

Our theory of art as revelatory, as giving insight into values, excludes many works. This theory may appear to be mired in a tradition that cannot account for the amazing developments of the avant-garde. Is the theory inadequate? Elitist and exclusionary? As you proceed with this chapter, ask yourself whether the distinction between art and artlike is valid? Useful? If not, what theory would you propose? Or would you be inclined to simply dismiss theories altogether?

The distinctions that we have listed in the chart are generalities, for exceptions (sometimes many) exist. And often the opposition between the traditional and the avant-garde is one of degree. For example, as indicated by the word "craft" stretched out across all of the eight types, craft is a pre-

FIGURE 14-1
Wax figures of former U.S.
presidents. Madame
Tussaud's Wax Museum.
(Courtesy Britain On View,
www.britainonview.com)

requisite of both the traditional and the avant-garde. But craft is usually less demanding in idea art, performance art, and shock art. In virtual art, however, craft of the highest order is generally required. Note that a distinction is being made between *craft,* or crafting, and crafts, or *craftworks*. Craft, or crafting, is the skillful use of some medium (even if, as in some performance art and shock art, the medium includes the maker's body). On the other hand, *crafts,* or *craftworks,* refers to the product of the crafting.

Illustration

REALISM

An *illustration* is almost always realistic; that is, the images closely resemble some object or event. Because of this sharing of realistic features, the following are grouped under Illustration in the chart: advertisement, folk art, popular art, propaganda, and kitsch.

The structure of an illustration portrays, presents, or depicts some object or event as the subject matter. Accordingly, a basically abstract painting or sculpture—for example Mondrian's *Composition in White, Black, and Red* (Figure 1-6)—is never an illustration. Nor is Pollock's *Autumn Rhythm* (Figure 3-2) illustrative, for although there is a suggestion of an autumnal event, there is no close resemblance, and the suggestion probably would not be even noticed without the title. On the other hand, we have no difficulty recognizing that these wax figures in a museum are meant to represent former presidents (Figure 14-1). But do realistic portrayals give us something more than presentation? Some significant interpretation? If we are correct in thinking not, then the forms of these sculptures only *present* their subject matter. They do not *interpret* their subject matter, which is to say that they lack content or artistic meaning. Such forms—providing their portrayals are realistic—produce illustration. They are not artistic forms. They are not form-content (Chapter 2).

FIGURE 14-2
Duane Hanson, *Woman with a Purse*. Rheinisches Bildarchiv, Koln, Germany. (Photo © AKG London. Art © Estate of Duane Hanson/ Licensed by VAGA, New York, NY)

PERCEPTION KEY   *Woman with a Purse*

Is Figure 14-2 a photograph of a real woman? An illustration? A work of art?

The following experience happened to one of the authors:

On entering a large room in the basement gallery of the Wallraf-Richartz Museum in Cologne, Germany, I noticed a woman standing by a large pillar staring at an abstract painting by Frank Stella. She seemed to be having an exceptionally intense participative experience with the Stella. After a few participative experiences of my own with the Stella and some other paintings in that room, I was amazed to find the lady still entranced. My curiosity was aroused. Summoning courage, I moved very close to find that the "woman" was in fact a sculpture—the *trompe l'oeil* was almost unbelievable, becoming recognizable only within a yard or so. Very few visitors in that gallery made my amusing discovery. And when they did, they too were amazed and amused, but no one's attention was held on this lady very long. Any concentrated attention was given to the technical details of the figure. Was the hair real? Were those real fingernails? We decided they were.

The form of the sculpture seemed to be less than artistic, apparently revealing nothing about women or anything else, except exceptional craftsmanship. The late Duane Hanson's *Woman with a Purse* is so extraordinarily realistic that it is a "substitute," a duplicate of the real thing. It is much better crafted than the wax presidents, and it makes a much better conversation piece. Is *Woman with a Purse* an example of art or the artlike? We will return to this question (see Perception Key, page 415).

ADVERTISEMENTS

Advertisements far outnumber works of art, and they are easily identified. They are mostly illustrative, mostly everywhere, and usually accompanied by brand names or logos that indicate their commercial purpose. The imitation of objects and events, especially when they are doctored up to be pleasant in appearance and association, evokes satisfaction, however fleeting. By juxtaposing a relevant and pleasing nonutilitarian image—for instance, a sensuous woman wearing sleek clothing—with an image of something utilitarian, positive associations with the former enhance the salability of the latter. Few indeed will describe such illustrations as works of art when they are presented in an advertising context—with product name, logos, labels, price, and so on. Yet, similar images transformed and taken out of an advertising context may be works of art (Pop Art); consider,

FIGURE 14-3
James Rosenquist, *I Love You with My Ford*. 1961. Oil on canvas, 82¾ × 93½ inches. Moderna Musset, Stockholm. (Photo © AKG London. Art © James Rosenquist/Licensed by VAGA, New York, NY)

for example, James Rosenquist's *I Love You with My Ford* (Figure 14-3). Conversely, works of art, such as Leonardo's *Mona Lisa*, can be transformed into illustrations when incorporated into an advertising context. Visual advertisements, in any case, are almost invariably illustrative, and often art-like, furnished with the color harmonies, symmetry, balance, and other elements of traditional art.

FOLK ART

There is no universally accepted definition of *folk art*. Most experts agree, however, that folk art is outside or below fine art or what we simply have been calling art. Unfortunately, the experts offer little agreement about why.

Folk artists usually are both self-taught and trained to some extent in a nonprofessional tradition. Although not trained by "fine artists," folk artists sometimes are directly influenced by the fine-art tradition, as in the case of Henri Rousseau, who was entranced by the works of Picasso. Folk art is never aristocratic or dictated to by the fashions of the artistic elite, and it is rarely fostered by patrons. Folk art is an expression of the folkways of the "plain society," the average person, the values of the unsophisticated. Often quite provincial, folk art generally is commonsensical, direct, naïve, and earthy. Almost everything that is carefully made and not mass-produced has a folk-art quality—dress, utensils, furniture, carpets, quilts, crockery, toys, *ad infinitum*. After a generation or two, such works often become antiques, and, in turn, increasingly valuable. The craft or skill that produces these things is often of the highest order. The products of a high degree of skill can be described as craftwork, although, of course, not all craftwork is folk art. Crafts do not necessarily express folkways, and usually craftspersons are professionally trained.

PERCEPTION KEY   Photography and Film

Every art seems to have its folk counterpart. Furthermore, every art—with the possible exceptions of photography and film—seems to have evolved from folk art, the dance and music being the most obvious examples. The artlike often precedes art. Why is it apparently problematic whether photography and especially film as art evolved from folk predecessors?

Sometimes there is a dynamic interplay between the "folk" and the "fine." Self-taught Henri Rousseau—called "le Douanier" in reference to his occupation as a customs clerk—accepted the advice of "high-art" painters, whom he greatly admired, to avoid professional training. Yet Rousseau was strongly influenced by the styles of contemporary painters. Conversely, Rousseau—who was treated as a kind of pet by the "professionals"—had important influence not only on Picasso but also on the fantasy painting of the Surrealists, such as Salvador Dali (see Figure 14-13). Folk art, like other art, is never created in total isolation from stylistic influences. Nevertheless, the folk artist, lacking the training of the professional artist, usually exhibits greater technical limitations. Picasso's technical achievements far surpass those of Rousseau. Awkwardness in a Picasso painting—*Guernica*, for example (Figure 1-4)—always appears intentional. Nevertheless, Rousseau developed, through "dogged work" as he described it, some exceptional skills, especially with color, light, and composition. Very few folk painters have been as skillful as Rousseau, although even his work shows lack of skill at times. Technical limitations are a clue to identifying folk art. Another clue is the more or less obvious attempt at realistic portrayals, especially in technologically developed societies. Because folk painters of these cultures tend to share the values of the common person, they usually paint with a commonsense directness things they see rather than ideas, and try to make these things look as they really are. Intentional distortion in this kind of folk art is usually frowned upon. Thus, when folk painting of technologically developed cultures is less than art but is artlike, it is almost always an example of Illustration—the portrayal of easily identifiable objects and events. On the other hand, the folk art of technologically undeveloped societies, such as the works of the North American Indians—the totem pole, for example—tends more toward the nonrealistic. What explains these different tendencies? Perhaps in developed societies, unlike the

FIGURE 14-4
Grandma Moses, *The Quilting Bee*. 1950. (K#883, M#1374). Oil on masonite, 20 × 24 inches. (Copyright 1950 [renewed 1978], Grandma Moses Properties Company, New York.)

FIGURE 14-5
Henri Rousseau, *Old Juniet's Cart*. 1908. Oil on canvas, 38 × 51 inches. (© Réunion des Musées Nationaux/Art Resource, New York)

FIGURE 14-6
Photograph of the Juniet Family and Their Cart, used by Rousseau for *Old Juniet's Cart.* (Courtesy Galerie St. Étienne, New York)

undeveloped, realistic images are everywhere, as in advertisements. That is not to claim, however, that in undeveloped societies realistic images are necessarily lacking; for example, on the totem pole, animals often are very realistically portrayed, as they are in the cave painting (Figure 1-1).

PERCEPTION KEY   Rousseau and Grandma Moses

Superior craftsmanship may or may not create art. The test should focus on the made, not the making.

1. Does *The Quilting Bee* (Figure 14-4) display lack of skill? Does it display exceptional skill?
2. Do you think *The Quilting Bee* was painted in front of an actual scene or from a photograph or from memory? Why?
3. In what basic ways does Grandma Moses's painting differ from Rousseau's (Figure 14-5)?
4. Is Grandma Moses's painting folk art? Whatever you decide, would you classify the painting as art or artlike? Does it present subject matter or does it reveal subject matter? What is the subject matter? If there is content, what is it?
5. We have asserted that Rousseau's paintings usually exhibit both great skill and, paradoxically, lack of skill. Do you find these characteristics in *Old Juniet's Cart?* Explain.
6. Study the photograph (Figure 14-6) that provided the schema for *Old Juniet's Cart.* Rousseau obviously made some drastic rearrangements. What are they? And why? Be as detailed as possible in your answers.
7. Is Rousseau's painting illustration or art? What is the subject matter? If there is a content, what is it?

FIGURE 14-7
Richard Estes, *Baby Doll Lounge*. 1978. Oil on canvas, approximately 36 × 60 inches. (Art © Richard Estes, courtesy Marlborough Gallery, New York. Photo © Artothek)

The Quilting Bee seems to be sharply realistic in intention. One senses that Grandma Moses (Anna Mary Robertson Moses, who started painting in her sixties and was still at it when she died in 1961 at 101) apparently wanted to get in every detail of her memories of the American farm and the rural lifestyle that has vanished, except with groups such as the Amish. This apparent aim toward realistic precision makes the technical limitations stand out. Observe, for example, the static quality of the figures who seem meant to portray movement, the cutout flatness of everything except the landscape, the improbable slant of the floor, and the inaccuracies of proportion and perspective. Compare the absence of technical limitations in Richard Estes' *Baby Doll Lounge* (Figure 14-7). Here the realistic intention is so skillfully crafted that at first sight we may think we are looking at a photograph rather than a painting. Nevertheless, despite the technical limitations, the colors of *The Quilting Bee* work together brilliantly, and the crowded goings-on make a lovely and lively pattern. There is a wonderful charm and innocence (perhaps enhanced by the technical limitations?), a heartwarming nostalgia. Self-taught by doing and isolated from the professional tradition, Grandma Moses is the paradigm of the folk painter. Her work has been almost completely ignored by critics, and those who have bothered for the most part describe her as an illustrator. Do you agree?

Old Juniet's Cart, like *The Quilting Bee,* seems to exhibit technical limitations: The lines and brownish bands of curb, street, and field cut strongly and diagonally to the left, converging in an inconstant way; the human figures and the dog, unlike the horse, look like cutouts; the figures in the cart are very improbably placed; and with reference to traditional perspective almost everything is a bit awry (for example, the footstep of the cart). But with this naivete (some innocent viewers have actually supposed that *Old*

Juniet's Cart was done by a child!), there is an astonishing sophistication. Compare again the composition of the photograph with that of the painting. In the painting the utterly still, self-contained inhabitants of the cart are outlined in a semicircle that is accented by the converse outline of the tree above, whose trunk, in turn, anchors the tree and earth to the cart and its riders. The tree on the right side of the photograph is eliminated, and in the open space in front of the horse the tiny dog, moved from the far left of the photograph, becomes the only moving feature in the frozen moment. The flat-patterned, sharply contoured smooth surfaces of the painting, unlike the surfaces of the photograph, grip together with a tightness that perfectly fits (except for the little dog) the petrified scene. One senses, as with the late piano sonatas of Mozart, that nothing should be changed. The technical deficiencies of *Old Juniet's Cart* are not artistic deficiencies—unlike, perhaps, those of *The Quilting Bee*—for they help create an unreal world, abstracted from the space and time of reality. And yet reality is also very much there. The people in the photograph, for instance, are identifiable in the painting. Thus the strange meeting of the unreal and real, joined as in a dream. There is a suggestion of danger—the little dog moving into the unknown. There seems to be a passionless order of some mysterious kind governing these doomed cart dwellers, so closely packed together and yet each so pathetically alone. Nevertheless, and paradoxically, they appear in harmony with nature—the tree above them is portrayed as unified with them, the whimsical dog in the cart that looks like a monkey is almost at their center, and the horse is friendly.

In this magical mix of the unreal and the real, Rousseau obviously relied upon observation, as the influence of the photograph on his painting shows. In this respect Rousseau is completely within the tradition of folk painting in technologically developed societies. In contrast, the drastic changes Rousseau made in his painting with reference to the photograph show that he painted his *conception* of what he observed, and in this respect Rousseau is more in the tradition of folk painting of technologically undeveloped societies. His imaginative and witty visions created, most critics agree, works of art of very high quality. His paintings may make a difference in our way of perceiving the world, as when sometimes we visually mix fantasy with reality in some strange way. Conversely, Grandma Moses's paintings have had little impact on either craftspeople or artists. Perhaps time will change this. Her paintings seem to be somewhere in a vague area on the boundary between art and artlike. At the very least, they are wonderfully pleasing to the eye.

POPULAR ART

Popular art—a very imprecise category—refers to contemporary works enjoyed by the masses, who presumably lack artistic discrimination. The masses love Norman Rockwell, dismiss Mondrian, and are puzzled by Picasso. Popular art is looked down upon by the "highbrows." Fine art is looked down upon by the "lowbrows."

FIGURE 14-8
Andy Warhol, *One Hundred Cans*. 1962. Oil on canvas, 72 × 52 inches. The Andy Warhol Foundation, Inc. (Photo © The Andy Warhol Foundation, Inc./Art Resource, New York. Art © 2003 Andy Warhol Foundation/ ARS, New York/TM Licensed by Campbell's Soup Co. All rights reserved)

The term *Pop* derives from the term "popular." In the 1960s and 70s Pop Art was at the front edge of the avant-garde, startling to the masses. But as usually happens, time makes the avant-garde less controversial, and in this case the style quickly became popular. The realistic showings of mundane objects were easily comprehended. Here was an art people could understand without those snobbish critics. We see the tomato soup cans in supermarkets. Andy Warhol helps us to look at them as objects worthy of notice (Figure 14-8), especially their blatant repetitive colors and shapes and their useful simplicity. For the masses, we finally have an art that seemingly is revelatory.

PERCEPTION KEY   Pop Art

1. Is Warhol's painting revelatory? If so, about what?
2. Go back to the discussion of Duane Hanson's work (Figure 14-2). If you decide that the Warhol work is art, then can you make a convincing argument that *Lady with a Purse* helps us really *see* ordinary people and thus also is a work of art? These are controversial questions. Discuss.
3. Do you think the Lichtensteins (Chapter 2) and the Rosenquist (Figure 14-3) are accurately described as Pop Art? Are they revelatory?

PERCEPTION KEY   Norman Rockwell's *Freedom from Want*

Next to Andrew Wyeth, Rockwell is probably the most popular and beloved American painter. A very modest man, Rockwell always insisted that he was

FIGURE 14-9
Norman Rockwell, *Freedom from Want*. 1943. Oil on canvas, 45¾ × 35½ inches. From the collection of The Norman Rockwell Museum at Stockbridge, Norman Rockwell Art Collection Trust. (Printed by permission of Norman Rockwell Family Agency. © 1943 The Norman Rockwell Family Entities)

only an illustrator. Does the folksy piety appear sentimental in *Freedom from Want* (Figure 14-9)? Is the scene superficial? Does the scene stir your imagination? Does the painting make any demand on you? Enhance your sensitivity to anything? Enlarge your experience? Is *Freedom from Want* art or illustration? Despite his popularity, Rockwell is almost universally described as an illustrator by the experts. They claim that his works are composed of pictorial clichés. Do you agree? Who anoints the experts? Discuss.

Professional work can be much more realistic than folk art. Professional technical training usually is a prerequisite for achieving the goal of very accurate representation, as anyone who has tried pictorial imitation can attest. Professionals who are realists are better at representation than folk painters, as Richard Estes' *Baby Doll Lounge* (Figure 14-7) demonstrates. Realistic painting done by professionals is one of the most popular kinds of painting, for it requires little or no training or effort to enjoy. Usually, very realistic paintings are illustrations, examples of the artlike. Sometimes, however, realistic painters not only imitate objects and events but also interpret what they imitate, crossing the line from illustration to art.

PERCEPTION KEY   Estes and Rosenquist

1. Does the sharp-focus realism (known as "photo realism" because it is based on photography) of *Baby Doll Lounge* make it an illustration?
2. Note the reflections in the store windows. Do we ever see reflections quite like that? If not, then can one reasonably argue that by means of such transformation Estes heightens our awareness of such "things as they are" in the cityscape?
3. James Rosenquist, one of our most important contemporary painters, worked for a number of years as a sign painter on the huge billboards above Times Square in New York City. Does Rosenquist's work as a billboard painter show in *I Love You with My Ford* (Figure 14-3)? If so, how can we be sure that this is not an advertisement? Have you ever seen a billboard that you would describe as a work of art?
4. Fragmented images are juxtaposed in *I Love You with My Ford*, as happens sometimes when we speed rapidly past billboards. What are the connections of these images? Does the title give a clue? What is the significance of the strange figure, apparently a profile of a man, bending down over the lips of the ashen-gray woman?
5. Is the painting a work of art?

Baby Doll Lounge, in our opinion, is a work of art. Estes worked from a series of photographs, shifting them around in order to portray interesting relationships of abstract shapes as well as the illusion of realism. Thus the buildings in the left background are reflected in the glass in the right foreground, helping—along with the long curving line on the roof of the building slightly left of center—to tie the innumerable rectangles together. A geometrical order has been subtly imposed on a very disorderly scene. Estes has retained so much realistic detail, totally unlike Mondrian in *Broadway Boogie Woogie* (Figure 4-10), that initially we might think we are looking at a photograph. Yet, on second sight it becomes apparent that this cannot be a photograph of an actual scene, for such a complete underlying geometry does not occur in city scenes. Moreover, people are totally absent, a possible but unlikely condition. An anxious, pervasive silence emanates from this painting. Despite the realism, there is a dreamy unreality. Take an early Sunday morning stroll in a large city, with the dwellers still asleep, and see if you do not perceive more because of Estes.

Rosenquist's painting is about sexual involvement (as suggested by the phallic form of the man above the woman and the title) and death (as suggested by the pallor of the woman and the ghastly spaghetti that in the context suggests disemboweled intestines). But is the woman being seduced? Or is she dead, hit by the car? Or are we being given a satirical set of images referring to the mechanization and commercialization of sex? Or is the painting about all of these possibilities and perhaps more? We think so. This painting is a work of art, transcending illustration despite the accurate renditions that are similar to the style of billboard advertising. A student told one of the authors that the painting was so effective it ruined spaghetti for her! This is surely an example of taking heightened sensitivity too far, but, in any case, the work is vividly haunting. The next time you see a man and woman speeding dangerously down a highway in a sleek car, ask yourself if you do not see the event differently because of *I Love You with My Ford*. Again we have an example of the sex–death theme of Shakespeare and Freud (Chapter 8) and Edgar Allan Poe.

The line between realistic painting that is illustration and realistic painting that is art is perhaps particularly difficult to draw with respect to the paintings of Andrew Wyeth, hailed as the "people's painter" and undoubtedly the most popular American painter of all time. His father, N. C. Wyeth, was a gifted, professional illustrator, and he rigorously trained his son in the fundamentals of drawing and painting. Wyeth was also carefully trained in the use of tempera, his favorite medium, by the professional painter Peter Hurd, a brother-in-law. So although a nonacademic and although trained mainly "in the family," Wyeth's training was professional. Wyeth is not a folk painter.

With the great majority of critics, Wyeth is not highly appreciated, although there are outstanding exceptions, such as Thomas Hoving, former director of the Metropolitan Museum of Art. Wyeth is not even mentioned, let alone discussed, in Mahonri Young's *American Realists*. Clement Greenberg, one of the most respected critics of recent times, asserted that realistic works such as Wyeth's are out of date and "result in second-hand, second-rate paintings." In 1987, an exhibition of Wyeth's work was held at the National Gallery of Art in Washington, D.C. Some critics demurred: Wyeth makes superficial pictures that look like "the world as it is," except tidied up and sentimentalized. They claimed that Wyeth is a fine illustrator, like his father, but that the National Gallery of Art should be used for exhibitions of art, not illustrations. Notice again, incidentally, the relevance of the question: What is art?

Wyeth's most beloved and famous painting is *Christina's World* (Figure 14-10). He tells us that

> When I painted it in 1948, *Christina's World* hung all summer in my house in Maine and nobody particularly reacted to it. I thought is this one ever a flat tire. Now I get at least a letter a week from all over the world, usually wanting to know what she's doing. Actually there isn't any definite story. The way this tempera happened, I was in an upstairs room in the Olson house and saw Christina crawling in the field. Later, I went down on the road and made a pencil drawing of the house, but I never went down into the field. You see, my memory was more of a

FIGURE 14-10
Andrew Wyeth, *Christina's World*. 1948. Tempera on gessoed panel, 32¼ × 47¾ inches. The Museum of Modern Art, New York. Purchase. (16.1949) (Image © The Museum of Modern Art, New York/Licensed by Scala/Art Resource, New York)

reality than the thing itself. I didn't put Christina in till the very end. I worked on the hill for months, that brown grass, and kept thinking about her in her pink dress like a faded lobster shell I might find on the beach, crumpled. Finally I got up enough courage to say to her, "Would you mind if I made a drawing of you sitting outside?" and drew her crippled arms and hands. Finally, I was so shy about posing her, I got my wife Betsy to pose for her figure. Then it came time to lay in Christina's figure against that planet I'd created for all those weeks. I put this pink tone on her shoulder — and it almost blew me cross the room.[1]

PERCEPTION KEY   *Christina's World*

1. Does Wyeth's statement strike you as describing the crafting of an illustrator or the "crafting-creating" of an artist? But is such a question relevant to distinguishing illustration from art? Is not *what is made* the issue, not the *making* (Chapter 2)?
2. Would you describe the painting as sentimental (Chapter 12)? Could it be that sometimes critics tag works as sentimental because of elitism?
3. Is this a pretty painting? If so, is such a description derogatory?
4. Try to imagine what the actual scene looked like. Is the painting very different from your image?

---

[1]Wanda M. Corn, *The Art of Andrew Wyeth* (Greenwich, Conn.: New York Graphic Society, 1964), p. 38.

5. Some critics claim that every painting that is a work of art is characterized by a noticeable surface that integrates with whatever is portrayed in depth. If the surface is not noticeably visible, then, in our terms, the form will not inform; then we have—provided the objects and events are realistically portrayed—illustration. With Rockwell's *Freedom from Want*, for example, the surface is invisible, like *transparent* glass. On the other hand, the surface of Cézanne's *Mont Sainte-Victoire* (Figure 2-4) is *translucent*. We do not see straight through the frontal plane of Cézanne's painting, because it affects the way we see everything in depth, somewhat like the way glass with noticeable scratches or tints transforms everything we see behind it. We see the surface as well as the background. One way of testing this, providing you can get to the originals and the lighting is right, is to stand somewhat to the side of the frame and look across the painted surface, ignoring whatever is portrayed in the background. If the surface is transparent, it probably will not make an interesting pattern. If the surface is translucent, it probably will make an interesting pattern. If you have an opportunity of seeing *Christina's World* at the Museum of Modern Art in New York City, decide whether the surface is transparent or translucent. Is it more like Rockwell's painting or Cézanne's?

6. Is *Christina's World* illustration or art? Until you see the original in the museum, keep your judgment more tentative than usual.

PERCEPTION KEY   Illustration and Other Arts

1. In one of his letters, James Thurber observes, "When all things are equal, translucence in writing is more effective than transparency." Do you agree? Find examples in Chapter 7 of translucency versus transparency.

2. The camera, more than any other medium, can produce images that very closely resemble reality. Do the images of the camera tend more to transparency than translucency? If so, does this make photography especially susceptible to the production of illustration rather than the creation of art? Is film equally susceptible? Discuss.

3. When pantomime is used in dance, is it necessarily illustrative of a subject matter, or can it be interpretive?

4. Do you know of any building that as a totality is illustrative?

5. Do you know of any music that as a totality is illustrative?

6. Is there any significant sense in which a poem or a novel can be said to be illustrative? What about drama?

PROPAGANDA

No species of the artlike is likely to be as realistically illustrative as *propaganda*, for mass persuasion requires the easy access of realism. The title of Figure 14-11—*They Are Writing about Us in Pravda*—immediately suggests Soviet political propaganda, for Pravda was the chief propaganda organ of the Russian Communists. Superficially, the painting—with its apparent innocence and realism—might appear to be an example of folk art. And yet it is too well crafted (professionally executed) to be folk. Note, for example, the skillful use of perspective.

FIGURE 14-11
Alexei Vasilev, *They Are
Writing about Us in Pravda.*
1951. Oil on canvas, 39 × 61
inches. (Courtesy Overland
Gallery)

Once the historical context of the painting is understood, one confronts political propaganda of the most blatant kind. The five young harvesters lunch on a beautiful day amidst the golden cornfields of Moldova (eastern Romania). A gleaming green motorcycle is parked on the right side, and on the far left in the middle distance a combine is reaping. Alexei Vasilev produced a picture that in Stalin's words is "national in form and socialist in content." These happy peasants, blessed with modern machinery and the Soviet government, are even happier because of their notice in Pravda.

Everything has been falsified: The Moldavian peasantry had been robbed by the Soviet state of their land, culture, and even language. Most of them were beaten, killed, or exiled. The painting is an artlike work with propaganda as its subject matter.

PERCEPTION KEY   Propaganda

1. If you were a Communist, do you think you would describe the Vasilev as political propaganda?
2. Try to see either *Triumph of the Will* (1936) or *Olympia* (1938) by Leni Riefenstahl (born 1902), a popular actress and film director who worked for Hitler. The camera work is extraordinarily imaginative. The narratives glorify Nazism. Can such a work be art? Discuss.

KITSCH

Kitsch refers to works that realistically depict easily identifiable objects and events in a pretentiously vulgar, awkward, sentimental, and often obscene manner. Kitsch triggers disgust at worst and stock emotions at best, trivializing rather than enriching our understanding of the subject matter. The crafting of kitsch is often minimal. Kitsch is the epitome of the bad artlike,

FIGURE 14-12
Anonymous, *The Girl with a Violin*. (Reprinted from "Pornography and Porno-kitsch," by Ugo Volli. In *Kitsch: The World of Bad Taste*, by Gillo Dorfles, New York: Universe Books, 1968.)

surpassed only, perhaps, by pornography. What possible insights about females or violins or seascapes or the sensuous or whatever are created by *The Girl with a Violin* (Figure 14-12)? Presumably none. Well, then, let us say, it is just non-art. That would not be inaccurate, but there are some minor formal achievements, perhaps, such as balance, symmetry, perspective, color, and linear harmonies. Despite the awkwardness and trashiness, it is at least arguable that the work shares some of the basic characteristics of art.

Study Salvador Dali's *Love and Death* (Figure 14-13). The subject matter is about Dali, sex, and death. Craftsmanship is much more evident than in *The Girl with the Violin*, but what does the extraordinary cleverness reveal about sex and death? It presents Dali as an egoist, hardly an earth-shaking discovery. Dali was associated with the Surrealists in the 1920s and 30s and did some paintings that generally are accepted as art.

> **PERCEPTION KEY** Dali and Rockwell
>
> 1. We have implied that the Dali is not a work of art. Do you agree?
> 2. If the Dali is artlike, is it also kitsch?
> 3. Compare the Dali with the Rockwell (Figure 14-9). Do they differ drastically? If so, in what ways? Is the Rockwell kitsch?

FIGURE 14-13
Salvador Dali, *Love and Death*. (Reprinted from "Pornography and Porno-kitsch," by Ugo Volli. In *Kitsch: The World of Bad Taste*, by Gillo Dorfles, New York: Universe Books, 1968.

Kitsch has been around for centuries, especially since the 1700s, but now it seems to be all pervasive. Bad taste greets us everywhere—tasteless advertisements, silly sitcoms, soap operas, vile music, superficial novels, pornographic images, and on and on. Where, except in virgin nature, is kitsch completely absent? According to Milan Kundera, "The brotherhood of man on earth will be possible only on the base of kitsch." Jacques Sternberg says, "It's long ago taken over the world. If Martians were to take a look at the world they might rename it kitsch." Are these overstatements? As you think about this, take a hard look at the world around you.

Decoration

Decoration is something added to enhance something else, to make it more prominent or attractive or suitable. Decoration is subordinate to what it decorates. Good decoration rarely calls attention to itself. If the decoration dominates a work of art, then as decoration it is inappropriate. Works of art usually control decoration, because the power of their content defies subordination. Sometimes something that often is decorated—such as the frame of a painting—may be an integral part of the painting. For example,

FIGURE 14-14
Raphael, *Madonna della Sedia*. Circa 1516, in a frame circa 1700. Oil on panel. Palazzo Pitti, Florence. (© Scala/Art Resource, New York)

Georges Seurat, the French impressionist of the late nineteenth century, sometimes painted tiny dots on his frames closely matching the dottings on the canvases. To describe the painting on the frames as decoration would be misleading. As you think about this, look at Raphael's *Madonna della Sedia* (Figure 14-14). The frame obviously is strikingly beautiful. Is it an integral part of the painting? Or is it decoration?

The Book of Kells was made in a monastery shortly after A.D. 800 on the island of Iona off the Irish coast, miraculously surviving ninth-century Viking raids of unprecedented destruction. Because Christians of the time believed that the Bible was divinely inspired, they regarded its letters, especially on the first page of one of the Gospels, as having miraculous religious potency. Thus, the letters were painted with special care. On the first page

FIGURE 14-15
Book of Kells, Chi Figure.
Circa A.D. 800. (Trinity College Library, Dublin, Eire/©
The Bridgeman Art Library)

of the Gospel of St. Matthew is a fantastic painting surrounding the Greek letter chi (Figure 14-15). Although the rest of the pages are beautifully printed, this first page is exceptional.

A letter functions as an element of language. The fabulous pattern of lines and colors around the chi enhances our interest in that letter. Thus, it would seem reasonable to assert that the pattern makes the chi more attractive and thus is decoration, is artlike.

PERCEPTION KEY   Book of Kells

Because of the beautiful crafting of its letters, the Book of Kells is often described as "illuminated," suggesting "to light up," "to enlighten." Does this suggest that the *illumination* we have here, at least on this page, is more than decoration? But if so, what is the subject matter? What is the content?

Perhaps on one level the subject matter is abstract, the sensuous, the swirl of lines in endless patterns of exquisite color. So vast are the mazes of patterns, it is impossible to take them all in simultaneously as a whole. Only by successive partial inspections, adding cumulatively, can we more or less comprehend the totality. Few if any works of art have more successfully revealed in such a small area (13 × 19½ inches) the dynamic linear rhythms and color patterns of certain kinds of intricate visual experience—for example, the walls of the Paris subway near the Louvre as one speeds by. Less obviously, there may be a deeper level of subject matter, undoubtedly more evident to ninth-century contemporaries—the awesome complexity and incomprehensibility of the divine. The apparent infinity of line encompassed within such a finite space, it can be argued, reveals something of the majestic mystery of the sacred.

Good decoration is always modest. Only when what is decorated is especially powerful can the decoration also be powerful, providing it still remains secondary in attraction. Consider, for example, Raphael's *Madonna della Sedia* (Figure 14-14). The radiant patterns of the gold-gilt frame—made long after Raphael's death and one of the finest frames of all time—are well worth attention. Yet, the painting is so overwhelming that the frame remains completely subordinate, and properly so. Its beauty enhances the beauty of the painting. Over the years one of the authors has taken a large number of students to the Pitti Palace in Florence to see this work. Afterward, some of them were asked whether there were any portrayals of human faces in the frame. There are four. No student ever noticed.

PERCEPTION KEY   Decoration and Realism

Do you think decoration and realism are easily combined? Why or why not?

For the most part, except when used with works of art of very high quality such as Raphael's *Madonna della Sedia*, decoration avoids realistic portrayals. Decoration and realism normally do not mix very well, because realism tends to distract our attention from what is being decorated. Decoration is rarely an illustration. Our survival depends upon recognizing objects and events, and so when we see them realistically portrayed, our attention automatically tends to focus upon them. Abstract decoration or highly stylized portrayals of things are better suited for the background, as with the Raphael.

Owen Jones, one of the best decorators of the nineteenth century, claimed in his *Grammar of Ornament* (1856) that "Flowers or other natural objects [realistically portrayed] should not be used as ornaments, but conventional [stylized] representations founded upon them should be sufficiently suggestive to convey the intended image to the mind." That principle has prevailed throughout the history of the best decoration. Observe, for example, how excellent interior decoration—wallpaper, furniture, carpets, and the like—tends toward the abstract, and objects, if included at all, are usually presented in highly stylized ways. Events are rarely portrayed, for they tend to be even more attention-grabbing than objects. We are curious beings. We want to know what is going on. Indeed, the abstract tendencies of decoration have been an important factor in the development of abstract painting and sculpture in the twentieth century.

Oscar Wilde, in a remarkable passage in *The Artist as Critic* (1890), both describes the effect of good decoration and foresees its influence on twentieth-century painting:

> The art that is frankly decorative is the art to live with. It is, of all visible arts, the one art that creates in us both mood and temperament. Mere colour, unspoiled by meaning, and unallied with definite form, can speak to the soul in a thousand different ways. The harmony that resides in the delicate proportions of lines and masses becomes mirrored in the mind. The repetitions of patterns give us rest. The marvels of design stir the imagination. In the mere loveliness of the materials employed there are latent elements of culture. Nor is this all. By its deliberate rejection of Nature as the ideal of beauty, as well as of the imitative method of the ordinary painter, decorative art not merely prepares the soul for the reception of true imaginative work, but develops in it that sense of form which is the basis of creative . . . achievement.

Yet, nothing is likely to annoy the abstract artist more than to be called a decorator. This is another indication, incidentally, of how important it is to be as clear as possible about the differences between art and the artlike.

Ideally we *attend* to works of art. Although we may not have time for the painting on the wall or the sculpture in the corner, we know they were meant to be participated with. Good decoration, on the other hand, makes no such demand. Its function is to provide a proper setting or background. Imparting no content, decoration requires no participation. We live comfortably with good decoration, find it fitting, and normally experience it with whatever fluctuating attention we can spare. Good decoration is restful, one of the most valuable amenities of civilized life.

Craftworks

To craft is to skillfully manipulate a medium. Both artists and the makers of the artlike engage in craft. But their crafting produces—granting all kinds of overlappings—different kinds of things. Craftwork usually brings forth an object, often utilitarian, as beautiful or attractive to the eye. Illustration, decoration, and art may or may not be beautiful. Illustration realistically portrays objects and events, depicting subject matter; decoration enhances the decorated; and art reveals subject matter.

The explicit separation of the artist from the craftsperson came to the fore in the practice and theory of the sixteenth century. Leonardo, Raphael, and Michelangelo proudly thought of themselves as artists, and they were recognized as such. Since then the artist generally has been regarded as superior to the craftsperson. In the nineteenth century, during the Industrial Revolution, which began around 1830, the craftsperson seemed to be becoming superfluous. Machine-made, mass-produced products increasingly took the place of craftwork.

Although crafts are often described as handicrafts, made by hand rather than machines, such a description is unduly restrictive. Machines are often used in crafting, and great skill can be involved, particularly with recalcitrant materials such as granite and marble. Craftwork is not, however, mass-produced. And in the late nineteenth century, a strong reaction developed against the mass-produced product. "Arts and Crafts" movements sprang up in America and Europe, especially in England, with John Ruskin and William Morris leading the way. There was a return to the pre-Renaissance conception of the identity of art and crafts.

PERCEPTION KEY   Crafts and Arts

1. Why do we rarely see "Crafts and Arts"? Is this significant? If so, why?
2. Go to a museum or exhibition or sale advertised as "Arts and Crafts." The name suggests that you will find works of art. Do you? If so, is there more art than craftwork?
3. High-quality craftwork presumably can be distinguished from low-quality work. Can you do this? If so, what criteria do you use in making such judgments?

High-quality craftwork generally is distinguished by four characteristics. First, a sensitive selection of and a loving care for the material is exhibited—the sort of thing we previously referred to as "truth to materials" (Chapter 5). In the chart on page 405, "chance avoided" is listed on the same side of the line as craftwork. We need to make an exception here. Good craftspeople often welcome chance—an unexpected twist in a grain of wood, for example—and take advantage of it in their forming. The craftsperson is the medium of the medium. William Morris, the Moses of craftwork, proclaimed in *Arts and Crafts Essays*, 1899: "Never forget the material you are working with, and try always to use it for doing what it can do best: if you feel yourself hampered by the material in which you are working, instead of being helped by it, you have so far not learned your business." Second, if the craftwork is utilitarian, then the form must follow function: The plate must hold the bread, the cup must hold the wine. Furthermore, if there is decoration, it will follow and be subordinate to the form. Third, craftwork, unlike the industrial product, is personal, and generally the more personal the better. Uniqueness of style makes craftwork stand out, makes it more memorable and special, a "signature work." Fourth, craftwork should be beautiful. Beauty as a feature of the craftwork is generally the ultimate aim of the craftsperson.

Crafts and the Other Arts

Crafting as the skillful manipulation of a medium presumably is necessary in the creation of any work of art. We speak of the fine crafting of a poem, for example, or of a piece of music. Yet it is much more natural to speak of the crafting of a medium that is three-dimensional, such as sculpture. Why is this?

Design

A maker of decorative patterns or monograms often is referred to as a designer. We are using the term *designer*, however, to refer to a planner—the maker of a "design" as a guide to the making of something else. In medieval times and before, artists rarely just designed. They often designed, of course, but normally they took part in the making. In the construction of the great Gothic cathedrals for instance, the designers were not called architects but master masons. They often modified their *designs* as they were carrying them out. Thus, during the construction of the Cathedral of Notre Dame in Paris in the thirteenth century, some of the flying buttresses on the upper level began to crack. The master masons on the scaffolds changed their design of these buttresses on the spot. In modern times, architects are almost always just designers. They make the plans: Then the carpenters, plumbers, electricians, bricklayers, and others, do the building, usually under the guidance of a contractor.

I. M. Pei, architect of the East Wing of the National Gallery (Figures 6-30, 6-31, 6-32), designed the John Hancock Building (Figure 14-16) in Boston, and it won a prestigious design award. The firm had little to do with the building process, as is the case with practically all major architectural firms today. The design called for a new material for the windows—double-layered reflective glass. And so it was done, and the winds blew, and the building twisted, and the glass came tumbling down. Now if Pei or his colleagues had been on the scaffolds, at least periodically, they might have corrected the problem, like the master masons of times past. But here is what Pei said during the huge liability case which he won:

> What I can tell you now with considerable satisfaction is that the cause of the glass breakage in the building is now known. It hasn't been tested yet in court, but we are almost certain it's going to be judged that way. That product (the glass) is no longer on the market. You can't buy it anymore. . . . Architects should only set forth performance specifications. The burden of proof should be on the manufacturers. They are the ones making money from it. I don't think architectural firms should be responsible for the testing of materials.

Designer Responsibility

Do you agree with Pei? Why or why not?

FIGURE 14-16
I.M. Pei, John Hancock
Building, Boston. 1976.
(Pei Cobb Freed &
Partners/Gorchev &
Gorchev)

It seems to us that in a way Pei is mistaken. No matter how busy an architectural firm, it should be able to provide continuing on-site guidance. Something of the old master-mason tradition might greatly improve contemporary architecture. Artists, no matter how creative their designing, abandon craftsmanship at their peril. Forms in general should follow the demands of their materials, and usually those demands declare themselves completely only as the work progresses. Even Wright's Kaufman house (Figure 6-13), great as it undoubtedly is, could have been greater if Wright had supervised the making more closely. He came to the site, after great pressure from Kaufman, only after the building was well on its way, and then only about once every six weeks. The interior, for example, is too dark in places, ventilation and humidity controls are often poor, and spaces are sometimes cramped by low ceilings. The cantilevered balconies dipped below the horizontal almost as soon as they were built, and recently they had to be completely rebuilt at enormous expense. There is a story that Kaufman called Wright complaining that water was dripping from the ceiling down on his desk. Wright replied, "Move the desk!" Even the greatest designer is unlikely to foresee everything. So the only remedy is either for the designer to be involved in the crafting or to have a craftsperson of great talent with the power to modify the design in the making. A design is the seed of a work of art. Crafting is its cultivation. In the case of architecture, no matter how original a design (and Wright's design is both exceptionally original and beautiful), it is usually still an example of the artlike on its way to art. The case is less clear with some of the other arts.

PERCEPTION KEY   Design and Other Arts

1. What arts in addition to architecture tend to separate design from the crafting of the work?
2. Do you think that most composers of the symphony, like Joseph Haydn, work with an orchestra as they are composing? If not, are they at a disadvantage? Why or why not? Is the completed score of a symphony a design that must be crafted into fulfillment by a conductor? And if this is the case, ideally, other things being equal, should the conductor be the composer?
3. Do you think that most choreographers of dance work with dancers as they are designing? If not, are they at a disadvantage? Why or why not?
4. Is a written poem a design to be crafted into fulfillment by a speaker? If so, should the poet be the speaker?

Idea Art

Idea art began with the Dadaists around 1916. Although never dominant, idea art has survived throughout the twentieth century by spawning "isms"—*Duchampism,* Conceptualism, Lettrism, New Dadaism, to name just a few—with little consensus about an umbrella name that indicates a common denominator. Idea art raises questions about the presuppositions of traditional art and the art establishment—that is, the traditional artists, critics, philosophers of art, historians, museum keepers, textbook writers, and everyone involved with the preservation, restoration, selling, and buying of traditional art. Sometimes this questioning is hostile, as with the Dadaists. Sometimes it is humorous, as with Marcel Duchamp. And sometimes it is more of an intellectual game, as with many of the conceptual artists. We will limit our discussion to these three species.

DADA

The infantile sound of "dada," chosen for its meaninglessness, became the battle cry of a group of disenchanted young artists who fled World War I and met, mainly by chance, in Zurich, Switzerland, in 1916. Led by the poet Hugo Ball, they assembled at the Cabaret Voltaire. In their view, humanity had forsaken reason—utterly. The mission of Dadaism was to shock a crazed world with expressions of outrageous nonsense, negating every traditional value.

Civilization was the subject of their violent attack, for it had produced maniacs murdering millions in World War I. The movement was joined by such outstanding artists as Hans Arp, Sophie Tauber, Hans Richter, Paul Klee, Francis Picabia, and Duchamp. Except for their talent and hatred of the bourgeoisie and the status quo, they had little in common. Yet, the Dada movement held together for about seven years, spreading rapidly beyond Zurich, locating especially in Paris and New York City. During those years the Dadaists for the most part tried to make works that were not art, at least in the traditional sense, for such art was part of civilization. They usually succeeded, but sometimes they made art in spite of themselves. The influence of the Dadaists on succeeding styles—such as Surrealist, Abstract, environmental, Pop, performance, body, shock, outsider, and conceptual art—has been enormous. Picabia announced:

> Dada itself wants nothing, nothing, nothing, it's doing something so that the public can say: "We understand nothing, nothing, nothing." The Dadaists are nothing, nothing, nothing—certainly they will come to nothing, nothing, nothing.
>   Francis Picabia
>   Who knows nothing, nothing, nothing.

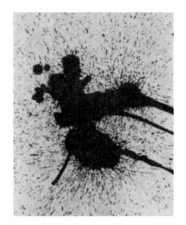

FIGURE 14-17
Francis Picabia, *The Blessed Virgin*, 1920. Ink. Collection unknown. (© 2003 Artists Rights Society [ARS], New York/ADAGP, Paris)

But there is a dilemma: To express nothing is something. Unless one remains silent (sometimes the Dadaists thought of their revolt as "nothing" but a state of mind), there has to be a crafted medium. Picabia's proclamation required the medium of language, and he obviously formed it to say something about "nothing," emphasized by its triadic repetition.

PERCEPTION KEY   Picabia and Schamberg

1. Is *The Blessed Virgin* (Figure 14-17) about nothing? Is the title significant? Is the work anticivilization? Is it a work of art according to the theory of art proposed in this text?
2. Is *God* (Figure 14-18) anticivilization? If so, how? Is it a work of art? Does it belong in a museum of art?

FIGURE 14-18
Morton Schamberg, *God.* © 1918. Wooden miter box and cast iron plumbing trap. Height 10½ inches. Philadelphia Museum of Art: Louise and Walter Arensberg Collection. (Photo by Graydon Wood, 1989)

Picabia dropped ink on paper, and the resulting form is mainly one of chance, one of the earliest examples of a technique later to be exploited by artists such as Jackson Pollock (Figure 3-2). The height of the drop; the type of ink; the color, texture, and dimensions of the paper were controlled, and the result is not entirely formless. Then there is the title. Is it entirely meaningless? If not, is the Virgin to be identified with the ink splash or the white paper? Is this blasphemy? An image of a bursting bomb? Splattered flesh and blood? Chance murder? Meanings gather. Given the social-political context of 1920, this work is surely anticivilization. It defied both social and artistic conventions. Yet, its very defiance obviously conveyed meanings. Unlike a traditional work of art, however, the meanings of *The Blessed Virgin* are suggested rather than embodied in the work. A glance or two suffices,

KEITH ARNATT IS AN ARTIST

FIGURE 14-19
Keith Arnatt, *Keith Arnatt Is an Artist*. Wall inscription exhibited in 1972 at the Tate Gallery in London. (Courtesy Tate Archive)

and that triggers ideas. The form is too loose to hold attention. There is no invitation to participate with *The Blessed Virgin*. We "think at" rather than "think from" (Chapter 2). *The Blessed Virgin,* according to the theory of art proposed in this text, is not a work of art but a work that makes us think about what is art. It is a clear example of idea art.

Schamberg's *God* is what Duchamp called "found art" or a "ready-made"—a plumbing trap upended in a miter box. The material is quite physical, of course, but of little intrinsic interest. It is "dematerialized" in the sense that its importance centers on the ideas it suggests rather than on the material. Notice that, as with *The Blessed Virgin,* the title is essential. Schamberg's title evokes a number of concepts, all hostile to bourgeois society: concepts such as "God has gone down the drain," "capitalism has made technology into God," and "to hell with art as beauty." This work, like *The Blessed Virgin,* is an attack on both society and traditional art.

Idea art does not mix or embody its ideas in the medium. Rather the medium is used to suggest ideas. Medium and ideas are experienced as separate. In turn, idea art tends to increasingly depend upon language for its communication. And in recent years idea art has even generated a species called Lettrism, or word art—see, for example, *Keith Arnatt Is an Artist* (Figure 14-19).

FIGURE 14-20
Marcel Duchamp, *L.H.O.O.Q.*
1919. Drawing, 7¾ × 4⅛
inches. (Photo © Camera-
photo/Art Resource, New
York. Art © 2003 Artists
Rights Society [ARS],
New York)

DUCHAMPISM

Dada, the earliest species of idea art, is characterized by the anger of its assault on civilization. Although Duchamp cooperated with the Dadaists, his
work and the work of those who followed his style (a widespread influence)
is more anti-art and anti-establishment than anticivilization.

> **PERCEPTION KEY**   *L.H.O.O.Q.*
>
> 1. Is *L.H.O.O.Q.* (Figure 14-20) an example of idea art?
> 2. Is *L.H.O.O.Q.* a work of art?

L.H.O.O.Q. is hardly anticivilization, but it is surely anti-art and anti-establishment, funny rather than angry. It is a hilarious comment upon the
tendency to glorify certain works beyond their artistic value. To desecrate
one of the most famous paintings of the Western world was surely a great
idea if you wanted to taunt the art establishment. And ideas gather. Sexual
ambiguity, part of both Leonardo's and Duchamp's legends, is evident in
Leonardo's *Mona Lisa*. By penciling in a mustache and beard, Duchamp

FIGURE 14-21
Marcel Duchamp, *Étant Donnés (Given: 1. The Waterfall, 2. The Illuminating Gas).* 1946–1966. Mixed media, height 95? inches. Philadelphia Museum of Art. Gift of the Cassandra Foundation. (Photo by Graydon Wood, 1996. Art © 2003 Artists Rights Society [ARS], New York/ADAGP, Paris/Estate of Marcel Duchamp)

accents the masculine. By adding the title, he accents the feminine. *L.H.O.O.Q.* is an obscene pun, reading phonetically in French, "Elle a chaud au cul" ("She has a hot ass"). The wit, at least for those not too set in the establishment, was compounded by Duchamp's taking *L.H.O.O.Q.* with him to New York in January 1921. And then Picabia, with Duchamp's permission, produced a remake for his magazine *391* but forgot the beard. Sometime later Hans Arp showed Duchamp the remake, and he added the missing beard and dutifully inscribed: "Moustaches by Picabia, beard by Duchamp." *L.H.O.O.Q.*, like *The Blessed Virgin* and *God*, is far more ideational than retinal. The visual details of the moustache and beard and the lettering of the title are of little concern. The concepts suggested by the work are the main interest, and they seem to have no end.

Perhaps the most famous (or infamous) example of Duchamp's idea art is the ready-made entitled *Fountain*. In 1917 in New York City a group of avant-garde artists, the Society of Independent Artists, put on an exhibition in which anyone could join and exhibit two works merely by paying six dollars. Duchamp submitted a porcelain urinal that he had bought, placed it on its back on a pedestal, and signed it "R. Mutt." Duchamp was claiming, with marvelous irony, that *any* object could be turned into a work of art merely by the artist labeling it as such. How amusing to nettle the jurors by challenging their libertarian principles! Predictably the jury refused to display *Fountain*. Anti-art conquered even the avant-garde. And the ready-made—Duchamp selected and placed on pedestals such things as bottle racks and bicycle wheels—posed the ever-recurring question: What is a work of art? For the art establishment, the whole issue has been destabilizing ever since the rejection of *Fountain* in 1917. Many of Duchamp's ready-mades are now ensconced in museums of art, the ultimate irony. They have great historical interest because of the originality of Duchamp's ideas, their humor, and the questions they raise; and for these reasons their placement in museums seems to be justified. But are they works of art?

Duchamp, like many idea artists, was not a particularly expert craftsperson. He was the consummate intellectual. So in his last years he played chess and did little work, the great exception being an extraordinary structure built for the Philadelphia Museum of Art. *Étant Donnés (Given: 1. The Waterfall, 2. The Illuminating Gas)* (Figure 14-21) is a sculptural environment closed to the public, according to his precise wishes, except for a peephole. The work inside the peephole is fanciful, erotic, and is never to be photographed. As we peep through the peephole, it is difficult to avoid being self-conscious—the next in line may be watching us. At the end of his career, Duchamp made us voyeurs with this work. And we are invited to think about what that means. There is sense in Duchamp's nonsense, much more than meets the eye. Although the retinal is subservient to ideation, perhaps, it seems that we have a work of art. Try to see this strange installation, and think about how you would classify it.

CONCEPTUAL ART

Conceptual art became a movement in the 1960s, led by Sol LeWitt, Jenny Holzer, Carl Andre, Christo, Robert Morris, Walter De Maria, Keith Arnatt, Terry Atkinson, Michael Baldwin, David Bainbridge, and Joseph Kosuth. There was a strategy behind the movement: bring the audience into direct contact with the creative concepts of the artist. LeWitt claimed that "a work of art may be understood as a conductor from the artist's mind to the viewer's," and the less material used the better. The world is so overloaded with traditional art that most museums stash the bulk of their collections in storage bins. Now if we can get along without the material object, then the spaces of museums will not be jammed with this new art, and it will need no conservation, restoration, or any of the other expensive paraphernalia necessitated by the material work of art. Conceptual art floats free from material limitations, can occur anywhere, like a poem, and often costs practically nothing.

In recent years LeWitt has modified his early Conceptualism. In an exhibition in 2001 involving a whole floor of the Whitney Museum in New York City, a vast array of color fields, mainly within large geometrical shapes, blazed out from the walls. LeWitt provided exact detailed blueprints to guide a dozen or so craftspeople. LeWitt did none of the work and very little supervising. He provided the ideas—the rest can be done by anyone with a little skill. The creativity is in the conceptual process that produced the blueprints. The crafting is completely secondary.

FIGURE 14-22
Walter De Maria, *The Broken Kilometer*. 1979. Solid brass bars, each rod two meters long. Long-term installation at Dia Center for the Arts, 393 West Broadway, New York City. (Photo by John Abbott. © Dia Center for the Arts)

PERCEPTION KEY   *The Broken Kilometer*

1. Is this work by Walter De Maria (Figure 14-22) an example of conceptual art?
2. Would its installation require the presence of the artist? The presence of a craftsperson?
3. Is there any way in which this work is derivative from Dada? From Duchamp?

The idea of this example of conceptual art is to put into some kind of visible, total pattern a kilometer of 500 solid brass rods, each two meters long. They can be installed anywhere and in any way, as long as the concept is communicated. The artist's directions are all that is necessary for installation, which can be carried out by janitors. The brass rods have some material interest, and this interest no doubt compromises the conceptuality of *The Broken Kilometer*. The work is more derivative from Duchamp than Dada, for there is protest not against society, as in Dada, but against traditional art, as in Duchamp.

Terry Atkinson and Michael Baldwin collaborated in 1967 on a work entitled *Air Show*. Here is Atkinson's description: "A series of assertions concerning a theoretical usage of a column of air comprising a base of one square mile and of unspecified distance in the vertical dimension." No particular square mile of the surface of the earth was indicated. If you can conceive the concept, you can think it anywhere you like. Harold Rosenberg, art critic at the time for the *New Yorker* magazine, wrote, "Art communicated through documents is a development to the extreme of the Action painting idea that a painting ought to be considered as a record of the artist's creative processes rather than as a physical object." No photographs can be made of *Air Show*. The only material is linguistic. Pure conceptual art, insofar as it seems possible, has been achieved.

Performance Art

Unlike conceptual art, *performance art* (as distinct from the traditional performing arts) brings back physicality, stressing material things as much as or more than it does concepts. There are innumerable kinds of performances, but generally they tend to be site-specific, the site being either constructed or simply found. There rarely is a stage in the traditional style. But performances, as the name suggests, are related to drama. They clearly differ, however, especially from traditional drama, because usually there is no logical or sustained narrative, and perhaps no narrative at all. Sometimes there is an effort to allow for the expression of the subconscious, as in Surrealism. Sometimes provocative anti-establishment social and political views are expressed, rooted in the demonstrations of the 1960s and early 70s against the Vietnam War. Sometimes what happens, like most of the so-called *happenings* of the 60s, cannot be categorized. Generally, however, performances are about the values of the disinherited, the outsiders. Liberals tend to be more sympathetic than conservatives to performances.

Chance is an essential element of the form, which is to say the form is open. There usually is some control that makes possible the unforeseen, the happenings that are not planned. Many performances have instructions for the takeoff, but none for the landing. Repetition of a performance is rare, and close repetition even rarer. Thus, photography may be essential to have some record of the events. The factor of chance may weaken the crafting; for crafting is ordering, and chance is likely to be disordering in a performance situation. Both the artist and the audience may be an integral part of the performance. They can become part of the medium, an extraordinary departure from traditional art. Interaction between artist and audience is often encouraged. According to the performance artist Barbara Smith, "I turn to question the audience to see if their experiences might enlighten mine and break the isolation of my experience, to see if my Performance puts them into the same dilemma." There is a sense of digging for the common, unarticulated experience, especially of oppressed communities. The performance denies its independence, for it implicates the audience in its working. And there is no way of knowing exactly how all of this interaction is going to work out. The performance is an open event, full of suggestive potentialities rather than a self-contained whole, determined and final.

Visual effects are usually strongly emphasized in a performance, often involving expressive movements of the body, bringing performance close to dance. In early performances, language was generally limited. In recent performances, however, language has often come to the fore. Thus Taylor

FIGURE 14-23
William Pope.L, *ATM Piece*.
1997. New York City.
(© Catherine McGann.
Used with permission of
William Pope.L)

Woodrow, a British performer, and two collaborators covered themselves
with spray paint, attached themselves to separate painted canvases by
means of harnesses, stood there for about six hours, and talked with the
curious.

PERCEPTION KEY   *ATM Piece*

William Pope.L offered this 1997 performance in New York (Figure 14-23). He
is festooned with a loincloth made of dollar bills and attached by a rope of
sausages to an ATM near Grand Central Station.

1. Does *ATM Piece* catch your attention? Would it hold your attention for a
   considerable time? Would you tend to "think at" it or "think from" it?
2. Is the anticapitalist subject matter made more meaningful? Would the performance have an impact on your banking activities? On your understanding of capitalism? Or on your feelings about the growing disparity between
   the rich and the poor in the United States?
3. Is the work art or artlike or simply non-art?
4. In many cities, especially the big ones, performances are common. What
   motivates these events? Experience a few. Then analyze and discuss.

We have been assuming that "thinking from" (the participative experience; see Chapter 2) takes time. If a work fails to hold our attention, then
presumably it is not a work of art, because there is insufficient time for anything to be revealed. There is surface recognition but no depth. But what
is sufficient time? This may vary greatly from person to person. For some,

perhaps a minute or so is enough. The ultimate test: Did the experience, however brief, make a significant difference in your understanding of values, of yourself and your world? Generally for most of us insight requires more than a few minutes of participation.

Shock Art

In recent years, works of a bewildering variety have been made that attract and then often astonish, scandalize, or repel. These works have been displayed—presumably as art—both inside and outside of museums. Many performances could also be classified as shock art.

The anti-establishment career of Paul McCarthy began with anti-Vietnam performances in the 1960s and 1970s, and in recent years he has become one of the most well known of the "shockers." McCarthy's work has gradually expanded to include painting, sculpture, architecture (installations), drama, photography, film, and combined media, including his own body. He attacks the sometimes saccharine, Disneyfied view of the world with vengeance, often with horrifying, stomach-churning repulsion. McCarthy probes the depths of the darkest side of the American psyche: fears, terrors, and obsessions. Since September 11, 2001, his work would seem to be increasingly relevant. Taboos, especially the erotic, and even excretion, incest, and bestiality, are portrayed with primal violence. In the carnage of his works—an ugliness that perhaps has never been surpassed—humor occasionally may glint with parody. But McCarthy's works nauseate most people. Try to see some of his work and experience it for yourself. However evaluated, his creations are so powerful that they cannot be dismissed as merely clever. And, surely, no one will be bored.

Much shock art seems to involve little more than clever gimmickry, grabbing but not holding our attention. We love to be shocked, as long as there is no danger. We look with curiosity and often bewilderment. For example, who would place on display a crucifix in a bottle of his urine? The answer is Andres Serrano. Why? And at a recent exhibition at the Guggenheim Museum in New York, someone neatly packaged a piece of his own excrement in a little box, carefully signed, dated, and authenticated. It was placed on a pedestal. Why? One answer might be that these makers lacked the craftsmanship and creativity to make anything better, and the making gains them money and notice, perhaps in a book such as this. But why would the museum directors display such objects? Perhaps because shock art draws crowds. Furthermore, much shock art challenges common assumptions about what is art, and may serve an educational function. Shock art catches our attention, sometimes more strongly than traditional art. But usually, after the initial draw, we do not participate. After the first excited seizure, we turn away and perhaps think (or joke) about the possible meanings. Shock art often are conversation pieces. Much shock art could also be classified as idea art.

In 2001 the Brooklyn Museum of Art presented an exhibition of photography that included the fifteen-foot panel *Yo Mama's Last Supper*, a color photograph of a nude black woman as Christ at the Last Supper. The woman shown is the artist herself, Renee Cox, and she is surrounded by twelve black apostles. The exhibition elicited a strong response from then mayor Rudy Giuliani (remember his reaction to the Museum's 1999 show *Sensation: Young British Artists*, Figures 3-5 and 3-6). Mayor Giuliani declared that he would appoint a commission to set decency (or perhaps indecency) standards — basically "Culture Cops." Do you agree or disagree with the Mayor's decision? These kinds of incidents and issues are becoming more prevalent. Discuss.

Virtual Art

Virtual art is based on computer technology, often producing a mixture of the imaginary and the real. For example, imagine a world in which sculptures act in unpredictable ways: taking on different shapes and colors, stiffening or dancing, talking back or ignoring you, or maybe just dissolving. At a very sophisticated computer laboratory at Boston University, a team of artists and computer craftspeople have created a fascinating installation called *Spiritual Ruins*. One dons a pair of 3-D goggles and grabs a wand. On a large screen a computer projects a vast three-dimensional space within which we appear to be plunged. Sensors pick up and react to the speed and angle of our wand. With this magical instrument, we swoop and soar like a bird over an imaginary or virtual park of sculpture. We are in the scene, part of the work. We have little idea of what the wand will discover next. We may feel anxiety and confrontation, recalling bumping into hostile strangers in the streets. Or the happenings may be peaceful, even pastoral. Embedded microchips may play sculptures like musical instruments. Or sometimes the space around a sculpture may resound with the sounds of nature. Exact repetition never seems to occur. Obviously we are in an imaginary world, and yet because of our activity it also seems real. Our participation is highly playful. If you are familiar with computer training simulators (golf for instance) and computer games and videos — interactive and multisensory — you are already well prepared for the complexities of virtual art.

1. Do you think *Spiritual Ruins* is art or artlike? Use your imagination, for no descriptions or photographs can begin to capture the interactive scenario. Try to see some examples of virtual art. More and more exhibitions are being presented, especially at the larger museums.

2. You will find that *Spiritual Ruins* belongs to only one of many species of virtual art. It should be fascinating to watch the new developments in this field. Ask yourself as it grows whether it is art or artlike.

3. The switch from the large screens of the computer laboratories and museums (six or so people can interact with *Spiritual Ruins* in its Boston

location) to your personal computer screen will make a dramatic difference, just as seeing *Titanic* in the theater is very different from seeing it on a video. Public space is reduced to private space. Although interactivity will still be present, do you think it will be a significant factor in your experience?

4. Frank Gehry, along with many other architects, is using the computer to discover the possibilities inherent in his designs. Computer-created sounds have produced new kinds of music, as in the work of Milton Babbitt. Do you think the computer can be useful in any of the other arts? If so, which ones? And how? Discuss.

5. We have claimed that to "get" the content of a work of art we must "think from" the work rather than "think at" it. If you activate a work by using a wand or a mouse, will this necessarily involve "thinking at"? Discuss.

Computer technology promises to have a powerful influence on the arts of the twenty-first century. Perhaps "computer artists" will become the artists of the future. It seems that technological advances inevitably generate new art forms. For example, photography had an impact on painting (Chapter 12) and led to film (Chapter 11).

At the Whitney Museum of American Art in New York City, in spring 2001, a large array of works was exhibited based on digital technology. Many of the works were more experimental than accomplished, artlike rather than art, but Jeremy Blake's *Station to Station* (Figure 14-24) was exceptional. Five boxlike panels, a couple inches in depth, were placed on a white wall, each panel about 3 × 2 feet and separated by about 3 feet from each other. They were animated by monitors in a left-right sequence. Here is the write-up: There is the suggestion of a "trip from an inner-city train station, through a transition zone of abstract colors and forms to a station located on the edge of a modular residential development high above a sprawling city. A recurring image of a wall of train-station lockers creates a unifying compositional grid upon which variations of locale, interior and exterior, and times of day are transposed." Blake describes these panels as "time-based paintings." Although there is no interactivity as in *Spiritual Ruins,* the sense of the paintings being caught in temporal sequences combines something of reality with what otherwise is an imaginary world.

The virtual reality and moving images of such works, however different in many other ways, associate them with film. The grids of Blake's work are reminiscent of Mondrian (Figure 1-6), and the subtle nuances of color are reminiscent of Rothko (Figure 4-11). The variations of moving shapes in the two panels between the three stations suggest something of what is seen from a moving train. The visual patterns continually change as one's eye moves almost hypnotically from panel to panel. The range of colors—the computer can make 16 million!—allowed Blake to create hundreds of extraordinary color combinations that appear unending. The temporal unfolding of imagery completely breaks down the "all-at-onceness" (pages 93–94) of traditional painting. It also breaks down our sense of the unreal as clearly distinct from the real. Try to see this amazing work and see if it does not make your next train ride more interesting.

PERCEPTION KEY   Classification

1. Return to the chart (page 405). Can you think of a better way of classifying the artlike? Be as detailed as possible.
2. Does the study of the artlike clarify your understanding of what art is? Discuss.

Summary

Artlike works share many basic features with art, unlike works of non-art. But the artlike lacks a revealed subject matter, a content that brings fresh meaning into our lives. The artlike can be attention-holding, as with illustration; or fitting, as with decoration; or beautiful, as with craftwork; or foreseeing, as with design; or thought-provoking, as with idea art; or attention-grabbing, as with performance art; or scandalizing, as with shock art; or fantasy absorbing, as with virtual art. Art may have these features also, but what "works" in a work of art is a revelation. The artlike generally does not lend itself to sustained participation (Chapter 2) and that is because it lacks revelatory power. Yet, what sustains participation varies from person to person. Dogmatic judgments about what is art and what is artlike are counterproductive. We hope that this provides a stimulus for open-minded but guided discussions.

Bibliography

Alberro, Alexander, and Patricia Norvell, eds. *Recording Conceptual Art*. Berkeley: University of California Press, 2001.

Battcock, Gregory, ed. *Idea Art*. New York: Dutton, 1973.

Bishop, Robert. *Folk Painters of America*. New York: Dutton, 1979.

Bishop, Robert, and Patricia Coblentz. *American Decorative Arts*. New York: Abrams, 1982.

Carlson, Marvin. *Performance: A Critical Introduction*. New York: Routledge, 1996.

Childs, Elizabeth C., ed. *Suspended License: Censorship and the Visual Arts*. Madison: University of Wisconsin Press, 1997.

Crowther, Paul. *The Language of the Twentieth Century Art: A Conceptual History*. New Haven, Conn.: Yale University Press, 1998.

Freeland, Cynthia. *But Is It Art?* New York: Oxford University Press, 2001.

Gale, Matthew. *Dada and Surrealism*. London: Phaidon, 1997.

Gottlieb, Carla. *Beyond Modern Art*. New York: Dutton, 1976.

Grillo, Paul Jacques. *What Is Design?* Chicago: P. Theobold, 1960.

Harrison, Charles. *Modernism*. New York: Cambridge University Press, 1998.

Henri, Adrian. *Total Art: Environments, Happenings, and Performance*. New York: Praeger, 1974.

Hosbaum, Eric. *Behind the Times: The Decline and Fall of the Twentieth Century Avant-Gardes*. New York: Thames and Hudson, 1999.

Jones, Amelia. *Body Art: Performing the Subject*. Minneapolis: University of Minnesota, 1998.

Lipman, Jean, and Alice Winchester. *The Flowering of American Folk Art*. New York: Viking, 1974.

Lucie-Smith, Edward. *The Story of Craft*. Ithaca, N.Y.: Cornell University Press, 1981.

Marling, Karal Ann. *Norman Rockwell*. New York: Abrams, 1997.

Sayre, Henry M. *The Object of Performance*. Chicago: University of Chicago Press, 1989.

Schwarz, Arturo. *The Complete Works of Marcel Duchamp*. New York: Abrams, 1970.

Self-Taught Artists of the Twentieth Century. San Francisco: Chronicle Books, 1998.

Siegel, Jeanne. *Artwords*. Ann Arbor, Mich.: UMI Research Press, 1985.

Smith, Paul J. *Craft Today*. New York: American Craft Museum, 1986.

Internet Resources

ABNORMAL ART

http://www.abnormalart.com/

AMERICAN FOLK ART MUSEUM

http://www.folkartmuseum.org

APPRECIATION OF ART

http://www.appreciation-of-art.com/

FANTASY ART

http://www.frankwu.com/

JOSE POSADA: MEXICAN FOLK ART

http://www.hawaii.edu/artgallery/posada.html

KITSCH ART

http://www.badtaste.nl/

MUSEUM OF BAD ART, BOSTON

http://glyphs.com/moda/

PAINT BY NUMBERS KITSCH

http://artscenecal.com/ArticlesFile/Archive/Articles1998/Articles0398/PaintBy NumbersA.html

ROYAL ONTARIO MUSEUM

http://www.rom.on.ca/

VICTORIA AND ALBERT MUSEUM

http://www.vam.ac.uk/

CHAPTER 15

The Interrelationships of the Humanities

The Humanities and the Sciences

In the opening pages of Chapter 1, we referred to the humanities as that broad range of creative activities and studies that are usually contrasted with mathematics and the advanced sciences, mainly because in the humanities strictly objective or scientific standards usually do not dominate.

Most college and university catalogs contain a grouping of courses called the humanities. First, studies such as literature, the visual arts, music, history, *philosophy*, and *theology* are almost invariably included. Second, studies such as psychology, anthropology, sociology, political science, economics, business administration, and education may or may not be included. Third, studies such as physics, chemistry, biology, mathematics, and engineering are never included. The reason the last group is excluded is obvious — strict scientific or objective standards are clearly applicable. With the second group, these high standards are not always so clearly applicable. There is uncertainty about whether they belong with the sciences or the humanities. For example, most psychologists who experiment with animals apply the scientific method as rigorously as any biologist. But there are also psychologists — C. G. Jung, for instance — who speculate about such phenomena as the "collective unconscious" and the role of myth (Chapter 8). To judge their work strictly by scientific methods is to miss their contributions. Where then should psychology and the subjects in this group be placed? In the case of the first group, finally, the arts are invariably listed under the humanities. But then so are history, philosophy, and theology. Thus, as the title of this book implies, the humanities include subjects other than the arts. Then how are the arts distinguished from the other humanities? And what is the relationship between the arts and these other humanities?

These are broad and complex questions. Concerning the placement of the studies in group two, it is usually best to take each department case by case. If, for example, a department of psychology is dominated by experimentalists, as is most likely in the United States, it would seem most useful to place that department with the sciences. And the same approach can be made to all the studies in group two. In most cases, probably, you will discover that clear-cut placements into the humanities or the sciences are misleading. Furthermore, even the subjects that are almost always grouped within either the humanities or the sciences cannot always be neatly cataloged. Rigorous objective standards may be applied in any of the humanities. Thus painting can be approached as a science—by the historian of medieval painting, for example, who measures, as precisely as any engineer, the evolving sizes of haloes. On the other hand, the beauty of mathematics—its economy and elegance of proof—can excite the lover of mathematics as much as, if not more than, painting. Edna St. Vincent Millay proclaimed that "Euclid alone has looked on beauty bare." And so the separation of the humanities and the sciences should not be observed rigidly. The separation is useful mainly because it indicates the dominance or the subordinance of the strict scientific method in the various disciplines.

The Arts and the Other Humanities

Artists are humanists. But artists differ from the other humanists primarily because they create works that reveal values. Artists are sensitive to the important concerns or values of their society. That is their subject matter in the broadest sense. They create artistic forms that clarify these values. The other humanists—such as historians, philosophers, and theologians—reflect upon, rather than reveal, values. They study values as given, as they find them. They try to describe and explain values—their causes and consequences. Furthermore, they may judge these values as good or bad. Thus, like artists they, too, try to clarify values; but they do this by means of analysis (see Chapter 3) rather than artistic revelation.

CONCEPTION KEY   Artists and Other Humanists

1. Explain how the work of an artist might be of significance to the historian, philosopher, and theologian.
2. Select works of art that we have discussed in this book that you think might be of greatest significance to these other humanists. Ask others to do the same. Then compare and discuss your selections.
3. Can you find any works of art we have discussed that you think would have no significance whatsoever to any of the other humanists? If so, explain.

In their studies, the other humanists do not transform values, as artistic revelation does. If they take advantage of the revealing role of the arts, their studies often will be enhanced because, other things being equal, they will have a more penetrating understanding of the values they are studying. This is basically the help that the artists can give to the other humanists. Suppose, for example, a historian is trying to understand the bombing of Guernica by the Fascists in the Spanish Civil War. Suppose he or she has explored all factual resources. Even then something very important may be left out: a vivid awareness of the suffering of the noncombatants. To gain insight into that pain, Picasso's *Guernica* (Figure 1-4) may be very helpful.

CONCEPTION KEY   Other Humanists and Artists

1. Is there anything that Picasso may have learned from historians that he used in painting *Guernica?*
2. Picasso painted a night bombing, but the actual bombing occurred in daylight. Why the change? As you think about this, remember that the artist transforms in order to inform.

Other humanists, such as critics and sociologists, may aid artists by their study of values. For example, in this book we have concerned ourselves in some detail with criticism—the description, interpretation, and evaluation of works of art. Criticism is a humanistic discipline because it usually studies values—those revealed in works of art—without strictly applying scientific or objective standards. Good critics aid our understanding of works of art. We become more sensitively aware of the revealed values. This deeper understanding brings us into closer rapport with artists, and such rapport helps sustain their confidence in their work.

Artists reveal values; the other humanists study values. That does not mean that artists may not study values, but rather that such study, if any, is subordinated to revealing values in an artistic form that attracts our participation.

PERCEIVING AND THINKING

Another basic difference between the arts and the other humanities is the way perceiving dominates in the arts whereas thinking dominates in the other humanities. Of course, perceiving and thinking almost always go together. When we are aware of red striking our eyes, we are perceiving, but normally our brain is also conceiving, more or less explicitly, the idea "red." On the other hand, when we conceive the idea "red" with our eyes closed, we almost invariably remember some specific or generalized image of some perceptible red. Probably the infant only perceives, and as we are sinking into unconsciousness from illness or a blow on the head it may be that all ideas or concepts are wiped out. It may be, conversely, that conceiving sometimes occurs without any element of perceiving. Descartes, the great seventeenth-century philosopher, thought so. Most philosophers and psychologists believe, however, that even the most abstract thinking of mathematicians, since it still must be done with perceptible signs such as numbers, necessarily includes residues of perception.

Perception and Conception

1. Think of examples in your experience in which percepts dominate concepts, and vice versa. Which kind of experience do you enjoy the most? Does your answer tell you anything about yourself?
2. Is it easily possible for you to shift gears from conceptually dominated thinking to perceptually dominated thinking? For example, if you are studying intensely some theoretical or practical problem — "thinking at" — do you find it difficult to begin to "think from" some work of art? Or, conversely, if you have been participating with a work of art, do you find it difficult to begin to "think at" some theoretical or practical problem? Do your answers tell you anything about yourself?
3. Select from the chapter on literature (Chapter 7) the poem that seems to demand the most from your perceptual faculties and the least from your conceptual faculties. Then select the poem that seems to demand the most from your conceptual faculties and the least from your perceptual faculties. Which poem do you like better? Does your answer tell you anything about yourself?
4. Which of the arts that we have studied seems to demand the most from your perceptual faculties? Your conceptual faculties? Why? Which art do you like better? Does your answer tell you anything about yourself?

It seems evident that perceiving without some thinking is little more than a blooming, buzzing confusion. Thus, all our talk about art in the previous chapters has been a conceptualizing that we hope has clarified and intensified your perception of specific works of art. But that is not to suggest that conception ought to dominate perception in your participation with a work of art. In fact, if conception dominates, participation will be weakened or prevented — we will be thinking at rather than thinking from. If, as we listen to the sonata form, we concentrate only on identifying the exposition, development, and recapitulation sections, we inevitably would lower the sensitivity of our listening. The harmonies, dissonances, rhythms, tone colors, contrast, and so on would not be clearly heard. Yet, if you were to ask trained music lovers after their listening, they probably could easily name the sections and tell you where such sections occurred, even though they had been thinking from the music. Perception holds us to the specificity of the work. In other words, to experience the arts most intensely and satisfactorily, conception is indispensable, but perception must remain in the foreground. When we come to the other humanities, conception comes to the foreground. The other humanities basically reflect about values rather than reveal values, as in the case of the arts. With the other humanities, therefore, concepts become more central than percepts.

Values

A value is something we care about, something that matters. A value is an object of an interest. The term *object,* however, should be understood as including events or states of affairs. A pie is obviously an object and it may be a value, and the course of action involved in obtaining the pie may also be a value. If we are not interested in something, it is neutral in value or valueless to us. Positive values are those objects of interest that satisfy us or give us pleasure, such as good health. Negative values are those objects of interest that dissatisfy us or give us pain, such as bad health.

When the term "value" is used alone, it usually refers to positive values only, but it may also include negative values. In our value decisions, we generally seek to obtain positive values and avoid negative values. But except for the very young child, these decisions usually involve highly complex activities. To have a tooth pulled is painful, a negative value, but doing so leads to the possibility of better health, a positive value. *Intrinsic values* involve the feelings — such as pleasure and pain — we have of some value activity, such as enjoying good food or experiencing nausea from overeating. *Extrinsic values* are the means to intrinsic values, such as making the money that pays for the food. *Intrinsic–extrinsic values* not only evoke immediate feelings but also are means to further values, such as the enjoyable food that leads to future good health. For most people, intrinsic–extrinsic values of the positive kind are the basis of the good life. Heroin may have great positive intrinsic value, but then extrinsically it probably will have powerful negative value, leading to great suffering.

CONCEPTION KEY   Participation with Art and Values

1. Do you think that the value of a participative experience with a work of art is basically intrinsic, extrinsic, or intrinsic–extrinsic? Explain.
2. Dr. Victor Frankl, a medical doctor and psychiatrist, writes in *The Doctor and the Soul,*

   The higher meaning of a given moment in human existence can be fulfilled by the mere intensity with which it is experienced, and independent of any action. If anyone doubts this, let him consider the following situation. Imagine a music lover sitting in the concert hall while the most noble measures of his favorite symphony resound in his ears. He feels that shiver of emotion which we experience in presence of the purest beauty. Suppose now that at such a moment we should ask this person whether his life has meaning. He would have to reply that it had been worthwhile living if only to experience this ecstatic moment.[1]

   Do you agree with Frankl, or do you consider this an overstatement? Why?
3. It has been variously reported that some of the most sadistic guards and high-ranking officers in the Nazi concentration camps played the music of Bach or Beethoven during or after torturings. Goering was a great lover of excellent paintings. Hitler loved architecture and the music of Wagner. What do you make of this?

Participation with a work of art not only is immediately satisfying but also is usually extrinsically valuable because it leads to deeper satisfactions in the future. To participate with one poem is likely to increase our sensitivity to the next poem. To participate in great moments in music is likely

---

[1]Victor E. Frankl, *The Doctor and the Soul,* trans. Richard and Clara Winston (New York: Knopf, 1955), p. 49.

to strengthen our courage to face the tragic side of existence. To participate with the dance may help us be more graceful. To participate with the visual arts may enhance our seeing and touching.

The most important gift of the arts to our practical life, however, is the understanding it gives us of others. This is especially the gift of literature, for it gives us a sounder orientation with others and deeper sympathy. Literature teaches us compassion, the profoundest of moral virtues. It is possible to compartmentalize one's feeling through acts of will. The insights of the arts can be separated from our moral life, but that seems to occur only rarely. In any case, our hope must be that compartmentalization will be avoided.

CONCEPTION KEY   The Origin of Value

1. Select the work of art discussed in this book that is the most valuable to you. Why is it so valuable?
2. Do you believe that value is projected into things by us, that we discover values in things, or that in some way value originates in the relationship between us and things? Explain.

Values, we propose, involve a valuer and something that excites an interest in the valuer. *Subjectivist theories of value* claim, however, that it is the interest that projects the value on something. The painting, for example, is positively valuable only because it satisfies the interest of someone. Value is in the valuer. If no one is around to project interest, then there are no valuable objects. Value is entirely relative to the valuer. Beauty is in the eye of the beholder. *Objectivist theories of value* claim, conversely, that it is the object that excites the interest. Moreover, the painting is positively valuable even if no one has any interest in it. Value is in the object independently of any subject. Jane is beautiful even if no one is aware of her beauty.

The relational theory of value—which is the one we have been presupposing throughout this book—claims that value emerges from the relation between an interest and an object. A good painting that is satisfying no one's interest at the moment possesses only potential value. A good painting possesses properties that under proper conditions are likely to stimulate the interests of a valuer. The subjectivist would say that this painting has no value whatsoever until someone projects value on it. The objectivist would say that this painting has actualized value inherent in it whether anyone enjoys it or not. The relationalist would say that this painting has potential value, that when it is experienced under proper conditions, a sensitive, informed participant will actualize the potential value. To describe a painting as "good" is the same as saying that the painting has positive potential value. Furthermore, for the relationalist, value is realized only when objects with potential value connect with the interests of someone.

Values are usually studied with reference to the interaction of various kinds of potential value with human interests. For example, criticism tends to focus on the intrinsic values of works of art; economics focuses on commodities as basically extrinsic values; and *ethics* focuses on intrinsic–extrinsic values as they are or ought to be chosen by moral agents.

Values that are described scientifically as they are found we shall call *value facts*. Values that are set forth as norms or ideals or what ought to be we shall call *normative values*. The smoking of marijuana, for instance, is a positive value for some. Much research is being undertaken to provide descriptions of the consequences of the use of marijuana, and rigorous scientific standards are applicable. We would place such research with the sciences. And we would call the values that are described in such research value facts. A scientific report may describe the relevant value facts connected with the use of marijuana, showing, for instance, that people who smoke marijuana generally have such-and-such pleasurable experiences but at the same time incur such-and-such risks. Such a report is describing what is the case, not what ought to be the case (that is, normative values). When someone argues that marijuana should be prohibited or someone else argues that marijuana should be legalized, we are in a realm beyond the strict application of scientific standards. Appeal is being made not to what "is" or to factual value—this the sciences can handle—but to the "ought," or normative value.

CONCEPTION KEY   Factual Value and Normative Value

1. Do you see any possible connection between factual and normative value? For example, will the scientific studies now being made on the use of marijuana have any relevance to your judgment as to whether you should or should not smoke marijuana?
2. Do you think that an artist can reveal anything relevant to your judgment about using marijuana?
3. Do you think humanists other than artists might produce anything relevant to your judgment about the use of marijuana?

There is a very close relationship between factual and normative value. If scientists were to discover that anyone who uses marijuana regularly cannot possibly live longer than ten more years, this obviously would influence the arguments about its legalization. Yet, the basis for a well-grounded decision about such a complex issue—for it is hardly likely that such a clear-cut fact as death within ten years from using marijuana regularly will be discovered—surely involves more than scientific information. Novels such as Aldous Huxley's *Brave New World* reveal aspects and consequences of drug experiences that escape through the nets of scientific investigation. They clarify features of value phenomena that supplement the factual values as discovered by science. After exposure to such literature, we may be in a better position to make well-grounded decisions about such problems as the legalization of marijuana.

The arts and the other humanities often have normative relevance. They may clarify the possibilities for value decisions, thus clarifying what ought to be and what we ought to do. And this is an invaluable function, for we are beings who must constantly choose among various value possibilities. Paradoxically, even not choosing is often a choice. The humanities can help enlighten our choices. Artists help by revealing aspects and consequences of value phenomena that escape scientists. The other humanists help by clarifying aspects and consequences of value phenomena that escape both artists and scientists. For example, the historian or sociologist might trace the consequences of drug use in past societies. Moreover, the other humanists—especially philosophers—can take account of the whole value field, including the relationships between factual and normative values. This is something we are trying to do, however briefly and oversimply, right here.

CONCEPTION KEY Value Decisions

1. You probably have made a judgment about whether or not to use marijuana. Was there any kind of evidence—other than the scientific—that was relevant to your decision? Explain.
2. Reflect about the works of art that we have discussed in this book. Have any of them clarified value possibilities for you in a way that might helpfully influence your value decisions? How? Be as specific as possible. Do some arts seem more relevant than others in this respect? If so, why? Discuss with others. Do you find that people differ a great deal with respect to the arts that are most relevant to their value decisions? If so, how is this to be explained?
3. Do you think that in choosing its political leaders a society is likely to be helped if the arts are flourishing? As you think about this, consider the state of the arts in societies that have chosen wise leaders, as well as the state of the arts in societies that have chosen unwise leaders.
4. Do you think that political leaders are more likely to make wise decisions if they are sensitive to the arts? Back up your answer with reference to specific leaders.
5. Do you think there is any correlation between a flourishing state of the arts and a democracy? A tyranny? Back up your answers with reference to specific governments.

Factual values are verified *experimentally,* put through the tests of the scientific method. Normative values are verified *experientially,* put through the tests of living. Satisfaction, for ourselves and the others involved, is an experiential test that the normative values we chose in a given instance were probably right. Suffering, for ourselves and the others involved, is an experiential test that the normative values we chose were probably wrong. Experiential testing of normative values involves not only the immediacy of experience but also the consequences that follow. If you choose to try heroin, you cannot escape the consequences. And, fortunately, certain novels—Nelson Algren's *Man with the Golden Arm,* for instance—can make you vividly aware of those consequences before you have to suffer them. Science can also point out these consequences, of course, but science cannot make them so forcefully clear and present and thus so thoroughly understandable.

The arts are closely related to the other humanities, especially history, philosophy, and theology. In conclusion, we shall give only a brief sketch of these relationships, for they are enormously complex and require extensive analyses that we can only suggest.

The Arts and History

Historians try to discover the *what* and the *why* of the past. Of course, they need as many relevant facts as possible in order to describe and explain the events that happened. Often they may be able to use the scientific method in their gathering and verification of facts. But in attempting to give as full an explanation as possible as to why some of the events they are tracing happened, they function as humanists, for here they need understanding of "the way things were" as well as and especially the normative values or ideals of the society they are studying. Among their main resources are works of art. Often such works will reveal the norms of a people—their views of birth and death, blessing and disaster, victory and disgrace, endurance and decline, themselves and God, fate and what ought to be. Only with the understanding of such values can history become something more than a catalog of events.

CONCEPTION KEY   The Arts and History

Suppose an ancient town were being excavated but, aside from architecture no works of art had been unearthed. And then some paintings and sculpture, and some poems come to light—all from the local culture. Is it likely that the paintings would give information different from that provided by the architecture or the sculpture? Or what might the poems reveal that the other arts do not? As you reflect on these questions, reflect also on the following description by Martin Heidegger of a painting by Van Gogh of a pair of peasant shoes:

> From the dark opening of the worn insides of the shoes the toilsome tread of the worker stares forth. In the stiffly rugged heaviness of the shoes there is the accumulated tenacity of her slow trudge through the far-spreading and ever-uniform furrows of the field swept by a raw wind. On the leather lie the dampness and richness of the soil. Under the soles slides the loneliness of the field-patch as evening falls. In the shoes vibrates the silent call of the earth, its quiet gift of the ripening grain and its unexplained self-refusal in the fallow desolation of the wintry field. This equipment is pervaded by uncomplaining anxiety as to the certainty of bread, the wordless joy of having once more withstood want, the trembling before the impending childbed and shivering at the surrounding menace of death. This equipment belongs to the earth, and it is protected in the world of the peasant woman.[2]

The Arts and Philosophy

Philosophy is, among other things, an attempt to give reasoned answers to fundamental questions that, because of their generality, are not treated by any of the more specialized disciplines. Ethics, *aesthetics*, and metaphysics (or speculative philosophy), three of the main divisions of philosophy, are

---

[2]Martin Heidegger, "The Origin of the Work of Art," in *Poetry, Language, Thought*, trans. Albert Hofstadter (New York: Harper and Row, 1971), pp. 33ff.

very closely related to the arts. Ethics in part is often the inquiry into the presuppositions or principles operative in our moral judgments and the study of norms or standards for value decisions. If we are correct, an ethic dealing with norms that fails to take advantage of the insights of the arts is inadequate. John Dewey even argued that

> Art is more moral than moralities. For the latter either are, or tend to become, consecrations of the status quo, reflections of custom, reenforcements of the established order. The moral prophets of humanity have always been poets even though they spoke in free verse or by parable.[3]

CONCEPTION KEY   Ethics and the Arts

1. In the quote above, Dewey might seem to be thinking primarily of poets when he speaks of the contribution of artists to the ethicist. Or do you think he is using the term "poets" to include all artists? In any case, do you think that literature has more to contribute to the ethicist than the other arts? If so, why?
2. Reflect on the works of art we have discussed in this book. Which ones do you think might have the most relevance to an ethicist? Why?

Throughout this book we have been elaborating an aesthetics, or philosophy of art. We have been attempting to account to some extent for the whole range of the phenomena of art — the creative process, the work of art, the experience of the work of art, criticism, and the role of art in society. On occasion we have avoided restricting our analysis to any single area within that group, considering the interrelationships of these areas. And on other occasions we have tried to make explicit the basic assumptions of some of the restricted studies. These are typical functions of the aesthetician, or philosopher of art. For example, much of our time has been spent doing criticism — analyzing and appraising particular works of art. But at other times, as in Chapter 3, we tried to make explicit the presuppositions or principles of criticism. Critics, of course, may do this themselves, but then they are functioning more as philosophers than as critics. Furthermore, we have also reflected on how criticism influences artists, participants, and society. This, too, is a function of the philosopher.

Finally, the aim of the metaphysicians, or speculative philosophers, roughly speaking, is to understand reality as a totality. Therefore they must take into account the artifacts of the artists as well as the conclusions and reflections of the other humanists and the scientists. Metaphysicians attempt to reflect on the whole in order to achieve some valid general conclusions concerning the nature of reality and our position and prospects in it. A metaphysician who ignores the arts will have left out some of the most useful insights about value phenomena, which are very much a fundamental part of our reality.

---

[3]John Dewey, *Art as Experience* (New York: Minton, Balch, 1934), p. 348.

The Arts and Theology

The practice of religion, strictly speaking, is not a humanistic activity or study, for basically it neither reveals values in the way of the arts nor studies values in the way of the other humanities. A religion is an institution that brings people together for the purpose of worship. These people share beliefs about their religious experiences. Since the beliefs of various people differ, it is more accurate to refer to religions than to religion. Nevertheless, there is a commonsense basis, reflected in our ordinary language, for the term *religion*. Despite the differences about their beliefs, religious people generally agree that their religious values—for example, achieving, in some sense, communion with the sacred—are ultimate, that is, more important than any other values. They have ultimate concern for these values. Moreover, a common nucleus of experience seems to be shared by all religious people: (1) uneasy awareness of the limitations of human moral and theoretical powers; (2) awe-full awareness of a further reality, a majestic mystery, beyond or behind or within the world of our sense experience; (3) conviction that communion with this further reality is of supreme importance.

Theology involves the study of religions. As indicated in Chapter 1, the humanities in the medieval period were studies about humans, whereas theology and related studies were studies about God. But in present times theology, usually broadly conceived, is placed with the humanities. Moreover, for many religious people today, ultimate values or the values of the sacred are not necessarily ensconced in another world "up there." In any case, some works of art—the masterpieces—reveal ultimate values in ways that are relevant to the contemporary situation. Theologians who ignore these revelations cannot do justice to their study of religions.

CONCEPTION KEY   Religious Values and the Arts

Reflect about the works of art you know best. Have any of them revealed ultimate values to you in a way that is relevant to your situation? How? Are they necessarily contemporary works?

Dietrich Bonhoeffer, in one of his last letters from the Nazi prison of Tegel, noted that "now that it has become of age, the world is more Godless, and perhaps it is for that very reason nearer to God than ever before." Our artists, secular as well as religious, not only reveal our despair but also, in the depths of that darkness, open paths back to the sacred.

At the end of the nineteenth century, Matthew Arnold intimated that the aesthetic or participative experience, especially of the arts, would become the religious experience. We do not think this transformation will happen because the participative experience lacks the outward expressions, such as worship, that fulfill and in turn distinguish the religious experience. But Arnold was prophetic, we believe, in sensing that increasingly the arts would provide the most direct access to the sacred. Iris Murdoch, the late Anglo-Irish novelist, describes such an experience:

Dora had been in the National Gallery a thousand times and the pictures were almost as familiar to her as her own face. Passing between them now, as through a well-loved grove, she felt a calm descending on her. She wandered a little, watching with compassion the poor visitors armed with guidebooks who were peering anxiously at the masterpieces. Dora did not need to peer. She could look, as one can at last when one knows a great thing very well, confronting it with a dignity which it has itself conferred. She felt that the pictures belonged to her. . . . Vaguely, consoled by the presence of something welcoming and responding in the place, her footsteps took her to various shrines at which she had worshipped so often before.[4]

Such experiences may be rare. Most of us still require the guidebooks. But one hopes the time will come when we no longer just peer but also participate. And when that time comes, a guide to the guidebooks like this one may have its justification.

Summary

The arts and the other humanities are distinguished from the sciences because in the former, generally, strictly objective or scientific standards are irrelevant. In turn, the arts are distinguished from the other humanities because in the arts values are revealed, whereas in the other humanities values are studied. Furthermore, in the arts perception dominates, whereas in the other humanities conception dominates.

In our discussion about values, we distinguish between (1) intrinsic values—activities involving immediacy of feeling, positive or negative; (2) extrinsic values—activities that are means to intrinsic values; and (3) intrinsic–extrinsic values—activities that not only are means to intrinsic values but also involve significant immediacy of feeling. A value is something we care about, something that matters. The theory of value presupposed in this book has been relational; that is, value emerges from the relation between a human interest and an object or event. Value is not merely subjective—projected by human interest on some object or event—nor is value merely objective—valuable independently of any subject. Values that are described scientifically we call *value facts*. Values set forth as norms or ideals or what ought to be we call *normative values*. The arts and the other humanities often have normative relevance: by clarifying what ought to be and thus what we ought to do.

Finally, the arts are closely related to the other humanities, especially history, philosophy, and theology. The arts help reveal the normative values of past cultures to the historian. Philosophers attempt to answer questions about values, especially in the fields of ethics, aesthetics, and metaphysics. Some of the most useful insights about value phenomena for the philosopher come from artists. Theology involves the study of religions, and religions are grounded in ultimate concern for values. No human artifacts reveal ultimate values more powerfully to the theologian than works of art.

---

[4]*The Bell*, by Iris Murdoch, copyright © 1958 by Iris Murdoch. Reprinted by permission of The Viking Press, Inc., New York, and Chatto and Windus Ltd., London, p. 182.

Bibliography

Bronowski, J. *The Ascent of Man*. Boston: Little, Brown, 1973.

Carroll, Noel. *A Philosophy of Mass Art*. New York: Oxford University Press, 1998.

Fleming, William. *Arts and Ideas*, 9th ed. Fort Worth: Harcourt Brace, 1995.

Greenberg, Clement. *Art and Culture*. Boston: Beacon, 1989.

Hall, James B., and Barry Ulanov. *Modern Culture and the Arts*, 2d ed. New York: McGraw-Hill, 1972.

Haskell, Francis. *History and Its Images*. New Haven, Conn.: Yale University Press, 1992.

Hauser, Arnold. *The Philosophy of Art History*. Evanston, Ill.: Northwestern University Press, 1985.

Heidegger, Martin. *Poetry, Language, Thought*. Translated by Albert Hofstadter. New York: Harper, 1975.

Kaprow, Allan. *Essays on the Blurring of Art and Life*. Berkeley: University of California, 1993.

Lanham, Richard A. *The Electronic Word: Democracy, Technology, and the Arts*. Chicago: University of Chicago Press, 1994.

Martin, F. David. *Art and the Religious Experience*. Cranbury, N.J.: Associated University Press, 1972.

Maslow, Abraham. *New Knowledge in Human Values*. Chicago: Regnery, 1970.

Murdoch, Iris. *The Fire and the Sun: Why Plato Banished the Artists*. New York: Oxford University Press, 1977.

Panofsky, Erwin. *Idea: A Concept in Art*. New York: Harper and Row, 1975.

Rader, Melvin, and Bertram Jessup. *Art and Human Values*. Englewood Cliffs, N.J.: Prentice-Hall, 1976.

Read, Herbert. *Education through Art*, 3d ed. London: Faber and Faber, 1958.

Scruton, Roger. *An Intelligent Person's Guide to Modern Culture*. South Bend, Ind.: St. Augustine's Press, 2000.

Wilson, Robert N. *The Arts in Society*. Englewood Cliffs, N.J.: Prentice-Hall, 1964.

Wolterstorff, Nicholas. *Art in Action*. Grand Rapids, Mich.: William B. Eerdmans, 1980.

Internet Resources

ARIZONA STATE UNIVERSITY HUMANITIES HUB

http://www.asu.edu/clas/humnews/

HUMANITIES PORTALS

http://gateway.library.uiuc.edu/hix/internet_resources.htm

HUMANITIES TEXT INITIATIVE

http://www.hti.umich.edu/

HUMBUL HUMANITIES HUB

http://www.humbul.ac.uk/

THE OXFORD TEXT ARCHIVE

http://ota.ahds.ac.uk/

THE VIRTUAL LIBRARY: HUMANITIES

http://vlib.org/Humanities.html

Glossary

A-B-A In music, a three-part structure that consists of an opening section, a second section, and a return to the first section.

Abstract painting Painting that has the sensuous as its subject matter. See *representational painting*.

Acrylic In painting, pigment bound by a synthetic plastic substance, allowing it to dry much faster than oils.

Adagio A musical term denoting a slow and graceful tempo.

Aerial perspective The indication of distance in painting by means of dimming light and atmosphere. See *perspective*.

Aesthetics A philosophy of art: the study of the creative process, the work of art, the aesthetic experience, principles of criticism, and the role of art in society.

Allegory An expression by means of symbols, used to make a more effective generalization or moral commentary about human experience.

Allegretto A musical term denoting a lively tempo but one slower than allegro.

Allegro A musical term denoting a lively and brisk tempo.

Ambiguity Uncertain meaning, a situation in which several meanings are implied. Sometimes implies contradictory meanings.

Andante A musical term denoting a leisurely tempo.

Appropriation In the arts, the act of combining the artist's basic medium with the medium of another art or arts, but keeping the basic medium clearly dominant. See *synthesis* and *interpretation*.

Arabesque A classical ballet pose in which the body is supported on one leg, and the other leg is extended behind with the knee straight.

Arch In architecture, a structural system in which space is spanned by a curved member supported by two legs.

Archetype An idea or behavioral pattern, often formed in prehistoric times, that becomes a part of the unconscious psyche of a people. The archetype is embedded in the "collective unconscious." The term comes from Jungian psychology and has been associated by Jung with myth. In the arts, the archetype is usually expressed as a narrative pattern, such as the quest for personal identity. See *myth*.

Aria An elaborate solo song used primarily in operas, oratorios, and cantatas.

Artistic form The organization of a medium that clarifies or reveals a subject matter. See *subject matter, content, decorative form*, and *work of art*.

Artlike Works that possess some characteristics of works of art but lack revelatory power.

Assemblage The technique of sculpture, such as welding, whereby preformed pieces are attached. See *modeling*.

Assonance A sound structure employing a similarity among vowels but not consonants.

Auteur The author or primary maker of the total film, usually the director.

Avant-garde Innovators, the "advance guard"—those who break sharply with traditional conventions and styles.

Axis line An imaginary line—generated by a visible line or lines—that helps determine the direction of the eye in any of the visual arts.

Axis mundi A vertically placed pole used by some primitive people to center their world.

B

Baroque The style dominant in the visual arts in seventeenth-century Europe following the Renaissance, characterized by vivid colors, dramatic light, curvilinear heavy lines, elaborate ornamentation, bold scale, and strong expression of emotion. Music is the only other art of that time that can be accurately described as Baroque. See *Rococo*.

Binder The adhering agent for the various media of painting.

C

Cadence In music, the harmonic sequence that closes a phrase.

Cantilever   In architecture, a projecting beam or structure supported at only one end, which is anchored to a pier or wall.

Carving   Shaping by cutting, chipping, hewing, etc.

Casting   The process of making a sculpture or other object by pouring liquid material into a mold and allowing it to harden.

Catharsis   The cleansing or purification of the emotions and, in turn, a spiritual release and renewal.

Centered space   A site—natural or human-made—that organizes other places around it.

Character   In drama, the agents and their purpose.

Chiaroscuro   Technique in painting that makes use of light and shade.

Chord   Three or more notes played at the same time.

Cinematic motif   In film, a visual image that is repeated either in identical form or in variation.

Classical style   In Greek art the style of the fifth century B.C. More generally the term *Classical* sometimes refers to the ancient art of Greece and Rome. Also, it sometimes refers to an art that is based on rational principles and deliberate composition. With a lowercase "c," *classic* can mean excellence, whatever the period or style.

Closed line   In painting, hard and sharp line. See *line*.

Coda   A passage added to the end of a musical composition to produce a satisfactory close.

Collage   A work made by pasting bits of paper or other material onto a flat surface.

Color   The property of reflecting light of a particular wavelength.

Color value   Shading, the degree of lightness or darkness of a hue.

Comedy   A form of drama that is usually light in subject matter and ends happily but that is not necessarily void of seriousness.

Complementary colors   Colors that lie opposite to each other on the color wheel.

Composition   The organization of the elements. See *design*.

Computer art   Works using the computer as the medium.

Conception   Thinking that focuses on concepts or ideas. See *perception*.

Conceptual art   Works that bring the audience into direct contact with the creative concepts of the artist; a de-emphasis on the medium.

Conceptual metaphor   A comparison that evokes ideas.

Configurational center   A place of special value, a place to dwell.

Connotation   Use of language to suggest ideas and/or emotional coloration in addition to the explicit or denoted meaning. "Brothers and sisters" denotes relatives, but the words may also connote people united in a common effort or struggle, as in the expressions "Brotherhood of Teamsters" or "Sisterhood Is Powerful." See *denotation*.

Consonance   When two or more tones sounded simultaneously are pleasing to the ear. See *dissonance*.

Content   Subject matter detached by means of artistic form from its accidental or insignificant aspects and thus clarified and made more meaningful. See *subject matter*.

Cool color   A color that is recessive, such as blue, green, and black.

Cornice   The horizontal molding projecting along the top of a building.

Counterpoint   In music, two or more melodies, themes, or motifs played in opposition to each other at the same time.

Craft   Skilled making.

Craftwork   The product of craft, usually utilitarian and beautiful.

Crescendo   A gradual increase in loudness.

Criticism   The analysis and evaluation of works of art.

▪ D ▪

Dada   A movement begun during World War I in Europe that was anti-everything. A precursor of shock art and Duchampism.

Decoration   An artlike element added to enhance or adorn something else.

Decorative form   The organization of a medium that pleases, distracts, or entertains but does not inform about values. See *artistic form*.

Denotation   The direct, explicit meaning or reference of a word or words. See *connotation*.

Denouement   The section of a drama in which events are brought to a conclusion.

Descriptive criticism   The description of the subject matter and form of a work of art.

Design   The overall plan of a work before implementation. See *composition*.

Detail   Elements of structure; in painting, a small part. See *region*.

Detail relationship   Significant relationships between or among details. See *structural relationships*.

Diction   In literature, drama, and film, the choice of words with special care for their expressiveness.

Dissonance   When two or more tones sounded simultaneously are unpleasant to the ear. See *consonance*.

Documentarists   Photographers who document the present to preserve a record of it as it disappears.

Duchampism   School of art that produced works that are anti-art and anti-establishment, but are funny rather than angry. See *Dada*.

Dynamics   In music, the loudness and softness of the sound.

■ **E** ■

Earth-dominating architecture   Buildings that "rule over" the earth.

Earth-resting architecture   Buildings that accent neither the earth nor the sky, using the earth as a platform with the sky as a background.

Earth-rooted architecture   Buildings that bring out with special force the earth and its symbolism. See *sky-oriented architecture*.

Earth sculpture   Sculpture that makes the earth the medium, site, and subject matter.

Eclecticism   A combination of several different styles in a work.

Editing   In film, the process by which the footage is cut, the best version of each scene chosen, and these versions joined together for optimum effect. See *montage*.

Elements   The basic components of a medium. See *media*.

Elements of drama (Aristotle's)   Plot, character, thought, diction, spectacle, and music. See entries under individual elements.

Embodiment   The meshing of medium and meaning in a work of art.

Emotion   Strong sensations felt as related to a specific and apparent stimulus. See *passion* and *mood*.

***En pointe* (on point)**   In ballet, a specific technique utilizing special shoes in which the dancer dances on the points of the toes.

Entasis   The subtle convex swelling near the center of a column.

Epic   A lengthy narrative poem, usually episodic, with heroic action and great cultural scope.

Episodic narrative   A story composed of separate incidents (or episodes) tied loosely together. See *organic narrative*.

Ethics   The inquiry into the presuppositions or principles operative in our moral judgments. Ethics is a branch of philosophy.

Evaluative criticism   Judgment of the merits of a work of art.

Expressionism   School of art in which the work emphasizes the artist's feelings or state of mind.

Extrinsic value   The means to intrinsic values or to further, higher values. See *intrinsic value*s.

■ **F** ■

F/64 group   In photography, the name derives from the small aperture, F/64, which ensures that the foreground, middle ground, and background will all be in sharp focus.

Fantasia   A musical composition in which the "free flight of fancy" prevails over conventional structures such as the sonata form.

Flaw in character (hamartia)   In drama, the prominent weakness of character that leads to the protagonist's tragic end.

Flying buttress   An arch that springs from below the roof of a Gothic cathedral carrying the thrust above and across a side aisle.

Folk art   Work produced outside the professional tradition.

Form-content   The embodiment of the meaning of a work of art with the form.

Forte   A musical team denoting loud.

Framing   The photographic technique whereby important parts of figures or objects in a scene are cut off by the edges of the photograph.

Fresco   A wall painting. Wet fresco involves pigment applied to wet plaster. Dry fresco involves pigment applied to a dry wall. Wet fresco generally is much more enduring than dry fresco.

Frieze   Low-relief sculpture running high and horizontally on a wall of a building.

Fugue   In music, a theme developed by counterpoint. See *counterpoint*.

■ **G** ■

Genre   Kind or type.

Genre painting   Subjects or scenes drawn from everyday life portrayed realistically.

Greek cross   A cross with equal vertical and horizontal arms. See *Latin cross*.

■ **H** ■

Happenings   Very impromptu performances, often involving the audience. See *shock art*.

Harmony   The sounding of notes simultaneously.

Hearer   One who hears music without careful attention to details or structure. See *listener*.

High relief   Sculpture with a background plane from which the projections are relatively large.

Historical criticism   The description, interpretation, or evaluation of works of art with reference to their historical precedents.

Hue   The name of a color. See *saturation*.

Humanities   Broad areas of human creativity and

study essentially involved with values and generally not using strictly objective or scientific methods.

I

Iambic pentameter   Type of poetic meter. An iamb is a metrical unit, or foot, of two syllables; the first unaccented and the second accented. Pentameter is a five-foot line. See *sonnet*.

Idea art   Works in which ideas or concepts dominate the medium, challenging traditional presuppositions about art, especially embodiment. In an extreme phase, ideas are presented in diagram or description rather than in execution. See *embodiment*.

Illumination   Hand-drawn decoration or illustration in a manuscript.

Illustration   Images that closely resemble objects or events.

Imagery   Use of language to represent objects and events with strong appeal to the senses, especially the visual.

Impasto   The painting technique of heavily applying pigment so as to create a three-dimensional surface.

Improvisation   Music or other performance produced on the spur of the moment.

Inorganic color   In painting, flat color, appears laid on the object depicted. See *organic color*.

Intentional fallacy   In criticism, the assumption that what the artists say they intended to do outweighs what they in fact did.

Interpretation   In the arts, the act of using another work of art as subject matter. See *appropriation* and *synthesis*.

Interpretive criticism   Explication of the content of a work of art.

Intrinsic value   The value of an activity or object involving the immediacy of feeling. See *extrinsic value*.

Irony   Saying the opposite of what one means. Dramatic irony plays on the audience's capacity to perceive the difference between what the characters expect and what they will get.

K

Key   A system of tones based on and named after a given tone—the tonic.

Kitsch   Works that realistically depict objects and events in a pretentious, vulgar manner.

L

Labanotation   A system of writing down dance movements.

Largo   A musical term denoting a broad, very slow, stately tempo.

Latin cross   A cross in which the vertical arm is longer than the horizontal arm, through whose midpoint it passes. Chartres and many other European cathedrals are based on a recumbent Latin cross. See *Greek cross*.

Legato   A musical term indicating that a passage should be played smoothly and without a break between the tones.

Libretto   The text of an opera.

Line   A continuous marking made by a moving point on a surface.

Linear perspective   The creation of the illusion of distance in a two-dimensional work by means of converging lines. In one-point linear perspective, developed in the fifteenth century A.D., all parallel lines in a given visual field converge at a single vanishing point on the horizon. See *perspective*.

Listener   One who listens to music with careful attention to details and structure. See *hearer*.

Living space   The feeling of the comfortable positioning of things in the environment that promotes both liberty of movement and paths as directives.

Low relief   Sculpture with a background plane from which the projections are relatively small.

Lyric   A poem, usually brief and personal, with an emphasis on feelings or states of mind as part of the subject matter. Lyric songs use lyric poems.

M

Machine sculpture   Sculpture that reveals the machine and/or its powers.

Mass   In sculpture, three-dimensional form suggesting physical bulk, weight, and density.

Media   The materials out of which works of art are made. These elements either have an inherent order, such as colors, or permit an imposed order, such as words; these orders, in turn, are organizable by form. Singular, *medium*. See *elements*.

Melody   A group of notes having a perceivable beginning, middle, and end. See *theme*.

Metaphor   An implied comparison between different things. See *simile*.

Middle Ages   The centuries roughly between the dissolution of the Roman Empire (circa A.D. 500) and the Renaissance (fifteenth century).

Mixed media   The combination of two or more artistic media in the same work.

Mobile   A constructed structure whose components

have been connected at the joints to move by force of wind or motor.

Modeling The technique of building up a sculpture piece by piece with some plastic or malleable material. See *assemblage*.

Modern Art The bewildering variety of styles that developed after World War II, characterized by the tendency for rejecting traditionally accepted styles, emphasizing originality and experimentation, often with new technologies.

Modern dance A form of concert dancing relying on emotional use of the body, as opposed to formalized or conventional movement, and stressing emotion, passion, mood, and states of mind.

Montage The joining of physically different but usually psychologically related scenes. See *editing*.

Mood A feeling that arises from no specific or apparent stimulus.

Motive In music, a brief but intelligible and self-contained unit, usually a fragment of a melody or theme.

Myth Ancient stories rooted in primitive experience.

N

Narrative A story told to an audience.

Narrator The teller of a story.

Neo-classical A return in the late eighteenth and early nineteenth centuries, in reaction to the Baroque and Rococo, to the Classical styles of ancient Greece and Rome, characterized by reserved emotions. See *Romanticism*.

New Comedy Subject matter centered on the foibles of social manners and mores. Usually quite polished in style, with bright and incisive humor.

Normative values Values set forth as norms or ideals, what "ought to be."

O

Objective correlative An image that is similar to a subjective awareness.

Objectivist theory of value Value is in the object or event itself independently of any subject or interest. See *relational* and *subjectivist theories of value*.

Oil painting Artwork where the medium is pigment mixed with linseed oil, varnish, and turpentine.

Old Comedy Subject matter centered on ridiculous and/or highly exaggerated situations. Usually raucous, earthy, and satirical.

On point See *en pointe*.

Open line In painting, soft and blurry line. See *line*.

Organic color In painting, color that appears deep, as if coming out of an object depicted. See *inorganic color*.

Organic narrative A story composed of separable incidents that relate to one another in tightly coherent ways, usually causally and chronologically. See *episodic narrative*.

P

Paradox An apparent contradiction that, upon reflection, may seem reasonable.

Participative experience "Thinking from" something, letting that thing initiate and control everything that comes into awareness. See *"thinking from."*

Pas de deux A dance for two dancers.

Pas de trois A dance for three dancers.

Passion Emotions elevated to great intensity.

Pediment The triangular space formed by roof jointure in a Greek temple or a building on the Greek model.

Perception Awareness of something stimulating our sense organs.

Perceptual metaphor A comparison that evokes images.

Performance art Generally site-specific events often performed with little detailed planning and leaving much to chance; audience participation may ensue. See *shock art*.

Perspective In painting, the illusion of depth.

Philosophy The discipline that attempts to give reasoned answers to questions that—because of their generality—are not treated by any of the more specialized disciplines. Philosophy is the systematic examination of our most fundamental beliefs.

Pictorialists Photographers who use realistic paintings as models for their photographs. See *straight photography*.

Pictorial space The illusory space in a painting that seems to recede into depth from the picture plane (the "window effect").

Picture plane The flat surface of a painting, comparable to the glass of a framed picture behind which the picture recedes in depth.

Pigment For painting, the coloring agent.

Plot The sequence of actions or events in literature or drama.

Pop Art Art that realistically depicts and sometimes incorporates mass-produced articles, especially the familiar objects of everyday life.

Popular art Contemporary works enjoyed by the masses.

Pornography Works made to sexually arouse.

Presentational immediacy The awareness of something that is presented in its entirety with an "all-at-onceness."

Presto A musical term signifying a rapid tempo.

Pretext The underlying narrative of the dance.

Primary colors Red, yellow, and blue. See *secondary colors*.

Print An image created from a master wood block, stone, plate, or screen, usually on paper. Many impressions can be made from the same surface.

Propaganda Political persuasion.

Proportion Size relationships between parts of a whole.

Proscenium The arch, or "picture frame," stage of traditional theater that sets apart the actors from the audience.

Protagonist The chief character in drama and literature.

▨ Q ▨

Quoins Roughly cut stones that accent the ends of a façade.

▨ R ▨

Realism The portrayal of objects and events in a highly representational manner. An important style of painting around 1840–1860.

Recitative Sung dialogue in opera, cantata, and oratorio.

Recognition In drama, the moment of truth, the climax.

Region In painting, a large part. See *detail*.

Regional relationships Significant relationships between regions. See *structural relationships*.

Relational theory of value Value emerges from the relation between a human interest and an object or event. See *objectivist* and *subjectivist theories of value*.

Relief With sculpture, projection from a background.

Renaissance The period in Europe from the fifteenth through the sixteenth century with a renewed interest in ancient Greek and Roman civilizations. See *Classical style*.

Representational Descriptive of portrayals that closely resemble objects and events.

Representational painting Painting that has specific objects or events as its primary subject matter. See *abstract painting*.

Requiem A mass for the dead.

Reversal In drama, when the protagonist's fortunes turn from good to bad.

Rhyme A sound structure coupling words that sound alike.

Rhythm The relationship, either of time or space, between recurring elements of a composition.

Ritardando In music, a decrease in tempo.

Rococo The style of the visual arts dominant in Europe during the first three quarters of the eighteenth century, characterized by light curvilinear forms, pastel colors, ornate and small-scale decoration, the playful and light-hearted. Rococo music is lighter than Baroque. See *Baroque*.

Romanticism Style of the nineteenth century that in reaction to Neo-classicism denies that humanity is essentially rational and the measure of all things, characterized by intense colors, open line, strong expression of emotion, complex organizations, and often heroic subject matter.

Rondo A form of musical composition employing a return to an initial theme after the presentation of each new theme—for example, A-B-A-C-A-D-A.

Rubato A style of musical performance in which liberty is taken by the performer with the rhythm of the piece.

▨ S ▨

Satire Literature that ridicules people or institutions.

Saturation The purity, vividness, or intensity of a hue.

Sciences Disciplines that for the most part use strictly objective standards.

Sculpture in the round Sculpture freed from any background plane.

Secondary colors Green, orange, and violet. See *primary colors*.

Sensa The qualities of objects or events that stimulate our sense organs, especially our eyes. See *sensuous*.

Sensuous In painting, the color field as composed by sensa. See *sensa*.

Sentimentalism Superficial emotional responses.

Setting In literature, drama, dance, and film, the time and place in which the work of art occurs. The setting is established mainly by means of description in literature and spectacle in drama, dance, and film.

Shape The outlines and contours of an object.

Shock art Attention-grabbing works intended to shock or repel, which usually fail to hold attention.

Shot In film, a continuous length of film exposed in the camera without a break. There are various ways the camera can be used for taking shots.

Simile An explicit comparison between different

things, using comparative words such as "like."

Sky-oriented architecture Buildings that bring out with special emphasis the sky and its symbolism. See *earth-resting architecture*, *earth-rooted architecture*, and *earth-dominating architecture*.

Soliloquy An extended speech by a character alone with the audience.

Sonata form In music, a movement with three major sections—exposition, development, and recapitulation, usually followed by a coda.

Sonnet A poem of fourteen lines, with fixed rhyming patterns, typically in iambic pentameter. See *iambic pentameter*.

Space A hollow volume available for occupation by shapes, and the effect of the positioned interrelationships of these shapes.

Space sculpture Sculpture that emphasizes spatial relationships and thus tends to de-emphasize the density of its materials.

Spectacle The visual setting of a drama.

Staccato In music, the technique of playing so that individual notes are short and are separated from each other by sharp accents.

State of mind An attitude or orientation of mind that is relatively enduring.

Stereotype A completely predictable character. See *type character*.

Straight photography Style that aims for excellence in photographic techniques independent of painting. See *pictorialists*.

Structural relationship Significant relationships between or among details or regions to the totality. See *regional relationships*.

Structure Overall organization of a work.

Style The identifying features—characteristics of form—of a work or group of works that identify it with an artist, group of artists, era, or nation.

Subjectivist theory of value Value is projected by human interest on some object or event. See *objectivist* and *relational theories of value*.

Subject matter What the work of art "is about"; some value *before* artistic clarification. See *content*.

Sunken relief Sculpture made by carving grooves of various depths into the surface planes of the sculptural material, the surface plane remaining perceptually distinct.

Surface relief Sculpture with a flat surface plane as the basic organizing plane of the composition, but with no clear perceptual distinction perceivable between the depths behind the surface plane and the projections in front.

Surrealism The painting style of the 1920s and 1930s that emphasized dreamlike and fantastic imagery.

Symbol Something perceptible that stands for something more abstract.

Symmetry A feature of design in which two halves of a composition on either side of an imaginary central vertical axis are more or less of the same size, shape, and placement.

Synthesis In the arts, the more or less equal combination of the media of one or more arts. See *appropriation* and *interpretation*.

■ T ■

Tactility Touch sensations, both inward and outward.

Technology A discipline that applies for practical purposes the theoretical knowledge produced by the sciences.

Tempera In painting, pigment bound by egg yolk.

Tempo The speed at which a composition is played.

Texture The surface "feel" of a material, such as "smooth" bronze or "rough" concrete.

Theatricality Exaggeration and artificiality.

Theme In music, a melody or motive of considerable importance because of later repetition or development. In other arts, a theme is a main idea or general topic.

Theology The study of the sacred.

"Thinking at" Thinking that is aware of its separation from what it is thinking about. See *"thinking from."*

"Thinking from" Thinking that is unaware of its separation from what it is thinking about. See *"thinking at"* and *participative experience*.

Thought The ideas expressed in works of art. Also, the thinking that explains the motivations and actions of the characters in a story.

Tone A sound that has a definite frequency.

Tragedy Drama that portrays a serious subject matter and ends unhappily.

Tragic flaw See *flaw in character*.

Tragicomedy Drama that includes characteristics of both tragedy and comedy.

Transept The crossing arm of a church structured like a Latin cross. See *Latin cross*.

Truth to materials Respect for the characteristics of an artistic medium.

Twelve-tone technique A twentieth-century atonal structuring of music—no tonic or most important tone—developed especially by Schoenberg.

Tympanum The space above an entranceway to a building, usually containing a sculpture.

Type character A very predictable character. See *stereotype*.

Value facts Values described scientifically. See *normative values*.

Values Objects and events that we care about, that have great importance. Also, in regard to color, value refers to the lightness or darkness of a hue; shading.

Vanishing point In linear perspective, the point on the horizon where parallel lines appear to converge.

Virtual art Computer-created, imaginary, three-dimensional scenes in which the participant is involved interactively.

Virtuoso The display of impressive technique or skill by an artist.

Warm color A color that is aggressive, such as red, yellow, and white.

Watercolor For painting, pigment bound by a water-soluble adhesive, such as gum arabic.

White light The mixture of all colors, which prevents any color from showing.

Work of art An artifact that informs about values by means of an artistic form. See *artistic form*.

Credits

ADDITIONAL PHOTO CREDITS

p. iii, © Superstock; **p. viii,** © Alinari/Art Resource, New York; **p. ix,** © Jack Vartoogian/FrontRow Photos; **p. xvii,** The Museum of Modern Art Film Stills Archive; **p. 1,** The Phillips Collection, Washington, D.C.; **p. 3,** © LeSeuil/Corbis Sygma; **p. 21,** © Superstock; **p. 53,** © AKG London; **p. 69,** Photograph © 1997 Whitney Museum of American Art. Art © Helen Frankenthaler; **p. 71,** © Alinari/Art Resource, New York; **p. 113,** © The Tate Gallery, London/Art Resource, New York; **p. 153,** © Christian Richters/Esto; **p. 202,** © Réunion des Musées Nationaux/Art Resource, New York; **p. 233,** Courtesy Berkeley Repertory Theatre. Photo by Ken Friedman, 1996; **p. 294,** © Jack Vartoogian/FrontRow Photos; **p. 320,** The Museum of Modern Art Film Stills Archive; **p. 353,** International Museum of Photography at the George Eastman House, Rochester; **p. 381,** Digital image © The Museum of Modern Art, New York/Licensed by Scala/Art Resource, New York; **p. 383,** © Scala/Art Resource, New York; **p. 404,** Photo © The Andy Warhol Foundation, Inc./Art Resource, New York. Art © 2003 Andy Warhol Foundation/ARS, New York/TM Licensed by Campbell's Soup Co. All rights reserved; **p. 445,** © Erich Lessing/Art Resource, New York

TEXT CREDITS

Maya Angelou, "Africa" from *Oh Pray My Wings Are Gonna Fit Me Well*. Copyright © 1975 by Maya Angelou. Used by permission of Random House, Inc.

e. e. cummings, "l(a" from *Complete Poems: 1904–1962 by e .e. cummings*, edited by George J. Firmage. Copyright © 1958, 1986, 1991 by the Trustees for the e .e. cummings Trust. Used by permission of Liveright Publishing Corporation.

Emily Dickinson, "After Great Pain a Formal Feeling Comes." Reprinted by permission of the publishers and the Trustees of Amherst College from *The Poems of Emily Dickinson*, Thomas H. Johnson, ed., Cambridge, Mass.: The Belknap Press of Harvard University Press. Copyright © 1951, 1955, 1979 by the President and Fellows of Harvard College.

Fyodor Dostoevsky, excerpt from *Crime and Punishment*, translated by Jessie L. Coulson. Oxford: Oxford University Press. By permission of Oxford University Press.

Robert Fagles, "The Starry Night" from *I, Vincent: Poems from the Pictures of Van Gogh* by Robert Fagles. Copyright © 1978 by Princeton University Press. Reprinted with permission of Robert Fagles.

Louise Glück, "Vespers" from *The Wild Iris* by Louise Glück. Copyright © 1992 Louise Glück. New York: Ecco Press/HarperCollins Publishers. Reprinted by permission.

Langston Hughes, "Ballad of the Landlord" from *The Collected Poems of Langston Hughes*. Copyright © 1994 by The Estate of Langston Hughes. Used by permission of Alfred A. Knopf, a division of Random House, Inc.

D. H. Lawrence, "Piano" from *The Complete Poems of D. H. Lawrence*, edited by V. de Sola Pinto & F. W. Roberts. Copyright © 1964, 1971 by Angelo Ravagli and C. M. Weekley, Executors of the Estate of Frieda Lawrence Ravagli. Used by permission of Viking Penguin, a division of Penguin Group (USA) Inc.

Tu Mu, "The Grave of Little Su" from *Poems of the Late T'ang*, by Tu Mu, translated by A. C. Graham (Penguin Classics, 1965). Copyright © 1965 by A. C. Graham. Reprinted by permission.

Tu Mu, "The Retired Official Yuan's High Pavilion" from *Poems of the Late T'ang* by Tu Mu, translated by A. C. Graham (Penguin Classics, 1965). Copyright © 1965 by A. C. Graham. Reprinted by permission.

Gabriel Okara, "Piano and Drums" from *The African Assertion*, edited by Austin J. Shelton. New York: Odyssey. Originally in *Black Orpheus #6*, 1959. Reprinted by permission of Gabriel Okara.

Publius Ovidius Naso, *The Metamorphoses*, translated by Horace Gregory. Copyright © 1958 by The Viking Press, Inc., renewed copyright © 1986 by Patrick Polton Gregory. Used by permission of Viking Penguin, a division of Penguin Group (USA) Inc.

Sylvia Plath, "Paralytic" from *The Collected Poems of Sylvia Plath*. New York: HarperCollins Publishers. Reprinted by permission. Reprinted in Canada by permission of Faber & Faber Ltd.

Ezra Pound, "In a Station of the Metro" from *Personae* by Ezra Pound. Copyright © 1926 by Ezra Pound. Reprinted by permission of New Directions Publishing Corp.

Index

O'Casey, Sean, 250
Ocean's Motion (Tharp), 316
"Ode on a Grecian Urn" (Keats), 202
Oedipus Rex (Sophocles), 236, 239, 312
Ofili, Chris, Holy Virgin Mary, 64, **64**
oil painting, 76–79
Okara, Gabriel, "Piano and Drums,"
   17–18
O'Keeffe, Georgia, *Ghost Ranch Cliffs*,
   87, **87,** 96
Old Juniet's Cart (Rousseau), **411, 412,**
   413–414
Olympia (Manet), **48,** 50
One Hundred Cans (Warhol), 415, **415**
opera, 383–385
organic color, 88
organic narratives, 209–210
O'Sullivan, Timothy, *Canyon de Chelley,*
   Arizona, 358, **359**
Overgard, William, **39,** 39–41, 44
Ovid, *The Metamorphoses,* 397–399
Owens, Wilfred, 386

P

Pain (Sanasardo), 294, **295**
painting, 71–112
   abstract, 94–97
   acrylic, 79
   "all-at-onceness" of, 93–94
   clarity of, 92–93
   color, 86–88
   compared to sculpture, 115–118
   composition, 89–91
   fresco, 75–76
   interpretation of dance and music,
      399–402
   interpretation of poetry, 394–397
   interpretation of the Madonna and
      Child, 98–105
   line, 80–86
   mixed media, 79
   oil, 76–79
   photography and, 359–362, 387
   representational, 97–98
   self-portraits, 107–110
   styles, 110
   subject matter, 94, 105–106
   tempera, 73–75
   texture, 88–89
   visual powers, 71–72
   watercolor, 79
Palace of Versailles, **173,** 174
Palazzo Farnese, Rome, 188–189, **189,**
   192
Panini, Giovanni Paolo, Interior of the
   Pantheon, 175–176, **176**
Panofsky, Erwin, 166–167
Pantheon, Rome, 175–177, **176, 177**
Paradise Lost (Milton), 16
"Paralytic" (Plath), 207–208, 210
Parmigianino, Francesco, *The*
   Madonna with the Long Neck, **77,**
   79, 103–105
Parthenon, 159–161, **160, 161,** 167,
   170–171, 173–174
participation, 27–32
   critics and, 54–55
   definition, 23
   film and, 324–326
   form and content and, 37–38

overview, 27–32
   values and, 449–450
participative experiences, 28
Paula (Stieglitz), **360,** 360–361
pavane, 301–302
Pei, I. M.
   East Wing of the National Gallery of
      Art, 191, **191**
   John Hancock Building, 429–430, **430**
Pelagos (Hepworth), 135, **135,** 137, 387
El Penitente (Graham), 312
perception, 14–16, 19, 22–23, 447–448
perceptual metaphor, 222
performance art, 438–440
perspective, 91
Phaedra (Graham), 312, **313**
philosophy, arts and, 453–454
photography, 353–380
   camera obscura, 353, **354**
   color, 376–378
   Documentarists, 362, 367–372
   Execution in Saigon (Adams), 24–28,
      25
   F/64 Group, 362, 364–366
   in film, 322, 327–329
   painting and, 359–362, 387
   pictorialists, 359–362
   representation through, 353–359
   snapshots, 372–376
   straight, 362–367
   as works of art, 27–28
"Piano" (Lawrence), 206–207, 210
"Piano and Drums" (Okara), 17–18
piano keyboard, 263, **263**
Piazza before St. Peter's, 154, **154**
Picabia, Francis, 435
   The Blessed Virgin, **432,** 432–433
Picasso, Pablo
   Composition Study (Guernica study),
      10, 11
   Guernica, **10,** 11–12, 58
   Nude under a Pine Tree, 45, **47,** 88
pictorialists, 359–362
"Pied Beauty" (Hopkins), 214
Pietà (Michelangelo), 120–124, **121**
pigment, 80
Pilobolus Dance Company, 294, 313,
   314
Plath, Sylvia, "Paralytic," 207–208, 210
plot, 236
poetry. *See* literature
point-of-view shots, 322
Pollack, Jackson, *Autumn Rhythm,*
   57–58, **58,** 79, 87, 89, 118
Ponti, Gio, 173
Pop Art, 110, 415
Pope.L, William, *ATM Piece*, 439, **439**
popular art, 414–420
Potemkin (Eisenstein), 339
presentational immediacy, 94
primary colors, 87
prints, 79
propaganda, 420–421
proscenium theatre, 242, **243**
protest against technology, 139–140
Proust, Marcel, 205, 349
Psalm 23, 229–230
Psycho (Hitchcock), 339
"punch effect," 91
Push Comes to Shove (Tharp), 316

Q

quest narratives, 210–212
The Quilting Bee (Moses), **411,**
   412–413
quoins, 188

R

Raggedy Dances (Tharp), 316
Rain Man, 336
Rambo, 325
Raphael, *Madonna della Sedia,* 424,
   424, 426
Rauschenberg, Robert, 385–386
   Winter Pool, 387, **388**
realism, in illustration, 407–408, 417
Reclining Figure (Moore), 133, **134,**
   136–137
Reclining Nude (Modigliani), 45, **47,** 82
Reclining Nude (Valadon), **49,** 50
Redford, Robert, *A River Runs*
   Through It, 329
Red Interior, Provincetown
   (Meyerowitz), 376, **377**
regional relationships, 57
relational theory of value, 450
"The Relic" (Donne), 219–220
relief sculptures, 118–120, 125
religion and the arts, 455–456
Rembrandt van Rijn, *Self Portrait,* **106,**
   107–108, 358
Renoir, Jean, *The Grand Illusion,* 327,
   327
Renoir, Pierre Auguste, *Bather*
   Arranging Her Hair, **46,** 50, 82, 88
representational painting, 97–98
Requiem (Mozart), 271
responses to art, 8–12
"The Retired Official Yüan's High
   Pavilion" (Tu Mu), 220, 223
reverse shots, 323
rhythm, 89–90, 264
Rickey, George, *Two Lines—Temporal I,*
   142–143, **143**
Riefenstahl, Leni, 421
The Rising of the Moon (Gregory),
   250–255
ritual, in dance, 297–300
Rivera, Jose de, *Brussels Construction,*
   137, **137,** 142
A River Runs Through It, 329
Rockefeller Center, New York City, 171,
   171
Rockwell, Norman, *Freedom from*
   Want, 415–416, **416,** 420
Rodin, Auguste, 127–128
   Danaïde, 128, **128**
Rohmer, Eric, *Claire's Knee,* 340
Rojo, Jerry, 256
Romeo and Juliet (Shakespeare),
   242–246, **244**
rondos, 275
Rosenberg, Harold, 437
Rosenquist, James, *I Love You with My*
   Ford, 409, **409,** 417–418
Rosso, Medardo, 134
Rothko, Mark, *Earth Greens,* 83, **84,**
   87, 96–97, 115–116
Rotterdam Construction (Gabo), **146,**
   146–147
Rousseau, Henri, 410